Building Home

The publisher gratefully acknowledges the generous contribution to the production of this book provided by Howard F. Ahmanson, Jr., and Pinatubo Press.

The publisher also gratefully acknowledges the generous support of the Ahmanson Foundation.

Building Home

HOWARD F. AHMANSON AND THE POLITICS
OF THE AMERICAN DREAM

Eric John Abrahamson

UNIVERSITY OF CALIFORNIA PRESS

BERKELEY   LOS ANGELES   LONDON

University of California Press, one of the most distinguished university presses in the United States, enriches lives around the world by advancing scholarship in the humanities, social sciences, and natural sciences. Its activities are supported by the UC Press Foundation and by philanthropic contributions from individuals and institutions. For more information, visit www.ucpress.edu.

University of California Press
Berkeley and Los Angeles, California

University of California Press, Ltd.
London, England

Library of Congress Cataloging-in-Publication Data

Abrahamson, Eric John.
    Building home : Howard F. Ahmanson and the politics of the American dream / Eric John Abrahamson.
        p.   cm.
    Includes bibliographical references and index.
    ISBN 978-0-520-27375-7 (cloth : alk. paper)
        1. Mortgage loans—California—Los Angeles—History—20th century.
    2. Savings and loan associations—Los Angeles—History—20th century.
    3. Ahmanson, Howard F.   4. American Dream—History—20th century.
    I. Title.
        HG2040.5.U5A627   2013
        332.3'2092—dc23

                                                            2012031151

Manufactured in the United States of America

21   20   19   18   17   16   15   14   13
10   9   8   7   6   5   4   3   2   1

In keeping with a commitment to support environmentally responsible and sustainable printing practices, UC Press has printed this book on Rolland Enviro100, a 100% post-consumer fiber paper that is FSC certified, deinked, processed chlorine-free, and manufactured with renewable biogas energy. It is acid-free and EcoLogo certified.

CONTENTS

Illustrations follow page 152

ACKNOWLEDGMENTS

·

WHEN HE DIED IN 1968, Howard Ahmanson Sr. bequeathed a fortune to his son, as well as an ambiguous legacy. In the years that followed, no biographer emerged to chronicle the life of one of America's most successful postwar entrepreneurs. And as his son Howard junior matured, the substance of his father's life seemed hidden behind the reflected glare of black-and-white publicity photographs and a veil of cigarette smoke.

I first met Howard junior in the mid-1990s in Perry, Iowa. He and his wife Roberta were working on a number of historical projects in the town where she had grown up. I was part of an interpretive team working to develop a museum to be housed in the old Carnegie Library. Howard told me then that he was collecting material about his father's life and hoping to find someone to write a biography, but it didn't occur to either of us at the time that I might be the author. Although I had done work in California history, I was in a PhD program at Johns Hopkins, and Howard was looking closer to home for a writer.

We connected again after a long break in December 2008 as the nation reeled from the meltdown in the mortgage market. I asked Howard what had become of the biography idea. He told me that the potential authors had turned down the project because of a shortage of archival material and a feeling that Howard senior's story would be of little interest to readers. I told Howard that in light of the mortgage crisis a look back on an earlier era in mortgage finance might have significant appeal to readers newly interested in the subject. Moreover, Howard senior's biography reflected the ethos and character of that era. Howard agreed to underwrite work on the project if a university press and outside peer reviewers also agreed that the idea had merit. He was not interested in supporting a hagiography of his father.

I delivered a book proposal and sample chapters to the University of California Press several months later. The press submitted the proposal to peer review. The peer reviewers expressed support for the project and provided useful ideas for framing the context and argument of the story. On the strength of their review, UC Press offered me a contract for publication pending peer review of the final manuscript.

Throughout the course of my research, Howard junior has expressed enthusiastic support for this work, even when the story did not cast his father a favorable light. The staff that works for him at Fieldstead, Inc. welcomed me during my visits to do research in the family archives. Research performed by Lisa Hausdorfer and interviews conducted by Marc Nurre as part of that earlier effort to enable a biography gave me vital sources to work with. Steven Ferguson and Fieldstead's attorney, John Fossum of Irell and Manella, played a major role in helping me to locate several important interviewees and constantly encouraged the project. At my invitation, Steven, John, and Howard junior read occasional drafts and provided me with additional information on possible sources. All the while, they left me free to interpret the story as I have come to understand it from the available evidence.

One of the major challenges of this project, as other potential authors warned Howard junior, has been the paucity of material in Howard senior's own voice. He left only a few boxes of his personal correspondence and memorabilia. Howard junior never played a role in the management of Home Savings, and after the company was sold to Washington Mutual in 1998, most of its records disappeared. Late in my research, archivists at JPMorgan Chase found and allowed me to review a few boxes of Home Savings corporate materials that provided some additional details but shed little additional light on Ahmanson.

Piecing together information about Ahmanson's life from many sources and relying on the importance of a larger contextual story to drive the argument and the narrative, I was aided considerably by various people who agreed to let me interview them over the phone or in person. I am grateful to all of the following: Beverly Adair, Howard Ahmanson Jr., Mary Jane Bettfreund, Susan Buffett, Warren Buffett, Lou Cannon, Martha Cates, Hernando Courtright Jr., Gene Crain, Richard Deihl, Robert DeKruif, Carolyn Dunning, Sandra Edwards, William Ficker, Kim Fletcher, Marvin Holen, Elbert Hudson, Melinda Hurst, Peter McAndrews, Dolores Morse, Suzanne Muchnic, Charles Munger, John Notter, Margo Leonetti O'Connell, and Rufus Turner.

Craig Chapman transcribed the taped interviews with extraordinary attention to the story.

Archivists and librarians at a number of institutions helped me find letters and documents that shed light on Ahmanson's life. I am particularly grateful to staff at the Bancroft Library, the California State Archives, and the National Archives and Records Administration. Special Collections librarians at the University of California Los Angeles, Loyola Marymount, the University of Southern California, Stanford University, the National Association of Home Builders, and the Los Angeles County Museum of Art were all helpful. Diana Stickler at the *San Jose Mercury News* went above and beyond the call of duty to provide me with copies of a series of stories written by Harry Farrell. Dalit Baranoff helped me to understand the history of the fire insurance industry. William Ahmanson and Karen Ahmanson Hoffman were especially gracious and allowed me to comb through the papers of their father, Robert Ahmanson, at the Ahmanson Foundation. The staff at the Foundation were always warm and welcoming.

As my wife and research colleague, Lois Facer, and I wandered the country in search of Ahmanson's story, many people went out of their way to help. Brian and Amy Watts, Hans and Cheri Facer, Susan Abrahamson and Brent King, and Grant and Doris Facer were all generous with spare rooms and moral support. Friends in Los Angeles—Rob Ball, Tom Hartman, Gloria Gerace, and David Farneth—shared meals, homes, and conversations.

I am especially grateful to the Krieger School of Arts and Sciences at Johns Hopkins University for a multiyear appointment as a fellow with the Institute of Applied Economics and Study of Business Enterprise that gave me access to important research materials. I am also grateful to the Regents of the University of California for permission to include material from an essay I wrote on mortgage finance for *Carefree California: Cliff May and the Romance of the Ranch House.*

A number of people graciously agreed to read and comment on the manuscript at various stages of its development. William Deverell and Kenneth Lipartito reviewed the initial proposal and helped steer me along important lines of inquiry. Edwin J. Perkins read and critiqued an early draft. I appreciate the very helpful comments provided by anonymous peer reviewers at the University of California Press. Adam Arenson, who is writing his own book on Millard Sheets and the art and architecture of Home Savings, read and critiqued the manuscript. In addition, over and over, he generously alerted me to possible sources.

Madeleine Adams and I had a chance to renew an old friendship as she edited the manuscript. Her suggestions and comments helped sharpen the narrative and improved the prose. Elisabeth Magnus's diligent copyediting improved the text and notes even more. Ernest Grafe created the index. At the University of California Press, my editor, Kim Robinson, was especially cognizant of the challenges associated with this kind of sponsored project. She was extraordinarily supportive, patient, and firm about our approach. I appreciate all of these qualities. Her team helped to shepherd this book through to production.

For many years now, Lou Galambos has provided wisdom and insight related to the processes of writing business and economic history. I remain deeply in his debt. I am also grateful to Sam Hurst, who listened and asked questions on many walks or afternoons when we both wished we were back in Southern California rather than hiding from the worst days of winter in western South Dakota. Sam read the manuscript with a critical eye and led me to sources that surprised both of us for their connection to this story.

For many years now, literary production in our house has been a social process. From their new homes in Washington, D.C., my sons Reed and Zachary shared ideas and read drafts. Lois Facer, my colleague, confidante, and collaborator in life, has pored over clumsy sentences and asked the right questions with patience beyond measure. I'm grateful for all their help and affection.

In writing the story of one man's life and trying to see through to the heart of his generation, I am painfully aware that everything that looks like truth changes shape or color under a different light. I take responsibility for any errors in judgment or in fact that remain despite the best efforts of all these good Samaritans.

Introduction

LIKE MOST AMERICANS THAT SUNDAY AFTERNOON, the three men at the Shoreham Hotel in Washington, D.C., were surprised and dismayed by the news. Crackling through the speakers and interrupting the music, the announcer proclaimed: "... Japanese planes have attacked the U.S. naval base in Hawaii..." Without much elaboration or detail, the station returned to its regular Sunday afternoon broadcast.

With cigarette smoke drifting among them, the suntanned and ruddy-faced California executives discussed what the news would mean to their businesses and their lives. They were on their way home from the annual convention of the U.S. Savings and Loan League in Coral Gables, Florida. At the convention, rumors had circulated that the federal government was planning to impose restrictions on the use of building materials in anticipation of war.[1] Restrictions would slow construction and diminish the demand for home loans, the bread and butter of the savings and loan business. Already, the government was beginning to build its own housing in Los Angeles for war workers. Many of the men at the convention chafed at these rumors, which seemed to signal a resurgence of what some described as the Roosevelt administration's command-and-control approach to the national economy.

As the men talked, their conversation reflected the national mood. Caught up in the development of their own businesses and personal lives, they blamed diplomats and politicians for failing to keep the peace. If the country had to be dragged into the conflict, they hoped it would be short-lived. A guest column written by an American admiral in that morning's *Washington Post* had asserted that if war broke out, the United States and its allies would quickly blockade Japan and isolate the island nation.[2] Others were not so confident. Japan's alliance with Germany made the threat of prolonged war real. With the attack on Pearl Harbor, Californians, who had imagined themselves safe in their domestic tranquillity and far from the conflict in Europe, suddenly felt vulnerable.

Charlie Fletcher, a tall, broad-shouldered man just shy of his fortieth birthday, was the oldest and had the most intimate knowledge of politics. His father, an enormously successful real estate developer, represented San Diego in the California State Senate. A Progressive Republican when he was first elected, Fletcher senior had defected to the Democratic Party during the Roosevelt years. Unlike his father, Charlie remained a hard-core chamber of commerce, Herbert Hoover Republican. As an undergraduate at Hoover's alma mater, Stanford University, Fletcher captained the water polo team to a national championship. He was a three-time All-American swimmer.[3] He did graduate work at Oxford and traveled through Europe, the Middle East, and Asia before returning to San Diego. In 1926, he married Jeannette Toberman, daughter of one of Hollywood's founders.[4] In 1934, seizing an entrepreneurial opportunity created by Congress to promote home ownership in America, Fletcher founded Home Federal Savings and Loan. It was the worst year of the Great Depression. Seven years later, Home Federal had barely $4 million in assets, but Charlie had the resources to be patient. He remained confident and optimistic.[5] Cool-headed and cautious by nature, he resisted the war fever brought on by the bombing of Pearl Harbor. With a wife and young children, as he told his companions that afternoon, he had no intention of being dragged off to fight. He would sell war bonds instead "so the other guys would have something to fight with."[6]

Howard Edgerton, or "Edgie" as his friends called him, provided a stark contrast to Fletcher's cautiousness. Born in Sulphur Springs, Arkansas, in 1908 and raised in Prescott, Arizona, and Los Angeles, the thirty-three-year-old Edgerton was a glad-handing westerner. At five feet ten inches tall, he had a muscular but trim build. He graduated from the University of Southern California in 1928, stayed on to earn a law degree in 1930, and then joined the Railway Mutual Building and Loan Association.[7] Within five years he had taken over management of the organization, converted it from a state to a federal charter, and changed its name to California Federal Savings and Loan. He became president and CEO in 1939.[8] By 1941, his company had assets of approximately $5 million. Financially, he was comfortable enough to be the part owner of an airplane but he was not rich.[9] Unlike Fletcher, Edgerton was eager to go to war. Facetiously he announced he "was all set to be a general."[10]

Howard F. Ahmanson was undoubtedly amused by the discussion between his two friends. A handsome thirty-seven-year-old man with deep blue eyes that "just looked right through you," he could be charming "and make you feel like you were the center of the world."[11] When angry, he was often imperious and caustic. An Omaha native, Ahmanson moved to California at the age of nineteen, studied business at USC, and made his first million dollars in the middle of the Depression by selling insurance. Living in a fine house in Beverly Hills, he and his wife, Dorothy "Dottie" Johnston Grannis, had been married eight years but had no children. By nature, he was not impulsive. He worried over business problems but understood the profit to be made by taking calculated risks. Savings and loan executives like Fletcher and Edgerton who steered customers to his insurance company were crucial to his success. They were also among his closest friends.

Ahmanson was cautious about the war. He had seen the rise of militarism in Germany and Japan firsthand. He and Dottie had traveled extensively in Europe during the summer of 1938, shortly after Hitler's annexation of Austria. Two years later, they had sailed to Japan.[12] At the time, the Japanese army was ruthlessly suppressing resistance in conquered territories in China and Southeast Asia. Though just a tourist, Ahmanson had observed it all. Now, with war assured, he insisted that, like Fletcher, he would have nothing to do with "this flag-waving uniform business." If the government wanted him, they would have to come and get him.[13]

As speculation and rumor fed the conversations at the Shoreham that afternoon, the rumble of taxis and the slamming of car doors could be heard from the lobby. Some of the hotel's permanent residents, including senators and congressmen, rushed off to the Capitol and the White House. That night, President Roosevelt met with congressional leaders from both parties. Bitter party rivalries dissolved in the face of the Japanese attack. As these leaders returned to the hotel in the small hours of the night, word spread that the president would ask for a declaration of war.

Fletcher and Ahmanson may have begun to change their minds about their own involvement in the war the next morning. Edgerton, and perhaps the other two, joined the crowds outside the Capitol plaza as police and Secret Service agents kept access clear. From the packed and tense galleries of the U.S. House of Representatives, Edgerton watched as the president, accompanied by his son, a marine lieutenant in uniform, lifted himself to the microphone-cluttered rostrum.

On a date "which will live in infamy," the president began, his words crackling through the speakers of millions of radios across the country, "the United States of America was suddenly and deliberately attacked by naval and air forces of the Empire of Japan."[14] The surprise offensive had included assaults on the Philippines, Malaysia, Hong Kong, Guam, Wake Island, and Midway. "No matter how long it may take us to overcome this premeditated invasion," Roosevelt said, "the American people will in their righteous might win through to absolute victory." Members of Congress and the audience rose to applaud. Within an hour, both houses of Congress, by a nearly unanimous vote, approved the declaration of war.[15]

The Japanese attack unified the nation in anger and accelerated the militarization of the economy. Ford, General Motors, and other automobile companies began turning out Jeeps and tanks. Kaiser, Bechtel, and other heavy construction contractors in California started building Liberty ships and military bases. Food processors like Del Monte and S&W Fine Foods began canning California peaches, cherries, and grapes for mess halls in Europe and the Pacific. In Southern California, Douglas Aircraft scrambled to increase their production of bombers. Indeed, Southern California and its economy would be permanently transformed by the war.

Across the country, men and women lined up outside military recruiting offices to volunteer. Many who didn't were drafted. Fletcher and Ahmanson eventually joined Edgerton in the armed forces. None of the three saw combat, but the war years crystallized for them a complicated perspective on the relationship between citizen and country, private endeavor and public service, that would shape their entrepreneurial lives and the social contract between American society and business for a generation. Their wartime experiences would also give them powerful insights into the growing military-industrial complex and its influence on the future of Southern California.

The war reshaped the country's culture. When it was over, the devastation in Europe and Asia ensured that American industries would face limited competition from foreign manufacturers. With a domestic market primed with wartime savings and shortages, consumption skyrocketed as American workers enjoyed an era of unprecedented prosperity. Government policies, especially the GI Bill, recognized the service of veterans and sought to ensure a smooth transition to a peacetime economy. The GI Bill promoted education and training, entrepreneurship, and—most important for Fletcher, Edgerton, and Ahmanson—home ownership.

In this postwar era, all three men would be enormously successful in the savings and loan industry and would contribute substantially to the growth of Southern California. They played a significant role in the region's politics and cultural development. Among them, however, Howard Ahmanson would prosper beyond all imagining, building the largest savings and loan in America and enabling millions of Californians to realize the American dream.

SUCCESS IN A MANAGED ECONOMY

Ahmanson made his fortune in the context of an industry and an economy that became highly managed by government in response to the Great Depression and World War II. In the managed economy, government harnessed the capacities of private enterprise to achieve social goals. In turn, private enterprise maximized its profits by using government to stabilize competitive markets.[16]

Financial services were at the center of the managed economy. Under this regime, commercial banks and savings and loans enjoyed limits on competition and received government protection from catastrophic risk. Regulation, fiscal policy, and the monetary initiatives of the Federal Reserve were the most important tools the government employed to protect the financial system from collapsing and to provide an economic safety net—and eventually the means to attain a piece of the American dream—for as many citizens as possible. In return, the government expected the banking system to provide a stable supply of credit and an efficient system to channel the nation's savings into investments.

The mortgage industry and home ownership grew tremendously in the era of the managed economy. Government loan guarantees and mortgage insurance provided by the Veterans Administration and the Federal Housing Administration lowered lenders' risk. With less risk, lenders could afford to make loans at affordable interest rates to younger borrowers with less savings and lower incomes.[17] New home construction exploded. By the end of the 1950s, a quarter of the nation's single-family homes were less than ten years old. Middle-class savers provided much of the capital to finance the mortgage market with their life insurance premium payments as well as their savings accounts, and their companies provided more with their pension fund investments.

Among all the institutions shaped by the managed economy, the savings and loans—or thrifts—were especially important for economic, cultural, and political reasons. They represented the blended ambitions of businessmen, regulators, and politicians. Regulators wanted to rationalize the financial system to create stability in the marketplace. Politicians saw in thrifts a return to cultural ambitions rooted deep in the Jeffersonian ideal. By extending the opportunity of home ownership to a majority of the nation's households, Congress and various presidents sought to reaffirm the roots of an independent citizenry in the rich tradition of property ownership. Although leaders in the savings and loan industry—including Ahmanson, Fletcher, and Edgerton—shared this belief in the social value of home ownership, they also saw the entrepreneurial opportunity that the American dream created and appreciated how government intervention limited their business risks.

During the era of the managed economy, entrepreneurs like Howard Ahmanson in industries ranging from communications to transportation to financial services succeeded because they understood the social contract between business and government. They took advantage of competitive opportunities, subsidies, or protections created by government. They artfully managed their relations with politicians and regulators to protect their state-created advantages and opportunities. At the same time, they deployed traditional entrepreneurial skills to create products, services, and organizations that fit the markets circumscribed by policy makers.[18]

Howard Ahmanson reflected many of the characteristics of the government entrepreneur in the era of the managed economy. After purchasing Home Building and Loan in 1947 (later renamed Home Savings and Loan and then just Home Savings), he understood and embraced the government's policy goals, particularly the central effort to promote home ownership. He cultivated relationships with legislators and regulators to protect the policy-driven business environment that made him and his companies successful. He invested part of his profits back into the community to reinforce the civic qualities of his entrepreneurial endeavors.

SHAPING POSTWAR LOS ANGELES

The success of Home Savings reflected the remarkable achievements of the savings and loan industry in Southern California. During the era of the managed economy, when savings and loans made the majority of loans to home owners throughout the country, thrifts in Southern California dominated the mortgage market far more than they did in any other region.[19]

The extraordinary success of the savings and loan industry in Los Angeles was anchored in a number of factors: the city's explosive growth in the postwar era, the underlying opportunities created by government programs for returning GIs and middle-income families, and a cadre of industry leaders who capitalized on these opportunities to propel their businesses. Through its real estate development entities and its lending practices, Home Savings and Loan and other thrifts in Southern California played a leading role in the postwar suburban explosion that made Los Angeles the quintessential postmodern city.

With their personal fortunes and egos so intertwined with the city's development, it's not surprising that Ahmanson, Edgerton, and other savings and loan executives exerted an important influence on the cultural development of Los Angeles as well. Through the unique art and architecture of its branches, Home Savings and Loan reflected a specifically Southern California perspective on the American dream. Through his philanthropy, Howard Ahmanson contributed to Los Angeles's transformation from a cultural backwater to a world-class city for the arts.

THE END OF THE MANAGED ECONOMY AND THE CONSENSUS SOCIETY

From the Great Depression to the Great Society, a majority of the nation's citizens and its leaders believed in government's efficacy and the idea of the managed economy. In 1964, for example, three out of four Americans agreed that the government would "do what's right" always or most of the time. Nearly two-thirds (64 percent) said that the government was run for the benefit of all. As the memory of the radio broadcast on December 7, 1941, faded, however, public trust and confidence in government declined dramatically. Civil rights and antiwar demonstrations in the mid-1960s reflected growing social unrest. Two years after Howard Ahmanson's death in 1968, barely half of the country was confident that the government would do the right thing and six out of ten people believed that the government primarily benefited special interests.[20]

The decline in public confidence in government was mirrored by a growing intellectual attack on the idea of the managed economy. Economists at the University of Chicago and other institutions highlighted inefficiencies in the regulatory system. These theorists, along with consumer advocates, charged that regulators were too often "captured" by the industries they were supposed to regulate.[21] As a result, these agencies reached decisions outside of the core democratic framework embedded in the Constitution.[22] Meanwhile, business leaders chafed at rules that prevented them from pursuing opportunities tied to their core assets or skill sets. Their voices added to a rising tide of popular antigovernment sentiment as the consensus forged by the war years faded in the nation's collective memory. In this political economy, a sweeping movement toward deregulation, or what one scholar has called "contrived competition," reshaped the landscape of many industries, including mortgage lending and financial services.[23]

The high tide of the deregulatory movement came in the late 1990s with the repeal of major elements of financial regulation that had been the centerpiece of New Deal reforms in the 1930s. Massive consolidation in financial services followed, with commercial and investment banks merging with insurance companies and brokerage firms. In 1998, long after Ahmanson's death, Home Savings was sold to Washington Mutual, and the combined entity instantly became one of the largest banks in the country. Washington Mutual's success in this new environment was short-lived. When the housing bubble burst in 2007, the value of mortgage-backed securities plunged. Weakened by these collapsing asset values, in 2008 the company was acquired by JPMorgan Chase in a fire sale that brought a sad end to an institution that had once epitomized Southern California success and stability in the era of the managed economy.

The collapse of Washington Mutual and the mortgage market challenged fundamental elements of both the managed economy and deregulation. Conservatives blamed policy makers, insisting that the drive to extend home ownership to more and more lower-income Americans had gone beyond the bounds of prudence and reason.[24] Others suggested that elaborate new strategies for risk analysis had encouraged overconfidence on Wall Street.[25] Demand for mortgage-backed securities grew so large that it led to dramatic declines in credit standards as lenders practically threw money at borrowers, knowing that mortgages could be quickly securitized and sold to investors. Much of this problem could be tied to the transformation of mortgage lending brought on by securitization and deregulation. As finger-pointing began and calls for a new regulatory framework in financial services grew, the history of the managed economy and the mortgage market in the postwar era seemed strangely forgotten.[26]

In the context of the mortgage market's collapse and of widespread disenchantment with the pattern of deregulation over the past three decades, this book offers a look back at a different era. It weaves together three stories. It is one part corporate and industrial history, using the evolution of mortgage finance as a way to understand larger dynamics in the nation's political economy. It is another part urban history, since the extraordinary success of the savings and loan business in Los Angeles reflects the cultural and economic history of Southern California. Finally, it is a personal story, a biography of one of the nation's most successful entrepreneurs of the managed economy—Howard Fieldstad Ahmanson.

Unlike tycoons of an earlier era, Ahmanson evidenced neither inventive genius nor the ability or desire to oversee a great technological enterprise. He did not control some vast infrastructure like a railroad or an electrical utility. Nor did he build his wealth by pulling the financial levers that made possible these great corporate endeavors. Instead, he made a fortune by financing the middle-class American dream.

Perceived as a risk taker by outside observers, Ahmanson was actually extremely careful. He studied problems—in business and on the high seas—and devoted himself to limiting risk. In his initial field of endeavor, insurance, he found the safest of all markets and profited by minimizing losses. In lending, he focused exclusively on single-family homes, believing that the American dream of home ownership was so powerful that it offered the lender an extra margin of safety. In a racist era when even the federal government officially countenanced segregation, he avoided neighborhoods of color, preferring to lend to the aspiring white, middle-class home buyers that he knew and understood.[27] He succeeded by sticking to the basics as he understood them: sound lending, low-cost operations, and economies of scope and scale.

In an era famous for faceless corporate control and organization men, Ahmanson evidenced numerous contradictions. He refused to sell stock in his various companies, maintaining total personal control. Yet he was also a delegator—assembling a close circle of lieutenants who managed the company's day-to-day operations according to his vision so that he could work from home and take a dip in the pool whenever he felt like it. Though he clearly wanted the limelight, he was reluctant to be inconvenienced by public attention. Despite owning the largest and most successful savings and loan in the country, he had little to do with his industry's trade associations. With his great wealth, he contributed substantially to the expansion of the cultural institutions in Los Angeles and was pleased to have galleries, theaters, and research facilities named for him and his family. But after a brief flirtation with politics in the mid-1950s, he let others manage his company's lobbying and political deal making and deemed party politics a waste of time.

Yet Ahmanson was hardly a recluse. From the 1930s on, he and Dottie appeared regularly in the society pages of the *Los Angeles Times*. With a drink and a cigarette in front of him, he played the piano or the organ for his fellow revelers. After he and Dottie separated in 1961, his friend Art Linkletter, the television show host, introduced him to Caroline Leonetti, a charm school entrepreneur and TV personality. Smitten by her energy, intelligence, and good looks, Ahmanson married her. Together they hosted the power elite and helped to build cultural and educational institutions that he hoped would begin a new era in the history of Los Angeles and Southern California.

On his boats and in his business, Ahmanson brooked no dead weight and demanded loyalty, integrity, intelligence, and hard work. He also was ferociously competitive. He and his crews won most of the major West Coast yachting races in the late 1950s and early 1960s. Some of his closest friends were business rivals. He could enjoy their companionship and yet take great pleasure in beating them on the ocean or in the marketplace.

Despite his high standing among the nation's wealthiest citizens and the headlines that he and his yachting crews made in the *Los Angeles Times*'s sports section, most Americans and even Southern Californians knew little about Howard Ahmanson. In the infrequent profiles that appeared in the press during his lifetime, Ahmanson mythologized his childhood, repeating the same stories from one interview to the next. The uneven paper trail he left survives because others, particularly his first wife, Dottie, kept some of his personal correspondence. Only a few of his close relatives, friends, competitors, and business associates remain to tell his story. Yet when the fragments of his life are fitted into the context of his times, his biography sheds light on an important era in America.

Father as Mentor

THE MINISTER OF THE NORTH PRESBYTERIAN CHURCH in Omaha undoubtedly reminded the worshippers on Easter Sunday morning in 1913 that they were in the house of the Lord—and what a house it was. Inspired by the neoclassical architecture of the 1898 Trans-Mississippi and International Exposition, which celebrated Omaha's heroic role in the opening of the American West, the new church reflected both the hope of the Resurrection and the republican ideals of ancient Greece and Rome.[1] Despite the glory of the space, the reverend often cautioned his congregation against hubris. God's will would be done despite all worldly precautions.

These sermons touched the faith of one man in the congregation who came frequently with his wife and two sons. William "Will" Ahmanson understood that ultimately the world and the afterlife were in God's hands, but he believed that in this world men should not tempt their maker. For the sake of their families, business partners, and creditors, men had a responsibility to insure their property and persons against the risks of fire, flood, and sudden death.

Ahmanson thought he knew how to manage those risks. An insurance man since he was a teenager, he had studied the laws of statistics and probability. He learned to pay attention to the details of circumstances and conditions. Like all actuaries, he had developed a godlike ability to know in the aggregate what would be lost and who would be saved in the event of a fire. Yet like all insurance men, he lived in fear of a great disaster that would overwhelm the predictable cycle of fires and minor floods.

After the service on Easter morning in 1913, the overcast skies began to clear. The dry brown front lawns and shrubs just beginning to bud after the winter smelled of earth and rain. Within the eight blocks between the church and the Ahmansons' modest home at 2516 North Nineteenth Street a diversity of architectural styles reflected the heritage of Omaha's first streetcar suburb. Most of the neighborhood's residents were native born, but there were also Scandinavian, Scottish, German, and English immigrants. The men had white-collar jobs. They were shop owners, postal and city clerks, a streetcar conductor, an orchestra musician, and a pharmacist.[2] Like Will Ahmanson, they were all hoping to get ahead in the world.

Like most of these middle-class proprietors and salary men, Will and his wife Florence had great hopes for their two sons, Hayden and Howard. At age fifteen, Hayden was away from home that Sunday attending the Kemper Military School in Missouri. So Will doted on Howard. At six years old, the boy exhibited a confidence and intellect that ignited Will's pride. He often brought the boy along when he went to meetings or to see customers.

By late afternoon, the day was bright and warm. Then shortly before six o'clock, the wind began to blow. At the Diamond Moving Picture Theater, in a neighborhood not far away that had become home to Omaha's growing African American population, a crowd of sixty people gathered to see the black-and-white silent film *Twister*. Those who were still outside noticed the sky to the southwest turn luminous, "a lurid brass-yellow" color.[3] A black funnel cloud appeared. As it swirled and twisted toward the city, the tornado slammed to earth and then bounced back into the air. One man said, "It came like a rushing and roaring torrent of water."[4] As the sound increased and the air pressure dropped, the Ahmansons' dog grew nervous and bolted from the house. Howard wanted to run after him, but his parents hurried him into the cellar.

Then suddenly the tornado was on them. The swirling dust and debris blocked the waning daylight. The fierce wind ripped homes from their foundations and lifted them into the air. It tore roofs off homes and trees from the earth and smashed brick buildings. As the walls of the Diamond Motion Picture Theater crumbled, the roof fell in.[5] Then the tornado roared east, crossing the Missouri River and slashing its way toward Council Bluffs.

In the eerie silence that greeted them when they emerged from the cellar, the Ahmansons discovered their house still standing. They could hear shouts, sparks, and explosions as broken gas lines and severed electrical wires ignited fires that danced in the particulated evening air. The bells of horse-drawn fire trucks followed as they raced through the debris-laden streets. Fortunately, a heavy rain began that lasted for almost an hour, making the firemen's jobs easier.

The path of devastation, two to six blocks wide, was so narrow and inter-mittent that people wondered if it had been inscribed by God. Some believ-ers said that he had sent the deadliest tornado in American history on Easter Sunday to punish Omaha for the drinking, gambling, and prostitution that were legendary in this western city. Others pointed out that among the 135 killed in the city were innocent children as well as aging sinners.[6] Plenty of God-fearing people had inhabited the more than two thousand homes de-stroyed by the whirlwind. The victims had simply succumbed to bad luck.

MAKING YOUR OWN LUCK

Will Ahmanson's family believed that luck could be shaped by hard work. Will's Swedish father, John, had converted to the Church of Jesus Christ of Latter Day Saints as a young man and had been jailed in Norway in 1852 for preaching the Mormon faith.[7] He helped organize a group of Scandina-vians, including his Norwegian wife, Grete Fieldstad, to come to America in 1856. They joined the Fourth Handcart Company, and John was chosen to lead the 162 Scandinavian members to Utah.[8]

Following a series of setbacks en route and a miserable winter in Utah, John grew dissatisfied with the Mormon hierarchy. The following year, he and Grete and their first child left the church and joined a wagon train re-turning east. When John tried to retrieve his belongings stashed at the Mor-mon outpost of Devil's Gate, however, church leaders wouldn't return them to him. Frustrated, John and his family continued on to Omaha, where they settled in 1859. John became a hardware merchant and then a grocer. He also sued Brigham Young and the Mormon Church.

John was rewarded for his temerity and persistence. The jury ordered Young to pay him $1,297.50. Young tried to force a new trial but ultimately agreed to pay Ahmanson $1,000.[9] With this payment, John moved his fam-ily to Chicago so he could study medicine. After completing his studies, he remained in the Windy City for nearly a decade.[10] In 1879, he returned to Omaha and began practicing as a homeopath.[11]

Of John and Grete Ahmanson's three children, Will was the youngest.[12] Born in 1872, three years after the completion of the transcontinental rail-road and four years before the Battle of the Little Bighorn, he grew up with Omaha as it developed from a wide-open frontier town into an agricultural shipping center and one of the Midwest's major cities.[13] When he left high school at the age of fifteen, one friend advised him to become a preacher; another suggested he go into insurance. He chose insurance.[14]

A handsome and elegant man, Will had a strong, square face with a cleft chin. Keeping with the style of the times, he parted his hair loosely in the center. His soft eyes communicated patience and understanding. He wore a starched white collar, a silk necktie, and expensive suits. Undoubtedly, his good looks helped to charm Florence Mae Hayden, a slight, strong-willed woman. Born in Pennsylvania, she had grown up in the Sandhills of western Nebraska.[15] Her Scotch-Irish family had been in the United States since the Revolutionary War. She married Will in 1897 and gave birth to Hayden a year later. A daughter died as an infant.[16] Several years passed and then Howard was born on July 1, 1906.[17] After Howard, Florence had no more children.

FATHER AS MENTOR

Will Ahmanson loved both of his sons, but he showered pride and attention on Howard, whom he called a genius. "Father and Bud were extremely close," Hayden once said, betraying more wonder than jealousy. "They couldn't seem to get to see enough of each other."[18] While Howard was still in elementary school, Will took the boy aside every evening after dinner. "While he smoked a cigar he'd talk over with me the events of the day—business affairs and finances—as if I had the maturity and judgment of a man of 50."[19] When Will played cards or shot pool with his friends downtown, Howard tagged along and listened to the talk of business and politics.[20] Meanwhile, Florence set high expectations.[21] She was smart and competitive, with a strong sense of right and wrong.

Howard received an enormous amount of attention from both his parents. In the second grade, his report card carried A's in every subject except deportment. Rather than let this single instance of imperfection slide, his parents took him to the University of Omaha to be part of a special study. The staff told the Ahmansons that Howard didn't have enough to do. Will and Florence decided Howard needed lessons in German and piano.[22]

On another occasion, when Howard came home from elementary school his father asked if his grades were the best in the class. Howard confessed they were not. A girl in his class was number one; he was number two. His father responded, "Hmm, how in the world did that happen?" This was typical of the way Will approached the issue of setting standards, said Howard. "He never criticized me. He led me by sheer devotion."[23]

Will also believed in giving his son extraordinary responsibilities. When Howard was twelve or thirteen years old, Will opened a brokerage account for Howard, bankrolled it, and told his stockbroker to let the young man decide his own trades. Howard bought Bethlehem Steel while his father bought U.S. Steel. "When my stock went up twice as much as his, he was the happiest man in Nebraska," Howard remembered.[24] Father and son also collaborated on research and sometimes invested in the same company.[25]

An automobile enthusiast in the earliest days of the Model T, Will let his fourteen-year-old son drive. Howard fixed the license plate to a hinge and ran a wire to the driver's seat so that if he saw a policeman he could raise the plate so it was horizontal to the ground and harder to read.[26] "I shouldn't even have been allowed to drive for another two years," Howard recalled years later, "but nothing was too good for me."[27]

Howard skipped a grade and entered high school in 1919 at the age of thirteen. He entertained his friends by playing the banjo, the piano, and the organ, but he showed no interest in the school's music groups.[28] A popular junior, he became increasingly distracted by girls. When his grades fell, his teachers sent home warnings. "We called them flunk notices," Howard remembered. One day, his mother confronted him with the notices and tucked them under Will's plate at supper with the rest of the mail. Howard waited for his father to say something. When he was done eating, Howard excused himself, saying he had a date. Will followed him out the door.

Unable to stand the suspense, Howard asked, "Did you read your mail?"

"You mean those flunk notices?" his father asked.

"Yes."

Will guided him to the car. As Howard slid into the driver's seat, Will closed the door and spoke through the open window. "You're going to make it, aren't you?"

"Oh sure," Howard responded.

"Well—Good night," his father answered.

According to Howard, "that was all that was ever said about it." It seemed to be enough. Howard brought his grades up. "After all," he said later, "what would you do with a father like that? You had to do what he expected you to do."[29]

Under Florence's influence, Howard became a member of the Presbyterian Church.[30] He was active in the YMCA, passing his Bible study course with high marks.[31] But religion never became an important part of his life. Fifty years later, when he had a son of his own, he told a reporter that he was taking his son to a different church every weekend "to find one that fit," as if religion were simply one more accessory to the good life.

Throughout his childhood, Howard's relationship with Hayden was somewhat distant. Eight years older, Hayden left home to attend the Kemper Military Academy just as Howard was starting school.[32] By the time Howard was in his teenage years, Hayden was in college at the University of Nebraska. When Howard was in high school, Hayden was working for his father's company as an assistant underwriter. After Hayden began dating Aimee Elizabeth Tolbod, she joined the family for dinner every Sunday night, introducing another subtle distance between the two brothers.[33]

Later in life, Howard would idealize his childhood in Omaha. He remembered twenty maple trees for climbing in the yard of his parents' house. He played with the neighbor kids. In the summer, the family vacationed at Lake Okoboji in Iowa. Yet Omaha, like the rest of America, was a complicated and sometimes troubled place in the first two decades of the twentieth century.

AN UNSETTLED CITY

The fourth-largest city in the trans-Mississippi West, Omaha lagged only San Francisco, Denver, and Kansas City. On the streetcars, Howard overheard the thick accents of Germans, Swedes, Hungarians, Danes, and Italians who had come to work for the railroad, the packinghouses, the distilleries, and a host of other industries that depended on the shipment and processing of agricultural products.[34]

In this era, the entrepreneurs of the frontier age gave way to business leaders who collaborated to promote the city and resist unionization. The city became a regional center for banking and insurance. Between 1916 and 1918, Omaha rose from sixteenth to fourteenth on the list of cities leading the nation in bank clearings.[35] Nebraska led the nation in the number of banks per capita—with one for every 1,207 people, compared to the national average of one for every 4,032.[36] In Nebraska, and Omaha particularly, managing and protecting capital was big business.

Despite its importance as a financial center, Omaha also had a dark side. As in many American cities, political control rested in the hands of a shadowy political boss. Gambling and saloons flourished even after national prohibition was adopted in 1919. By one estimate, Omaha had twenty-six hundred prostitutes in 1910. Providing sex and liquor to cowboys, railroad workers and other men, the city's houses of ill repute netted $17.5 million a year.[37] In addition to crime, liquor, and prostitution, Omaha also experienced inter-ethnic and racial violence. A mob of a thousand men attacked the Greek section of town in 1909, looting, burning buildings, and attacking residents.[38] Ten years later, as race riots flared in midwestern cities, an African-American packinghouse worker was arrested and accused of assaulting a nineteen-year-old white woman and her companion. A mob stormed the courthouse, nearly lynched the mayor, and then seized the defendant. He was hanged, mutilated, and dragged through the streets with a rope around his neck. His bullet-riddled body was burned as the crowd cheered and posed for photographers.

If he didn't witness the murder, thirteen-year-old Howard Ahmanson certainly heard about it. His neighbor and high school classmate, actor Henry Fonda, was so seared by what he saw that he became a lifelong advocate of racial equality and social justice.[39] The chamber of commerce decried the violence and the breakdown in civil order.[40] But the lesson that Howard seems to have taken from this event was far more practical: in investing or taking risks, avoid the fault lines of society—the boundaries between races—where friction could lead to cataclysm.

SELLING FIRE INSURANCE
IN A VOLATILE COMMUNITY

Howard frequently discussed the stock market, grain prices, land deals, the insurance industry, and politics with his father.[41] These conversations undoubtedly influenced Howard's thinking about risk, management, and regulation.

In the 1920s, the American economy was in the midst of a critical transition that had begun well before World War I. New technologies and organizational strategies enabled a great merger movement that concentrated economic power.[42] Giant corporations like Standard Oil, United States Steel, American Telephone & Telegraph, and American Tobacco—known to many as "the trusts"—employed thousands of workers and made millions of dollars in profits. Populists resisted this economic power and called for trust-busting and regulation. Under Presidents Theodore Roosevelt, William Howard Taft, and Woodrow Wilson, the federal government's role in the economy grew significantly. In various state capitals, new regulatory commissions and agencies proliferated to protect consumers and stabilize chaotic markets.[43] Fire insurance, like virtually every other industry, was affected by the increasing scope and scale of business activity and government's growing role in managing the economy.

Fire insurance companies started as mutual or cooperative organizations, and this heritage was important to the way they operated and were regulated. It would also be important to the first fortune that Howard Ahmanson would make in the insurance industry and to the second fortune he earned in savings and loans. The first associations were created after the Great Fire in London in 1666, when property owners banded together to provide financial protection to one another in case of fire. Their "mutual" property insurance concept was replicated in the American colonies by Benjamin Franklin, who organized the first association in 1735.

With a mutual, risk was managed by familiarity. Members knew one another and the properties they were covering. Excess profits were returned to the members, so the insured was less inclined to worry that shareholders or owners were exploiting the policyholder. These associations—along with savings banks and building and loan associations—were part of a fabric of cooperative community institutions that proliferated in the United States in the eighteenth and nineteenth centuries.

The success of the mutuals attracted entrepreneurs who understood that insurance companies amassed enormous quantities of capital that could be invested. Earnings on this capital that exceeded the costs of paying policyholders' claims could be pocketed by shareholders. Success depended on making smart investments and limiting insurance risk—especially catastrophic risks like the Chicago fire of 1871 and the San Francisco earthquake and fire of 1906.

Large insurance companies enjoyed a competitive advantage in insurance. With greater numbers of policyholders and accurate statistics, the number of claims was much more predictable. By developing networks of agents and offices in the age of the telegraph, some insurance companies enjoyed the kind of economies of scope and scale associated with large industrial companies like railroads, power, and telegraph companies at the end of the nineteenth century.[44]

Will Ahmanson's career developed in tandem with the insurance industry in the United States. Omaha became a major insurance center—a kind of Hartford of the Midwest.[45] Most of the fire insurance companies were stock companies. By 1913, these for-profit enterprises covered nearly 93 percent of the $790 million in fire and property insurance written in the state.[46] These were profitable businesses. The combined income of all Omaha insurance companies topped $23.5 million in 1917.[47]

In a regional center like Omaha, leading insurance men often worked as agents or managers for several companies. Will Ahmanson's various affiliations between 1906 and 1919 reflected the fluidity of the business. Between 1906 and 1914, he was the assistant secretary of the Nebraska Underwriters Insurance Company, worked for the State Insurance Company of Nebraska (which was acquired by the National Fire Insurance Company of Hartford in 1912), and then joined Columbia Fire Underwriters in 1913.[48] He was also the assistant manager of the German Fire Underwriters of Omaha.[49] All of this movement reflected the still-unsettled state of the industry as consumers, companies, and politicians sought to use government to strengthen their respective positions in the marketplace, ensure "fair" treatment for everyone involved, and forge a political consensus.

REGULATING FIRE INSURANCE

Like businessmen in many industries, fire insurance agents tested their relationship with government on many fronts. On the one hand, they resisted proposed laws that were at odds with the fundamental economics of their industry. On the other hand, they turned to government to stabilize their business environment.[50] Thus insurance leaders exhibited the same conflicted perspective on regulation that characterized many industries at the beginning of the twentieth century.

Reckless competition posed the biggest threat to the stability of the fire insurance business. Upstanding companies were often undersold by naive or fraudulent firms that didn't have the means to pay claims if disaster struck. These "wildcatters" sparked rate wars. Although established insurance companies promoted their stability and trustworthiness to counter the wildcatters' price competition, customers had little ability to discern what fair rates for fire insurance should be and often selected companies on the basis of the price of their premiums rather than their reliability.

Incumbent insurance companies responded to this market competition by lobbying for limited regulation. They urged state governments to require new companies to post bonds, but these efforts to create state-sanctioned barriers to entry were largely unsuccessful in the late nineteenth century.[51] Insurers also tried self-regulation or cartelization.[52] In various states and nationally, they created underwriting boards to collect data and assess the level of risk associated with different kinds of buildings and uses. They then established systems of uniform rates. The best-known of these organizations, the National Board of Fire Underwriters, was launched after the Civil War by seventy-five companies from the East and the Midwest.[53]

Cooperative rate setting, however, prompted an outcry from customers. Some states accused the underwriting boards of violating state and national antitrust laws. In Nebraska, the legislature passed a law in 1897 barring insurance companies from combining to set rates or commissions paid to agents.[54] Although these efforts to apply antitrust laws to insurance were generally unsuccessful in the courts, state legislators introduced bills banning insurance compacts in thirty-three states between 1885 and 1900, and in sixteen states these bills were adopted into law.[55]

Frustrated, some customers turned to government. In 1909, Kansas adopted a law giving the state superintendent of insurance the power to approve rates. Insurers challenged the law, but in 1914, in *German Alliance Ins v. Lewis,* the U.S. Supreme Court upheld the state's authority.[56] Many other states followed Kansas. In Nebraska, the legislature passed a "New Insurance Code" in 1913 to establish comprehensive insurance regulation. The new structure withstood both judicial and electoral challenges in part because of an emerging consensus that regulation was a reasonable means to avoid various scenarios that would put the government in control of the marketplace as an agent of either labor or corporate interests.[57]

Even as they resisted efforts to bar them from collaborating and fought state rate regulation, fire insurance companies saw how they could benefit by working with government. Research developed by the fire insurance underwriting boards led to the development of model building standards and codes that lowered the risk of fire. Insurers pressured communities to adopt these standards and to develop and maintain fire departments. Where cities fell behind on their investments in fire departments, the industry raised rates or threatened to withdraw altogether. Will Ahmanson served on the Nebraska State Committee in 1918 as a volunteer building inspector looking for potential fire hazards. Altogether, these efforts to prevent fires represented the epitome of Progressive reform: collecting data, addressing underlying causes, marshaling citizen volunteers, often soliciting compliance and sometimes compelling it through state-enforced regulation.

A LOCAL COMPANY TO TAKE THE PLACE
OF EASTERN CAPITAL

Will Ahmanson watched all of these developments with an eye to his own opportunities and a growing frustration that his hometown was so dependent on East Coast insurance interests. In April 1919, he saw an opportunity to launch his own local company. But the effort nearly cost him his reputation.

In the securities markets of the 1910s and 1920s, stock scams were common and often targeted rural investors. Will Ahmanson must have known this, but for some reason he trusted the two stock promoters who came to him with the idea of creating National American Fire Insurance.[58] They appealed to his personal and civic aspirations and convinced him and other investors that they could create "the largest insurance company west of the Mississippi."[59] To reassure investors, they wanted Will to serve as president and become a major owner. Will agreed and recruited a friend and colleague, James Foster, from Columbia Fire Underwriters, to serve as secretary-treasurer.[60]

The stock promoters traveled throughout Nebraska and Iowa selling shares to farmers and small-town merchants and bankers. They bought full-page ads in the *Omaha World-Herald* promising profits and security. "No more attractive investment ever has been offered the public of the west," the ads exclaimed. "Sound, substantial, and certain of profit." The writers explained, "The state sees that the company's capital, which you helped to furnish, is kept intact."[61]

The promoters offered liberal terms to investors—half of the money down, with the rest due in six months at 6 percent interest.[62] Patriotic farmers and citizens were allowed to exchange their deflated Liberty Bonds, purchased during World War I, at full par value for National American stock. Some buyers were even offered seats on the board.[63] Using all of these tactics, in six months the promoters sold $1.115 million worth of stock to bankers, merchants, and farmers in towns and cities scattered across Nebraska.[64]

Will Ahmanson apparently didn't realize that the promoters were more interested in extracting capital than launching an insurance business. He was dismayed when an insurance examiner for the State of Nebraska found that nearly $142,840 had to be written off for "organization expense." This was money the promoters had skimmed for themselves.[65]

Ahmanson worked hard to redeem the investors' trust and protect his own good name. National American Fire Insurance leased an entire floor in downtown Omaha and recruited nearly three hundred agents in the surrounding territory.[66] In its first year, the company wrote policies for fire, tornado, automobile, hail, and marine insurance; it had gross premium income of more than $26,000 and net losses of only $1,210. It turned a small profit.[67] The chamber of commerce gushed that the company's success was yet another sign of Omaha's growing maturity and place among the nation's great cities. "At the end of its second year [National American] shows a remarkable growth which proves that Western men are beginning to have confidence in Western institutions."[68]

With this success, Will Ahmanson imagined his boys becoming executives with the company. He suggested to Howard that after college he might become National American's vice president and treasurer.[69] He moved his family to a new home in a part of town that would both reflect his position and epitomize all that he and Florence prized—family, community, responsibility, and stability. The neighborhood they chose was full of like-minded families in pursuit of the American dream.

THE MIDWESTERN IDEAL

The neighborhood of Dundee epitomized the suburban ideal at the beginning of the 1920s, and it would play an important part in Howard Ahmanson's vision of the relationship of home, community, and the economy in his later career. Established as an autonomous community just west of Omaha, it was served by a streetcar that carried businessmen like Will Ahmanson from home to office and back every day.

Advertisements for the development in its early years noted the "high dry pure and clean air," in contrast to the stench of the stockyards and factories on the city's south side.[70] Covenants precluded commercial development and barred all immoral and illegal businesses, including the sale of spirits or malt liquors.[71] In short, Dundee offered a refuge from the crowds and corruptions of urban life.

Unlike the suburban tracts that Ahmanson would finance in California, Dundee proudly proclaimed that it had been built "one house at a time." Prairie-style architecture featuring big porches and hipped roofs rose alongside Colonial, Georgian, Craftsman, Tudor, and Italian Renaissance-style homes. Covenants brought some uniformity to the look and feel of the community, however. The homes had twenty-five-foot setbacks to allow for tree-shaded front lawns. Garages were located at the rear of the lots. Alleys provided service access for trash collection and ice and grocery deliveries. Large municipal parks maintained a sense of nature in the neighborhood and served as community gathering places for picnics, concerts, and church revivals.[72]

The house that Will and Florence chose, at 5106 California, was a two-story bungalow with a portico front porch and a dormer window that commanded a view of the street.[73] Only a narrow driveway separated the home from the neighbors'. It was more house and a finer neighborhood than many families could afford, but the ranks of home owners in Omaha were growing.

Streetcars, low-priced land, and an adequate supply of mortgage credit helped make Omaha a city of home owners by 1920. As a building boom increased the number of dwellings in Omaha by 70 percent between 1900 and 1920, the percentage of owner-occupied residences rose from 27.7 to 47.2.[74] Only a handful of other midwestern cities had higher rates.

Home owners in Omaha depended on a variety of formal and informal sources for mortgage capital. Many people borrowed from family members or local merchants. The more affluent turned to commercial banks and mortgage brokers who loaned from their available pools of deposits or acted as agents of large eastern life insurance companies looking for investment opportunities. For the salaried and wage-earning classes, however, the greatest source of mortgage capital was the building and loan, a cooperative institution whose members pooled their savings and invested these funds in mortgages on one another's homes.

As the president of a fire insurance company, Will Ahmanson kept in close contact with the mortgage lenders in Omaha. They were an important source of business and information. Insurance risks and credit risks were often interrelated, and the more Will knew about the trustworthiness of a potential customer, the more he could measure the potential insurance risk.

Attending chamber of commerce meetings as a teenager with his father, Howard Ahmanson met many of these leaders of Omaha's financial sector. From his father he understood that Omaha's high rate of home ownership reflected a well-functioning commercial system, and he aspired to become a part of this system.

SEEKING A PROFESSIONAL EDUCATION IN BUSINESS

Howard already had a sense of himself as a business professional by 1923. He had learned from his father and from his apprenticeship in the offices of National American after school and during the summers. Graduating from Omaha's Central High School on the eve of his seventeenth birthday, he wanted to go east to Yale for college. But his father was not in good health, and Howard was uneasy about the idea of going so far away. Instead, he enrolled at the University of Nebraska to study business.[75]

Business administration was a relatively new academic discipline, and the University of Nebraska was quite proud of its school. As a "Bizad" major, Ahmanson joined the University Commercial Club. He flirted with journalism and worked on the *Cornhusker* yearbook.[76] But he was already a student of entrepreneurship.

He and his friends frequented a short-order restaurant called the White Spot, where crowds of college students and town folk lined up to buy hamburgers. Ahmanson admired the owner's success, especially after he opened six or seven additional White Spot restaurants around town. But Ahmanson also noticed that shortly after the owner added steaks, lobster, and other fancy dishes to the menu, he went broke. "Had he stuck with his original idea of making the best hamburger in town," Ahmanson would later point out, "he'd probably have been quite successful."[77]

A PROGRESSIVE BUSINESS CULTURE

Howard began his college career during a critical transition in the history of business-government relations in the United States. Through the end of the nineteenth century and into the early decades of the twentieth, myriad industries in the American economy became increasingly concentrated as entrepreneurs took advantage of the growing national transportation system to increase the scope and scale of manufacturing and to ship products throughout the country.[78] This economic integration fed the growth of cities, as factories swelled with workers fresh off the farm or the boat from Europe. A loose coalition of social reformers and business leaders known as Progressives sought to rationalize government's management of the infrastructure of society and the economy.[79] In cities like Omaha, Progressives campaigned to end machine politics and put decision making in the hands of nonpartisan "experts" and committees. At the national level, a series of Republican administrations focused on cooperation with big business rather than regulation.

Among the leaders of this Republican movement, none was more important than the Iowa-born Herbert Hoover. A mining engineer and successful businessman by World War I, he earned worldwide respect and admiration when he oversaw an international effort to provide food to Belgium's starving people during World War I. Appointed U.S. secretary of commerce in 1921, he made his philosophy clear: "The Department of Commerce should be in the widest sense a department of service to the commerce and industry of the country. It is not a department for the regulation of trade and industry. In order to do service to great advantage, I wish to establish a wider and better organized co-operation with the trades and commercial associations."[80]

Hoover transformed his agency in an effort to establish a new model for the ways in which government could support private efforts to strengthen the economy and society.[81] He created bureaus to deal with new industries, including aeronautics and radio. He restructured the Bureau of the Census to aid business by publishing more data. He expanded the government's role as convener and coordinator, urging business leaders to join trade associations to address public policy issues in a coordinated manner. "We are passing from a period of extreme individualistic action," he said in 1924, "into a period of associational activities."[82] Hoover envisioned a system in which public policy would be made by experts, technicians, and professionals deeply immersed in their subjects, who would collaborate voluntarily for the greater good of society, leaving traditional patronage politics to the history books. Under this framework, the federal government would become more "elaborate and permissive," serving as "a clearinghouse for business compromise" and widening the dialogue among communities of interest.[83]

As a business student at the state university in 1925, Howard was exposed to the ideology of Hoover-style Progressivism. He read Warren G. Harding's *Our Common Country: Mutual Good Will in America,* noting the late president's call for a better understanding between business and government.

Ranked in the top ten in his class, Ahmanson seemed destined to become one of Hoover's professional managers, but the greatest loss of his life would lead to an entirely different future.[84]

A PERSONAL CRISIS

Will Ahmanson suffered from goiter, an enlargement of the thyroid. In many patients, the condition created a swelling in the throat that made it hard to talk or swallow. Sometimes it was associated with an increased heart rate or an irregular heartbeat and muscle weakness. Researchers suspected that goiter resulted from an iodine deficiency. In the 1920s, however, popular culture blamed a variety of factors ranging from the stresses of modern life to jazz music.[85] In regions far from the ocean like the Great Lakes, the Missouri River valley, and the upper Midwest, the malady was so common that these areas were called "goiter belts."

Will's health had already affected the lives of both of his children. Hayden had proposed to Aimee on the eve of his graduation from law school. They had planned to marry in the spring of 1924, but Will was so often bedridden that they postponed the ceremony. Instead of launching his career as a lawyer, Hayden returned to National American as an underwriter so he could monitor his father's interest in the business.[86]

In the fall of 1924, Will seemed to be getting better. Aimee and Hayden married in a simple ceremony at the house officiated by the minister from Dundee Presbyterian Church. Then Will and Florence left to spend the winter in California.[87] In Los Angeles they visited many former Nebraskans who had moved to the Golden State. Under the California sun, and perhaps with more seafood in his diet, Will's health improved.

While his parents were gone, Howard spent his weekends and vacations with Hayden and Aimee.[88] They talked about the situation at National American. In 1924, Will and a couple of partners had launched another business, making loans on automobiles.[89] This new company, like National American, was growing as the economy in Omaha and around the country enjoyed good times. But with Will away, the company needed leadership. James Foster was well qualified for the job, but Will may have hoped that one of his sons would succeed him, and the brothers apparently expected this as well.

After Will and Florence returned to Omaha, a rare heat wave struck in the middle of May. Will lay in bed struggling to breathe, while Florence tried to keep him cool. When it was clear that there was no other option, he was admitted to the hospital to have his thyroid removed. The surgery was not successful. On the evening of May 22, Howard's father died.

LEGACY TAKEN AWAY

Will's death unraveled the family's control of the businesses that he had helped to build. "Everything he was into, somebody took a swipe at," Howard told a reporter many years later.[90] On the morning of the funeral, the directors of National American Fire Insurance met without the family and chose Foster to succeed Will as president.[91] Meanwhile, the banks cut off credit to the auto loan company and forced the Ahmansons to sell their interest in the business to the surviving partners.[92]

The family was hardly destitute. The *Omaha World Herald* reported that Ahmanson's estate was worth $75,000 (nearly $961,660 in 2011 dollars). Florence was left with a substantial sum of money and fifteen hundred shares in National American Fire Insurance.[93] Each of her sons received one hundred shares.[94] Howard also had the investments in his own brokerage account, which were worth nearly $20,000 in 1925 (nearly $258,000 in 2011 dollars)— a fortune for a teenager.

Howard returned to the University of Nebraska to begin his junior year, but shortly after the term started Florence became ill. Howard raced back to Omaha. With memories of Southern California still fresh in her mind and the doctor's recommendation that she move to a gentler climate, Florence and Howard decided to move to California. Howard loaded his roadster with his belongings and left that night for Los Angeles to find a place for them to live and make arrangements for Florence to join him.[95]

Deeply affected by his father's death, Howard confessed that it "made me do funny things for a long time."[96] He swore that one day he would regain control of National American. "I am a worshipper of my father," he told a reporter. "He used to tell me the world's your oyster. Nothing's impossible to you."[97] Witnessing his father's betrayal led him to "the crazy idea that anything I got into, I was going to control. . . . Having seen my father's dreams all shot to pieces because he was so trusting, I decided that the worst thing in the world was partners, and that being liquid was the best."[98]

TWO

Among the Lotus Eaters

ARRIVING IN LOS ANGELES in the fall of 1925, Howard Ahmanson discovered a city like Omaha. It was full of progressive, middle-class midwesterners, who had come after selling their farms and businesses. In many ways they had recreated a community they knew and understood, with "state societies" like the Iowa and the Nebraska clubs. They called themselves "Hawkeyes" or "Cornhuskers." They socialized with others from their home states and attended enormous annual picnics celebrating the history and culture of the Midwest.

Everyone seemed to be a recent transplant. Nine out of ten residents had been in Los Angeles less than fifteen years.[1] Without a rigid social structure—at least for white native-born Americans—the city offered opportunity to the entrepreneur and a boosterish political culture that blended public purpose with private gain and a social setting suited to Howard's ambition.[2]

Writer Carey McWilliams, who arrived in Los Angeles from Colorado with his mother and brother three years before Ahmanson, became convinced that these midwesterners never really adjusted to life in Southern California. Just as European immigrants in Eastern cities expressed nostalgia for the Old World and clung to tight-knit communities of immigrants in the New, midwesterners in Los Angeles lived within their transplanted communities at the edge of the Pacific.[3]

As he oriented himself, Howard discovered a community bursting with its own sense of destiny. In quarter-page newspaper advertisements, the Department of Water and Power, which was "owned by the citizens of Los Angeles," extolled the vision of an earlier generation in building the Los Angeles Aqueduct from the Owens River. The ads touted the promise of Boulder

Dam on the Colorado River, which would store more water than all the other dams in the world combined and would ensure water and power for the city "for all times."[4] The business section was devoted to news of the booming oil industry. Meanwhile, the flood of newcomers fueled an ever-expanding real estate market. As the *Los Angeles Times* pointed out, the city was on track to triple its population in a single decade to become the largest city in the West and the fifth-largest city in the country. "More people means that many square miles of new residence districts will spring up—that existing districts must be built more compactly—that many business sections now unknown will come into being—that many a sparsely settled country road will become a city thoroughfare."[5]

Like Omaha, Los Angeles advertised its commercial success and touted its embrace of the newest technologies and ways of living. The city had more automobiles per capita than any metropolis in the country; Omaha ranked second.[6] Omaha had more telephones per capita—284 for every 1,000 residents—than any other city, but Pasadena ranked second.[7] In the arena of home ownership, Omaha led Los Angeles by a substantial margin—48.4 percent compared to 34.7 percent—despite L.A.'s famous suburban expansion.[8] The two cities also shared a strong commercial link. Oranges and lemons grown in Southern California traveled by rail to Omaha, the headquarters of the Pacific Fruit Express, and were reshipped east to be sold on the streets of New York, Philadelphia, and Boston.[9]

Tourists, retirees, and relatively affluent citrus growers had fueled various boom and bust cycles of real estate speculation and economic growth in Los Angeles. Under the influence of a civic and commercial elite, the city had expanded its public infrastructure for water, power, and transportation ahead of demand, using these investments to attract industry. A vast system of streetcar lines had promoted suburban development of communities that seemed as familiar to Howard as Dundee.[10]

At the time of Howard's arrival, industrial growth in Los Angeles had reached the takeoff point. Over the next two years, the city's manufacturing sector expanded more quickly than that of any city in the nation except Flint, Michigan. By 1927, the dollar value of manufacturing output trailed only New York, Flint, and Milwaukee.[11] Working together, business leaders and local officials successfully promoted the region's development for public benefit and private gain.[12]

The business networks that fueled L.A.'s growth were often rooted in midwestern communities like Omaha. White-collar, native-born, Anglo-Saxon "men on the make" crowded the sidewalks of Spring Street downtown. According to historian Clark Davis, they were "largely a self-selected class of people willing to relocate far away in order to reap the region's many rewards."[13] They changed jobs frequently in search of opportunity, creating a system of loose friendships and business relationships that sparked innovation and growth. For young men, many of these relationships began while they were students at the region's still emerging universities.

FOOTBALL AND COMMERCE

Howard Ahmanson's enrollment at the University of Southern California (USC) resulted from a casual miscommunication. Newly arrived in the City of Angels in October 1925, he hailed a cab and instructed the driver to take him to the University of California's Southern Branch (later renamed UCLA). When the driver dropped him at USC, Ahmanson, none the wiser, found the registrar's office and enrolled. The mistake would eventually be worth millions to the university.[14]

USC catered to the aspirations of L.A.'s white Anglo-Saxon elite in the mid-1920s. Its ambitious president, Rufus Bernhard von KleinSmid, recognized that the city needed a professional elite to run its businesses, courts, and government. He expanded the two-year-old College of Commerce and Business Administration, opened a new law school building in 1925, launched a college of engineering, and in 1929 created the nation's second school of public administration. These changes kindled rapid growth in enrollments. The school became a hotbed for the emerging view of government championed by Progressives and technocrats. To promote alumni loyalty and giving, KleinSmid made football a central part of the USC experience.[15] The team became a national powerhouse. Ahmanson became a lifelong fan.

Howard's enrollment coincided with the university's move to expand the business program. Adding new requirements and classes, the university offered a full four-year degree. A record-setting class of 485 students, including 45 women, fostered a special camaraderie and sense of purpose among the students and faculty.[16] Among his classmates, Ahmanson found friends, including the indefatigable Howard Edgerton, who wrote for the school newspaper and was a class officer, and Joe Crail, who would later create the largest savings and loan in Los Angeles—until Howard Ahmanson entered the business.

In the faculty, Ahmanson also discovered a brilliant mentor and trusted advisor. Thurston Ross was a Signal Corps veteran who had served as a pilot in World War I. An engineer by instinct, he helped develop the timing technology that allowed fighter pilots to fire machine-gun bullets through the gaps between the spinning blades of their propellers. After the war, Ross moved to Los Angeles and earned a master's and a doctorate at USC in economics. Asked to join the faculty, he created the university's first course in real estate appraisal.[17] An efficiency expert, Ross was an advocate for the professionalization of management. In short, he was the kind of social engineer that Herbert Hoover and other Progressives liked.[18]

Ross and Ahmanson developed a mutual admiration. According to Ross, Ahmanson dazzled the faculty "with his terrific physical stamina and his brains." "He worked like a Trojan, taking twice as many courses as the rules allowed" and graduating ahead of schedule, in 1927.[19]

When he first arrived at USC, the university had no housing available, so Howard joined a fraternity at UCLA.[20] There he met Gould Eddy, a tall, thin fraternity brother who shared exactly the same birthday and year. They became good friends and soon business colleagues. He also met Dorothy "Dottie" Johnston Grannis, a "yell girl" or cheerleader and English literature major.

A HOLLYWOOD ROMANCE

Dottie personified the Jazz Age in Los Angeles. With bright, penetrating brown eyes, finger-wave curled blonde hair, and a diminutive 110-pound figure, she vibrated with energy. The daughter of Laura "Johnnie" Johnston and Frank Grannis, a real estate developer and opera devotee, Dottie was president of her class at the Hollywood School. After graduating in 1924, she was admitted to the University of California, Southern Branch.[21] Over the next six years, she attended the university off and on. Meanwhile, she worked as a social secretary to the young but enormously ambitious Paramount executive David O. Selznick.[22]

It's not clear how or when Howard and Dottie met, but by the time he graduated in 1927, they were already in love. The week after graduation, playing tourist in San Diego, he dispatched what he described as his "first written epistle." It was a chatty note, full of the confidences of young lovers. He talked about visiting scenic points and Southern California missions but complained about being too far from her. Already committed to a postgraduation trip with his mother to Omaha, he dreaded the excursion because it would take him farther away from Dottie.[23]

Howard's mother was delighted with his new girlfriend. As he reported from Omaha that summer, "The family would keep you in my mind if I didn't myself. . . . You have their unqualified endorsement from your picture," which was placed on the mantel of the family home on California Street.[24]

Howard's letters to Dottie that summer and during the course of his travels for family and business over the next several years evidence the family dynamic that influenced his entrepreneurial career as well as his continuing affection for his hometown. He noted that Florence was wrapped up in Hayden and Aimee's two children: William, who was nearly two, and Robert, who was just five months old. According to Howard, they were "probably the two 'swellest' boys in the United States, if not the world."[25] Back among family and old friends, he revealed his continuing attachment to the Midwest and Omaha. It was good "to know the butcher and baker and candlestick maker and all that," he wrote to Dottie. "What a change from Los Angeles. It does seem after all like home." In Omaha, he socialized with girls from his past and visited his fraternity brothers in Lincoln. In his letters to Dottie, he described these outings as obligations to old friends. Over and over he wrote that she was the only girl for him.

Dottie could understand Howard's Omaha nightlife, even if it made her nervous about his loyalty. She was high-strung, needed the attention of men, and craved the banter and drink of society to avoid what Howard would call "the gremlins" in her head. While he was away, she kept up an active social life, going to parties and nightclubs with friends from college and planning charity events with her sorority sisters. Yet despite the social distractions, Howard and Dottie increasingly depended on each other.

Howard also kept her informed of his efforts to redeem his father's dream. "Whenever he came to call," she said, "the first thing he'd tell me was that he'd picked up a couple more shares of National American."[26]

AN IDEA AS SIMPLE AS A SAFETY PIN

The memory of how his family had been treated following his father's death energized Ahmanson's entrepreneurial initiatives, yet it did not turn him against the company his father had founded and lost. Howard had begun selling fire insurance for National American while he was still at USC. Despite his youth, he knew the business and the institutional players. He knew that big insurance companies on the East Coast and in Britain were sitting on great piles of money. He believed he could persuade these companies to make him their agent.

Some in the industry warned that he was swimming against the tide. Seeking greater operational control over their far-flung businesses, many large fire insurance companies were replacing independent general agents with salaried managers. In January 1926, *Pacific Underwriter and Banker* predicted that general agents would soon disappear.[27]

The youthful Ahmanson ignored these warnings. He launched H. F. Ahmanson & Company as a managing general insurance agency in 1927, while he was still enrolled at USC. For working capital, he cashed a check for $588.21 that he had received from selling several insurance policies.[28] Renting an office downtown at 315 West Ninth Street, in the Pacific National Bank building, he hired a secretary and recruited his fraternity brother Gould Eddy to join him.[29] After receiving permission from the State of California, he issued one thousand shares of stock in the company. With his father in mind, he kept all of the shares to himself.

In Omaha after graduation, Howard tried to convince National American's two senior executives, James Foster and Roy Wilcox, to dump their existing agency and name him as the company's exclusive agent in Los Angeles.[30] Wilcox supported him, but Foster was reticent, no doubt disinclined to promote the precocious, if not pushy, twenty-one-year-old spoiled son of his former boss. Nevertheless, Howard was confident. He wrote Dottie that he was "on my way to putting across my 'big deal.'" Before he left Omaha, National American had agreed to make him the company's general agent in California.

NEVER SIT DOWN

With the National American logo on his stationery, Ahmanson began traveling to San Francisco, San Diego, and other California cities to build his clientele. He went to New York and Massachusetts to establish business relationships with big East Coast insurance companies. His brightest prospects were the brokers who arranged mortgage loans on behalf of the life insurance companies. Howard liked working with these agents. They were the most sophisticated risk managers, so they minimized his own risks of insuring a property.[31]

Nevertheless, the first couple of years in business were challenging. He was spending his own capital, and the volume of business didn't keep pace with expenses. Agents for the old-line fire insurance companies in San Francisco characterized him as a maverick.[32] Though he was able to get in the door with the big mortgage lenders, many were already locked into business relationships with other underwriters. As a newcomer to Los Angeles, he tried to recreate the social networks that his father had exploited in Omaha. He joined the Junior Division of the Los Angeles Chamber of Commerce and got himself nominated to the elite and sumptuous downtown Jonathan Club on South Figueroa.[33] But business relationships took time to mature.

He developed a selling strategy. Visit ten potential customers a day. Make sure each is a decision maker, a vice president at least. "When you visit, stand up, never sit down, and never pass the time of day," he later coached his salesmen. "Always leave them something they can use, and then get out." Building a relationship was the key to Ahmanson's strategy. He said, "Never 'point' a new prospect." In other words, never make a sales pitch "until you've called on him for at least a year."[34]

Ahmanson proved remarkably competent at selling and controlling risk. He reported to National American that premiums earned by his California agency in the first six months of 1929 were double what they had been for the same period in 1928. More astonishing to his former mentors in Omaha, his loss ratio was barely 2 percent in 1928 and 3 percent in 1929, far below the industry average. These numbers suggested that the policies he wrote were far more profitable for the underwriter, as well as the insurance agency.[35]

Ahmanson also made mistakes. Realizing that his youth was a disadvantage in working with older, more experienced insurance agents, Howard hired a veteran California insurance man in the fall of 1927 to manage his network of agents. Fred Garrigue had worked in insurance in Chicago and then moved to San Francisco to be a fire insurance adjustor. After serving in the Royal Canadian Air Force in World War I, he returned to insurance.[36] He worked for Ahmanson for only a short time, but four years later, after he and Howard had parted ways, Garrigue was arrested as the mastermind of a fire and earthquake insurance fraud ring engaged in attempted murder and grand theft.[37] Fortunately, H. F. Ahmanson & Co. was not drawn into the conspiracy.

The close call with Garrigue underscored Ahmanson's frustration with his efforts to build his company via head-to-head competition in well-established insurance markets. Searching for greater competitive advantage, Howard focused on residential property insurance. This market was "chicken feed" to most insurance agents. Howard believed he could make it profitable if he kept his expenses low.

Howard also came up with an idea that he later said was "as simple as a safety pin, only no one had ever thought of it before."[38] When lenders foreclosed on a property in the late 1920s, the fire insurance became null and void because insurance companies feared empty houses would become targets for arson. The lenders, however, were still exposed to the risk of fire until they could find a new buyer. Ahmanson believed the insurance companies' fears were unfounded. He reasoned that lenders, anxious to sell these foreclosed properties, would actually take good care of the buildings and that potential insurance losses would be minimal. He proposed to offer a new product—insurance on foreclosed properties.

To sell this new insurance policy, Ahmanson looked for a partner. Howard went to see Morgan Adams, the president of Mortgage Guarantee, which was the largest mortgage lender in Los Angeles. Curious about both the plan and the salesman's character, Adams said: "You seem like a bright young man. Who are you?"[39]

Howard explained that his father was president of National American Fire Insurance in Omaha. He may have left the impression that Will was still alive and in that position. Or he may have emphasized the substantial equity the family held in the business, his brother Hayden's role as an executive, or Howard's own experience in fire insurance dating back to the age of thirteen. In any case, Adams was impressed.

He asked Howard if he could find underwriting for his proposed venture. Howard boasted, "Of course."[40]

Actually, he had no idea if the men who had taken control of National American would go along with this novel concept. Alternatively, he could approach one of the big East Coast insurance firms. Still concerned that his youth was a problem in face-to-face negotiations, he turned to the Northern Assurance Company of England. Conducting the deal by mail, he convinced the Brits and at least one other company to back him. The companies made him their general agent for Southern California and offered him the usual 15 percent commission on each premium, plus 25 percent of the company's profits on any policies he wrote.[41] For Howard, this structure turned out to be lucrative. With a greater volume of business, his loss ratio rose to 8 percent, but this was still far below the industry average of 40 to 45 percent.[42] Since he shared in the profits on policies written with low loss ratios, he was soon making good money for a twenty-three-year-old entrepreneur.

A year after his initial conversation with Morgan Adams, Howard was summoned back to Mortgage Guarantee. Aware of Howard's success and seeking to bring his business in house, Adams offered Howard a job and a salary of $10,000 a year ($135,000 in 2011 dollars), "which is a lot of money for someone your age." Howard replied, "Go jump in the lake." Offended by Ahmanson's impertinence, Adams canceled all of Mortgage Guarantee's policies with H. F. Ahmanson & Co. Undeterred, Howard borrowed $15,000 from a banker friend, made deals with four other mortgage lenders, and was soon back in business.[43]

Ahmanson continued to innovate in ways that threatened his more established competitors. Most fire insurance companies wrote policies for residential and commercial property. Commercial property had a higher risk, but it was also more competitive, so insurers subsidized discounts for businesses by charging excessive fees to home owners. Ahmanson focused exclusively on residential policies and cut his rates accordingly. Competitors complained that this was "unfair" competition, but they soon followed suit. One prominent Los Angeles insurance agent later quipped, "Residential premiums in this area have gone down by as much as 45 percent since that joker came over the ridge."[44]

Howard recognized another unfilled niche in the insurance market in 1933 when a 6.4 magnitude earthquake slammed the Long Beach area, killing 115 people and causing forty million dollars' worth of property damage. Many mortgage lenders were forced to take a loss when borrowers failed to pay back loans on properties without earthquake insurance. To meet this market need, Howard developed a special "single-interest" policy defined to cover only the lender if a mortgaged property was damaged by earthquake. Cleverly, Howard wrote the policy so that it required the lender to foreclose to activate the insurance. He reasoned that rising land values in the Los Angeles area guaranteed that much of the loss on the structure would be mitigated by the appreciated value of the land. Thus his insurance risk was minimal.[45]

Ahmanson refused to write commercial insurance. He preferred the inherent diversification of risk that came from writing many small policies as opposed to the concentrated risk associated with a major liability for a corporate account. Also, corporations always wanted to negotiate their premiums.

Ahmanson didn't like negotiating over prices, whether he was buying or selling. Home buyers weren't in a position to bargain. Ahmanson preferred it that way.[46]

Innovation and self-confidence fueled Ahmanson's success. To impress potential clients and customers, he happily cultivated an image of wealth. He drove a Pierce Arrow automobile and, like his father, dressed in elegant suits. As he traveled around the state to meet with lenders, he would roar into town, slam on the brakes, and come to a stop in a cloud of dust in front of the local bank or building and loan. The manager would look out his plate-glass window and see Ahmanson just getting out of his car. Then Howard would go inside to get the lender's insurance business.[47]

On the road, Ahmanson stayed at the best hotels—the Palace in San Francisco and the Del Monte in Monterey. At Christmas, he sent lavish gifts to his clients. The child of one manager of a savings and loan remembered, "We all sat around the Christmas tree and opened the gift from Howard Ahmanson. It was always the best gift the family ever got. So I knew the name of Howard Ahmanson long before I ever met him."[48] Established downtown businessmen like Morgan Adams marveled at Ahmanson's acumen and sales-manship. Ahmanson's son would later say that, like Lyndon Johnson, Howard had the ability to see into the heart of whomever he needed to win over and to manipulate him on the basis of his deepest longings and fears.[49] Yet he was midwestern enough to use these insights, together with hard work, to satisfy the customer as well as himself. In the years before the start of the Great Depression, his charm and diligence made him successful, and his attention to the world around him made him cautious.[50] But his "chicken feed" strategy also alerted him to a fundamental transition taking place in the mortgage industry.

THE CHANGING WORLD OF THE BUILDING
AND LOAN

Home ownership was on the rise in the 1920s. Across the country, a building boom was under way and potential home owners needed mortgages. To find these loans, many turned to the kind of hometown building and loan immortalized by Jimmy Stewart in *It's a Wonderful Life*.

As an institution, the building and loan was also rooted in the rise of co-operative financial institutions in Europe and the United States in the late eighteenth and early nineteenth centuries. An increase in wage labor and the concentration of urban populations during the Industrial Revolution created a demand for financial institutions to serve wage earners new to the market economy. Without productive assets of their own, these wage earners needed to save cash to insure themselves against personal disaster or provide for the construction of a home. Commercial banks did not offer general savings accounts for workers.[51] Mutual self-help cooperatives were organized to promote thrift among the working class.[52]

After the Civil War, in a period of rapid economic expansion, building and loans became increasingly popular in the United States, particularly in capital-poor regions like the Midwest and Far West.[53] Most were small and local and run by part-time managers who often had other sources of income. The average institution included about 314 members who owned an average of $303 worth of stock.[54] Some served only a single neighborhood or a tight-knit ethnic or religious group.

The building and loan represented a revolution in mortgage finance to the working and middle classes. Prior to this time, home buyers who sought financing from institutional lenders generally had to provide at least 50 percent of the cash needed for the transaction and faced a large balloon payment for the remaining principal after only a few years. The building and loan offered members a way to protect their savings, earn interest on their balances, and access mortgage capital.

Lending money for first mortgages on residential property proved to be a remarkably safe investment, and it paid a relatively high return to the investor. Even during the financial crisis of 1893, building and loans enjoyed a low rate of failure. As a result, they became attractive to a variety of local investors, ranging from workers putting aside small savings each week to widows and merchants with capital to invest. Unlike commercial banks, thrifts offered fixed-rate loans with longer terms (up to twelve years) and higher loan-to-value ratios (60 to 75 percent). These institutions gave millions of Americans their first real chance to own a home. By the mid-1890s, they held nearly a quarter of all the residential mortgage debt extended by financial intermediaries in the United States.[55]

The spirit of mutualism and thrift that had characterized the building and loan represented a pragmatic, cooperative solution to the lack of mortgage capital available to the middle class. With success, thrifts also reflected a widespread reaction to the negative aspects of large-scale capitalist enterprise that worried many Americans at the end of the nineteenth century. Cooperatives seemed to be more aligned with the idea of community.[56]

A CORPORATE THREAT

An increasingly integrated national economy, however, posed a series of fundamental threats to the local, mutual ethos of the building and loan. The resolution of these threats would pave the way for a substantial and abiding role for government in the mortgage industry, lead to one of the most important and successful examples of cooperation between business and government in the managed economy, and, in the end, help make Howard Ahmanson rich beyond imagination.

The crisis for the local building and loans began in the 1890s, when a handful of for-profit "national" savings and loans entered the market. These companies believed that by diversifying their lending risk over broad geographies, they could prevent a crisis in one community from jeopardizing the company's health. By being able to look at credit patterns among a larger pool of borrowers, they would also lower their credit risks. By standardizing lending practices and agent-training systems, they would achieve operational efficiencies and diminish the risk that a rogue agent would underwrite a portfolio of bad loans.

Unfortunately for the nationals, in an era when the telegraph still dominated long-distance communication, local associations enjoyed competitive advantages that trumped those that could be generated by a large organization. In an era when credit history was largely by word of mouth, local thrift managers knew which individuals were hardworking, thrifty, and creditworthy. They knew the local economic conditions that might affect the loan's riskiness. And they understood the local politics.[57] When the national economy suffered in the late 1890s, the national companies failed while the local building and loans survived.

Building and loans responded to the threat of the nationals by organizing the U.S. League of Building and Loans to campaign for their movement.[58] To win political support, they made home ownership a central tenet of the American dream. Seymour Dexter, the league's first president, borrowed from Thomas Jefferson, who had believed that independent farmers, as owners of productive property, would sustain the independence and virtue of the citizenry and the health of the democracy. In Dexter's reconstruction, the home rather than the farm became the locus of this civic virtue.[59]

Dexter described the enormous economic transition under way in the nation and the challenges it posed to democratic institutions. Industrialization brought centralization and the growth of cities. Forced to live near factories where they were employed, wage earners occupied rented rooms or houses. In Dexter's view, this situation fundamentally corrupted the American political system. "The one and only power to confront and overcome these dangers in the future" was not the return to Jefferson's family farm or Franklin's independent artisan but rather "the American Home."[60] Under Dexter, the league adopted the motto: "The American Home: The Safe-Guard of American Liberties."

Dexter also saw the nation's salvation in the suburbs. "Rapid transit," he said, was making it possible for the wage earner to live "fifteen to twenty-five miles from the place where he works." As a result, families could

go out into the suburbs of the city, where land can be had at a reasonable price and homes erected at a reasonable cost. There [the wage earner] can rear his family in pure air, have a grass plot in his front yard, with its flower-beds and shrubbery. There he can have a home; there he can have true family life and comfort and see his children, away from the din, the dirt, the scenes and foul influences of the busy mart. There during the week the free school shall open to them its doors, and on Sundays, the influences of the church surround them.

In Dexter's view, the pillars of society would be solid: "true family life," "the free school," and "the church" would sustain the American republic.

Leaders in the savings and loan movement also believed that increased home ownership, enabled by mutual building and loans, could mediate "the growing conflict between capital and labor" that posed the most "vexing economic question" of the day and the most serious threat to the American republic. As property owners, workers would take pride in their neighborhoods and communities and be less inclined to violently oppose the interests of business owners. As members of a mutual, these workers, like stockholders, would also earn dividends on their invested capital.

The transformation of the home into the centerpiece of a new republican ideal was ironically assisted by builders and real estate agents who made the home the focus of consumer culture and consumption the ideal civic act. Modern advertising and merchandising promoted a new democracy in

America—the democracy of desire—with its promise of equal access, not to power, but to consumer goods and a complicated vision of happiness based on consumption.[61] As retailers plastered "Buy Now, Pay Later" banners across their store windows and developed installment plans for major purchases, debt was no longer associated with the improvident and the poor but was increasingly a marker of middle-class respectability.[62] Going into debt to buy a home brought the consumer status and a sanctuary.

Building and loan officials were often ambivalent about the changing attitudes toward thrift and consumption. The rise of the consumer society and especially consumer credit threatened to undermine the basic value of thrift on which the building and loan movement had been built. "We are being educated to be a nation of spendthrifts," some building and loan leaders complained.[63] A "wave of extravagance prevails," complained a writer in the *American Building Association News* in 1923, as men sacrificed the dream of owning their own home for the pleasures of an automobile.[64] "When we reflect upon the comparative value of the home and the automobile to our citizenship," another writer wrote, "we wonder if the quality of American character is deteriorating."[65]

Traditionalists in the building and loan movement fought to preserve the small-scale, cooperative character of the institution. They were often dismayed to discover proponents of the new approach to consumption and credit within their own midst. These modernists embraced professional management, marketing, consumerism, and above all growth. If larger associations could achieve economies of scale that would benefit borrowers and investors alike, then "it is right, proper and our duty to enlarge our usefulness by increasing our assets."[66] To build those assets, manager L. L. Rankin suggested, building and loans should employ the tools of modern advertising.[67]

As some thrifts grew large enough to demand permanent, full-time staff managers, Rankin insisted that he and his peers "should give all their time, thought and energy to the companies they serve and for such services they should receive abundant compensation."[68] In essence, he argued that building and loan managers should join the growing ranks of business executives who looked upon their work as a profession with skills that could be taught and an ethic that could be cultivated over the course of a university education.[69]

These tensions in the building and loan movement were at their peak in the late 1920s as Howard Ahmanson visited thrift managers to convince them to place their property insurance with his company. Large fire insurance companies often ignored these local institutions. The small profits didn't seem to be worth the effort. But Ahmanson saw something different. Across the country, thrifts were enjoying unprecedented success. By 1930, they managed the savings of more than ten million Americans and underwrote two-thirds of all the residential mortgages in the country.[70] In California, they were growing even faster. From 1920 through 1928, total assets climbed from $47.9 million to $297 million.[71] The largest of these institutions wrote two hundred first mortgages a month, which meant two hundred fire and hazard insurance policies.[72] In this market there was room for Ahmanson and the thrift managers to make a little money.

INSURANCE ON THE SIDE

Ahmanson knew that many managers of these savings and loans were paid very little. If they ran a mutual, all the profits flowed to the depositors. Quite often, however, thrift managers found a way to supplement their salaries by selling property hazard insurance to their mortgage customers.

These side insurance businesses generated controversy. While many building and loan boards of directors countenanced the practice because it meant they didn't have to pay their managers as much, independent insurance agents protested. They argued that lenders with the power of credit could strong-arm customers into paying too much for insurance. At a large meeting of the Los Angeles Fire Insurance Exchange in 1925, for example, attendees voted to deny membership to banks, building and loans, and building and loan officials.[73]

In direct opposition to the majority in his industry, Ahmanson chose to make it easy for thrift managers to write fire insurance policies. All the manager needed to do was create an insurance agency and staff it with a clerk or a secretary. H. F. Ahmanson & Co. did most of the paperwork. Howard's one-day turnaround on new policies helped the lender finalize the loan, lock in the customer, and build goodwill for everyone involved.[74] H. F. Ahmanson & Co. frequently produced the invoices for the premium payer and recorded the payments. If the premium buyer had a particular issue that required insurance expertise, the lender/agent's secretary called the offices of H. F. Ahmanson & Co. to find out what to do. Howard's lieutenants would often go to an agent's office once a month to add up the receivables and close his books for him. No other insurance company would provide that kind of service, in part because it operated in a gray area of the law, especially regarding the qualifications of the secretaries who were the "agents" of record in the transaction. Because all of these services kept the savings and loan/insurance manager's overhead low, they stuck with Ahmanson.[75]

Ahmanson cultivated his relationships with the lenders to get their insurance business. When lenders brought him their insurance business, he benefited. But lenders also made him aware of investment opportunities, and at the age of twenty-three, Ahmanson was already a savvy investor.

A TIMELY EXIT

Throughout his career, Howard Ahmanson displayed an uncanny ability to observe the economic landscape and understand how trends were likely to shape opportunities. During his senior year at USC he interviewed a number of workers about their personal finances and then wrote a senior thesis titled "The Coming American Debacle." He concluded that the average skilled worker was overspending his income by about 22 percent. This trend toward debt was likely to result in trouble for the worker and for the economy.[76]

After he graduated in 1927, several small events added to Ahmanson's concern. Sometimes when he traveled, for example, he empowered his secretary to trade stocks for him. After one trip he discovered that she had approved the purchase of shares in a new fire insurance company. "Now here was a business I knew a lot about," Ahmanson later recalled, and he knew that it took several years to begin making money. So he was surprised when his $30 shares rose quickly to $50 even before the company had opened its doors. "If people were acting crazy about a business I knew about," he thought, "maybe they were acting just as crazy about a business I knew nothing about."[77]

The last straw came when an elevator boy stopped the lift midway between two floors to pitch Howard on another insurance stock. If elevator boys were investing in stocks, Howard reasoned, it was time to get out. In the middle of 1929, months before the great crash, he sold all of his holdings except for National American Insurance, netting nearly forty thousand dollars. He had doubled his money in four years and was now "beautifully liquid."[78]

After the crash in October 1929, with cash in a depressed market, Howard bought Chrysler shares and searched for other bargains. He became part owner and an officer and director in Victor Oil.[79] He acquired property, invested in oil, and continued to grow his insurance business.[80] Between 1930 and 1935 he also acquired nearly a half million dollars' worth of real estate. Many of these properties he later sold for four or five times what he had invested. With his increasing wealth he bought a new home at 203 North Rexford Drive in Beverly Hills.[81] Having consolidated his financial position in the world, he was at last ready to formalize another longtime partnership.

A LONG COURTSHIP

Howard and Dorothy Grannis had dated for nearly seven years by 1933. It's unclear why they didn't marry earlier. Certainly it wasn't because of Howard's financial situation. Both of them were smart, headstrong people. Howard's surviving letters evidence his tendency to imperial egotism. She lashed out at him when he neglected her. They were both opportunistic, and perhaps there was a part of each that was waiting for someone more perfect to come along. But in the end, they also needed and loved each other. Howard paid attention to Dottie's feelings and fears and strove to protect her, something she longed for. Dottie supported the part of Howard's workaholic and sometimes reticent personality that embraced the sybaritic lifestyle of L.A.'s beaches, clubs, and night life.

Perhaps Howard wanted to wait until he had become a millionaire ($17.5 million in 2011 dollars). As others throughout the nation struggled to feed their children or keep from losing their homes, Howard approached this financial milestone toward the end of 1932. That Christmas he traveled to Omaha without Dottie, but he made special arrangements. On Christmas morning, a messenger delivered an engagement ring to her home. She accepted.

The subsequent wedding invitation reflected the couple's sense of humor and disdain for formality. Designed to look like a court summons, it was signed by "Dan Cupid, Clerk of the Courts." Guests were to appear on Saturday, June 24, 1933, at the La Venta Inn at the end of the Palos Verdes Peninsula. The mission-style complex with gardens designed by the Olmstead brothers offered a commanding view of the Pacific. With a black-tie restaurant for Hollywood stars, the place was home to the Los Angeles elite. After the wedding, Howard and Dottie drove to San Pedro. Her parents and his family waved good-bye as the honeymooners stood on the deck of the Grace liner *Santa Elena* bound for the Caribbean.[82]

Despite a long and luxurious honeymoon, Howard remained committed to his pursuit of capital. He and Dottie agreed to limit their spending to 10 percent of the income they received from their personal holdings only—in other words, from Howard's side bets in real estate and the stock market. They would leave the earnings and dividends from H. F. Ahmanson & Co. in the business to grow.

With his personal investments, Ahmanson developed a conservative strategy. He put 90 percent of his reserves in cash or cash-equivalent short-term government bonds. "If you've got cash available," he said, "your gun is always loaded." He invested the rest "in the wildest cats and dogs. If the beasts are good," he said, "they'll go up twenty times. If they're sour, they'll go down to two, but I'll still have the cash."[83] With the nation and the world sinking deeper into economic depression, Ahmanson's cash was king.

THREE

Undertaker at a Plague

THE LOS ANGELES TIMES BLAMED home buyers. A "careful study of conditions," the *Times* reported in July 1931, revealed that most home owners going through foreclosure had only themselves to blame for "attempting more than they can handle" or for having "overextended themselves in an effort to 'keep up with the Joneses.'" Most foreclosed homes were "not those of the moderate-priced class, but are the more expensive type residence bought by persons in a 'flush' financial period." In some cases, the *Times* conceded, the "downright dishonesty" of either the contractor or the lender was also to blame. But *Times* readers needn't worry. In middle-class and suburban areas, foreclosures were practically unknown.[1]

Despite the *Times*'s efforts to downplay the crisis, foreclosures affected many home owners in Los Angeles and the lenders who carried their loans. The president of the Los Angeles real estate board in 1932 called for legislation to protect home owners from rapid foreclosure and eviction. One Hollywood assemblyman asked Governor Rolph to convene a special session of the legislature "to enact laws providing for a year's moratorium on foreclosures to give homeowners a breathing spell in order to readjust themselves to the present economic condition."[2] Rolph refused, asserting that relief was better addressed at the local level.[3] Meanwhile, the American Legion and local women's organizations, supported by local realty boards, launched a fund-raising effort to amass a two-million-dollar revolving loan fund to help home owners on the brink of foreclosure.[4]

Despite these efforts, the pace of foreclosures increased. Each time a lender took a house back and left it empty, H. F. Ahmanson & Co. had an opportunity to write an insurance policy. Sometimes, when even the lender didn't have the cash necessary for the insurance, Ahmanson paid the premium and let the lender run a tab. When these debts grew high enough, the banks gave him properties to settle the debt. While others struggled, Ahmanson amassed a small fortune in cash and property. "It was like being an undertaker at a plague," Ahmanson said later. "The worse things got, the better I was."[5]

FINANCIAL REFORM SHAPES
THE MORTGAGE MARKET

While Ahmanson ran his own personal bailout program for lenders with distressed properties on their hands, President Herbert Hoover began to reframe the government's role in financial services and the mortgage industry as a way to ease the crisis of the Great Depression. The reforms he initiated were continued and deepened by his successor. They created enormous entrepreneurial opportunities for Howard Ahmanson and other lenders in the years following World War II. During the Depression, however, the presidents aimed to stem the crisis.

Throughout his years in Washington, Hoover had sought to make home ownership and housing development a federal priority. As secretary of commerce, he created a Division of Building and Housing to promote the "Own Your Own Home" movement.[6] As the Republican nominee for president in 1928, he professed that the American home was the most important foundation stone in the structure of modern civilization.[7] Following the stock market crash of October 1929, Hoover labored to adapt his philosophy of cooperation and associationalism to the nation's growing economic crisis and to the issues facing home owners across the country.

Early in the Depression, Hoover gathered the nation's top CEOs and persuaded them to accelerate construction and maintenance projects to stimulate spending to avert large-scale unemployment. He encouraged states to do the same. He won high praise for his activism. Within his cabinet, however, some believed that the crash was good for the country. Treasury secretary Andrew Mellon was convinced that the Depression "will purge the rottenness out of the system. People will work harder, live a more moral life. Values will be adjusted and enterprising people will pick up the wreck from less-competent people." Mellon was joined in this perspective by the governors of the Federal Reserve, who refused to pump cash into the economy and, in fact, raised interest rates in October 1931, exacerbating the shrinkage of the money supply.[8]

Hoover never subscribed to the laissez-faire ideologies of these bankers. But in the early years of the Depression, he relied on presidential cajoling and corporate cooperation to promote prosperity. Initially his strategy seemed to work. In the spring of 1930, Hoover told members of the U.S. Chamber of Commerce: "We [are] past the worst."[9]

In reality, the nation's problems were just beginning. Throughout 1930 and 1931 unemployment increased and incomes plummeted. As credit tightened, corporate giants and whole industries stood poised on the brink of failure. To solve the credit crisis, Hoover once again promoted a cooperative approach. In a secret meeting in October 1931, he asked top banking executives to create a private fund of five hundred million dollars to be known as the National Credit Corporation to aid struggling financial institutions. Shocked when the bankers asked for government intervention instead, Hoover soon gave up on this voluntary strategy.[10] In his State of the Union address in December, he urged Congress to create the Reconstruction Finance Corporation (RFC) to provide up to two billion dollars in emergency financing to banks, railroads, and insurance companies.[11] He also asked Congress to address the growing credit crisis in home ownership.

The Depression threatened to undermine home ownership in America. Across the country, foreclosures rose from an annual rate of 75,000 per year prior to the stock market's collapse in 1929 to 273,000 in 1932.[12] Nearly one in six mortgages slipped into foreclosure between 1930 and 1934.[13] Since building and loans held roughly a third of the home mortgages in the United States in 1930, these foreclosures put enormous pressure on their working capital.[14] Unable to sell many of these properties, they carried them on their balance sheets and paid the taxes, maintenance, and, of course, property insurance.[15] As loan payments slowed, the value of the assets in their portfolios declined and creditors made demands. Many building and loans failed.

Hoover organized the White House Conference on Home Building and Homeownership in 1931 to confront the crisis. Addressing the assembled members, Hoover echoed the rhetoric of Seymour Dexter and successive leaders in the U.S. League of Savings and Loans:

> Next to food and clothing, the housing of a nation is its most vital social and economic problem. . . . I am confident that the sentiment for homeownership is so embedded in the American heart that millions of people who dwell in tenements, apartments and rented rows of solid brick have the aspiration for wider opportunity in ownership of their own homes. To possess one's own home is the hope and ambition of almost every individual in our country,

whether he lives in hotel, apartment or tenement. . . . This aspiration penetrates the heart of our national wellbeing. It makes for happier married life. It makes for better children. It makes for confidence and security, it makes for courage to meet the battle of life, it makes for better citizenship. There can be no fear for a democracy or self-government or for liberty or freedom from homeowners no matter how humble they may be.[16]

Continuing, Hoover announced that the time had come to consider what role the federal government might play in facilitating home ownership.

Initially, Hoover's call for action seemed to fall on deaf ears. Building and loan leaders hoped Hoover would allow thrifts to become members of the Federal Reserve system, giving them access to credit, but commercial bankers attending the White House conference rejected this idea and failed to support any substantial changes in the mortgage finance system. Congressional leaders also scorned the idea of creating a federal institution to provide a credit facility for mortgage lenders. Even Hoover was reluctant to put the nation's home mortgage system in the hands of the Federal Reserve's governors, whom he saw as a "weak reed for a nation to lean on in time of trouble."[17] So savings and loan officials dusted off an old proposal.

After World War I, the league had proposed the creation of a federal home loan bank to provide credit to the nation's thrift institutions. Congress, focused on shrinking the size of the federal bureaucracy, showed little interest. The league abandoned the effort. With the Depression, however, the league's plan was revived, and Hoover offered it to Congress in November 1931.[18]

Hoover pointed to three primary constituencies that the Federal Home Loan Bank (FHLB) would address: mortgage lenders facing a liquidity crisis, home owners in danger of losing their property to foreclosure, and workers unemployed because of the drop in demand for construction.[19] On Capitol Hill, the building and loans asserted that a federal home loan bank would bring stability to the mortgage credit system and provide liquidity during the economic crisis. The league also suggested that the bank would help standardize lending practices in the building and loan community, which would also strengthen the financial system.[20]

Opponents asserted that borrowers and inflated real estate prices were to blame for the home ownership crisis. They insisted the system would naturally self-correct. Imprudent buyers and lenders would be disciplined by foreclosures and bank or building and loan failures. If the Federal Home Loan Bank Act passed and building and loans gained access to government resources, thrifts would tend to lend too much, leading to overbuilding and inflated home prices.[21]

Despite the arguments against the bill, lobbying efforts by the building and loan associations, combined with the pressures of the economic crisis and widely shared support for the ideology of home ownership, convinced Congress to approve the bill.[22] Hoover signed it into law on July 22, 1932. Moving quickly, the administration had the FHLB up and running in a matter of weeks. Hoover optimistically declared that the mortgage credit crisis was over.[23]

The new law reflected an emerging paradigm of financial industry regulation that would be consolidated under Hoover's successor, Franklin Delano Roosevelt. Under the overarching philosophy of this reform, large categories of financial services would be separated from one another by federal rules. In exchange, the government would provide incentives and protections to make these sectors successful.[24] This kind of regulatory paradigm reflected the essence of what would become the managed economy, a system in which business adopted the government's public policy goals in exchange for the stability of limited or bounded competition in the marketplace.

During his reelection campaign in 1932, Hoover touted the strength of this vision as a way to preserve the capitalist system. As he crisscrossed the country campaigning that fall, Hoover insisted that everything his administration was doing for the economy was intended to address the needs of ordinary Americans. "We are a nation of 25 million families living in 25 million homes," he said, "each warmed by the fires of affection and cherishing within it a mutual solicitude for kinfolk and children." Within the nation's homes, schools, and churches, Hoover continued, the nation's ideals and character were formed. They were part of the promise of America, "and those promises must be fulfilled."[25] Roosevelt echoed this ideology of home ownership. As many Americans worried about whether they could keep a roof over their heads, he asserted that "a nation of homeowners, of people who own a real share in their own land, is unconquerable."[26] Home mortgages, he said, were the "backbone of the American financial system."[27]

Unfortunately for Hoover, the country, and America's home owners, the crisis grew worse. Many thrifts failed to take advantage of their new ability to borrow from the FHLB and refused to refinance troubled home loans. Real estate agents in California were furious. Hayden Jones, the president of the California Real Estate Association, blasted the thrift industry for lobbying for the creation of the bank and then failing to use it. "They are not keeping faith with the citizens of their communities," he said.[28] Herbert Hoover undoubtedly agreed.

In November, Hoover was overwhelmingly defeated by Franklin Roosevelt. During the four-month interregnum between the election and Roosevelt's inauguration, Hoover continued to advocate banking reform, urging Congress to take action in his December State of the Union address. He especially wanted to federalize the banking system and override state regulations that promoted the proliferation of small and weak local banks, but Roosevelt refused to cooperate.[29]

The nation's economy crumpled. Bank failures reached unprecedented levels. By 1933, more than nine thousand banks had collapsed since the stock market crash.[30] Trading on Wall Street slowed to a trickle as the number of investment and brokerage firms that had been forced out of business by the crisis rose to two thousand.[31] Meanwhile, unemployment skyrocketed to 25 percent. Farm foreclosures in the Midwest grew so dire that Iowa farmers banded together to prevent foreclosure auctions. In Howard Ahmanson's home state of Nebraska, thousands of singing and shouting farmers marched on the legislature demanding an end to foreclosures and evictions.[32] A rebellion against the entire credit system seemed to be in the offing.

For home owners the picture was also bleak. According to the federal government, 43 percent of all first mortgages were in default. On average, borrowers were fifteen months behind in their payments. Lenders were foreclosing at a rate of twenty-four thousand homes a month. Even this rate was held down by the fact that many lenders, already "suffocated with foreclosed property," were reluctant to take action against delinquent borrowers because it would mean they would have to book a loss on their own shaky balance sheets.[33]

In his inaugural address on March 4, Roosevelt tried to reassure the nation: "The only thing we have to fear is fear itself." The calamity of the Depression did not reflect any inherent flaw in the people's character or America's productive potential, nor did it evidence any inherent weakness in the system of government. The crisis, he said, should be laid at the feet of the money changers. "The rulers of the exchange of mankind's goods have failed through their own stubbornness and their own incompetence." The money changers "have admitted their failure and abdicated," he said. Fortunately, they had been driven from "the high seats in the temple of our civilization," their practices "indicted in the court of public opinion, rejected by the hearts and minds of men." In the collective effort to restore the nation's economic health, he called for "safeguards against a return of the evils of this old order: there must be a strict supervision of all banking and credits and investments; there must be an end to speculation with other people's money, and there must be provision for an adequate but sound currency."[34]

Roosevelt made it clear that he would act. In the hundred days that followed, he and his administration pushed for sweeping reforms that included strong federal regulation of the financial system, with various financial services divided from one another. The Banking Act of 1933, sponsored by Senators Carter Glass and Henry Steagall, separated investment banking from commercial banking to protect deposits from speculators. The Home Owners Loan Act established federally chartered savings and loans that could only collect savings and make loans for homes.[35]

The following year, Congress created the Federal Housing Administration (FHA) and empowered that agency to provide mortgage lenders with insurance against default on loans that met FHA standards. To encourage savers to deposit their money with savings and loans, the government guaranteed the safety of these funds by creating the Federal Savings and Loan Insurance Corporation (FSLIC) in 1934.[36] State-chartered as well as federally chartered thrifts were eligible for this deposit insurance. With Roosevelt's encouragement, Congress also created the Federal National Mortgage Association (later known as Fannie Mae) to promote the development of a secondary market for home loans.[37] In theory, a government-sponsored secondary market made it easier for banks and savings and loans to sell long-term mortgages for cash and a quick profit. With this liquidity, they would be able to offer new loans to their customers. An amendment to the National Housing Act that year also eased credit terms for newly constructed small homes.

Overall, the establishment and expansion of federal housing programs under Hoover and Roosevelt reflected bipartisan support for a federal role in promoting home ownership in America through the institution of the savings and loan. Within the new financial system, stability and security for savers, lenders, and home buyers was the overriding goal.[38]

Many bankers, insurance company presidents, stock brokers, mortgage dealers, and corporate leaders complained about the new managed economy that emerged from the crisis of the Depression, but they gradually adapted to the new regime. Historians Louis Galambos and Joseph Pratt have characterized the new relationship between business and government as a "corporate commonwealth" that served business and the public alike by fostering greater economic stability.[39]

With regard to savings and loans, the new laws reflected a secondary theme in much of the New Deal's lawmaking. Suspicious of private capital, Congress strengthened the competitive hand of the nation's producer and consumer cooperative and mutual organizations. Savings and loans were not the only institutions to benefit from this new regime. Agricultural cooperatives received exemptions from antitrust rules, credit unions were given tax exemptions, rural electric cooperatives were empowered to deploy public capital to build electrical grids. In the grand spirit of American cooperation, savings and loans would make home ownership possible for millions of Americans.

Ironically, the government's effort to support building and loans as cooperatives created a framework in which these institutions could become enormously profitable. In the middle of the Great Depression, that wasn't obvious to many people. In fact, many state-chartered savings and loans in California took out federal charters and became mutuals under the umbrella of the new federal laws. But after World War II, when demand for housing skyrocketed, a handful of entrepreneurs would amass extraordinary wealth within this system. No one benefited more than Howard Ahmanson.

AHMANSON'S PERSPECTIVE ON REFORM

As an undertaker at a plague, Howard Ahmanson did not sit around the kitchen table with home owners struggling to keep up with their mortgage payments as a doctor might attend a patient at her bedside. He listened to building and loan managers, mortgage lenders, and bankers talk about their efforts to minister to the growing ranks of hopelessly indebted families, but he had no responsibility for trying to save the patient. He arrived after the foreclosure, like the undertaker dressing the lifeless body, to offer lenders insurance on the empty house. Undoubtedly he had thoughts on the plague, but his views have not survived.

Some sense of his perspective on the role of government is revealed in a speech he gave in 1933 after joining the newly formed Economic Round Table of Los Angeles. A group of leading businessmen and academics organized to discuss the issues of the day, the Round Table represented the emerging power elite of a new generation in Los Angeles. Over breakfast at the University Club, men like "Bud" Haldeman, John McCone, Reese Taylor, Preston Hotchkiss, Emerson Spear, and Frederick Warren Williamson shaped their perspectives on the future of the region's growth and the policies and leadership that would realize their vision.[40]

Howard's speech was titled "Buyer Beware," and it focused on the need to strengthen the Pure Food and Drug Act of 1906. Divided into two sections, the talk blasted the advertising industry for misleading consumers in a variety of industries and criticized lawmakers for succumbing to the interests of manufacturers in the food, drug, and cosmetic industries. He didn't spare Congress, the president, or his administration.

Ahmanson began by making it clear that he was on the side of the consumer. "New deals, old deals or what-not," he said, "to an ever increasing degree we seem to be plucking our greatest benefactor, good old John Consumer. And inasmuch as we are all both producers and consumers, we go madly forward giving ourselves a bad break." In Ahmanson's view, advertising had played an enormously beneficial role in the development of national companies by allowing economies of scope and scale that lowered production costs for the consumer and increased profits for the shareholder. Without advertising, these companies would not have been able to expand their manufacturing processes and distribution networks. But advertising, he said, "appears to have become a veritable Frankenstein and has taken a firm hold upon his former master, Production."

Ahmanson detailed the ways in which the advertising profession misled rather than informed. He criticized the tobacco industry, which had the temerity to pretend that it was reducing prices when it actually was shrinking the amount of tobacco in a cigarette. He blasted the cosmetic industry for its insidious efforts to insinuate that a woman would lose her man if she used the wrong soap or failed to apply the right makeup. He took on the makers and advertisers of toothpastes, automobiles, antiseptics, laxatives, and Jell-O. "All of such examples of quackery and just plain bunk," he said, "bring to the mind of the curious what tools we have for combating the ever-increasing wave of undependable advertising, and useless if not dangerous products promoted thereby."

Ahmanson looked to government to protect the public, but he was frustrated by both the existing body of law and the resources devoted to enforcement. "We are operating under the Food and Drug Act of 1906," he said, "whose woefully weak provisions are even more weakly policed." He noted that "less than one cent per person per year is spent by the Federal Government in guarding the interest of the consumer." He also pointed out that "the average fine for the successful prosecution of a violation of [the Act] is

$6.00—this amount including the value of the seized goods." Implicitly, he argued, the government, under its duty to provide for the public safety, should do more.

From the evils of advertising, Ahmanson turned to the corruptions of interest group politics. In an allusion to Roosevelt's inaugural address, he recalled the president's assurance that "the money changers would be driven from the temple." Roosevelt and his undersecretary of agriculture had promised "that the food and drug industries would be purged of adulterators, poisoners and quacks." But the "sell-out of the consumer started almost immediately." The administration's proposal had been developed with the input of industry. In Congress, it had been watered down by politicians who were cooking the bill with the adulterators. After describing in detail the painful legislative process, Ahmanson concluded with apparent disgust "that the whole problem of giving the consumer some measure of protection against fraud, trickery and dishonesty is getting exactly no place."[41]

Ahmanson's speech to the Economic Round Table was hardly designed to provide a coherent synthesis of his view of the role of government in structuring markets, nor was it a call for popular revolt, but it does offer important perspectives on his values. Clearly, he supported the government's authority to intrude into the marketplace in the context of protecting public safety. Toothpaste with toxic ingredients, for example, should be banned. But Ahmanson seemed to go further. The government should also protect the consumer from product claims that were simply fraudulent—motor oil that did nothing, despite the manufacturers' claims, to extend the life of a car's engine, or laxatives that were "doctor-recommended" when they weren't. Thus the government had a role to play in a market where buyers and sellers had unequal access to information.

Ahmanson also made it clear that government regulation should not be left in the hands of politicians. Explicitly, he expressed his support for the Progressive model of regulation by experts insulated from the political process. An effective pure food and drug law, he said, should be administered by "qualified technicians interested primarily in consumers' welfare and safety." Implicitly, he believed that such experts should be protected from the influence of manufacturers and other interest groups.

It's not clear from the speech whether Ahmanson believed that the government had a positive role to play in the marketplace—to promote hygiene or good health, for example. He didn't suggest that the alternative to false claims in a free market was government approval in a managed economy. He didn't outline a plan for the government to encourage manufacturers to make one kind of drug over another or reward grocery stores for selling broccoli rather than Jell-O. Likewise, his speech didn't touch on the growing number of federal programs designed to support food producers—like agricultural cooperative marketing programs or price supports—without concomitant efforts to protect consumers.

Delivered in the first year of Franklin Roosevelt's presidency near the low point of the Depression, when unemployment, labor unrest, and a collapsing financial system threatened to undermine capitalism itself, Ahmanson's remarks have to be taken within the context of the times. Nevertheless, they were his times. He was twenty-seven years old and already a highly successful entrepreneur. His audience of academics, business leaders, and "men on the make" shared in the common experience of the era. Roosevelt had equated the Depression to a war. Soon business leaders like Ahmanson and his friends Charlie Fletcher and Howard Edgerton would discover that a real war could pose an even greater challenge to the management of the economy.

BUSINESS AND HIGH SOCIETY

Fortunately for Ahmanson, the regulatory reforms of the New Deal had little impact on the fire insurance industry. The U.S. Supreme Court continued to hold that insurance was for the states, not the federal government, to regulate. In California, Ahmanson's main regulatory threat came from independent insurance agents. They complained that mortgage lenders should not be allowed to steer borrowers into buying property insurance from favored companies—like National American Insurance. They claimed that these arrangements were fraught with conflicts of interest, were "coercive" in nature, and served as a barrier to entry and competition. The independent agents lobbied the California legislature to pass an "anticoercion" law, but Ahmanson's friends in the savings and loan industry, including Howard Edgerton and Charlie Fletcher, were able to kill these proposals.[42]

Meanwhile, Ahmanson continued to cultivate an image of success as a critical component of his sales strategy. "He always wanted us to drive a good car so we looked successful," remembers Robert DeKruif, who began working for the company in 1941. "And he wanted us to dress immaculately: wing-tip shoes, white shirts, blue shirts, and everything like that."[43] But while he cultivated the image of success, Ahmanson also stuck to the basics of building and sustaining relationships. Working with his secretary, Evelyn Barty, for example, he maintained an elaborate "birthday list" that included customers, friends, employees, and politicians. Every month, Barty gave him a list and he would handwrite cards to everyone on the list.[44] He worked eighteen hours a day. His aunt, who lived in Los Angeles, complained that he was "a hard man to find in his office." Howard, she said, had told her "he loses money when he's in."[45] It was far better to be out calling on customers.

But Howard also paid attention to the cost of doing business. As a manager, he found ways to stimulate productivity. He ordered desks without drawers "so people, when they got policy orders or anything like that couldn't stick them in their drawer." When he walked around at night he could see if staff was keeping up with the work. When he hired a new typist, "he would put that typist next to the gal that typed the fastest," DeKruif remembers. Ahmanson also didn't believe in private offices. At one point early in his career, DeKruif realized that a lot of his competitors were schmoozing potential clients on the golf course, so he suggested to Ahmanson that maybe he should join a golf club. "Bob, let me tell you," Ahmanson replied, "while you're playing one game of golf, you can call on five agencies." So DeKruif stuck to Ahmanson's Calvin Coolidge approach—persistence.[46]

As hard as he worked, Ahmanson also enjoyed his wealth. While the rest of the nation struggled through the Great Depression, he and Dottie frequented the Jonathan Club downtown, the Bel Air Bay Club in Santa Monica, and the Los Angeles Stock Club. In the fall of 1935 they began an annual tradition, hosting a spectacular champagne brunch before the football game between USC and UCLA. Howard chartered buses for his guests—many of them savings and loan clients. With banners waving and the sirens of a police escort screaming, "Southland's younger set" rode to the Los Angeles Coliseum.[47]

Dottie threw herself into an endless series of society luncheons and charity events. Howard participated to a limited extent. He helped organize the Boys Club Foundation of Los Angeles and served on its board. Dinners with other couples to play cards or badminton were noted in the society pages of the *Los Angeles Times*. The Ahmansons were regulars at nightclubs like the Cocoanut Grove, the Biltmore Bowl, and Ciro's. In addition to enjoying the high life at home, Dottie and Howard traveled widely. A year after their honeymoon cruise through the Caribbean, they went to Mexico. In 1938, they sailed on the *Queen Mary* to Europe for a six-week tour of the continent with screen star Don Ameche and his wife.[48] In 1940, with the United

States watching the path of Japanese aggression across the Pacific, Howard and Dottie impulsively visited Japan. Arriving in Yokohama in May, Howard told the *Japan News-Week*, "We are the only honest-to-goodness tourists in Japan."[49] Howard and Dottie toured the countryside and visited Tokyo without a guide or interpreter. Howard entertained the locals by playing the piano. The memory of that trip would soon seem surreal.

After Pearl Harbor, fear seized the West Coast as newspapers speculated on whether the Japanese would bomb and strafe the mainland next. Fresh headlines hit the newsstands several times a day. With dark humor, Dottie joked that Howard was to blame for the war: the Japanese had attacked Pearl Harbor, she said, as a way to put an end to Howard's piano playing.[50]

REORGANIZING FOR THE DURATION

In one respect, the war came at just the right time for both Howard Ahmanson and his good friend Howard Edgerton. Both had gotten in trouble with regulators and the law. With six other men, including a prominent Los Angeles physician, Edgerton had been indicted by a federal grand jury in June 1941 for devising a scheme to defraud investors in the Railway Mutual Building and Loan Association.[51] According to the charges, victims of the scheme who were Railway depositors were told that they would have to wait for some time to withdraw their money from the association. If they wanted their money sooner, they could go to a company called First Security Deposit Corporation, which would give them only eighty or ninety cents on the dollar but would give them cash immediately. Customers who chose this option sold their Railway Mutual shares (deposits) to First Security. According to prosecutors, Edgerton was the primary owner of First Security Deposit Corporation, and as soon as these accounts were transferred, Edgerton received full value for the accounts he had paid for at a discount.[52]

As the rest of the nation organized for all-out war, Edgerton and his fellow defendants went on trial in February 1942.[53] On April 5, 1942, after thirty hours of deliberation, a jury convicted him and a codefendant on a number of counts related to mail fraud. The jury was unable to agree on the guilt or innocence of four other men. One other man was found completely innocent. All were judged innocent on the charge of conspiracy.[54] Three weeks later, a federal judge sentenced Edgerton to two and a half years in a federal penitentiary.[55] While the rest of the nation turned to the business of war, Edgerton was released on his own recognizance pending his appeal.[56]

Howard Ahmanson's brush with the censure of state government in 1942 threatened far less serious consequences, but it was troubling nonetheless. The details are sketchy. He ran into trouble with the Insurance Commission on business transactions with Thomas Mortgage Co., a business run by two brothers, H. B. and Luther Thomas, out of Los Angeles and Long Beach. The brothers, as agents for Prudential Life Insurance Company, advertised their services in the classifieds of the *Los Angeles Times*.[57] They offered FHA Title II and Title VI loans and handled real estate sales. They also seemed to offer fire insurance through H. F. Ahmanson. At the time, Anthony Caminetti, a former judge from Amador County, was the state insurance commissioner. Appointed by Democratic governor Culbert Olson in 1939, he was known as a crusader.[58] In 1940, he had seized a dozen life insurance companies, asserting that they were being mismanaged and that assets to benefit policyholders were being diverted to stockholders and directors.[59] It's unclear what brought the Thomas brothers and Ahmanson to Caminetti's attention, except to quote from Ahmanson, who later blamed it all on "one careless, fiery-tempered red-head."[60] It's also unclear what actual charges were leveled against the Thomas brothers and Ahmanson. All apparently faced possible suspensions.

Ahmanson and the Thomas brothers caught a break in September 1943, when Governor Earl Warren announced that he would not reappoint the controversial Caminetti. Instead, he tapped Pasadena attorney Maynard Garrison. The thirty-eight-year-old Garrison had graduated from Loyola University Law School in 1932 and had practiced insurance law as an employee and associate general counsel for the Automobile Club of Southern California for eleven years. He had served as vice chairman of Warren's campaign in Southern California.[61] He was also good friends with the attorneys handling the case for the Thomases and Ahmanson.[62]

With Ahmanson already in navy basic training on the East Coast, the Thomases' preliminary hearing took place on November 29, 1943. Asked to offer a plea, the brothers asserted that they were unaware of the events that led up to the charges.[63] The hearing was then postponed until December 10. Before the 10th, the attorneys for the Thomases negotiated a thirty-day suspension for the brothers, who pled guilty to several minor citations. All other charges were dropped. Gould Eddy thought this was a remarkably favorable outcome. Howard apparently received only a five-day suspension. Writing to H. B. Thomas after the decision, he gave credit to the lawyers but also concluded that the lightness of the sentence reflected "the reputation of the good old Thomas Mortgage Company and some of your and my personal acquaintances."[64]

Military service offered Ahmanson and Edgerton a way to put some distance between them and the law. Even before Pearl Harbor, Congress had approved a broad military draft that eventually encompassed every able-bodied man under the age of forty-five. Edgerton joined the Air Corps as a civilian flight instructor.[65] To Ahmanson and Fletcher he expressed his delight in being able to graduate from his Piper Cub to the 450-horsepower trainer aircraft that he flew "with a cadet in the other cockpit that doesn't know a damned thing about the airplane and is scared to death of its size." Despite the bravado of his aerial exploits, however, "the shadow of the gray prison walls" followed him. In November 1943, as he waited for the oral hearings on his case before the Ninth Circuit Court of Appeals, he confessed that "this particular period before the deadline is a rather tense one and is a fitting climax to the past 3½ years during which period of time I have been investigated, indicted, tried, convicted, wooed, screwed and tattooed."[66]

Despite his statements in 1941, Howard chose to enlist in the U.S. Navy rather than wait to be drafted. In his application for a commission, he included yachting among his leisure activities. Curiously, he also noted that he had performed "investigation along lines required by Naval Intelligence."[67] Perhaps this referred to information he had supplied after touring Japan. In any case, in May 1943 he was appointed as a lieutenant in the U.S. Naval Reserves with the understanding that he would go to Rhode Island for basic training and then be assigned to duty.

Before leaving for boot camp, Ahmanson reorganized his businesses to create a simplified structure. Although H. F. Ahmanson & Co. was his primary focus, he had a number of other active investments and property to be managed, including his real estate and oil wells. As the result of a winning hand in a poker game with Morgan Adams, he was also the owner of the once-famous Mayan Theater in downtown Los Angeles, where live stage performances included African American song and dance troupes, Jewish comedies, and solo performances by singers and comedians.[68] Howard could easily leave the oil wells and the real estate in the hands of developers and property managers. He asked Ted Crane, the head of the Inland Marine Department

at H. F. Ahmanson & Co., to keep the theater rented. H. F. Ahmanson & Company, however, was more complicated.

As he put it, H. F. Ahmanson & Company had "become involved in so doggone many kinds of businesses that my examiners and the like were going nutty trying to figure out who was doing what to who[m]—and so was I." For the duration of the war he put the day-to-day operations into a company called Insurance Managers, which was owned by H. F. Ahmanson & Company, Inc. He turned management of the new company over to Gould Eddy. Then he began packing for basic training.[69]

DEPRESSION LEGACIES

War ended the long nightmare of the Depression even as it slowed all of the industries dependent on the residential real estate market. Private construction came to a virtual standstill in the face of the government's need for construction materials. Nevertheless, the institutional legacies of the Depression reflected substantial changes in the government's approach to increasing the supply of residential mortgage capital and promoting the role of home ownership in strengthening American democracy and capitalism. New government institutions brought stability to the market by diminishing risks for savers, borrowers, and lenders alike. These institutions had been formed from the coalescence of Hoover's associationalism with the strong hand of Roosevelt's New Deal. During the Depression, these new agencies had staved off even deeper trouble. After the war, they would provide the foundation for a resurgent and redefined American Dream, a dream that would reshape the pattern of cities across the nation and would lead savings and loan executives like Howard Ahmanson to great fortune.

FOUR

The Common Experience

SOCIOLOGISTS AND HISTORIANS often point to the equalizing effect that military service had on men in America. It gave them a common experience, a frame of reference for every conversation. It reinforced the appeals to civic duty made by President Roosevelt in his fireside chats and echoed by civic and political leaders across the country. It fortified a fundamental sense of a social contract between the individual and the state that incorporated basic entitlements, including Roosevelt's "freedom from want." It also heightened awareness of the personal and collective responsibilities of citizens for the preservation of a free society.[1]

In the popular imagination, the entitlements flowed especially to soldiers and citizens engaged in the national defense—marines in bunkers on the beaches of Corregidor and Rosie the Riveter attaching the cockpit shell of a B-17 bomber in Seattle. But Howard Ahmanson's military experience hardly fit the popular imagination.

For starters, when most men left for basic training, it didn't make the society pages of the *Los Angeles Times.* "Instead of waiting to see what his classmates would look like [in uniform]," wrote columnist Lucy Quirk, "he had them over for a preview showing and get-together party." Most were members of the Beverly Hills social set. Dottie greeted them at the door wearing a Tahitian print with a tropical blossom in her hair, as if they were all bound for a South Sea vacation.[2]

Charlie Fletcher was no doubt chagrined when he arrived in his navy blues, his broad swimmer's shoulders pushing at the seams. Unlike Ahmanson and Edgerton, who saw the war as an opportunity to escape the glare of official scrutiny of their business activities, Fletcher entered the military from the limelight of public service. Since the attack on Pearl Harbor, he had been elected president of the California Savings and Loan League. True to his vow at the Shoreham Hotel, he had launched a major bond drive to help finance the war. But like Ahmanson, he was not old enough to escape the draft so he had chosen to enlist.[3]

If Howard reminded him of his emphatic assertion that he would not go to war, the point was lost in a new reality. Since the attack on Pearl Harbor and that morning at the Shoreham, the world had changed. In Europe, the Pacific, and North Africa, men were fighting and dying. At home, families had pulled up stakes and moved to work in factories and shipyards making the airplanes and vessels needed to wage war. More subtly, the relationship between business and government had undergone a profound shift. The tensions between corporate America and Washington that colored the years of the New Deal were giving way to a new partnership that depended on seasoned executives like Fletcher and Ahmanson.

BASIC TRAINING IN QUONSET, RHODE ISLAND

Considered the "birthplace" of the U.S. Navy during the Revolutionary War, Quonset, Rhode Island, was teeming with activity when Howard arrived in 1943. Land- and carrier-based antisubmarine squadrons trained offshore while British, Canadian, and American pilots roared into the air. Arriving roughly a year after another Southern Californian, Richard Nixon, had completed his training at Quonset, Howard and Charlie joined a class full of lawyers, business executives, and other professionals on the fast track to become officers.[4]

Despite the flip attitude that his send-off party might suggest, Howard seemed to revel in the eight-week basic training experience. He wrote Dottie that he couldn't sleep for the first few days in the barracks but felt "swell." His bunkmates ranged from "excited kids to old time blasé naval officers." Although he did well on his written exams (memorizing aircraft and naval vessels), his fellow swabbies kidded him "about being the worst driller in the place." "My mind wanders," he confessed, "and I have a strong tendency to look at the scenery. I drill about like I drive a car, half conscious I guess." He didn't mind the running or physical fitness program and enjoyed playing baseball, basketball, and touch football, though he was "lousy" at sports. On the one occasion when he snagged a high fly ball to win a baseball game, he reported the details to Dottie like a schoolboy crowing to his mother.[5] He even looked forward to going to church—a rare event for him—on his first Sunday in Rhode Island because it would give him the opportunity to wear his dress blues and not have to walk in formation.[6]

Dottie wrote him frequently and grew exasperated when he didn't write back soon enough. She worried that he was having too good a time without her, that he would be unfaithful. He tried to reassure her. Meanwhile, Gould Eddy, who had been rejected by the draft board, kept Howard posted on business issues—a major fire in Malibu that had destroyed a number of homes, unrest among the women in the accounting office who were lobbying for raises, and the latest gossip among the company's main clients in the savings and loan industry.[7] Armed with Eddy's news, Ahmanson sent a stream of chatty letters to his clients and customers.

Howard worried about where the navy would send him. He was told he would serve either as an administrative officer at a naval air station or as a materials expediter. Since most of the rest of his class was headed to "fighter direction" or "air combat intelligence," Howard was happy with his possibilities, but he also hoped that an old friend might be able to land him a position in Southern California.[8]

Never one to enter unknown waters without a chart, Howard showed rare vulnerability when he wrote to a longtime mentor for advice and influence. Robert Frank Gross worked as a vice president of Mortgage Guarantee in Los Angeles. A generation older, Gross had graduated from the U.S. Naval Academy in 1907 and served on active duty through the end of World War I, retiring as a lieutenant commander. After the war, he entered the mortgage business in Los Angeles and helped finance new suburbs in the 1920s. Throughout these years, Gross maintained his navy connections, serving as an officer in the Naval Reserve and retiring in 1941 with the rank of commander.[9] The thin correspondence that survives between Ahmanson and Gross suggests the complexity of the relationship and highlights the close personal ties between the defense industries in Southern California and local financial institutions.

With Gross's help, Ahmanson was assigned to the Bureau of Aeronautics in Washington as a lieutenant junior grade (JG). As chief expediter for the Aircraft Products Division, he worked with parts manufacturing companies to ensure a steady supply of components to the aircraft manufacturers—most of which were located in Southern California. "As you might well guess," he wrote to a friend, "for the first thirty days I was completely baffled, never having been inside an airplane." By January 1944, however, he reported that "I now find myself building them with the greatest of ease."[10] With characteristic humor, Ahmanson wrote to a friend in Beverly Hills:

> I came down here expecting to be a nice kind-faced file boy for some guy in the Production Division, find out at the beginning of work the first day that I'm in a whole new end of the work known as the Modification Program, and am the assistant to the head man, and at the end of the day find that the head man is being moved, so I'm it. . . . It has turned out to be more fun than I could imagine a Navy job to be. I have no superiors to read the multitudinous instructions I send out hither and yon. . . . If you could see the reckless abandon with which I am spending your money, you would probably start a tax fight. . . . I find myself surrounded by quite a bevy of near and not-so-near tycoons like young Rockefeller, Firestone, Van Eck, the ex-president of Pontiac Motors, the president of a Boston bank, a guy who owns a bunch of New England knitting mills—along with a Ford dealer from Punk Center, Oregon and a guy who ran a general store in Pine Bluffs, Arkansas. They're all heads or assistants of various sub-sections in the Production Division and truly a swell, patient and hard-working bunch of guys.[11]

Howard's initial enthusiasm for his work in Washington did not last. By January 1944, he was complaining that it was "a little wearisome being a glorified file boy in Washington." Eighty percent of the things he did could be managed by his trusted secretary, Barty. For the other 20 percent, "no one but a fool would have the courage." Meanwhile, his friends Charlie Fletcher and Thurston Ross were flying around the world on secret missions and organizing invasions.[12]

Ahmanson's perspective changed when it seemed he might get a position in the office of the undersecretary of the navy, but he was torn between ambition and a deep desire to return to California. Gross wrote to say that with the growth of aircraft manufacturing in Southern California, the navy was going to open a new procurement facility in Van Nuys. Ahmanson could hope for a senior management position at this facility.[13]

FOXHOLE AT THE SHOREHAM

With housing in short supply and Dottie coming to live with him in Washington, Ahmanson secured a room at his old haunt—the Shoreham Hotel. Missing their usual Christmas festivities in California, he and Dottie bought a "two for a nickel" eighteen-inch tree for their hotel parlor and piled presents around it.[14] Howard wrote to the staff at National American back in Omaha that he was sorry to miss the annual Christmas extravaganza. He said he had started to feel a little sorry for himself, but "all of a sudden I thought of ten million other guys spread all over creation wondering what goes on when the fracas is over, and I decided that I'm the luckiest guy in the world—as usual."[15]

Indeed, midshipmen in the Pacific avoiding the gunfire of Japanese Zeros would hardly have recognized the sailor's life that Ahmanson led. Tongue in cheek, Howard wrote his college classmate Joe Crail, the head of Coast Federal Savings and Loan, "I know that my discomfiture and self-sacrifice at fighting the war from my foxhole in the Shoreham would wring from you deep expressions of sympathy." Then he jokingly chastised Crail for growing his business "while I'm not around to keep track" or "defend myself."[16]

In Washington, Howard and Dottie bonded with other Southern Californians. Charlie Fletcher and his wife, Jeannette, had moved their family from San Diego to Chevy Chase, Maryland. Jeannette managed a house full of kids while Charlie flew to Europe and the Pacific organizing logistics to support the invasions of North Africa and later Saipan.[17] The Californians often gathered together. In May 1944, Howard attended a dinner party hosted by Colonel and Mrs. Ed Shattuck. A longtime Republican activist in California, Shattuck served as general counsel to the Selective Service System. After the war, Shattuck would become deputy city attorney in Los Angeles and run for attorney general of California. That night, the Shattucks' guests included Major General Lewis Hershey, the head of the Selective Service; Harold Judson, an attorney from Los Angeles who had joined the Solicitor General's Office and would soon be promoted to chief counsel to the president; as well as Howard's longtime business mentor Morgan Adams, the head of Mortgage Guarantee. (After Ahmanson had told Adams to "jump in a lake" rather than allow him to buy out H. F. Ahmanson in the late 1920s, the two men had become friends again and Adams had returned to the occasional role of mentor.) Adams was in Washington to serve as an advisor to Secretary of the Navy James Forrestal, who oversaw shipyards across the country that were furiously producing vessels for the war.[18] Lieutenant Harrison Chandler, son of *Los Angeles Times* publisher Harry Chandler, also joined the party. Charlie Fletcher should have been there but he was overseas on a special mission.

From the company at this dinner table, as well as his day-to-day work at the Aeronautics Bureau, Ahmanson gained considerable insight into the growing military-industrial complex. This perspective helped him understand that aviation and aeronautics would be important in the postwar economy. These social interactions also deepened his connections with a group of Southern Californians in Washington who would play a pivotal role in the region's postwar development.

Howard moved out of the Shoreham after Dottie returned to Los Angeles. He rented a large house, brought in a piano, and told Dottie that he had been spending "99.44 percent" of his waking moments playing music. To complete his life of Riley, he had his butler, Marshall, come from Los Angeles to live with him.

Howard wrote to Dottie multiple times a week and cajoled her to write him more. Although both of them consumed prodigious amounts of alcohol, Howard never seemed outwardly drunk. Dottie, however, seemed increasingly dependent. He worried about her state of mind and encouraged her over and over not to live alone.

New responsibilities in May 1944 kept him working late and skipping lunches. In June, he visited the radar school at the Massachusetts Institute of Technology in Cambridge.[19] The work sparked ideas, which were resisted all too often by his superiors and his subordinates. He tried to suppress his own entrepreneurial bent and his growing commitment to the collective war effort. His own "gremlins," he told Dottie, were buzzing around 10 percent too fast in his head. "Each night I resolve—no more of this monkey business.... [H]undreds of guys are sitting on their fanny—you're a [lieutenant] j.g.—the war effort was doing dandy without you et cetera, et cetera—and damn it the next morning at 0805 something comes up that looks kind of important to me and we're off."[20]

At night in his splendid rented home near Rock Creek Park, he played the piano and the organ. He listened to his favorite radio show—*Amos 'n' Andy*. He drank and he smoked. He socialized and flirted with college girls.[21] His wife and his mother worried about his "morals." Florence accused him of dragging the Ahmanson name through the mud with his drinking. Dottie was sure he was having too good a time in Washington with other women, despite his constant assurances to the contrary. They argued on the phone and then wrote contrite letters apologizing. Often these tensions were rooted in Howard's larger ambitions.

Florence may have accused him of abandoning the morals she and Will had tried to impart to their two sons, but Howard had not forgotten his father's lessons or legacy. Howard remembered the pain his father experienced when he discovered in 1919 that National American's stock promoters had oversold the company and when farmers and merchants who had purchased the company's stock for one hundred dollars discovered that it was worth only one-fifth of that price. He remembered how his father had worked to redeem his good name and had sought to deliver high-quality service to insurance customers and earnings to stockholders. At the time of Will's death, National American had only just begun this process of redemption.

Seventeen years later, National American was in trouble. The men who were running the company were the same executives, led by James Foster, who had taken control after Will's death in 1925. From 1921 to 1937, they paid dividends to shareholders in all but one year—1933. From 1938 to 1943, the company paid a dividend only once. When the state of Nebraska's Department of Insurance examined the company's records in October 1943, it found that the total amount of dividends paid had "consumed the earnings of the company together with a considerable portion of the original contributed surplus."[22] The company was still growing, but not by much. Total net assets increased only 4.4 percent between 1940 and 1943 to just under two million dollars.[23] Attempting to adjust to declining circumstances, the company had slashed executive pay beginning in 1939. Hayden's salary was cut nearly 20 percent.[24] But cost cutting was not turning the company around.

For years, Howard had worked to secure control of his father's company. National American's stock was not traded on any exchange. Local brokers in Omaha handled sales and purchases privately. All through the 1930s, Ahmanson had purchased stock from farmers and merchants scattered across Nebraska and Iowa. By 1943, he had accumulated 33 percent of the outstanding shares, but there were still approximately six hundred shareholders who held various blocks of the company's twenty thousand outstanding shares.[25]

Before entering the navy, Howard had traveled to Omaha to investigate the situation. "Everyone has a different idea" about what needed to be done, he reported to Dottie. Top management wanted to sell out.[26] Howard thought this was crazy. Loss ratios on the business he wrote in California averaged only 24.3 percent from 1940 to 1942, compared to loss ratios well over 50 percent in Colorado, Nebraska, and Minnesota.[27] Meanwhile, administrative overhead in Nebraska was high because the home office supervised approximately 475 separate agencies in just two states—Nebraska and Iowa. In California, Howard worked with only 55 different agencies and wrote insurance for a very limited number of risks: fire, earthquake, and marine.[28] In fact, his business accounted for a large percentage of National American's total volume and profits.

There were other management problems that also must have troubled Howard. The Nebraska Department of Insurance found that real estate assets were on the books for values far above their actual market value.[29] In 1942 the company caught its real estate mortgage loan manager pocketing rent and other collections from clients that should have been paid to the company. The loan manager was fired and the company was reimbursed by the fidelity bond insurer, but the incident provided evidence that Hayden and others in Omaha were not at the top of their game.[30]

Howard was confident that he could turn the company around. Unfortunately, the stock was still scattered "from hell to breakfast." Hayden encouraged Howard to be patient.[31] But with the longtime executives of the company talking about selling out, Howard decided to be more aggressive.[32] Fearing that if word got out the price of the shares would rise or the company's senior executives would sabotage his efforts, he kept his plans secret. "The pals . . . are determined to sell out," he wrote Dottie, "and equally determined that I don't get control."

The fight was complicated by a family crisis. Hayden was not in good shape "mentally, morally, spiritually and financially." Three or more times a week, he drank too much and stayed in bed to recover. His wife, Aimee, struggled to keep her household together with one son graduated from high school and the other about to graduate. Meanwhile, Florence was beside herself and ready to "jump out a window."[33] Howard empowered Ray Stryker, a junior executive at National American who was loyal to the Ahmansons, to look after the family's interest in the business while Howard worked to find a way to ameliorate the situation.[34]

Howard was determined, as he wrote Gould Eddy, "that the best seventeen years' work I've ever done" should not be ruined by either his adversaries or a few anxious stockholders.[35] He recruited Ted Crane from H. F. Ahmanson & Co.'s office in Los Angeles to travel to Iowa and Nebraska to track down stockholders and buy them out. In June 1943, Crane went to eastern Iowa on the train and spent three days talking to stockholders.[36] Pointing to recent reports from state insurance departments in Nebraska, Iowa, and California, he told potential sellers that the regulators "not only took issue with some of the values at which assets had been carried, but also went on record as stating that several of the later dividends paid by the company were illegal in that the company hadn't earned them." All of this was true. Crane even told at least one stockholder that he didn't see how the company "could pay another dividend for ten years."[37] Having bad-mouthed the stock, he offered to pay $20 a share (a fifth the stock's initial value) if they were willing to sell.

Finally, a week before he was scheduled to enter the navy, Howard learned that James Foster, the man who had succeeded his father as president, was ready to retire. Foster had rivals who wanted to take over the company, but he felt this would hurt the many longtime farmer shareholders who had patiently stayed with the business since the 1920s. Foster and another executive agreed to sell their 20 percent stake to Howard if Ahmanson would protect the interests of these shareholders.[38]

Still "beautifully liquid," Ahmanson was able to move quickly. When the transaction was complete, his equity in National American topped 51 percent, a stake worth $733,540 ($9.4 million in 2011 dollars). He would later say his decision to pay top dollar (about three times the market value of the shares) was "my silliest business venture."[39] He did it out of respect and affection for his father.

With majority control, Ahmanson planned to reconfigure the board of directors.[40] Unable to leave Washington, he let Gould Eddy and Hayden orchestrate the fight with two remaining dissident shareholders.[41] Certain that he had the shares and proxies to be successful, he focused on arranging the company's balance sheet so that results under his management would be almost guaranteed to be positive. As he bragged to a friend in Southern California, he had been "cutting the gizzard out of everything, to the point where they're carrying Government bonds at under par, real estate at half of what it's worth, unpaid losses about double of what really should have been, etc. etc. I am going to have the unusual pleasure of taking over officially with a few sprinters tucked away in the barn instead of the usual process of having to pay for dead horses."[42]

Howard's financial strategy made the former management look even worse. Hayden constantly reminded him that the men in Omaha resented these moves. Howard didn't care.[43] "What we're trying to sell," he wrote, "is the fact that the new regime is different from the old."[44] The new regime would practice more conservative bookkeeping and money management and give Howard more capital to work with.[45]

Ahmanson wanted the world to know of his success. He asked Gould Eddy and his associates to "dream up some idea of publicizing in a big way the advent of H. F. Ahmanson as president of the National American Fire Insurance Company. The National American isn't very important and neither am I, but inasmuch as the two of us are only going to get together once, I believe this is an opportunity which should make us both better known."[46]

Behind this desire for publicity lay a deeper motivation. Howard had partially redeemed his father's memory. As president of National American, he would now have the opportunity to fulfill the promise with which the promoters had saddled his father: he would make the company profitable. Those who stuck with him and the company would reap their reward. For those who wanted to sell out, he was more than happy to buy their shares— at the cheapest price possible.

GOING HOME

Bored with his work in Washington, Howard reported to Dottie in the summer of 1944 that he struggled to get up in the mornings. Charlie Fletcher had moved in with him after Jeannette and the children moved back to San Diego. The two men often had breakfast with other friends at the office. One time, after a mad dash to get Fletcher to a plane, he wrote: "Good old Charlie—he is the most delightful roommate a guy could imagine—but a little energetic for me."[47]

"Getting out is the sole subject of conversation around here," Howard wrote to Dottie at the end of August.[48] While American forces in Europe and the Pacific were fighting some of the heaviest battles of the war in the fall of 1944, Howard and Charlie, like others in Washington whose lives were caught up in planning, sensed victory and began to make plans for their own futures. By the end of July, the government had begun to cut back on aircraft production and Howard and his crew found themselves with less and less to do.[49] Howard wrote Dottie that men who were over the age of thirty-eight (he was thirty-eight) were getting approved to go on inactive duty, especially if they had "something special to do on the outside."[50]

At first, Howard didn't think he would be able to get out until the war with Germany was over, but he was convinced that Germany's surrender would come before Thanksgiving. In fact, he was so sure that he sold all of his stock on the assumption that the market would plunge when the war ended.[51]

He complained about the heat, the humidity, and the rain in Washington and "perspiring buckets all night." He was jealous of Charlie, who could fall asleep instantly, standing or lying down. Howard often lay awake much of the night planning. Longing for relaxation, he fantasized about going to Mexico with Dottie. "It's the only place in the world that's not all this war business."[52] At one point he proclaimed that he was going to stop visiting folks from California. "They are all homesick by nature—and it is contagious."[53]

Fletcher and Ahmanson were each driven by more than just the desire to return to private life. Charlie had been infected by his time in Washington and was considering a run for Congress. Meanwhile Howard, aware that the reconversion of the economy was already under way, wanted to get back to business.

Howard's desire to go home was made urgent by the other member of the threesome, Howard Edgerton. Still in Southern California and keeping an eye on business, Edgerton had appealed to the federal circuit court after being sentenced to prison for his role in the Railway Mutual scheme. On September 26, 1944, the circuit court reversed the judgment of the lower court and ordered the entire indictment dismissed.[54] With the specter of incarceration removed and the end of the war in sight, Edgerton was understandably excited about the future and anxious for his good friends and business associates to return to California.

"Edgie" hounded Gould Eddy for information about Howard and Charlie's plans. On October 31, 1944, he wrote to both men to let them know that a looming fight in the legislature and the industry association needed their attention. Mixing the ribald character of their friendship with hard news about business, he chided Ahmanson and Fletcher for their lack of communication—not even a postcard from a nightclub. He needed to know their plans, he said, so that he could "guard my company against any shock it might receive from the public reaction. Bringing Stillwell home from Burma or replacing Roosevelt with Dewey will create only slight public diversion compared to Ahmanson and Fletcher pulling out of Washington at the same time."[55]

"On the home front," Edgerton continued, "we are carrying on as good stooges should. From a business standpoint we are continuing to shove National American fire policies down the throats of both willing and unwilling borrowers, and on the political horizon we are letting the public get a bellyful of the present group of candidates waiting for Fletcher to come home and run for something really serious."

Edgerton went on to highlight the news from the savings and loan industry. After describing the petty arguments and displays of bravado at a recent meeting of the California Savings and Loan League, Edgerton noted that "it was my first group meeting since returning to civilian life," and he was appalled by the lack of discipline and focus. "It just goes to show, Charlie, that you have got to come back and start running this damned league again so that we can worry more about defeating our business competitors and less about sticking a knife in each other's backs."[56]

Edgerton followed his letter with a trip to Washington several weeks later. He socialized with Fletcher and Ahmanson and talked about his own postwar plans. He had served as part-time president and CEO of California Federal Savings & Loan since 1939, but with the boom that all three men expected in the housing market in Southern California, he knew that he needed "to decide whether to continue practicing law and hire a chief executive for the Association, or take over full-time management responsibilities and hire lawyers." Ahmanson and Fletcher encouraged him to become a full-time corporate executive.[57]

COOPERATING FRIENDS

Working in different markets, with Home Federal based in San Diego and California Federal in Los Angeles, Fletcher and Edgerton could strategize together on their investment strategies. They could also collaborate on regulatory issues. Shortly after he returned to California, for example, Edgerton found out that there was a move afoot in the legislature to restrict one of their main sources of profit—the tie between lender and property insurer.

Once again, independent insurance agents were trying to pass a law forbidding lenders from engaging in exclusive contracts with an insurance agent and forcing borrowers to buy fire and property insurance from only one agency. Although Howard and his best clients in the mortgage industry had been able to kill this proposal in previous years, Gould Eddy told Edgerton that it looked as though they were in for a "tougher scrap" in 1945. The mortgage bankers were lining up to support the bill, along with the independent insurance agents. Even their longtime allies at Mortgage Guarantee, including Morgan Adams and Frank Gross, would provide only "behind-the-scenes support after the matter got into committee." Edgerton bemoaned the fact that Ahmanson and Fletcher were not on the scene to help with lobbying. He complained about the lack of support from other mortgage lenders. "They are the ones who will yell the loudest if this bill ever passes," he wrote, "and every damn insurance agent representing the large mortgage companies loses thousands a year in commissions as a result of this legislation."[58]

Fortunately, Ahmanson already had one foot out the door of the navy. He was waiting only for a resolution from the board of National American attesting that the company needed to have him on the job. Hayden was working on this paperwork. Morgan Adams had agreed to help push the paperwork through—"my first and only request for influence," Howard wrote home to Dottie.[59]

LOOKING FORWARD

Much has been made of the effect of the Depression and World War II on the lives of what some have called the "Greatest Generation." The Depression taught them to be conservative about money, to avoid debt and favor savings, and to take care of one another in hard times. The war brought the nation together, smoothed some of the edges of social, racial, and ethnic boundaries, and conditioned a generation to think of the common good. Howard Ahmanson's experiences during this era ran counter to the usual story. The Depression made him rich. Managing the home front from a desk in Washington, D.C., was at times fascinating and at other times boring and frustrating. Still, the defining era of his generation changed him as it did so many others.

Ahmanson's experiences shaped his perspective on government. Like many Americans, he saw it as necessary and well intentioned, though not always efficient. In one letter he marveled at "the way that American industry has produced all the big and little items that we require."[60] Yet he was genuinely proud of his department's ability to aid the war effort. In January 1944, when James Foster, the president of National American, wanted to send a circular to the company's agents criticizing Roosevelt and his administration, Howard reacted strongly: "Being personally sympathetic to many Administration reforms and agencies," he wired Hayden, "I for one would resent capricious literature on subject from any public corporation."[61]

Historian James Sparrow has described the transformation of the relationship between business and government during World War II as a "new iteration" of the associational state that Herbert Hoover had championed in the

1920s. Corporate interests gained powerful positions in what Dwight Eisenhower would later describe as the military-industrial complex, and corporate influence extended to the administrative offices of virtually every regulatory body as well. But the government was not simply "captured" by this process, as Sparrow points out: "If federal power became critically dependent on business in the war the reverse was also true, making those business figures who entered public service at least as much creatures of the state as they were servants of capital."[62]

By the end of the war, Howard, Charlie Fletcher, and Howard Edgerton had tired of the military bureaucracy but had gained greater respect for government and the stronger sense of public purpose that Sparrow describes. This doesn't mean they were any less self-involved, ambitious, or eager to continue building their fortunes, but in the years ahead these experiences shaped their approaches to business, politics, and philanthropy.

FIVE

Building Home

WHILE SOME SOLDIERS and sailors moved home with their parents, doubled up in apartments, or lived in converted garages, Howard and Dottie Ahmanson arrived at the Beverly Hills Hotel on New Year's Eve, 1944, intending to stay for a while.[1] Day and night, the hotel was a social center, a community forum, and a watering hole for Hollywood stars. Women's groups held their luncheons and charity events in the ballroom. Hollywood regulars included Humphrey Bogart, Marlene Dietrich, and Katherine Hepburn, as well as the already reclusive Howard Hughes.[2] Poolside during the day or sipping cocktails in the Polo Lounge at night, Howard and Dottie were pampered by Howard's college friend, hotel manager Hernando Courtright. Yet the scene was strangely surreal.

The war was not over. Although the Allies were closing in on Germany, the invasion of Japan was expected to be bloody. With the military focus on the Pacific Theater, many people anticipated that Los Angeles would expand even further as it continued to serve as the major West Coast embarkation point and manufacturing center and to receive the battered bodies of the nation's heroes.

In preparation for the last phase of the war against Japan, policy makers worried about housing an even greater number of war workers. "Scores of men and women [are] sleeping in all-night or past-midnight theaters because of lack of conventional quarters," the *Los Angeles Times* noted.[3] Charities and government agencies appealed to home owners to open spare rooms to families desperate for shelter.[4] Mayor Fletcher Bowron wrote to President Roosevelt to say that "more than 100,000 unfilled applications for housing are now on file with the Los Angeles War Housing Centers."[5] The federal government, which controlled the supply of building materials, approved the construction of six thousand new homes in areas of Los Angeles near shipyards and aircraft factories. But this allocation represented only a small step toward meeting the demand.

The need for housing reflected one of many ways in which the city and region that Howard Ahmanson returned to at the beginning of 1945 had been transformed by the war. Nearly a half-million new residents had arrived to assemble aircraft, build ships, forge steel, refine petroleum, make machine tools, and manufacture a host of other vital war matériel. At its peak, the Los Angeles area produced 10 percent of the goods needed to wage the war. Large military installations at Terminal Island, San Pedro, Long Beach, and El Toro also brought soldiers, sailors, airmen, and marines passing through on their way to the Pacific.[6]

Despite this growth, L.A.'s postwar future was not clear. When builder and developer Mark Taper tried to get a construction loan in 1942 to build government-insured FHA homes, the first bank he approached turned him down. "The bank told me they thought this would be a ghost town once the war ended."[7] When Howard Edgerton went to Chicago to borrow money so California Federal Savings & Loan could buy more government bonds, a senior executive from Continental Illinois eerily told him the same thing: "We do not care to invest our money directly or indirectly in any Southern California enterprise at the present time because we are convinced that when the war is over Los Angeles is going to become a ghost town."[8]

Taper and Edgerton weren't convinced, and neither were Howard Ahmanson and Charlie Fletcher. "We already had evidence that some of the war workers who had come here during the peak production periods had decided to stay," Edgerton recalled later. "What we didn't anticipate was that they would send for all their relatives and friends."[9]

For those lucky enough to survive the war, the memory of Southern California was compelling. "A lot of guys had been here and seen what it was not to have snow in their ears," remembered one local resident.[10] The ocean, the mountains, the citrus groves, and the region's bustling wartime economy were all attractive.[11] When they returned after the war, these new residents sparked a gold rush in real estate, construction, and mortgage lending. For a handful of entrepreneurs who saw how the government had, intentionally and unintentionally, created profitable opportunities to finance that gold rush, the postwar suburban boom produced massive personal and corporate fortunes.[12]

Southern California's growth before, during, and after the war was phenomenal. More people and better wages fed a booming economy. The population of Los Angeles County alone rose more than 50 percent in the 1940s, climbing from 2,786,000 to 4,374,000.[13] Before the war, in contrast to most other large American cities, residents had worked in trade, services, and agriculture. With the war, trade and services grew 51 and 35 percent, respectively, but manufacturing jobs more than doubled, adding nearly 213,000 positions. As citrus groves and bean fields were bulldozed to make way for factories and homes, agriculture lost nearly three thousand jobs. Meanwhile, employment in construction increased 88 percent, providing work for another sixty thousand people. The burgeoning field of aeronautics contributed substantially to the growth of L.A.'s manufacturing sector. By 1953, aviation accounted for one in four manufacturing jobs in the region.[14]

These new jobs came with good wages. Between 1940 and 1951, average income in the area tripled.[15] Median family income in Los Angeles County in 1951 was 19 percent higher than the national median for metropolitan regions.[16] And like most Americans, Angelenos had saved money during the war.[17] Across the country, liquid assets of businesses and individuals had increased 252 percent; in California, they had increased nearly 300 percent.[18] In short, households in Los Angeles after the war had income and savings to spend on new homes.

Demographic changes also fed the demand for housing. During and after the war, marriage rates soared. "The nation has fewer bachelors and old maids than in former years," the Census Bureau reported in 1946. More marriages led to an increase in the birthrate. Even before the end of the war, for every soldier or sailor killed in battle, six "war babies" were born over and above the prewar birthrate.[19]

Los Angeles was particularly affected by the marriage and baby boom. The migration to California, and especially Southern California, was overwhelmingly youthful, with the great majority of new residents under the age of forty-five. More likely to reproduce, these young newcomers contributed to a 40 percent increase in the birthrate between 1940 and 1950, compared to an increase of 31.3 percent for the country as a whole.[20] In Los Angeles, the population of children ages zero to five rose 150 percent during the 1940s.[21] All of these new families fueled an overall increase in household formation and a concomitant decline in the number of multigenerational households.

Policy makers across the country anticipated a demand for millions of new homes. In Southern California, the commission charged with planning estimated that Los Angeles County alone would need one hundred thousand family-dwelling units in the first five postwar years.[22] Most of these homes would need to be modestly priced, between six thousand and ten thousand dollars, to be affordable to young families. To fill this need, a new breed of home builder emerged with experience rooted in the construction of dams, ships, and communities for farm and war workers. By catering to their need for capital, Howard Ahmanson would build an empire.

A REVOLUTION IN HOME BUILDING

American mass production, in tandem with a remarkably prolific system for industrial research and innovation, played a critical role in winning World War II.[23] With the end of the war, industrial leaders and journalists predicted that it would enhance the quality of life of all Americans, especially as increasingly flexible production systems allowed manufacturers to achieve economies of scale while producing goods for a variety of niche markets and tastes.[24] In housing especially, expectations were high. Insiders writing in the trade journals and even the popular press predicted that new materials and new methods of construction would speed the process of home building and lower the cost of home ownership.

Mass production depended on standardized building materials and components, which had been under development for decades. As late as the mid-nineteenth century, most homes were built as one-of-a-kind products. Highly skilled craftsmen cut or shaped materials at the site, and each was supervised by a builder or contractor who was often a former craftsman.[25]

This system of home construction began to change at the end of the nineteenth century. Factory-made components and materials accelerated the process of construction and reduced the need for highly trained craftsmen. A premilled door simply needed to be hung. Precut and sanded floor boards were simply attached to the joists at the job site.[26] Soon whole facades for homes were manufactured in cities like Chicago and shipped to communities throughout the country. Catalog companies like Sears and Montgomery Ward loaded precut components of homes onto railroad flatbeds for delivery to customers hundreds of miles away.[27] Nevertheless, through the 1930s, the vast majority of American homes were built by their owners or by small-scale contractors who erected an average of only five to twenty homes a year.[28]

The Depression brought new players and techniques to home construction. A handful of pioneers experimented with the idea of prefabricated homes. Foster Gunnison, who launched Gunnison Magic Homes, adapted the newly developed waterproof, plywood, stressed-skin panel created by the U.S. Forest Products Laboratory to make standardized wall panels. Gunnison offered prefabricated model homes for different income groups and hoped to become the "Henry Ford of housing." Unfortunately, according to historian David Hounshell, "all of his houses looked very much alike, and they did not satisfy the idiosyncratic, highly personalized tastes of the American home buyer."[29]

In the West, innovators focused more on streamlining construction. On the Colorado River, the Six Companies, which included Henry J. Kaiser as a partner, pioneered in situ mass-production techniques when they built the Hoover Dam and housing for workers in Boulder City in the early 1930s. They later adapted these techniques to revolutionize the process of wartime shipbuilding and housing construction.[30] Meanwhile, planners and builders working for the Farm Security Administration in California developed new strategies for low-cost housing construction to meet the needs of migrant workers.[31]

With defense mobilization, the federal government began to finance the construction of new facilities to make tanks, airplanes, and ships. To shelter this workforce, Congress authorized the construction of seven hundred thousand public housing units in key defense industry communities, including Southern California.[32] Given the urgency of the situation, Congress and federal policy makers expected that these units would be built by large-scale contractors, like Kaiser, who had political connections and extensive experience with federal projects.[33]

Traditional home builders feared that they would go out of business if these large contractors won all the government work. Traveling around the country to talk to contractors, Howard Ahmanson's friend Fritz Burns helped to organize the Home Builders Emergency Committee. Their lobbying effort paid off when Congress passed Title VI of the Housing Act in March 1941. The new law offered builders direct, guaranteed loans of up to 90 percent for the construction of homes in 146 industrial areas that were deemed to be critical to the nation's defense. The success of this effort led to the creation of the National Association of Home Builders in 1942 and Burns's election as the association's president.[34] It also helped put Los Angeles at the forefront of mass production in home construction as Burns and other builders erected some of the first low-cost, mass-produced tract homes in communities like Westside Village in Mar Vista, Toluca Wood in North Hollywood, and suburban Westchester near aircraft manufacturing facilities owned by Douglas Aircraft, Lockheed, and North American Aviation.[35]

With the end of the war, many people anticipated that "better and less expensive homes would be coming off assembly lines by the thousands."[36] Only days after the Nazi surrender in Germany in May 1945, Kaiser announced plans to build ten thousand low-cost homes on the West Coast as soon as war restrictions on building materials were lifted. Fritz Burns would serve as president of the newly organized Kaiser Community Homes.[37]

Kaiser and Burns represented a new kind of home builder.[38] In Los Angeles, New York, and other major urban areas, these "minor Henry Fords," described as "operative" or "merchant" builders, developed assembly lines on the job site and used mass-production strategies to cut costs even below the prefabricators.[39] Employing vertical integration strategies to manufacture many of their building materials and preassemble components, they constructed hundreds of homes at a time. At the Kaiser plant in Los Angeles, floor and wall sections were made in the factory, along with ceilings and cabinets. Workers prepainted in spray booths before these components were trucked to the job site.[40]

The operative builders also adapted the multidivisional structure of the corporate world to keep subcontractors engaged full time. These subcontractors learned the builders' systems and provided continuity from tract to tract. These subcontractors didn't have to bid on jobs. Instead, they were offered negotiated fees. In essence, they operated as divisional managers, but they had a financial stake in the success of the project.[41]

With new materials, assembly-line production, and new labor arrangements, tract home builders cut construction costs dramatically. On Long Island in 1947, William Levitt built homes for around seven dollars per square foot at a time when most metropolitan builders incurred costs between ten and fifteen dollars per square foot for non-custom-built homes.[42] By 1955, three out of four houses under construction in metropolitan America were being built in housing tracts. In Southern California, the sound of carpenters hammering housing frames together rang out in new bedroom communities in the San Gabriel and San Fernando valleys and along the path from downtown Los Angeles to the coast.

As developers and builders rushed to meet the demand for these affordable single-family homes, the scale of these new projects increased dramatically. Kaiser pledged to build a hundred thousand homes—fifty times the number that Fritz Burns had constructed during World War II, when he was one of the nation's most productive home builders.[43] In just two years, between September 1, 1946, and September 1, 1948, Kaiser Community Homes made an aggressive start on this goal by erecting 5,319 homes in the Los Angeles metropolitan area, including 1,295 in Westchester, 562 in Monterey Park, 471 in Ontario, 430 in Compton, and 300 in Westside Terrace.[44] In 1947, Kaiser Community Homes developed plans to build a new "City within a City" on the Panorama Ranch in the San Fernando Valley, complete with homes, factories, and shopping centers for "living, work and play."[45]

At Lakewood, developer Louis H. Boyar bought 3,375 acres of farmland near Long Beach. With builders Mark Taper and Ben Weingart, he began planning a community of seventy thousand people housed in 17,500 homes.[46] Located only a short commute from jobs at Douglas Aircraft and at the port, the project attracted twenty-five thousand people on the day the sales office opened to the public.[47] At the height of construction, Taper and Weingart and their crews built fifty houses a day.[48]

Construction at Panorama City and Lakewood reflected only the most dramatic aspects of an unprecedented building boom in Los Angeles. Throughout the region, other builders and developers launched projects ranging from a few dozen to several hundred new homes. During the five years that followed the Japanese surrender, 327,598 new single-family homes were built in Los Angeles County alone, increasing the overall stock of homes by 45 percent. Few other metropolitan regions in the country rivaled this production.[49]

None of these new homes would have been possible without construction loans and mortgage capital. But many lenders were intimidated by the risks associated with large projects. Prior to 1938, for example, when Fritz Burns experimented with mass production at Westside Village, no subdivision developer or builder in Southern California had ever received a construction loan for more than 40 units, much less the 788 that Burns proposed to build.[50] With the end of the war, builders rushed to follow in Burns's footsteps, but finding lenders to back them remained a challenge. In this situation, Howard Ahmanson recognized a major opportunity.

Charlie Fletcher wanted to talk politics. He was running for Congress in September 1946, and Howard ostensibly was his campaign manager. With two months left before the election, they had lunch together at the Stock Exchange Club in the heart of L.A.'s financial district. With their voices muffled by the dark paneled walls of the English club room, Howard smoked and listened as Fletcher talked.

Charlie believed he was gaining on the incumbent, Democrat Ed Izak. As an officer in the San Diego Amvets organization, he hoped to win the GI vote. Given his father's twelve-year stint in the California legislature, he was sure to have good name recognition. And it helped that across the country pollsters were predicting a Republican resurgence. Howard offered his support and advice.

As they were walking back to Howard's office, Charlie casually mentioned that he knew a savings and loan manager who wanted to get out of the business. The association was for sale. He suggested Howard should buy it.

"How much is it?" Howard asked.

"Sixty thousand."

"Where is it?"

"Highland Park," Charlie replied.

Howard considered the area and the opportunity. Located along the Arroyo Seco just west of Pasadena, Highland Park included some of the oldest homes in Los Angeles. The thrift had been established on November 24, 1924, as the Los Angeles American Building and Loan Association by Walter Giddens Tomlinson, who had served as secretary and manager and now wanted to retire.[51] For some unknown reason, the company was in the process of changing its name to North American Savings and Loan Association.[52] Howard decided to take a chance.

"Come on up to my office," he told Charlie.

Upstairs, Howard wrote out a check to Tomlinson and asked Charlie to make the deal for him. Characteristically, he was not interested in negotiating. If the price was fair, he paid it. If it wasn't, he walked away.[53]

In telling this story years later, Ahmanson made it sound impulsive, as if nothing that came before had prepared him for that moment. In fact, he was anything but impulsive. As one of his longtime employees recalled, "Howard explored every facet of everything before he made a decision."[54] In fact, Ahmanson had spent years studying the savings and loan industry. He owned more than 28 percent of one thrift and served on the board of directors of Hollywood Savings and Loan. He had also spent months thinking about the postwar future of Los Angeles.[55]

Ahmanson knew the demand for housing in Los Angeles was explosive. He was already positioned to take advantage of this growth by selling residential fire and hazard insurance, but he wanted to increase his bet.[56] He bought stock in cement companies because new homes needed foundations. He continued to buy real estate because developers and builders had to have land. But he also recognized that tract builders would need financing and that savings and loans were uniquely positioned in the postwar era to provide construction loans and mortgages.

Ahmanson knew that most savings and loan managers didn't see the opportunity. For too long they had been focused on surviving. Hit hard by the Depression, nearly one in four in California had gone out of business. Those that remained carried large portfolios of delinquent loans and foreclosed properties through the 1930s. By the end of the war, only 101 state-chartered savings and loans and 73 federally chartered thrifts were still in business in California.[57] The total assets held by the industry amounted to $642 million, compared to $511 million in 1930. With this weak growth over fifteen years, the industry had failed to keep pace with the state's increase in population or the expansion of real estate lending.[58]

Within the industry, the federally chartered institutions, like Howard Edgerton's California Federal and Charlie Fletcher's Home Federal in San Diego, were the strongest. Statewide, they accounted for 59 percent of total assets.[59] In Los Angeles, the federals, which were all mutuals, commanded much greater resources than the nearly moribund state-chartered institutions. The leader, Coast Federal Savings and Loan, managed by Howard's USC classmate Joe Crail, had nearly $42 million in assets in August 1945.[60] The next largest, Western Federal, had just over half that amount.[61] Meanwhile, most of the state-chartered, stockholder-owned thrifts had barely $1 million left on their books. With so little money, these thrifts weren't in a position to finance major housing projects. Savings and loans also lacked the skills needed for these kinds of deals. According to builder Mark Taper, "They didn't know what good plans or good locations were."[62] Taper had to get his first tract loan from Bank of America, which dominated the mortgage market and the banking sector, with more than $1 billion in outstanding loans in 1945.[63]

Savings and loans in California also seemed disadvantaged by public policy that favored commercial banks. Mutual savings banks, the leading source of home loans on the East Coast, had not been enabled by the California legislature, so commercial banks played a greater role in the mortgage market in California than they did on the East Coast.[64] California was also unusually permissive with regard to branch banking, which weakened the competitive position of strictly local institutions.[65] As a result, Bank of America, the nation's largest commercial bank, had been able to achieve enormous economies of scope and scale.[66]

Despite all of these drawbacks, Ahmanson saw potential. States and the federal government regulated savings and loans as mutual or cooperative organizations. Given thrifts' quasi-nonprofit status, lawmakers were inclined to give them competitive advantages. For example, in 1947, savings and loans were completely exempt from federal income taxes if they made substantially all of their loans to their own depositors.[67] Given the high federal tax rates still in place in the immediate postwar era, this was a substantial advantage.

Since regulators wanted to ensure that banks would remain liquid enough to meet demands for deposits—especially if there was a run—banks weren't allowed to loan more than a certain percentage of their capital long term for real estate. Commercial banks had to maintain sufficient cash reserves to meet the daily demands of their depositors. Cash tied up in vaults couldn't be invested. Savings and loans could invest more of their cash. State and federal laws made it difficult for depositors to withdraw money from savings and loan accounts. They did this to minimize the risk of a run on the association's deposits.[68]

Savings and loans also enjoyed other significant competitive opportunities. They could attract savings by advertising the dividend rates (interest) paid on deposits; banks were not allowed to do this.[69] This privilege was especially important because, under Regulation Q, the Federal Reserve controlled interest rates paid by banks on savings deposits. Savings and loans had greater freedom to set their own rates.

All of these advantages would have meant little to Ahmanson if all savings and loans in California operated as mutual or cooperative organizations, as they did in most states.[70] But in California, entrepreneurs had a unique opportunity to own a savings and loan and profit from its success. In 1909, the California legislature had passed an unusual law that essentially transformed state-chartered thrifts into stockholder, rather than mutual, corporations.[71]

Some California entrepreneurs had taken advantage of this structure, but the Depression and World War II stifled the industry's growth. Very few entrepreneurs paid attention to the ways in which New Deal legislation, especially government-sponsored mortgage insurance programs, had diminished the risks and enhanced the potential profits of the business.[72]

Passage of the GI Bill, with mortgage guarantees for veterans, made the business of mortgage lending even more attractive. Officially titled the Servicemen's Readjustment Act, and signed by President Roosevelt on June 22, 1944, the GI Bill offered financial assistance for education, employment, housing, health care, and insurance to veterans returning from the war. The law authorized the Veterans Administration (VA) to guarantee loans for the purchase, construction, alteration, or improvement of homes, farms, or businesses.[73] Borrowers could finance the entire purchase price and move in with no down payment.[74]

All of these government incentives to lenders and particularly to savings and loans, coupled with the latent demand for home ownership in Los Angeles, suggested enormous opportunity to an entrepreneur in California, particularly to a government entrepreneur who saw the potential for profit in aligning his business to achieve public policy objectives. In Washington, Ahmanson had seen men like Donald Douglas and Henry J. Kaiser get rich by focusing on the government's priorities. With the war over, the government no longer needed as many bombers and battleships. Now it wanted homes and mortgages.[75] Ahmanson would build a business to meet this demand.

BUYING AND BUILDING HOME

Characteristically, since he was always a delegator, Ahmanson made Gould Eddy president of North American Savings and Loan and named himself chairman. With permission from the Los Angeles office of the California building and loan commissioner, he moved the main office to 9631 Wilshire Boulevard in Beverly Hills.[76] To get access to additional capital, North American joined the Federal Home Loan Bank in 1947. It also purchased insurance from the Federal Savings and Loan Insurance Corporation (FSLIC) program to reassure depositors. Then Ahmanson and Eddy began an aggressive campaign to attract deposits.[77]

Though he had criticized the field of advertising in his speech to the Economic Round Table in the 1930s, Ahmanson shared many of the instincts of the professional ad men. By today's standards, his appeals were very tame, focusing on safety and security, but he was willing to invest in marketing. By the end of 1947, with new customers and deposits and infusions of capital from friends and associates, he had more than tripled North American's assets to just over $6 million.[78] He was still far behind Edgerton's California Federal, which was twice as large, and Joe Crail's Coast Federal, which dwarfed all the others with nearly $43.5 million.[79] But Howard began to think about catching his friends.

Ahmanson heard about another savings and loan for sale—Home Building and Loan.[80] It was hardly a thriving entity in 1947. With its office on West Ninth Street in downtown Los Angeles, the company had seen its assets fall from $610,000 in 1930 to $249,000 by 1940.[81] Although it recovered slightly after the war, it still had less than $1 million and had only four employees.[82]

But Home's intangible assets were very attractive to Ahmanson. The thrift had a name that customers could associate with all of the intangibles they imagined would come with the purchase of a house. Home also had a very valuable charter. California law allowed most thrifts to make loans only in a relatively small area near their offices. Savings and loans, like Home, that had been founded before the law took effect and made loans over a broader geography could continue to do business in a larger territory. This meant Home had growth potential that younger savings and loans did not have.[83] Howard also liked the marketing value of Home's track record. The thrift had an unbroken history of paying dividends to depositors. This was a story Howard could sell to working- and middle-class savers who had lived through the Great Depression and seen banks and thrifts fail, with depositors losing their life savings.

Ahmanson bought Home Building and Loan's name and assets for $162,000. Over the next nine months, he restructured the board of directors and brought in new management from among his friends in the insurance industry, including Jack Kuhrts, an insurance broker who was already a business partner on a massive six-hundred-acre, $25 million mixed-use apartment and retail shopping complex near Crenshaw and La Brea. Relative to a project of this size, Home Savings hardly seemed like a racehorse.[84] In fact, Ahmanson told his young assistant Robert DeKruif that he would be happy if the company eventually reached ten million dollars in assets.[85]

To grow both of his new associations, Ahmanson needed deposits. He decided to go after the savings bonds that Angelenos, like many other Americans, had accumulated during the war. Some of these bonds had reached maturity, but they were not especially liquid. Many people were eager to cash them and deposit the proceeds in a bank or savings and loan. Ahmanson liked to tell the story of how he borrowed a tactic from a friend. He mailed pennies to thousands of potential customers, using the coin to highlight the difference between the rates that banks paid on savings and the rate that Home would pay. Ahmanson also gambled and offered an interest rate that was 25 percent higher than what most thrifts were offering.[86] The marketing effort worked beautifully and helped lure more than three million dollars in new deposits.[87]

Ahmanson's aggressive pursuit of deposits posed two major risks. The first was intrinsic to the operations of all savings and loans. The second was unique to H. F. Ahmanson & Co., the legal owner of Home Savings' stock. To be able to afford to pay depositors a higher rate of interest, any association had to have lower costs or a higher rate of return on its loan portfolio. To achieve this goal, Ahmanson focused on increasing the volume of lending and selling these loans to the Federal National Mortgage Association ("Fannie Mae") for a quick profit.[88] In 1947 and 1948, Home lent money for small developments in Compton and Buena Park, but Ahmanson also favored Westside areas, including Westwood and Brentwood, where relatively high prices could be expected to hold their value in times of depression or recession. Lending aggressively in a strong market and taking advantage of these government programs, Ahmanson quickly increased the assets and earnings of the association. Within a year of his acquisition of Home, Ahmanson had increased lending tenfold from dozens of loans a month to hundreds.[89]

The other major business risk was unique to Ahmanson's situation. By raising the interest rate paid on deposits above what other savings and loans were paying, Howard put market pressure on many of his best insurance customers—other savings and loans. They were not happy. Some stopped doing business with H. F. Ahmanson & Co. altogether. Howard had anticipated this. He encouraged his salesmen to maintain their sales efforts, even if the door was slammed in their face. By ensuring that thrift managers earned good commissions, he believed he could continue to grow his insurance business. For some thrift managers who were both customers and rivals, this was enough. Joe Crail, for example, owned two insurance companies on the side, but in 1958 he still gave H. F. Ahmanson & Co. plenty of business. Ahmanson "gave good service," Crail said. "He still does, or I'd drop him in a minute. It's not only that he sends out his policies the very next day after he gets them, instead of in the usual week or so. He'll send an appraiser around to the property for a quote the same day, even if he's called at 5:00 p.m."[90]

TRACT LENDING

While he coached his salesmen to be persistent, Ahmanson the entrepreneur focused on a once-in-a-lifetime opportunity in mortgage lending. Two years into the postwar era, it was already clear that there was money to be made by financing tract housing construction. Construction loans were highly profitable, and they offered the lender an inside track on permanent loans for home buyers. Ahmanson would later say this strategy gave Home Savings and Loan the ability to "manufacture mortgages" with potential economies of scale from high-volume production.

The GI Bill and VA loans were critical to Ahmanson's strategy. Although some savings and loan managers grumbled about the interest rate cap on VA loans or chafed at the idea of government intervention in the housing market, Ahmanson saw only opportunity. With a conventional-market loan, a thrift could lend up to 80 percent of the appraised value of the home. The loan would then go on the balance sheet, but the lender could book profits only as the borrower made payments. With a VA loan, by contrast, the lender was allowed to underwrite 100 percent of the value of the house, thus putting more money to work at interest, and the VA made the first payment on behalf of the borrower. Lenders could book this first payment immediately as profit. A smart lender, like Ahmanson, could use these immediate profits to build capital reserves. With more reserves, under the regulatory system, a thrift could lend more—and earn even greater profits.

Although mortgage lending to GIs offered quick profits, construction financing promised even bigger returns. Under the rules in place in 1948, Home or North American could charge a major tract builder as much as ten points (10 percent) on a construction loan. When the loan was recorded, the savings and loan could book the ten points as an immediate profit. Meanwhile, the actual cash for the loan would sit at Home Savings for months as the builder received only progress payments as construction was completed. It was as if a person had a ten-thousand-dollar line of credit at the bank and the bank subtracted the full interest cost on the full value of the line before the borrower had taken the money out of the bank.[91]

Tract builders were willing to pay these points because most did not have the capital they needed for such large projects. Banks were too busy with more secure investment opportunities. Equity financing would require giving potential profits to other investors. In addition, the potential profits were so good that most builders calculated that they could easily absorb the lenders' high fees.

The rewards for tract lending were good because the risk was high. Builders were notoriously undercapitalized, and many of them were not ready for the scale of operations contemplated in the postwar years. To protect himself, Ahmanson decided that he would limit the size and type of tract loan he would make. As an extra protection, he hired an appraiser to evaluate the properties to make sure the builders were actually constructing homes that would sell.[92]

Despite his precautions, one of Ahmanson's first forays nearly ended in disaster when a friend Ahmanson recruited from the insurance industry overcommitted the firm by nearly a million dollars on a single project and failed to tell Ahmanson.[93] The Riviera Housing Corporation planned to build relatively expensive homes on a tract in Palos Verdes. When Howard found out about the project in the summer of 1948, the homes were already under construction and supposed to be 75 percent complete. When he visited the site, however, Howard discovered the project was way behind schedule. Furious, he fired the executive in charge and the company's appraiser. The builder then abandoned the project, leaving Ahmanson to pick up the pieces.[94]

Ahmanson faced the prospect of a half-million-dollar loss, an amount equal to twice the association's capital reserves. With this kind of loss, the regulators could have forced Home to stop taking deposits or making loans. Even worse, the state could have seized control or forced the company into bankruptcy. To keep the regulators at bay, Howard assured Milton Shaw, the deputy commissioner of the California Department of Savings and Loans, that he would personally compensate Home for any losses.[95] When Shaw agreed to give Ahmanson a chance to salvage the situation, Howard called Thurston Ross, his former economics professor from USC. Ross recommended that Howard hire someone who understood the worlds of real estate and construction.[96]

Like Ahmanson, Ken Childs was a product of the Midwest. Born in Herington, Kansas, in 1901, he was a big man with a dry sense of humor, a sharp mind, and "an instinct for the jugular."[97] With square shoulders, a crew cut, and a broad, open face, he prided himself on his efficiency. He had been working in construction and real estate in the Beverly Hills area since 1925. During the war, he served four years in the army air forces. Afterward, he went to work for the Harry Kem Company, self-proclaimed realtors to the stars.[98] "He knew every trick that a builder would try to take advantage of a lender," remembers one longtime Home employee.[99] And that was what Howard Ahmanson needed.

Childs presented his analysis of the situation to Ahmanson and Home's board of directors on September 21, 1948, and the board agreed to let Childs's Commerce Building Company take over the project. They also extended additional loans to complete construction and capped new lending on other projects until the situation could be resolved.[100] Over the next year, Childs oversaw the completion of the Palos Verdes project and the sale of the homes. He was so successful that Home's total liability on the project shrank to about $100,000 ($937,000 in 2011 dollars). Howard paid this amount into the company's reserves from his personal funds, honoring his pledge to the California regulators.[101]

The Riviera project was a disaster, but it wasn't the only tract development to go into default in 1948. The board had to deal with a handful of smaller projects that ran into similar troubles. In response, Ahmanson restructured Home's management and board of directors. In November, he terminated the association's president and personally took charge. Impressed with the way Childs had handled the Riviera project, he put Childs on the board and tapped him to serve as executive vice president. At the same time, he retained his onetime business school professor Thurston Ross as a loan consultant and created a loan committee composed of Ross, Childs, and Ahmanson to tightly control future lending.[102] Ross joined Home Savings's board of directors six months later, consolidating Ahmanson's tight circle of trusted advisors.[103]

To ensure that no builder ever took advantage of Home Savings again, Ahmanson and Childs also introduced a number of innovative management systems and business strategies. Childs organized a department that built one hundred to two hundred homes a year. This department gave Home a better understanding of the costs of construction, which allowed the company more closely to monitor tract builders receiving loans.[104] The group also gave Home the ability to complete a project if a builder ran into trouble or if costs started to exceed the builder's estimates.[105]

To keep a tighter control on cash, Childs established a loan disbursement department. Builders had to show receipts for supplies. An inspector ensured that the supplies had actually been used on the project and that subcontractors had finished their work before the builder was reimbursed. For this service, Home charged 1.5 points on the construction loan.[106]

Ahmanson also worked with his attorney Thomas Webster to develop a new form of construction mortgage. This agreement gave Home a comprehensive claim on *all* the houses in a development, rather than individual liens on specific properties.[107] This way, if a project ran into major trouble, Home could quickly take over the entire project.

All of these innovations reduced Home's risk and increased Ahmanson's willingness, even eagerness, to lend to tract developers. By 1950, North American and Home Savings and Loan were reportedly financing more than five hundred housing tracts in Southern California.[108] Over the next several years, Home continued to lend aggressively. In 1952, Joe Crail acknowledged, "My bet was that the housing boom was over, and I didn't want the risk." Ahmanson thought differently. He continued to lend and as a result became the major financier for tract builders.[109]

Commercial banks also seemed to leave the whole field of tract lending wide open to innovators like Ahmanson. They could have doubled their total real estate loans in the first five years after the war and still remained under the federal limit for non-government-insured loans, but they had better options.[110] With California cities, school districts, and the state undertaking massive construction projects to keep pace with the growing demand for public infrastructure, and the state's private companies and corporations spending to increase their productive capacity, banks had plenty of investment alternatives that didn't require tying up their money for decades.

Ahmanson also seemed to understand that the postwar years offered a limited opportunity to make extraordinary profits while the demand for housing was high and the supply extremely limited. At some point, he knew, the pent-up demand for housing would be satiated. Continuing immigration to the Golden State would drive growth, but the greatest profits would go to those who moved quickly.

SIX

Scaling Up

THE OLD GUARD was leaving the savings and loan industry in the early 1950s. Managers and owners who had weathered the Depression and the war were ready for retirement. Few had gotten rich. If they had equity in a thrift, they couldn't get it out. Liquidating would hurt depositors, many of whom had personal relationships with the savings and loan managers. Meanwhile, as Robert DeKruif recalls, "No one wanted to buy a savings and loan."[1] Except Howard Ahmanson.

Ahmanson, like A. P. Giannini, the founder of Bank of America, realized that additional branches would leverage his investment in advertising, create efficiencies in lending, and, most of all, provide a bigger pool for aggregating savings, which could be invested in more tract homes. To open branches he had two options: petition the state for permission or acquire an existing savings and loan and merge it with the two thrifts he already owned. If he took the latter route, he needed to find a way to help the current owners exit gracefully.

"All these guys were like my father," says Richard Deihl, whose father ran the Pico Rivera Savings and Loan. "They were good, honest, hardworking people who were happy with their involvement in their neighborhood and community." Many of them also depended on the income they made from selling insurance on the side through H. F. Ahmanson & Co. They liked Howard and believed he understood their business.[2]

Howard and his lawyer Thomas Webster developed a creative way to buy out this older generation. The arrangement cost Home Savings and Loan almost nothing, but it put cash in the owner's pocket and provided Home with a way to grow. Essentially, the liquidating company would transfer its loans and its deposits, which usually were nearly equal on the balance sheet, to Home Savings and Loan. The liquidating company would then be left with its reserves, which included paid-in capital plus accumulated earnings. This amount was then distributed back to the association's shareholders as part of the liquidation.[3] These deals gave longtime owners of small stock savings and loans a tax-friendly way to cash out and retire. They also ensured that customers and employees of the liquidating thrift would be taken care of. Meanwhile, Home Savings increased its assets and acquired a new branch without paying a premium. By law, Home Savings had to raise its reserves in conjunction with the increase in deposits, but this was rarely a problem. Because Howard never withdrew profits from the business and earnings kept accumulating, Home Savings and Loan's reserves were already high.

With this strategy, Ahmanson was uniquely positioned to choose which thrifts to buy. He had spent nearly twenty years on the sidelines of the mortgage industry in Los Angeles. He knew which savings and loans had the best customers and locations. He knew which companies had piled up cash during the war. He also knew which local organizations had good managers, who would help Home continue to grow.

Ahmanson began a buying spree in January 1951, when he announced that Home would acquire the Long Beach Building and Loan Association, which had a main office in Long Beach and a branch in Huntington Park. The deal increased the number of Home offices from three to five and expanded the association's total assets to just under $30 million.[4] At this level, Home still lagged far behind Joe Crail's Coast Federal ($111.8 million) and Howard Edgerton's California Federal ($50.6 million), but it was suddenly the largest of the state-chartered institutions in Los Angeles, and, with five offices, it served more territory than any other thrift in the region.[5]

Ahmanson realized that it made no sense to maintain North American's operations as a separate savings and loan, so he transferred North American's accounts and assets to Home in 1951. He kept North American as a corporate entity to be the conduit for his own real estate investments and to handle proprietary tract development, but he terminated its charter with the state as a savings and loan. With the consolidation, Home's total assets rose to nearly $53 million.[6] Most important for the ever-competitive Ahmanson, Home edged out Howard Edgerton's California Federal Savings and Loan as number nineteen among the nation's largest savings and loans, up from forty-fifth a year earlier.[7] Suddenly, in the Los Angeles area only Joe Crail's Coast Federal was larger.

Home continued to grow in 1952, when Howard acquired Occidental Savings and Loan Association. The deal added another $20 million in assets, making Home the largest "capital-stock" savings and loan in the world.[8] It also had the most branches in the country—six—a testament to how local the thrift industry was in 1952.[9] Then, in the first week of January 1953, Ahmanson finalized an agreement to acquire the assets and accounts of Arcadia Savings and Loan, worth approximately $8 million, raising Home's total assets to more than $100 million.[10] Only six years after Howard had acquired the business, Home ranked among the top five savings and loans in the country.[11]

With continued growth and new acquisitions, Home doubled its size again over the next year. In February, the company acquired the Burbank Savings and Loan Association in the fast-growing San Fernando Valley. The oldest thrift in the valley, Burbank had tripled its assets to $10 million in the early 1950s.[12] The same month, Home announced that it would buy United Savings and Loan of Glendale, a $40 million company with twenty thousand depositors and borrowers. When this deal was completed on March 1, 1954, with $190 million in assets, nearly seventy thousand depositors, and twenty thousand borrowers, Home moved past the Perpetual Building Association of Washington, D.C., to become the largest savings and loan in the United States.[13]

With these acquisitions, Ahmanson challenged the dominant paradigm for savings and loans, most of which did not have branch operations. Older managers bristled at Ahmanson's aggressive tactics, but if state officials were concerned by Home's growth, they failed to show it. On several occasions, Lieutenant Governor Goodwin Knight and California building and loan commissioner Milton O. Shaw were on hand to join in Home's celebrations.

BUILDING AN ORGANIZATION

Building an empire by acquisition was one thing. Integrating all of these businesses and making the combined organization a success was something else. Like many entrepreneurs, Ahmanson hired people he trusted as well as talent he encountered. His approach to both reflected his personality as well as his business acumen.

When he met new people, Ahmanson explored their interests and passions, often searching for ideas he could use and an understanding of how their minds worked. He had what David Hannah called "an uncanny ability to seize on a good idea, maybe an idea you had but never implemented. Howard would take that good idea and put it to practice."[14]

Ahmanson proudly told reporters that the executives he hired were all younger than he was. Except for Ken Childs, he did not want to pay for experience or expertise. He was always on the lookout for good employees. When he bought a savings and loan, he often promoted its younger managers who were ready for more responsibility. He would also visit the commercial banks in the area. "He stood in the lobby and watched to see which tellers had the longest line," remembers Bob DeKruif. Those were the tellers that the customers liked. "So he would go and hire them because he was so sold on service."[15]

Generally, Ahmanson proved to be a good judge of talent and disposition. "Howard's genius was in picking people and putting them in the right slots," remembers John Notter, who managed several offices in the early 1960s.[16] "He said the most damaging thing you can do to a person is get them out of their niche in a business," remembers DeKruif. "If you get them out of their niche, the first thing they do is damage themselves. The second thing they do is damage the company."[17]

Ahmanson's judgment of character was important because he was not a micromanager.[18] Once he hired someone and gave him directions, he let the employee work. "If you screwed up," Notter says, "you heard about it." Ahmanson would want to know why and what you were going to do about a problem. Although he could be tough, manipulative, and even mean at times, he also displayed a gift for empathy.[19]

Ahmanson offered good salaries to his key executives but rarely a stake in the business. Instead, he let them participate in his side deals, a real estate development, for example.[20] In this way, he cultivated their entrepreneurial and risk-taking sensibilities.

In addition to the talent he recruited, Ahmanson continued to trust the advice of mentors from the 1920s, especially Thurston Ross. During the war, Ross had joined the navy as a captain. He was deployed on special missions in Africa, Europe, and the Pacific. He represented the United States as a logistics expert at the Yalta and Malta conferences.[21] He was on the U.S.S. *Missouri* when General MacArthur received Japan's official surrender.[22] After the war, Ross did not return to USC but opened his own real estate consulting firm in Beverly Hills.[23] To those he encountered, he was a genius.

To Howard, Ross was a weatherman, someone who could anticipate the tornado on the horizon even on a clear blue day.

Howard also made a place for and relied on his family. In Omaha, nearly ten years had passed since Hayden had hit bottom with his drinking. Remarkably, he had turned his life around. He continued to oversee the operations of National American Fire Insurance, although Howard remained president.[24] In 1952, however, when Hayden became next in line to be president of the Omaha Chamber of Commerce, Howard decided that the time had come to acknowledge and reward his older brother for his "moral victory." He made Hayden president, reserving for himself the title of chairman. Hayden's wife, Aimee, wrote to her brother-in-law, "You just haven't any idea what it has done for his ego already. He has had so many flowers and letters of congratulations that he is fairly walking on the clouds these days."[25] In her letter, Aimee also expressed her gratitude for all that Howard and Dottie had done for her sons, William Hayden Ahmanson and Robert Howard Ahmanson.

Married for more than sixteen years with no children of their own, Howard and Dottie had lavished attention on Howard's two nephews. Bill, the older and more difficult of the two, had been born just four months after his grandfather's death in 1925.[26] Bob was born on Valentine's Day in 1927. As they came of age during the war years, Howard tried to pull strings to get Bill into an officer training program in the navy. The war ended before he was deployed. Bob, the easygoing nephew, graduated from high school near the end of the war and moved to California to go to college near Howard and Dottie and be mentored by his uncle. Bill joined his younger brother at UCLA when the war was over.

"The kids," as Howard and Dottie referred to their nephews, introduced a new element to the Ahmanson household that recalled the college days that Howard and Dottie had enjoyed so much. Howard was patient, even after Bill was reprimanded by the university for his "hoodlumism" in engaging in a panty raid on a sorority house.[27] To help amuse the young men, Howard and Dottie bought a twenty-six-foot Luder sailboat. Before long the foursome was racing. In 1947, they entered twenty-eight regattas, winning twenty-three and placing second in the other five. After graduating from college, both nephews went to work for their uncle: Bill in the insurance business, Bob on construction projects within Home's growing collection of branches.

Howard's relationship with his nephews was close, but they were not the executives at the center of the business. The organization of the late 1940s traced its roots to Howard's two years at USC. The first of his key lieutenants was his longtime friend Gould Eddy, who had done an outstanding job in the insurance business.[28] Nearly twenty-five years after the founding of H. F. Ahmanson & Co., Eddy and his wife, Lucia, were still good friends with Howard and Dottie, and Eddy continued to play a key role in the insurance business. Thomas Webster, Howard's personal attorney, was a direct, low-key, and extremely creative lawyer who was not afraid to challenge Howard.

Evelyn Barty was equally bold. She joined H. F. Ahmanson & Co. in 1942 and soon became the masterful, if often irascible, secretary who managed the details of Howard's life. Born with the last name of Bertanzetti, she had come to Hollywood from Pennsylvania with her family in 1928. Musically inclined, she and her sister Dolores ("Dede") toured in a vaudeville act in 1934 with Billy, a "little person" who reached three feet nine inches as an adult. Billy had already become a Hollywood star at the age of ten, and his parents had shortened his last name to "Barty." The act was known as "Billy Barty and Sisters."[29] As an adult, he appeared on television and in nightclubs. Evelyn gave up her performing career in 1942 to go to work for Ahmanson, but she sometimes joined Howard at the piano for employee events.

As his businesses grew, Ahmanson recruited a whole generation of leadership right out of college. Robert DeKruif had been born in Iowa and brought to California as an infant "in a clothes basket." He grew up in the mid-Wilshire District, attended Los Angeles High School, went to college at USC, and graduated with a degree in business administration in 1941. His older sister and her husband were friends with Howard and Dottie. One night, shortly before graduation, he had dinner with the four of them. Characteristically, Howard quizzed DeKruif on what he was studying. Then he offered DeKruif a job. Ineligible for the military because of ear problems, DeKruif stayed with the insurance business through the war. Rising early in the morning, he worked in the shipyards until midafternoon and then made insurance calls.[30] Eventually, DeKruif would become president of H. F. Ahmanson & Co. and play a key role as Howard's political liaison.

The most important contributor to Ahmanson's success, however, was Ken Childs. A teetotaler and practicing Christian Scientist, Childs ran the day-to-day operations of Home Savings and Loan.[31] Like Ahmanson, Childs was not typical of the managers described by William Whyte in *The Organization Man*. He ignored the world of organization charts and frequently disrupted the chain of command, but his commitment to Home gave Ahmanson the ability to focus on the strategic needs of the business and to manage his overall portfolio, including his insurance company, his oil investments, and real estate.[32]

Both men worked feverishly. Eighteen-hour days were the norm, as Ahmanson left the house in the early morning and rarely came home before ten at night. Ken Childs kept pace. North American and Home Savings underwrote hundreds of tract loans for builders like Milton Kaufmann and Sandee Seness. Ahmanson and Childs shifted cash and equity between various corporations and legal entities in a constant effort to keep income away from the tax man and available as capital for continued growth. In his letters to Howard, Childs referred to himself jokingly as "your man Friday." Childs's leadership proved critical when Ahmanson suddenly became very ill and his doctors advised him to get away for a while. While Howard and Dottie and his nephew Bob embarked on an extended vacation through North Africa and Greece and then went on to Norway in February, 1951, Childs kept the money rolling in.[33]

A FETISH FOR COST CONTROL

Ahmanson and Childs also exhibited a near fetish for cost control.[34] Ahmanson organized the sales staff so that he paid almost exclusively for production. He compensated his salesmen with commissions paid by the borrower. These "solicitors," as John Notter remembers, "were like a mortgage broker, except they were working for us. They would go to all the real estate offices and hustle business for us. We did the underwriting."[35] The commission system drove loan sales and kept costs in line with production. Under Ahmanson's system, an ambitious salesman could make good money. When Richard Deihl became a salesman, for example, he earned $30,000 a year in the early 1960s ($224,000 in 2011 dollars). "I worked Saturdays. I worked nights," remembers Deihl, "because I was on commission and this was the only way I got paid."[36]

Ahmanson also leveraged the time of these commissioned agents by having them do most of the work that an appraiser would do. A certified appraiser would then follow up, but since he was only checking the information provided by the loan agent, it took him far less time to complete his appraisal. Deihl laughs when he remembers wondering why Ahmanson organized the work this way. "Then it dawned on me," he says. "It wasn't because we were so bright. It was because we were doing it on our own time. We were on commission. The appraisers were getting paid by the hour."[37]

Although Ahmanson built an aggressive loan sales organization by using commissioned salespeople, he and Childs protected Home's balance sheet by relying on loan officers to approve all mortgages. In other associations, the function of the sales agent and the loan officer were often combined in one individual. This created a potential conflict of interest. The loan officer had a financial interest in making the loan no matter how risky the borrower. At Home Savings, "It was a separation of church and state," Deihl recalls.[38]

All of these cost containment strategies helped keep Home's overhead among the lowest of all its competitors—according to some analysts, 50 percent lower than the average stock savings and loan.[39] With this kind of advantage, Home could be far more aggressive in the marketplace.

MARKETING PEACE OF MIND

Howard once described Home's business as 90 percent lending and 10 percent promotion. "He was a salesman," Richard Deihl remembers. "Selling was in his blood. He was always selling somebody something—a job, a low salary, whatever."[40] The public face of Home's sales campaign, however, was almost entirely devoted to depositors. They were the customers who provided the working capital to invest. They were the ones who needed to trust the institution with their life savings.

Fortunately, deposit customers were plentiful. As the nation prospered in the early 1950s, Americans enjoyed the best of both worlds: consumer spending rose dramatically and so did savings and investments. Even as middle-class families bought refrigerators, furniture, and automobiles, they stashed money into savings accounts. By 1954, savings and loans spent $20 million a year on advertising, while commercial banks, with seven times the assets, spent just $45 million. To cultivate the children of the baby boom, savings and loans offered special accounts for children and delivered lessons in thrift to local schools. In 1954, three hundred savings and loan associations promoted television's first western series, *Hopalong Cassidy,* to attract youngsters to their doors. While the adults in the family appreciated the attention lavished on their children, they also liked the interest paid on their accounts. In 1954, the average savings and loan paid 2.8 percent on savings deposits, compared to 1.75 percent paid by banks.[41]

These advertising campaigns helped drive a major shift in the way middle-class Americans invested their savings. At the end of the war, 31.5 percent of all savings in the United States were invested in government bonds and only 5.4 percent were in savings and loans. A decade later, only 21.4 percent of savings were invested in government bonds, while savings and loans had increased their share of the national piggy bank to 13.8 percent.[42] Nationally, savings and loans steadily took market share from commercial banks. Between 1952 and 1961, savings and loans increased their share of savings deposits held by commercial banks and thrifts from 23.7 percent to 40.9 percent. In California, the shift was even more significant. Thrifts moved from 22.0 percent of savings deposits to 49.7 percent in the same period.[43] Meanwhile, in Southern California, the success of the savings and loans was nothing short of astonishing. By 1962, Los Angeles County thrifts held a 59.9 percent market share compared to banks; in Orange County it was 63.3 percent.[44]

Savings and loans captured this larger market share because they advertised more, created more customer-friendly environments, and offered better returns than commercial banks. Ahmanson and Home, in particular, stressed customer service. In everyday life, he noted, most people were friendly. In the office or retail environment, however, they seemed to lose their natural conviviality. He blamed the boss. "When you find rudeness in any business institution, look for the boss, and you will find an autocratic fat head carefully insulated from the outer world by a maze of push buttons and crisp, insolent secretaries." As early as 1956, he noted that the average savings and loan spent eighteen dollars on advertising to get a new customer to walk in the door or pick up the phone. That investment was squandered if the customer didn't receive good service when he or she walked in or called.[45]

Home Savings and Loan spent heavily to get that customer to walk through the door. With characteristic ironic self-deprecation, Ahmanson told one reporter that his company's advertisements were "dull as dishwater, but they work."[46] Home emphasized stability and security. Almost every ad in the *Los Angeles Times* noted the company's founding in 1889 and the fact that deposits were insured by the federal government. One display ad in January 1951 featured a photograph of Los Angeles' city hall in 1898 and reported that Home's account holders had already received eighteen earnings payments by that date.[47] Other ads proclaimed: "No One Ever Lost a Penny" and "There's No Place Like Home."[48] Around 1952, Howard began adding the slogan "Peace of Mind since '89" to Home's promotional materials and advertising.[49]

After Home acquired Occidental Savings and Loan later in 1952 and the company became the largest capital stock thrift in the nation, advertisements included a new tagline: "One of America's oldest, largest, strongest financial institutions." With more branches than any other savings and loan, the company also highlighted the convenience of access.[50]

Howard frequently told the press that he didn't buy other savings and loans simply to increase the company's asset base. "We've never made an acquisition just to get size," he said. "We only want branches in exactly the right location."[51] To him, location encompassed a number of factors. He wanted communities where people were likely to be savers. In Ahmanson's judgment, those were the middle-class families in the flatlands of the Los Angeles region. "You can't get savers from the mountainsides," he said. Those people had stockbrokers. Ahmanson also saw location in terms of its advertising value. He watched where the billboard companies put their signs. He thought the billboard company Foster and Kleiser was particularly savvy about traffic and eyeballs. He favored corner locations or spots with special advantages. In Pasadena, he bought a savings and loan, in part, because it offered a particularly good view of the Rose Parade. He then used the venue to throw a major party every New Year's Day for H. F. Ahmanson's insurance brokers and agents, politicians, and other business associates.[52] In Glendale, Ken Childs urged him to buy a site downtown, but Howard preferred a location alongside the proposed Ventura freeway. "The advertising is worth millions to Home Savings," he said.[53]

Ahmanson did not tout Home's dividend rate in the early years. Commercial banks weren't allowed to advertise their rates, so rather than focus on price competition, which might lower his margins, Ahmanson sold security, safety, and service.

Most important, Home Savings focused on projecting an image of strength. In some industries, being the biggest makes a company a target for competitors. Size can discourage customers who think they will receive poor service. "That doesn't apply to a saver," says Deihl. "A saver equates size with strength."[54] Shortly after Home Savings became the largest in the country, Home began stressing this size and strength message. Full-page newspaper advertisements featured dramatic images of Mt. Whitney, "the largest in America," linking Home to this tallest mountain in the lower forty-eight states. Other ads incorporated images of Hoover Dam, the Golden Gate Bridge, the Grand Canyon, Niagara Falls, the General Sherman giant sequoia, the U.S.S. *Midway* aircraft carrier, and the Los Angeles Coliseum—all the "largest in America."[55]

Being the "largest in America" also gave Home other advantages. In any financial category that would offer reassurance to the saver, Home was bound to be the largest. The most assets. Highest reserves. Richest aggregate payment of dividends.[56] For these reasons, Ahmanson aggressively protected the company's position as the front-runner. "We would have gone through fire to remain America's largest," says Richard Deihl.[57]

While many savings and loans focused on attracting the accounts of relatively high-income households, Ahmanson cultivated the man in the street. Most depositors, in Ahmanson's mind, hadn't learned the lesson offered by George Bailey in the movie classic *It's a Wonderful Life*. "I'm not sure that everybody knows that [savings deposits] go into somebody's house," Ahmanson told his staff.[58] So he didn't want a lot of advertisements focused on lending. Loans were to be sold by salespeople.

To the saver Ahmanson offered reassurance even in the design of the company's facilities. "We built fortresses," says Deihl, describing Home's "mausoleum-style" branches. "They looked like they were going to be there for not just a hundred, but a thousand years."[59] Ahmanson reinforced this sensibility sometimes by incorporating enormous bank vault doors into the interior design of a branch. Often, there was no big vault on premises, remembers Rufus Turner, who worked on the architecture. "It was just for show." Everything in the design was meant to suggest to savers that their money was safe and available.[60] The greater irony from a public policy-making point of view was that in reality the bank vaults and imposing architecture were far less important to the safety of a customer's deposits than the little sign in the window: "Insured by FSLIC."

THE MASS PRODUCTION OF MORTGAGES

As Howard Ahmanson recognized, standardization and advertising were critical to mass production. Standardization allowed the manufacturer to make millions of cigarettes, boxes of cereal, or cans of soup that were all alike. Advertising generated the outsized demand for a product that justified the investment in enormous factories or facilities. With this large-scale production, the cost of producing each unit dropped. These economies of scale enhanced profits that turned companies like American Tobacco, Quaker Oats, and Campbell Soup into corporate behemoths at the beginning of the twentieth century.[61] Howard believed these same mass production and distribution techniques, anchored in the idea of standardization, could generate economies of scale for Home Savings as well.

Ahmanson and Childs understood that the government had taken the first step in standardizing home loans with the creation of the Federal Housing Administration (FHA). FHA's regulations stipulated construction and design guidelines that frustrated many architects and home buyers but benefited the mortgage lender as well as the builder. As long as the design and construction techniques were approved at the front end to avoid a systemic design flaw affecting all the homes in a development, these rules and techniques eliminated uncertainties for the lender. Without the need to check the design of each home in a development and with the knowledge that all or most of the loan was guaranteed by the federal government, lenders could spend less time reviewing and processing loan applications.[62]

Under Ahmanson and Childs, Home Savings capitalized on all of these market conditions and focused relentlessly on lowering the costs of lending. Other thrifts wrote loans from each of their branches under the time-honored assumption that the lender closest to the borrower would be best able to understand the borrower's creditworthiness. Ahmanson and Childs understood that with mass production and government guarantees, credit reviews were less dependent on personal knowledge of the borrower. Therefore, Home centralized its lending operations in two primary facilities where Ahmanson and Childs employed their most capable loan officers. This strategy minimized risks and maximized efficiencies.[63]

Home was sometimes criticized for this strategy because it often meant that the company collected deposits in a community but failed to make loans in that area. California Federal had a deeper commitment to the communities in which it operated, according to Howard Edgerton. CalFed's branches "become part of the community," Edgerton said. He encouraged his managers to join local civic organizations. "This boosts our overhead a little," he said, backhandedly painting Ahmanson as a scrooge. Ahmanson was unabashed. In the first place, "Civic affairs and religion are a man's own business." In the second place, "If a bad downturn comes the only thing our depositors are going to be interested in is whether they can get their money. They'll forget about all this community-chest stuff."[64]

In construction lending, Home Savings continued to rely on Ken Childs's superior knowledge of the industry and the community to avoid making loans for flawed developments. It was rumored in the industry that when Childs went on vacation, Home Savings didn't lend money. "That was brilliant," says

Warren Buffett, who was keeping track of the industry in those days. "If you've got low-cost money [deposits] and you don't get in trouble on the asset side [loans], the sky is the limit."[65]

Ahmanson also strategized savings on the service side on the basis of his observations of human nature. He determined that it cost Home eight times more to accept a loan payment over the counter in a branch than by mail. Part of the difference was the cost of employee time spent chatting with the customer. So he took loan servicing out of the branches and centralized it in a location away from most of his customers, making it difficult for borrowers to pay in person.[66] All of these initiatives contributed to Home's very low cost of operations.

LENDING PHILOSOPHY

If there was a core element to Howard Ahmanson's strategy in the 1950s, it was his single-minded focus on single-family homes. "His theory of lending was on homes always, always," remembers Robert DeKruif.[67] Ahmanson remembered his family's move from the north side of Omaha to the idyllic suburb of Dundee. He knew that home ownership was more than a financial transaction; it had everything to do with an individual's standing in the community. Americans would sacrifice greatly before they failed to make mortgage payments.

In the insurance business, Ahmanson had seen how people protected their homes. Risks were lower for residential property than for commercial buildings. Fires, tornados, and earthquakes didn't go away, but if pride of ownership lowered the percentage of negative outcomes—fires or foreclosures—it could make a huge impact on profits.

Ahmanson was also aware that widespread political support for home ownership reduced his risk as well. Politicians protected the institutions that promoted home ownership because home ownership had become essential to how Americans measured the health and vitality of their communities. These factors made single-family homes a conservative bet, safe enough that he could afford to bet big.

Often Ahmanson was encouraged to diversify, but he resisted commercial lending, which cost more and carried more risk. "You had to hire much more expensive people," says John Notter, "and you didn't make as much money. So why go into something you're not really good at?"[68] Always the memory of the White Spot restaurant in Nebraska stayed with Ahmanson: a limited menu done well could bring enormous success. Ahmanson and Childs kept the menu at Home extremely limited. By the end of 1955, 99.7 percent of the loans in Home's enormous $270 million real estate portfolio were for single-family residences.[69]

Although borrowers were critical to Ahmanson's sense of the safety of mortgage lending, he also emphasized the quality of the property. "He wanted homes in good areas because he figured everybody wanted to move up," says DeKruif.[70] He was often willing to bet on the house over the borrower. "That doesn't mean 'no-doc' or 'low-doc' loans," says Richard Deihl, "but he wanted a good house because the house was the security." If a borrower ran into trouble, a good house could always be resold. As a result, Ahmanson was often willing to make loans to people who had been marginalized by the industry. The first loan Richard Deihl made as a junior loan officer in 1960, for example, was to a divorcee with two children who had a sales job where she was paid on commission. In those days, single women had a hard time getting banks to lend to them. "Nobody would touch her," Deihl remembers, "but the house was good." So he made the loan.[71]

Ahmanson was also more than willing to look at a high loan-to-value ratio. He did not try to undercut the competition on price (lower interest rates) but preferred to win the borrower by offering a bigger loan. Although this meant taking more risk because the borrower had less of his or her own money in the house, Ahmanson had confidence in the abiding and constantly increasing value of California real estate.

As he often told reporters when he was sharing his big ideas about the world, the managed economies of democracies tended toward inflation. Under political pressure, democratic governments always printed more money, and when the economy boomed they didn't have the discipline to tax enough to pay down their debts.[72] It was an idea he had picked up in college and subscribed to all his life. "Years ago, you couldn't get any financier or hard-money man to say anything in favor of an unbalanced budget," he said, "but times have changed."[73] Lenders were vulnerable to interest rate risks in this political economy since the value of their assets would be eroded by inflation while the price of the debtor's asset, the home, rose. Ahmanson hedged this equation by betting on the property rather than the borrower and offering a larger loan as a percentage of the total value of the house. If housing values were rising, the slight additional risk on the larger loan would be balanced by the greater profit.

Like most lenders, Ahmanson avoided neighborhoods where values were not rising. In the "war room" of the main office of Home Savings in the late 1950s, a huge map of the Los Angeles area hung on the wall. A red line bounded hash marks drawn over certain neighborhoods, Richard Deihl remembers. When he was a loan agent, "we were told not to lend in those areas."[74] Those areas were affected by poverty and real estate values were considered unstable. In the segregated society of the era, many of these neighborhoods had higher concentrations of African and Mexican Americans.

For many years, with the encouragement of the federal government, lenders, appraisers, real estate agents, and developers subscribed to the theory that homogeneity was the key to reducing mortgage risk. In the 1930s, the Home Owners Loan Corporation (HOLC) had institutionalized the practice of racial and economic segregation in housing development and residential lending. HOLC's "property security maps" classified neighborhoods on the basis of the average age of the structures, the maintenance of the homes, the number of rentals, and the presence of "undesirable elements," which included members of racial minorities.[75] Social segregation continued to permeate public policy during and after the war, and the FHA explicitly perpetuated racial discrimination in mortgage lending. When the Community Homes cooperative in Reseda sought FHA approval to finance 280 single-family homes in 1947, for example, it was turned down by the government because the cooperative refused to adopt racial restrictions. Responding to the group's appeal of his staff's decision, FHA commissioner Raymond M. Foley explained that if racial integration increased the financial risk to the lender, then "we are not warranted in accepting the risk."[76]

In the immediate postwar years, federal officials, builders, and lenders sought to show their support for communities of color by promoting a separate-but-equal ideology that was friendlier than the outright ostracism that had characterized race relations throughout the history of the Golden State. In January 1945, the National Housing Agency announced that it would build twelve hundred houses for Negro war workers in Los Angeles and planned to develop communities for Chinese, Mexican, and Japanese American residents as well.[77] In December 1948, the *California Savings and Loan Journal* highlighted the first-ever VA tract development for Mexican Americans. But by the late 1940s this separate-but-equal ideology was already under assault.

African Americans had organized chapters of the National Association for the Advancement of Colored People (NAACP) and the Urban League as early as 1913 and 1921 to battle against employment and housing discrimination. These efforts were generally unsuccessful through the 1930s. In 1930, seven out of every ten black residents of Los Angeles lived in one assembly district.[78] As the black population nearly tripled during the war, growing from 4 percent to 9 percent of the total population in Los Angeles, discrimination became a bigger issue.[79] During the war, this growing black community fought to end employment and housing discrimination, but victories were limited.[80]

After the war, the NAACP and other civil rights organizations in Los Angeles challenged racial covenants in court.[81] In October 1947, in a case involving three African American families seeking to buy homes in the mid-Wilshire District, Los Angeles Superior Court judge Stanley Mosk ruled that racial covenants were unenforceable. He likened these covenants to the racist policies of the Nazi regime and noted that one of the defendants in the case had fought in World War II and earned a Purple Heart. "This court would indeed be callous if it were to permit him to be ousted from his own home by using 'race' as the measure of his worth as a citizen and a neighbor."[82]

The California cases broke legal ground for the NAACP's arguments before the U.S. Supreme Court. Seven months later, in May 1948, the Court ruled in *Shelley v. Kramer* that government enforcement of private racial covenants violated the equal protection clause of the Fourteenth Amendment to the U.S. Constitution. When that ruling was amplified by further decisions, the concept of racial covenants seemed doomed.[83] The *Los Angeles Sentinel* proclaimed that "Jim Crow is just about dead in California."[84]

The Supreme Court's decisions foreshadowed the end of overt racial discrimination in housing developments, but its impact was blunted by the lack of laws proscribing discrimination. Months after U.S. Supreme Court's decision, when singer Nat King Cole paid $75,000 for a home at 401 S. Muirfield, blocks away from where Howard and Dottie lived, the Hancock Park Property Owners offered him $100,000 for his home. When Cole refused the offer and moved in, the word "nigger" was burned into the lawn and someone poisoned the family dog.[85]

Howard Ahmanson defended Nat King Cole's right to live in the tony Hancock Park community, but without Home Savings lending records from the 1950s, it's impossible to know whether his defense of an individual black family reflected any change in the pattern of Home Savings' treatment of nonwhite applicants for loans. The growth of savings and loans owned and operated by African Americans, however, provides powerful evidence of the unmet market need in Los Angeles. By 1958, thrifts like Broadway Federal, Liberty, Safety and Watts savings and loans were among the top twenty-five African American thrifts in the country.[86]

As the civil rights movement swelled in the early 1960s, many California thrifts insisted that they did not discriminate; at the same time, they rationalized policies that prohibited making certain loans to people of color. When one Los Angeles savings and loan surveyed its customers in the early 1960s, for example, it received an inquiry asking whether the institution would ever make a loan to a black home buyer who wanted to move into an all-white neighborhood. "We would definitely *not* consider such a loan application," a spokesperson for the company wrote back, "for the reason that it would be extremely disturbing to existing property owners and initially at least would tend to cause a deterioration of property values due to distressed selling." But according to the author, "We should like to make it clear however, that our attitude is not based in any sense upon racial prejudice, but solely on sound economics and a desire to preserve existing community attitudes and values. In areas where the residents are predominantly those from minority groups we have no hesitancy in considering loans."[87]

NATIONAL LEADER IN A TRANSFORMED INDUSTRY

With Thomas Webster's help, Ahmanson developed an elaborate corporate structure to maximize his legal and tax advantages. The master holding company until the mid-1960s was H. F. Ahmanson & Co., which controlled Home Savings and Loan and National American Insurance. Occasionally, Ahmanson also bought thrifts that he did not merge with Home Savings and Loan. If he could not acquire 100 percent ownership, he kept these companies separate and used them as a training ground for talented young managers. John Notter, for example, got to run a business on his own when Ahmanson moved him from Home Savings to run Victory Savings and Loan in Van Nuys.

With this corporate structure, Ahmanson operated with a great deal of freedom. He was uninhibited by partners or shareholders. He could make decisions on his own, which was the way he liked it. Someone once asked him what his ideal corporate board would look like. His response spoke volumes about his attitudes toward race and class in America. He said he would prefer four colored porters and himself. When they asked him where he would have his board meetings, he replied: "In a phone booth."

Ahmanson was also extremely conservative financially. The company's reserves were sometimes double that of other savings and loans. His good friend Howard Edgerton was far more aggressive and at times ran into problems with regulators because of it. When California Federal sought permission to open two new branches in the fall of 1953, regulators at the Federal Home Loan Bank Board rejected the plan because the company had not made sufficient progress on an agreement to strengthen its liquidity.[88]

As a strategist, Ahmanson kept his eye on the horizon. Already an accomplished yachtsman by the mid-1950s, in business as well as on the open ocean he had the ability to change direction, "to go where the wind was," if things weren't going as he wanted.[89]

Although many people saw the profit possibilities in various aspects of the home ownership industry in Southern California, Ahmanson bet more aggressively and his timing was superior. As it turned out, the best entrepreneurial opportunities in the savings and loan industry were available in the first ten years after the end of the war. Those who waited found their growth and profits constrained by higher prices for land and capital, increasing regulatory barriers and costs, and growing competition for management talent and customers.

By the late 1950s, many of Ahmanson's rivals had come to appreciate Home's enormous competitive advantages. Some called Ahmanson "the octopus," a reference to the title of Frank Norris's 1901 novel about the Southern Pacific Railroad, which dominated the state's economy and politics in the late nineteenth century. Bill Ahmanson defended his uncle: "The worst that can be said about 'Unc' is that he lives to build capital—and to run his own show."[90] Howard Ahmanson didn't mind his jealous rivals. "I could be wrong," he said with characteristic false modesty, "but I'm probably accumulating money—and by money I mean cash and easily converted assets, not debts—at a faster rate than any other man in America."[91]

In many ways, Home's growth reflected the national success of the postwar savings and loan industry and the spectacular characteristics of the Los Angeles market. At the beginning of the war, savings and loans held only 24.4 percent of the total residential mortgage debt on one- to four-unit buildings in the United States.[92] By 1955, they had emerged to play the leading role in residential mortgage credit in the United States, especially in the market for middle- and working-class families and among borrowers taking advantage of the government's home loan programs.

The success of the savings and loans nationally was amplified in California, and especially in Southern California. At the end of the war, the savings accounts in commercial banks were ten times greater than the deposits in savings and loans.[93] In 1947, banks held about 45 percent of all residential mortgages in California. Their market share fell dramatically over the next ten years to 19 percent. Meanwhile, savings and loans in the Golden State increased their residential mortgage market share from 17 percent to 36 percent in the same period. This was exactly the era when Home Savings and Loan engineered its dramatic growth to become the nation's largest thrift.[94]

The rise of savings and loans helped the nation achieve a significant increase in the rate of home ownership. Nationally, nonfarm home ownership rose from 43.6 percent to 61.9 percent between 1940 and 1960. Although California did not keep pace with the nation, it produced very significant gains: from 43.4 percent in 1940 to 58.4 percent in 1960.[95] In the Los Angeles–Long Beach metropolitan area, given the success of the savings and loans, one might have expected an even more dramatic increase, but this was not the case. With a 56.4 percent rate of home ownership in 1960, the region lagged the state, the nation, and even the average of all metropolitan regions. Some speculated that higher mortgage rates in the area kept some buyers from being able to afford a home, but Orange County reported a home ownership rate of 71.8 percent.[96]

Many factors affected the increases in home ownership: smaller and more affordable homes, new technologies and materials that lowered the costs of construction, incomes that rose faster than the cost of housing. As we have seen, not all segments of the population benefited from these policies. But there was no denying that in many communities across the country, including Los Angeles, the transformed Jeffersonian vision that home owners would make up the majority of citizens had become a reality, and it was this dream that had made Howard Ahmanson rich.

SEVEN

Home and the State

AS THE SAVINGS AND LOAN INDUSTRY in Southern California grew in the postwar years, it was elaborately integrated with a system of state and federal regulations.[1] The system, like the *Titanic,* was designed to be unsinkable, with separate compartments, so that if one was punctured the others would keep the massive ship afloat and on keel.[2] It was a system designed by politicians during the Depression to ensure stability regardless of the cost to competition and efficiency. It favored entrepreneurs who understood both the legal and the political purposes of the law and who worked well with lawmakers and regulators to achieve common goals. This climate of cooperation reflected business's embrace of what has been called the "interventionist state," the "corporate commonwealth," or the managed economy.[3]

Some academics have argued that the comfortable relationship between business and government in the postwar years reflected a tendency for businesses to "capture" the agencies created to regulate them. Without a doubt, Howard Ahmanson found ways to influence this system to promote his economic interests. But even when his influence was strongest, he did not always get what he wanted. In reality, as Stephen Adams has described the relationship between government entrepreneur Henry J. Kaiser and federal bureaucrats, the story was "of neither battle nor capture, but rather a process of continuous negotiation."[4]

From the earliest days of the American republic, the regulation of financial services reflected tensions between state and federal priorities. These tensions were deeply embedded by the end of World War II. Federally chartered banks and thrifts competed with their state-chartered cousins in local communities on the basis of what lawmakers and regulators allowed. A customer could open a checking account at a commercial bank but not at a savings and loan. By law, a thrift could offer a saver more interest than a commercial bank. A prospective automobile buyer could get a consumer loan from a bank but not from a savings and loan. Advertising copy was strictly controlled by state regulators.[5]

To influence this complex system of laws and regulations, savings and loans individually and collectively developed relationships with regulators and politicians. In Washington, the U.S. Savings and Loan League, with members and customers in nearly every congressional district in the country, exerted a powerful influence on Congress. Closer to home, the California Savings and Loan League drafted legislation and often collaborated with regulators on the development of new rules.

Howard Ahmanson and his companies maintained an ambiguous relationship with these trade associations. While his close friends Charlie Fletcher and Howard Edgerton served terms as president of the California league and Edgerton rose to be president of the national trade association, Ahmanson declined to take a leadership position in either association after 1948. He almost never spoke at an industry gathering, although he did often foot the bill for food and festivities. Usually, Ahmanson let Ken Childs and Robert DeKruif carry the water on most of Home's government relations. At the highest levels, however, he personally cultivated relationships with regulators, legislators, and governors who were critical to Home's success.

THE INFLUENCE OF THE STATE

Because Home was a state-chartered institution, its growth and business opportunities were dictated first by lawmakers in Sacramento and bureaucrats employed in the office of the California commissioner of savings and loans. State regulators approved applications for charters and branches. They monitored lending activity to ensure that an association was not incurring imprudent risks—checking loan-to-value ratios, visiting properties to ensure that valuations were fair and accurate, tracking capital ratios to prevent an association from becoming too highly leveraged. If an association got into trouble on any of these measures, the state could seize the association and operate it, sell it, or liquidate the assets to repay the depositors.

Like most states, California had regulated the industry since the late nineteenth century, largely at the behest of the industry itself. Leaders of the thrift movement initially sought state regulation to ensure best practices and honest management to protect the good name of building and loans. They also hoped that with the state's help they could standardize elements of their operations, which would further increase public confidence in the building and loan concept. And like many industries in the late nineteenth century, thrift leaders turned to the legislature for statutory competitive advantages—particularly in relation to commercial banks.

Formal state supervision began in 1891, after the California legislature passed a law providing for a special form of incorporation for building and loan associations and putting them under the supervision of the state's Board of Bank Commissioners. The act reflected the legislature's belief that thrifts were to serve a public purpose. The law required that articles of incorporation stipulate that "the association is formed to encourage industry, frugality, home building and the accommodation of savings."[6]

The bank commissioners, however, did not retain their authority very long. In 1893, they recommended that Governor Henry H. Markham establish a separate regulatory system for building and loans, and the legislature created the Board of Commissioners of the Building and Loan Associations.[7] Thereafter, like most savings and loans across the country, California thrifts operated under state regulation with little or no supervision by federal authorities.

With the collapse of credit and sweeping federal reforms of the banking system during the Depression, the federal government stepped dramatically into the world of savings and loans. New laws provided for federal charters and access to credit through the newly created Federal Home Loan Banks. The Federal Savings and Loan Insurance Corporation (FSLIC) offered deposit insurance to both federally chartered and state-chartered institutions.

In a very real sense, the New Deal legislation created parallel and competing systems of regulation in California and other states, and over the next several decades savings and loan entrepreneurs would watch the evolution of laws and regulations in each system with an eye to maximizing their competitive advantage. In California, existing savings and loans lobbied for changes that would help them take advantage of the new federal law. "Under the sponsorship of the league, and with the untiring work of league officers, staff and committees," California Savings and Loan League president Howard

Stevens later proclaimed, "the *Building and Loan Association Act* was entirely rewritten and became law in 1931."[8] During the time that the Federal Home Loan Bank Act was drafted, California league officials worked closely with the U.S. Savings and Loan League to shape this legislation. In subsequent years, as the National Housing Act was revised and renewed, California league officials continued to press the legislature to adapt California's laws to the new federal guidelines.[9]

The savings and loan industry also exerted influence over the operations and management of the office of the California commissioner of building and loans. When Commissioner Leroy Hunt wrote to Governor Warren in 1953 to suggest a reorganization of his department, he noted that he had consulted with "various state officials, the Division of Building and Loan staff and many members of the California Savings and Loan League" in the process of developing his recommendations.[10] The close interaction between regulator and regulated was enhanced by the fact that the expenses of the division were paid for by the industry, not taxpayers, through an assessment based on each association's total assets.[11]

Thus the relationship that developed between regulator and regulated by the early 1950s was often collaborative and mutually supportive. Regulators believed that a major part of their job was to protect the health of the industry as well as the consumer or depositor. When changes needed to be made in the law, industry officials often drafted the new legislation, and legislators in Sacramento and Washington often accepted their recommendations with little other public input.[12] When influential regulators retired, they often became owners, managers, or consultants to savings and loans.[13] Meanwhile, many legislators owned shares or served on the boards of local savings and loans.

The self-regulatory atmosphere of the 1950s was also evident when individual companies or bad actors got into trouble and threatened to provoke negative public reaction to the whole industry. In 1953, for example, builder Harold Shaw (no relation to Commissioner Milt Shaw) acquired United Savings and Loan of Glendale but ran afoul of the regulators. Leaders from the industry met in the league's office in Pasadena with Milton Shaw and discussed what should be done. The leaders urged the commissioner to ban all new deposits with United if the company didn't straighten itself out. Ultimately, to make the problem go away, Howard Ahmanson agreed to buy United and turn it around.[14] Howard Edgerton confided in a letter to Governor Goodwin

Knight that Commissioner Shaw "should be commended and not criticized for the manner in which he has handled a couple of sore spots that could have been real headaches for our business."[15]

THE HOME THAT SHAW BUILT

Of the various commissioners who ran the California Division of Savings and Loans from 1945 to 1965, none was more important to Home Savings than Milton Otis Shaw. A thin, grizzled man in the 1950s, Shaw was born in Ohio and served in the army during World War I. After the war, he earned a degree in business administration and accounting from Ohio State University and then came to California in a Model T Ford roadster in 1923. Smitten with the climate, he became an auditor with the Division of Corporations and was admitted as a certified public accountant in 1927. He joined the Division of Building and Loans in 1930 as a chief examiner. On his first audit in Southern California, Shaw uncovered an eight-million-dollar embezzlement scheme—at the time, the largest building and loan theft in history. Shaw rose through the ranks to become assistant commissioner in 1947, in charge of the office in Los Angeles. When Commissioner Frank Mortimer retired in 1951, Shaw became acting commissioner for nearly a year and a half. After a brief return to his job as deputy commissioner, he finally became commissioner in his own right under Governor Goodwin Knight on January 1, 1954.[16]

Some in the industry said that Home Savings and Loan was "the house that Shaw built" because he was so permissive of Home's acquisitions. By the mid-1950s, no other savings and loan in Southern California or the state as a whole had been allowed to acquire so many other thrifts and convert them into branches. In 1958, *Fortune* asserted that Shaw had "once helped Ahmanson out of a serious jam," referring to the Palos Verdes episode. The magazine did not provide details, nor did it note Ahmanson's pledge to cover any shortfall from his own personal bank account.[17]

There is also considerable evidence that Ahmanson and Home Savings and Loan did not get everything they wanted from Commissioner Shaw. In 1954, for example, the company's applications to open branches in Torrance and Culver City were denied.[18] The following year, when Ahmanson challenged the regulatory conventions by trying to acquire a San Francisco–based thrift, he was rebuffed by Shaw and federal regulators.[19] Without question, however, the commissioner's office often aligned with Home Savings and other successful thrifts, especially on complaints.

COMPLAINTS

As Ahmanson, Edgerton, and other entrepreneurs in the savings and loan industry transformed a business once anchored in localism and mutual ownership into one characterized by aggressive competition and profit making, some objected. In January 1952, Governor Earl Warren received an anonymous letter warning that a building and loan scandal was going to "blow up in your face whenever there is a slight recession, unless something is done to correct it *NOW.*" The writer asserted that North American, Home, Occidental, "and especially the United" (all Ahmanson-controlled companies) were paying excessively high rates on deposits and charging "usurious loan fees . . . without regards for the real value of the property" to fuel rapid growth and high profits. Without referencing Ahmanson, the author, a self-described "old-timer" among the state-chartered companies, erroneously suggested that "a paltry original investment of less than $100,000 in both the North American and the Home" had been transformed into $4.5 million in only five years. "Things just don't happen that way in a well-regulated business." Fearing retribution, the writer refused to sign the letter but did conclude by saying that he or she was acting in the public interest "as well as for the protection of the good name of associations that have been operating soundly since the last depression—and we don't want what happened then to happen again, and I don't believe you do either."[20]

Though the letter was not signed, the governor's staff took the issue seriously enough to refer the matter to Milt Shaw, who was then acting commissioner. Shaw's report to the governor highlighted some of the tensions within the industry. After dismissing the specific accusations, he turned to what he suspected was the real issue for the writer—the fact that Home and a number of other thrifts were aggressively pursuing deposits by advertising higher rates. "Banks and other associations paying a lesser rate continually criticize the 3½ percent associations," Shaw noted, but he also pointed out that there were twenty associations in Southern California offering this rate. Shaw suggested that there were two ways the state could deal with the issue: ban the advertising of rates or set the rates. He artfully noted, however, that the governor had spoken out strongly against state interference in competitive markets.[21] The governor's personal secretary answered Shaw with a bureaucrat's and a politician's tact. He instructed Shaw to take all necessary steps "to protect the public interest in connection with the activities of Building and Loan Associations" but made clear his understanding "that this would not involve an attempt to control advertising practices, except as they may be regulated by statute or where, in your opinion, the public interest is endangered."[22]

Still, complaints continued to come in. In 1953, A. T. Purtell wrote to Governor Warren about the interest rates on loans charged by Joe Crail's Coast Federal Savings and Loan and its aggressive profit making. "My understanding has always been that the whole purpose behind the creation of Building and Loan Associations was to enable frugal people to buy homes on reasonable terms."[23] Ahmanson and other entrepreneurs in the industry dismissed these complaints as sour grapes from an earlier generation of industry leaders out of touch with the modern exigencies of the business.

Records of the investigations into these complaints provide some evidence of Ahmanson's competitive advantage in the marketplace. Audits by state and federal examiners, for example, highlighted the fact that Home Savings and Loan's average loan-to-value ratio (59.5 percent in early 1952) was significantly higher than that of other savings and loans in the area (52 percent). These higher loan-to-value ratios reflected two factors. First, Home's growth had been fast. Therefore, its portfolio was not "aged." Home buyers had made relatively few payments and had not reduced their principal balances. The high loan-to-value ratio also reflected Ahmanson's willingness to bet bigger than many of his competitors on the home and the borrower. Home's ratios were still within the regulatory limits, but to further inspire confidence in regulators and depositors, Home balanced this greater risk by maintaining reserves that were well above government requirements.[24]

Federal regulators also fielded occasional complaints engendered by Home's aggressive expansion. In the fall of 1954, Howard Ahmanson and Howard Edgerton were scrutinized by the Federal Home Loan Bank Board after complaints were filed with the Veterans Administration asserting that the two companies were charging builders fees of 10 percent on VA construction loans. In a personal letter to Chairman Walter McAllister, Edgerton suggested that "the complaints, in our case, at least, are completely without foundation." Eastern mutual savings banks, operating through brokers, dominated the market for construction financing in Southern California. "All we do is compete with them to keep our builders' business." California

Federal received a gross income of 6 to 7.5 points on interim financing and the VA takeout (or long-term, fixed-rate) loan on a piece of property. But the company often didn't have enough cash to meet the demand. Eastern companies charged even more. Edgerton noted that the market in the fall of 1954 was becoming increasingly competitive, squeezing the company's earnings.[25]

Home Savings followed a somewhat different strategy that reflected Ahmanson's tolerance for risk and Home's competitive advantages as a state-chartered institution. According to Edgerton, Home had "intentionally taken some of the weaker builders who have to pay a higher price for their financing because they cannot get it from the local commercial banks or savings associations like ours." He also explained that under California law Home had the ability to buy land and "set up a deal for a builder on a much more elastic basis than a federal savings and loan can do. As a consequence, they have been able to get higher fees."[26]

THE FEDERAL HOME LOAN BANK BOARD
AND THE FSLIC

As a state-chartered thrift, Home Savings and Loan was not directly regulated by the Federal Home Loan Bank Board (FHLBB), but state-chartered associations that enrolled in the FSLIC agreed to be bound by the FSLIC's rules, and the FHLBB worked closely with the FSLIC to keep state associations in line.

Deposit insurance was one of the most important supports that the federal government offered the savings and loan industry, but not every thrift took advantage of the insurance program. Six years after the creation of the FSLIC, for example, only one in three state-chartered savings and loans across the country had enrolled.[27] Some didn't want to be controlled by Washington. Others decided that as public confidence in banks and thrifts began to return in the mid-1930s, the premium for insurance was too high.[28]

Even if they didn't become members of the FSLIC, state-chartered institutions, especially in California, benefited from the more cumbersome regulatory structure that the FHLBB imposed on the federally chartered savings and loans. Some federal savings and loan managers, particularly Howard Edgerton, felt these disadvantages acutely. The federal system did not allow for stockholder-owned companies, for example. Federal thrift executives could be paid handsomely and enjoy significant perks paid for by the thrift's profits, but they could not accumulate an ownership interest. More than once, Edgerton tried to convert to a state-chartered stock association, but regulators turned down California Federal's applications and resisted these conversions in general.[29]

Federal regulators also tended to be less sensitive to local market conditions, which posed a major disadvantage to a Los Angeles–based company operating in the most unusual market in the country. Federal regulators were slower making decisions on branches and charters and were deferential to state regulators for political reasons. As a result, Edgerton and the leaders of other federal savings and loans often felt they were unable to grow as fast as the state-chartered institutions.

Edgerton maintained particularly close relationships with the various chairmen of the FHLBB, especially during the years when he served in top leadership roles in the U.S. Savings and Loan League.[30] These friendships provided the basis for a more informal regulatory approach. After Bert King, the head of the Veterans Administration, passed on complaints he had received regarding the high rates that California Federal and Home Savings were charging for VA construction loans, FHLBB chairman McAllister wrote to Edgerton to suggest that he might look into the situation. "Don't look on this as an official complaint," McAllister said. "I merely point out to you that Bert is sensitive and hopes that this doesn't reach, for instance, Senator Homer Capehart."[31]

As a former savings and loan executive, McAllister also shared his own ambivalence over his regulatory role and his reluctance to interfere in the market. "If the builder can't find someone else from whom to get his money and pays you 10 percent instead of 5 percent, the going rate, if such it is, then either you are taking a terrific risk with that builder, or else your competitors are sound asleep, or else there is something particularly stupid about the builder." Pragmatically, McAllister suggested that since Edgerton was good friends with Ahmanson, he ought to talk the situation over with him and clear up any misunderstandings with the VA. "Bert is very friendly," McAllister noted, "but I know that he doesn't want any explosion."[32]

California Federal and Home Savings handled the situation directly and discreetly. Edgerton wrote to King to explain California Federal's loan policies. Ahmanson sent Ken Childs to Washington to meet with the VA's top administrator. Well briefed, King told McAllister at the FHLBB that he was completely satisfied.[33]

McAllister's support and encouragement for the savings and loan indus- try reflected his political philosophy and a developing awareness of the com- plexities of government's relationship with private enterprise. In a speech to savings and loan executives in Los Angeles in the fall of 1953, he noted that for twenty years he had been a critic of the government's regulatory ap- proach. With Eisenhower's election, champions of limited government faced their first opportunity in two decades to reduce government interference in the daily lives of the nation's citizens. Yet he also noted that in his first year in office he had faced "innumerable requests to get a regulation passed to pro- hibit this, that or the other thing. We Americans just naturally want to correct the other fellow by passing a law. We would like to squash competition by a regulation." In this sense, the industry was often its own worst enemy. Even in the Eisenhower administration, "All of us are constantly subject to influ- ence and the advocates of a managed economy are fighting as never before to resume their place in the sun," McAllister said.[34]

A deeply conservative man, McAllister continued to struggle with his own sense of how to balance the role of government and private enterprise in the mortgage market. But he was very clear on what the government should *not* do: build or own public housing.

THE THREAT OF PUBLIC HOUSING

During the war, the government had exercised unprecedented control over the nation's economy, dictating prices and wages, controlling construction and manufacturing, and focusing the nation's productive system on build- ing airplanes, bombs, tanks, and other implements of destruction. To some, this era seemed to suggest that tentative New Deal experiments with social democracy might come to full fruition after the war. But many Americans were eager to get rid of the thinly tolerated systems of rationing and price controls once the war was over.

For many, public housing proved to be the battle line between two alter- native views of American society. To the champions of social democracy, public housing, like public roads, schools, libraries, and parks, represented a natural extension of the communitarian and cooperative aspects of American culture. To others it posed a dramatic threat to the ideal of private home own- ership and free enterprise. When public officials in Los Angeles proposed to solve the postwar housing crisis by building government-owned apartments and homes, the opponents of social democracy rebelled.[35]

Charlie Fletcher was one of the leaders of the rebellion. Victorious in his bid for Congress in 1946, he arrived in Washington the following January prepared to fight for an end to price and rent controls and a ban on the development of public housing. Fletcher joined many young World War II veterans, including two future presidents—John Kennedy and Richard Nixon—in the so-called Class of 1946. His victory helped the Republicans gain fifty-six seats in the House. Coupled with a gain of thirteen seats in the Senate, the election set the stage for a new conservative resurgence that was determined to reduce the federal government's role in the economy, weaken the influence of labor unions, and fight the spread of communism.[36]

Fletcher's self-appointed role in realizing this new agenda was to block the construction of public housing. During a series of hearings that he chaired in San Francisco and Los Angeles, he deplored slums and agreed that something needed to be done about them, but he also noted the housing shortage affecting communities across the country. He favored the establishment of a national building code, especially for rental housing. He expressed confidence that private builders and lenders would be able to meet the nation's needs. Speaking to members of the Los Angeles Chamber of Commerce, he was more partisan. He warned of creeping socialism. "You've all seen what has happened in England," he said. "I don't want any part of it."[37]

Charlie's critics suggested that he was "a tool for the real estate lobby," which included land developers, builders, and lenders.[38] This group launched a major battle over public housing in Los Angeles, much of it centered on a roughly four-hundred–acre site in Chávez Ravine. At the end of the war, housing officials had studied the community's housing stock and identified eleven "blighted" areas, including Chávez Ravine. The city council approved a plan in October 1950 to spend $110 million to construct ten thousand housing units to be built in these areas.[39]

Scored with dirt streets and walking paths, the old wooden houses of Chávez Ravine were home to a large community of Mexican Americans. City officials commissioned noted architects Robert Alexander and Richard Neutra to design a complex of 24 thirteen-story towers and 163 two-story buildings that would be owned and managed by the city's housing authority.[40]

Private builders and lenders quickly organized in opposition to the city's plan, calling it "creeping socialism" and branding the director of the city's housing office a communist. Under mounting political pressure, the city council narrowly voted to cancel plans to build the development. When the housing authority appealed this decision to the courts, the city council put the issue on the ballot for June 3, 1952. The vote seemed to be obviated when the California Supreme Court ruled that the city could not cancel its contract for the project, but voters rejected the project anyway by a three-to-two margin. To honor the will of the electorate, California's senators, William Knowland and Richard Nixon, pushed for a federal law that would allow the city to cancel the contract.[41]

Opposition to the public housing projects continued to swell in the fall of 1952 as anticommunism swept the nation. After three of the city housing authority's top officials refused to testify before the California Senate Un-American Activities Committee in the fall of 1952, all three were fired. The following spring, Norris Poulson, a five-term Republican congressman, challenged the incumbent mayor, Fletcher Bowron, a supporter of public housing, and won.[42] Soon after he took office, Poulson canceled the Chávez Ravine project.[43]

The California Savings and Loan League supported the fight against public housing. Waving the flag of antisocialism in 1950, the league created a committee on governmental relations "to encourage high caliber men to run for public office, to back them in their campaigns and to help them with their problems after they have attained public office."[44] It's not clear that Home officials shared this belief that the country was on a downward slope "toward the welfare state," but Ken Childs served on this new committee. Howard's friends Mervyn Hope, of Hollywood Savings and Loan, and Joe Crail, of Coast Federal Savings and Loan, ran the Southern California branch of the committee.[45] Two years later, these members were succeeded by a new group of leaders that included Charlie Fletcher. This group invited another of Ahmanson's friends, Henry A. Bubb, to speak to the midyear meeting of savings and loan executives.

A tall, lean, handsome man right out of a Norman Rockwell painting, Bubb was the president of the Capitol Federal Savings and Loan Association in Topeka, Kansas. He later became a member of the board of directors of Home Savings and Loan. He had started with Capitol Building and Loan in 1926, when it was still a state-chartered institution, and had become president in 1941 after the organization converted to a federal charter. Under his leadership, Capitol Federal had become the largest federally insured association in Kansas.[46] In his 1952 speech, Bubb encouraged California savings and loan leaders to march at the forefront of "an alert, aggressive movement of political conservatism in this country." Harkening back to the early days of the building and loan movement, when leaders had seen themselves as a defense against the rising tide of consumer credit, Bubb suggested that building and loan managers who did not join such a movement "are shirking our responsibilities to our savers, to our borrowers, and to ourselves" if "we fail to do everything in our power to elect conservatives to public office." Bubb insisted that "Washington planners" were promoting inflation and threatening private home ownership in America by building public housing. "Public housing is a scandal," Bubb declared. He encouraged thrift leaders to campaign against any politician who advocated it and to urge their customers to vote for conservative candidates. By doing so, he said, "we'll put a rope around the public housers yet."[47]

While Bubb, Fletcher, and other leaders in the savings and loan movement railed against public housing, Howard Ahmanson said little about his own position on the issue. Some thrift leaders expressed equal concern about the government's role in mortgage lending, but not Ahmanson and Childs. They made government-guaranteed loans a centerpiece of their strategy.

FEDERALLY GUARANTEED LOANS

Thrift industry leaders had helped write the mortgage-guarantee components of the GI Bill. They underwrote 80 percent of the VA loans issued during the first year of the program's operation.[48] But the program's cap on interest rates soon became a problem. "How can we tie up our money at such a low interest rate for such a long time?" some lenders asked. "What are we going to do when we have to pay higher dividends to attract savings?"[49]

Terms and conditions also proved difficult. The original GI Bill, for example, prohibited the lender from accessing the government's guarantee if the purchase price of the home exceeded a "reasonable normal value" determined by a proper appraisal. Legislators had inserted this provision to try to keep the market honest. In fact, "reasonable normal value" came to be interpreted as the home price absent high demand or an inflationary market, which was unrealistic in the postwar economy. Millions of people wanted to buy homes and prices were rising.

Congress amended the law in December 1945 to fix some of these problems. It increased the maximum loan amount from two thousand to four thousand dollars. It changed "reasonable normal value" to "reasonable value," which allowed lenders to accept an appraisal based on current market conditions. Congress also extended the maximum term of the loan from twenty to twenty-five years, enhancing the affordability of the program. Responding to complaints from veterans and lenders, the VA streamlined procedures. "Supervised lenders," for example, including financial institutions subject to state or federal oversight, were allowed to automatically write government-guaranteed loans to eligible veterans without prior VA approval. Congress gave veterans ten additional years to exercise their rights under the bill. It also allowed the VA to pay lenders 4 percent of the amount of the guaranty upon completion of the loan—a first payment on the veteran's behalf.[50]

Still, many bankers and lenders continued to be more concerned than excited by the law. One thrift manager asked: "Should Government be called upon to make good those guarantees there will be some excitement.... Who will be blamed for making the poor loans that caused the loss to the Government and a drain on the taxpayers' money? What do you imagine the electorate will think of a financial system that collects income and profits on its loans but transfers losses to the Government?"[51]

Some lenders balked because the rules kept changing. Years later, Howard Edgerton noted that "the housing authorities in Washington issued directive after directive" regarding federal mortgage insurance and loan programs. "Life was never boring" in this environment, "but it was a bit difficult to make business plans as much as 30 days in advance."[52]

Given these problems, some savings and loan leaders avoided the federal programs. In fact, two-thirds of all single-family residential loans made by the nation's savings and loans were conventional loans without any government guarantee. Walter Ray, the president of the U.S. Savings and Loan League, warned his peers that if government guarantee programs "should ever become the sole and exclusive avenue through which mortgage credit was available, we would be at the point in the game where Uncle Sam would be able to tell a home buyer where he should buy his house, what kind of house it should be, and how much he should pay for it."[53]

Despite this dire warning, government-guaranteed loans were popular with Americans and seemed like a prudent investment to many people. In March 1954, the National Association of Home Builders noted triumphantly the biggest mortgage burning in history when the FHA commissioner delivered a check for $16.45 million to the U.S. Treasury to pay off loans the federal government had provided to the FHA in the darkest days of the Great Depression.[54]

One prominent builder also reminded thrift managers that when their industry had failed to embrace the FHA's programs during the Depression they had left the door wide open for mortgage brokers who increased their market share significantly. If banks and savings and loans refused to make loans to veterans, they were also "lending weight to the eventual entry of the government into the field of direct loans to veterans."[55]

Despite these warnings, thrifts showed a declining interest in VA loans in the mid-1950s. They wrote only about 20 percent of all VA loans in the country in 1955, at a time when VA and FHA loans accounted for nearly half of all new mortgages. As predicted, mortgage brokers and insurance companies rushed back into the business after Congress gave new freedom to Fannie Mae to buy and sell government-backed mortgages.[56] In 1956, *Barron's* noted that in the savings and loan industry, "the more enterprising [institutions] avoid VAs and FHAs entirely."[57]

Veterans groups lobbied hard for the government to fix the program. Los Angeles County supervisor John Anson Ford received a brochure from the Veteran's Organizations Council of Altadena titled *The Big Promise*. Echoing the prose rhythms of the novelist John Dos Passos, the brochure depicted the men who had preserved the nation, who "flew down the cloud-lined slots of sudden death" or "charged the bullet-laced Siegfried Line." In gratitude, the nation had promised them "a share of the fullness of America, of the dreams of America: Was not every man's home his castle, and did not every man dream of a home of his own. Then, this you do for the men who preserved a nation; you promise them a home of their own."[58]

The promise came with the GI Bill. But with the competition for money in the postwar economy, the incentives to lenders were too slim. Fewer than twenty-five thousand veterans a month were able to obtain the home loans they wanted, while "twelve million veterans cannot get GI Home Loans today." The solution: "The Congress must incorporate features which make the GI Home Loan competitively attractive in this age of atoms and economic worlds within worlds; adjust the interest rate on GI Home Loans to the average market level."[59]

The U.S. Savings and Loan League also lobbied for changes to make VA loans more amenable to lenders. Home Savings played a major role in this effort, although Howard never became directly involved. When the league began a campaign to raise the interest cap in 1953, Ken Childs led the charge. He told reporters that a raise was desperately needed because "the percentage of GI lending to the total volume of home financing had dropped to the lowest level since the close of World War II." Childs insisted that the industry wanted to help the program "get back on its feet."[60] He didn't tell reporters that an increase in the maximum interest rate would benefit Home Savings more than any other lender in the nation.

HOME SAVINGS, VA LOANS, AND SOUTHERN CALIFORNIA

Los Angeles was the capital of the VA loan program in the postwar years. More VA home loans had been written in Los Angeles County by the fall of 1954 than anywhere else in the country—245,035 total, for a combined value of nearly $2 billion. These loans accounted for 7 percent of all VA loans in the country and more than half of California's 12.5 percent share of the national total.[61]

Home Savings and Loan wrote a huge share of these loans. Across the country, GI loans made up only 18 percent of the total loan portfolio of the average savings and loan in the mid-1950s, but they accounted for 68.2 percent of the value of Home's $377 million portfolio in 1956, increasing to 70 percent in 1958.[62] The numbers were staggering. As Howard told reporters, this was the largest such portfolio in the United States.[63]

Ahmanson and Childs relied on the safety of VA loans to balance the risks they were taking with tract lending and development.[64] With hundreds of millions of dollars invested in very safe but low-yielding government-insured loans, they could afford to buy big undeveloped pieces of property. Some financial analysts marveled at this strategy. While good conventional uninsured mortgages were earning 6 percent, the overwhelming majority of Home Savings and Loan's mortgages were earning closer to 4.5 percent. Ahmanson said he didn't mind. Commenting on the company's overall financial conservatism in 1958, he pointed out: "With the kind of reserves and the insured loan portfolio that we've got, we could stand a double 1929."[65] In other words, real estate values could plummet, yet Home's asset base would be secure.

Howard also recognized a key opportunity in VA loans that many other lenders didn't see. As we saw in chapter 5, conventional loans went on the books at 100 percent of the value of the loan. The lender might earn a point or two in fees, but the major profits on the loan were amortized over the life of the loan. In contrast, VA loans went on the books for 92 percent of their value, and the lender was allowed to book as much as 8 percent of the loan immediately as earnings. This 8 percent margin enhanced Home's capital, allowed the company to grow more quickly, and gave the company greater lending capacity.[66]

Beyond the direct subsidy and guarantee inherent in the VA program, Ahmanson and Childs recognized other benefits from the government's involvement with housing. Historically, many savings and loans wrote loans and then held them for the duration of the loan. During the Depression, the government had tried to introduce greater liquidity by creating the Federal National Mortgage Association (FNMA) to buy and hold loans originated by certified lenders. Many savings and loans were skeptical of FNMA, but Childs and Ahmanson saw what most grocery store owners understood: the fastest way to profits was in the turnover of stock on the shelves. If they could book a profit from selling a loan to FNMA and then make a new loan to another builder, profits would be higher. Childs, for example, made that clear to his boss in 1951, when he expressed frustration that he could not offer more loans to tract builder Milton Kauffman because North American had reached the legal lending limit based on its capital. If he could deliver a new batch of loans to FNMA fast enough, North American would be able to finance an additional 118 homes.[67]

BUILDING CODES AND MASS PRODUCTION

In addition to providing liquidity, as described earlier, the federal government's mortgage loan guarantee programs increasingly standardized the way homes and neighborhoods were designed and built. This trend toward standardization and mass production received additional support at the state and local level as communities adopted and enforced building codes after World War II.

Since the early part of the twentieth century, California, and especially Los Angeles, had led the nation in the development of building codes and standards along with the adoption of the nation's first zoning laws.[68] In 1917, the first single-family home standards were adopted and the legislature authorized the creation of city planning commissions.[69] In 1923, the legislature consolidated its various housing statutes, and California became the second state in the Union (after Michigan) to enact a comprehensive statewide housing law.[70] The new law delegated great power to local authorities, but this power was lightly used. Only four California counties enforced local building standards, for example, in 1938. After the war, local standards and building codes became much more prevalent in urban areas and had a substantial influence on the process and pattern of suburbanization.[71]

Sometimes these codes accelerated the pace of innovation; at other times they slowed it down. As contractors integrated new building products like aluminum siding and roofs, electric heat, insulated glass, and treated lumber, for example, some building inspectors were leery of these new materials. They remembered the inadequacies of "victory plumbing" products, for example, which had been substituted for conventional copper or cast iron during the war.[72] To convince building inspectors that these new products were effective and durable, manufacturers provided product-testing data and pushed for broad and standardized revisions to building codes. These revisions made it easier for tract home builders to move from community to community replicating their construction strategies. They also decreased the lender's risk and thus lowered the costs of underwriting. For Ahmanson and Home Savings, all of these factors produced a simple but timeless equation: earn a small margin on a high volume and get rich in the process.

POLITICAL COMPETITION

Unlike most of his peers in the savings and loan industry, Howard Ahmanson had created a strategy that was deeply dependent on government initiatives. Like the legendary griffon, part lion and part eagle, who guarded the treasuries of the ancients and was the chosen emblem of H. F. Ahmanson & Co., government guarantees protected his huge store of assets from changes in interest rates and the money supply that put his peers on edge. With such security, he could bet on "the wildest cats and dogs," tract developers willing to pay anything to get the cash they needed to build Southern California's burgeoning automobile suburbs.

Yet despite his dependence on the decisions of policy makers, Ahmanson lived at arm's length from the trade associations that lobbied on behalf of his business. While smaller savings and loans relied on the California and U.S. leagues to protect their interests and ensure that regulators maintained a balanced and profitable environment for their companies, a competitive entrepreneur like Ahmanson often found that his interests diverged from the majority in the league. Home Savings did not need regulators to intervene to manage dividend rates or giveaways, for example; it had the scale and scope to win pricing wars on its own. Focusing on growth as a way to increase profitability, Home favored more permissive licensing for branches, while smaller associations used the regulatory process as a way to impede potential competitors. As political appointees, regulators were inclined to align themselves with the interests of the largest number of industry players, represented by the league, rather than the handful of larger associations like Home Savings or California Federal. But Howard Ahmanson had his own singular source of competitive advantage in the regulatory and political arenas. He had deep pockets with lots of loose change.

EIGHT

Political Economy

THROUGHOUT HIS LIFE, Howard Ahmanson flirted with the limelight. In college, he evidenced a powerful intelligence but he had no interest in becoming an academic. He liked to theorize about the world and occasionally wrote a speech offering his views on the economy or society, but he had no desire to become an intellectual leader. When he acquired control of National American Fire Insurance in 1943 and was elected president of the company, he told Gould Eddy and his brother, Hayden, that he wanted to get some publicity for this accomplishment—an unusual move given his usual preference for a low public profile—but their efforts yielded only a few minor notices in insurance industry publications. After the war, when he entered the savings and loan industry, perhaps thinking for a short time that he would follow Fletcher and Edgerton into a visible leadership position in the industry, Howard agreed to serve as president of a Los Angeles County association of savings and loan executives. But as soon as his term was over, he stepped down and never held a leadership position in the industry again. The pattern reflected a deep ambivalence in the man. He longed for recognition and admiration from the public as he had from his father when he was younger. But he clung to privacy and avoided the encumbrances and responsibilities of leadership. Circumstances combined in 1954 to offer him a new and very public opportunity to resolve his ambivalence.

POLITICAL HISTORY

Ahmanson may have become involved in Republican politics in California as early as the 1930s. He certainly knew some of the right people. His wartime friend Ed Shattuck had been a founder of the California Republican Assembly, a group of "Young Turks" who set out in the mid-1930s to wrest control of the party from its aging Progressive-era leadership. Earl Warren, who would go on to govern the state and, ultimately, lead the U.S. Supreme Court, joined the group. So did Goodwin Knight.

Knight and Ahmanson became friends around 1934, when they both had offices in a building at Seventh and Spring Streets.[1] Knight, or "Goodie" as he was called by his friends and the press, was ten years older than Ahmanson. He had come to Los Angeles from Utah with his parents. After graduating from high school, he worked for a year as a miner in Southern Nevada and then enrolled at Stanford University. World War I interrupted his college career. He served in the navy aboard a sub-chaser in both the Pacific and the Atlantic Oceans. After the war, he graduated from Stanford and enrolled at Cornell University in Ithaca, New York, as a Telluride Scholar. Returning to California, he joined the state bar in 1921. Thereafter, Knight and a partner developed one of the most successful legal practices in the state. Knight added to his growing fortune in the 1930s by buying gold mines in Kern County. He also became increasingly active in politics. His support for Frank Merriam's run for governor led to a superior court appointment in 1935. From the bench, Knight presided over several famous divorce cases and became known as the "Hollywood divorce judge." He also hosted a radio show that aired in Los Angeles and San Francisco, which helped him build a following in the two major urban areas of the state.[2]

Knight embarked on his first political campaign in 1946. With Earl Warren on the ticket running for reelection as governor, Knight defeated state senator Jack Shelley in the race for lieutenant governor.[3] Ambitious, charismatic, and sometimes temperamental, Knight thought he had an opportunity to succeed Warren in 1948, when the Republicans tapped Warren to be New York governor Thomas Dewey's running mate in the campaign against Harry Truman for president. Truman's victory astonished the pundits and sent Warren back to California.

Knight waited. He and Warren easily won reelection two years later. With the ascent of an ambitious Southern California congressman named Richard Nixon, Knight seemed to find new support for his own bid for governor. Nixon had made a national name for himself with the House Un-American Activities Committee and his personal efforts to expose State Department official Alger Hiss as a spy. Running for the U.S. Senate in 1950, with battles raging on the Korean peninsula, he played to voter fears of communism. He also rallied conservatives, who were increasingly frustrated by Warren's liberalism. Nixon's base saw Knight as a conservative alternative to the incumbent governor. Knight hoped that these conservatives would help convince Warren not to run again in 1954.

While Knight waited, he and Howard Ahmanson corresponded occasionally on personal and political topics. Ahmanson sent a postcard from Europe in the spring of 1951 depicting the leg of a booted farmer pushing an American shovel into plowed ground. "Thought you'd get a kick out of the cards they give away in the post office for Greeks to send to the U.S.A.," Ahmanson wrote. "We're definitely keeping them and they love it." Knight wrote back that he was "immensely interested in your comments concerning the practical application of the Marshall Plan. We are not only keeping them, but I'll bet they enjoyed using your good American dollars and were stinging you with high prices if they got the chance." Knight also told Ahmanson that he would be in Sacramento for the legislative session. "If there is anything I can do for you, I am as close to you as the telephone."[4]

Knight's offer may have been in the back of Ahmanson's mind that July when he wrote to recommend Milt Shaw for building and loan commissioner. Sardonic as always, Ahmanson told Knight, "The only thing that makes me stand out as a duly constituted voter in the State of California is that I don't believe that I have ever written a letter to you—or the Governor, for anything." He had "meticulously stayed away from any effort to stick my nose in the affairs of the Building and Loan Commissioner's office—or even discuss the subject with anyone in Sacramento, including yourself." But efforts by the "recalcitrants" in the savings and loan industry to lobby for the appointment of "incompetents of the Home Loan Bank System" had aroused his ire. He characterized the work of the building and loan commissioner's office under Governor Warren and the retiring Frank Mortimer as "the most scrupulously honest government function that I was ever able to observe in operation." "I have no ax to grind whatsoever," Ahmanson said, "other than the fact that I am revolted by some of the names being suggested by the [savings and loan] industry." Reflecting his genuine lack of political entrée, he told Knight that he would "like to know how and to whom I can best say what I really think—namely, the best possible candidate for the job of Building and Loan Commissioner for the State of California from every standpoint is already acting in that capacity."[5] The letter apparently had little effect. Warren waited almost two years before selecting a permanent replacement for Mortimer and did not choose Shaw. Instead, he picked a four-star general and longtime friend with no previous background in the savings and loan industry.[6]

Other events suggest that in politics Ahmanson boxed well below his weight. In December 1952, Home's assets broke the one-hundred-million-dollar mark. The company asked Governor Warren to pose for a publicity photo with Ahmanson and Ken Childs. The governor's staff passed the request to Acting Commissioner Shaw and asked him to offer his "appraisal of this institution and your recommendation as to whether [the governor] should participate in such a photograph."[7] There's no record to indicate whether Warren posed for the photo, but Knight showed no hesitation. As lieutenant governor, he was often on hand when Home celebrated the takeover or opening of a branch.[8]

Knight's opportunity to become governor finally arrived in the summer of 1953.[9] Warren had not indicated whether he would stand for an unprecedented fourth term as governor. Knight was so eager that he made it clear that he would run regardless. Warren finally demurred and announced in the early fall that he would not be a candidate. Soon after this announcement, on September 8, Chief Justice Fred Vinson of the U.S. Supreme Court died. Three weeks later, Eisenhower picked Warren as the new chief justice of the United States.

"Hot diggity-dog," Knight said, when reporters told him the news.[10] He immediately began to solidify his control of the state Republican Party. He cemented his alliances with the state's two Republican U.S. senators— William Knowland and Thomas Kuchel. He sought Warren's and Nixon's endorsements for the 1954 gubernatorial race, and he began raising money.

Knight asked Ahmanson to be his finance chair and campaign manager in Southern California. Ahmanson was clearly pleased. He told reporters that Knight understood the "tremendous developments required to meet the needs of the constant stream of people coming into our state [and] to make it an even better place to live in for those already here."[11]

Ahmanson worked closely with the pioneers of political consulting in California, Clem Whitaker and Leone Baxter. Taking advantage of California's cross-filing laws, Whitaker and Baxter helped ensure that Knight won the Republican primary in June by a ten-to-one margin and nearly tied the Democratic contender in the Democratic primary.

With a substantial lead in the governor's race that summer, Knight and his campaign staff began to look farther down the road. Knight hoped to convince the national Republican Party to hold its nominating convention in California in 1956. If that happened, he wanted to ensure that he was in control of the state party. That meant electing a vice chairman (who would become chairman in 1956) who would be loyal to him. Ordinarily, this was an easy task. Party leaders usually deferred to the governor's choice. But in 1954 there was too much at stake for Knight's plan to go unchallenged.

Dwight Eisenhower hadn't committed to a second term. Indeed, he seemed to be leaning against it. In a letter to his brother Milton in mid-1954, he suggested that he planned to step down after one term. Facetiously, he told his brother that if he showed signs of changing his mind, Milton should "please call in the psychiatrist—or even better the sheriff."[12] With the president's plans uncertain, a number of potential GOP candidates quietly began positioning themselves to run, including Richard Nixon.

Knight was not a Nixon fan. As lieutenant governor, he had watched Nixon undercut Warren's favorite-son bid for the presidency in 1952 and then was famously snubbed by Nixon in a photo opportunity later that year.[13] Meanwhile, Nixon did not want Earl Warren's friends, including Senator Knowland and Governor Knight, to control the California delegation.[14] He wanted those votes if Eisenhower decided not to run. And if Eisenhower did run, Nixon wanted to be sure he could block any effort to dump him from the ticket.

Knight wanted Howard Ahmanson to chair the party in 1956. He was loyal, smart, and rich. During a trip to the East Coast in July 1954, Knight tried to secure Nixon's and Knowland's reassurance that they would support his nominee. He later said that Nixon "told me any fine person the State committee might select would be satisfactory to him."[15]

Reassured, Knight, a widower, turned his attention to his upcoming wedding to Virginia Carlson, a smart, charming, and unflappable writer and television producer whose first husband, an air force bombardier, had been killed in World War II. Anticipating that state party officials would do his bidding at the Central Committee meeting in August, Knight planned to be honeymooning with Virginia on a friend's yacht when the meeting took place.[16]

Before "Goodie" and Virginia could say their vows, opposition to his leadership team materialized.[17] The *Los Angeles Times* reported that Lieutenant Governor Harold J. Powers supported another candidate. The paper also suggested that Nixon was not happy. Knight called Nixon, who apparently reiterated his support for whomever Knight might endorse.[18] But the vice president's California friends in Congress said they were "miffed" that they hadn't been consulted.

For a week, the newspapers followed the split within the Republican Party over the Ahmanson issue. According to Representative Carl Hinshaw of Pasadena, Ahmanson was "an unknown" who lacked party experience. Northern California congressmen told the *Los Angeles Examiner:* "We don't know anything about Ahmanson. He hasn't passed the test of fire as far as we're concerned." With their Southern California brethren, a number of California Republican congressmen announced their support for Ray Arbuthnot, a La Verne citrus grower who had a long track record of activism and leadership within the party and, not coincidentally, was also a Nixon loyalist, having served on the vice president's campaign staff in 1952.

Knight wouldn't back down. He pledged a "fight to the finish." According to reporter Morrie Landsberg, he showed "a rare burst of anger" when he accused the Nixon loyalists of "breaking an agreement" over the issue. Senators Knowland and Kuchel backed Knight in this internecine battle. With Knight's wedding just five days away, Knowland tried to stop the intraparty fight by putting out a press release acknowledging his support for Ahmanson.[19] One newspaper reported that Knight had even taken the issue to Eisenhower, arguing that the controversy could jeopardize the GOP's chances to hold and gain congressional seats in California.[20]

With the battle still raging, Knight and Carlson were married in a small private ceremony. They had a reception at Hernando Courtright's Beverly Hills Hotel. Then they boarded a private yacht bound for Santa Cruz Island off the coast of Southern California. But while Knight and his wife enjoyed their time away, Nixon's operatives continued to lobby the members of the state's central committee. Furious when he learned about these efforts, Knight cut short his honeymoon.[21]

Back in Sacramento only two hours after he landed, Knight called a press conference to defend Ahmanson. "Seldom has the capitol press corps seen Knight so wrought up over a political situation," wrote one columnist. To belie the argument that Ahmanson was a newcomer to Republican politics, the governor recited Howard's political résumé: an original member of the California Republican Assembly in 1934, campaign manager for Charlie Fletcher's congressional campaign in 1946, member of Richard Nixon's congressional campaign organization in 1946, general chairman of Edward Shattuck's campaign for attorney general, active in Knight's campaign for lieutenant governor in 1950, and general chairman of Knight's Southern California primary campaign for governor. Blasting his political rivals, Knight asserted, "Some of those circulating the rumors that Ahmanson is new to GOP politics in California may not know these facts because they haven't been in the party that long, themselves."[22] After the press conference, Knight also called Republican members of the California Assembly, who made up a majority of the members of the Republican Central Committee. He made it clear that patronage for their districts would depend on their vote on the party leadership.[23]

With this kind of pressure, Ahmanson was elected by acclamation. The opposition was not able even to nominate Arbuthnot. In a biting speech, Congressman Patrick J. Hillings warned the Republican Party against "machine politics." Knowland responded to this criticism by saying that it was standard practice for governors to choose the heads of their parties. Satisfied with his victory, Knight told reporters he had not backed down because "I just had to demonstrate a few things: First, that I keep my promises, and secondly, that I am the Governor. Some people lost sight of that fact temporarily."[24]

Throughout this fight, Ahmanson said little publicly in his own defense. The criticisms, however, were withering to a man who had anticipated a triumphant entrance onto the grand stage of politics. Congratulating him on his election, Clem Whitaker and Leone Baxter acknowledged, "You may feel that you are entitled to commiseration, rather than congratulations, but we do want you to know that we think your election will be a great boon to the Party."[25] Shortly after the vote was taken, Ahmanson had breakfast with the governor in Los Angeles.[26] If Knight offered any words of solace or encouragement to his old friend, they went unrecorded. They were both soon immersed in the governor's general election campaign, which was expected to be a cakewalk.

The growing divide within the California Republican Party, however, grew serious enough that President Eisenhower came to Los Angeles in late September to campaign for unity.[27] He warned that the bickering might undermine Republican chances of keeping control of Congress and would jeopardize his own agenda.[28] His remarks were prescient, but these divisions would be particularly damaging, not in 1956, but when Knight would have to run for reelection in 1958.

The results of the party election and the Knight team's confidence during the fall campaign seemed to feed Ahmanson's tendency to swagger in public. With Knight headed for an easy victory in November, Ahmanson stood before a group of insurance executives that fall, his Norwegian blue eyes cold with determination, and declared, "When the time comes to appoint the insurance commissioner, I will appoint him."[29]

This bravado dismayed Knight supporter Nathan Fairbairn, the president of the California Compensation Insurance Company and Great Western Fire & Marine Insurance Company. "I have told these insurance executives repeatedly that the Governor has told me that the insurance companies should submit at least three names of the best insurance men qualified as an honest and impartial commissioner," Fairburn wrote to Clem Whitaker. The governor had reassured him that he would appoint one of the people recommended by the industry—and not the one chosen by Howard Ahmanson. Ahmanson told Whitaker that it was Fairbairn who was out of line. Nevertheless, he wrote, "I am not sore—I am not even upset, I am a Fairbairn fan and would marry him if he wasn't one of those repulsive characters who uses a power boat instead of sails."[30]

Knight stayed close to Ahmanson and to his good friend Howard Edgerton in the final months of the campaign. In the last week of August, at Edgerton's suggestion, Knight spoke at the Jonathan Club in Los Angeles to the Home Builders Committee.[31] Over the next several weeks, Knight and Ahmanson met several times to go over campaign finances. In November, when Knight trounced his Democratic opponent, Richard Graves, the entire team celebrated. Two weeks later, when Howard Edgerton was elected president of the U.S. Savings and Loan League at a convention held in Los Angeles and the league acknowledged Home Savings and Loan as the new national leader in the industry, the old friends who had listened together to the first news of the attack on Pearl Harbor in 1941 no doubt felt they were on top of the world.[32]

With the election over, Home Savings and Loan growing rapidly under Ken Childs's extraordinary management, and Milt Shaw installed as California commissioner of savings and loans in 1955, Ahmanson plunged into political organizing with his eye on the 1956 convention. He served as the California member of the Republican National Finance Committee.[33] In February, the Republican National Committee announced that the party would hold its convention in San Francisco. Asked about his role in influencing the decision, Ahmanson was coy. "I think the national party was impressed by our work in the last elections, but we can't leave out the attraction of our climate."[34]

THREE FRIENDS AND THE POLITICS
OF HOME OWNERSHIP

Ahmanson's deep involvement in Republican politics on the national and state levels and his close relationship with the incumbent governor were often viewed cynically by his critics and competitors. It's unclear how much he benefited from these connections. In 1955, the Antitrust Division of the U.S. Justice Department launched an investigation of H. F. Ahmanson and Home Savings. Certainly, it didn't hurt to have the ear of the governor of California or a Republican in the White House at this moment, but it also seems clear that there was hardly a case for the government to build on. Though National American Fire Insurance had become the leading residential property insurance company in Los Angeles, and Home Savings had become the largest thrift in the country, the links between these two businesses were not compelling in the context of the overall market, and the Justice Department quickly dropped its investigation. In other matters, Ahmanson, Home Savings, and the savings and loan industry didn't clearly find political or regulatory advantage. In January 1956, for example, President Eisenhower called for an end to the GI Bill's loan guaranty program. Noting that 4.5 million World War II veterans had acquired homes with help from the program, he suggested that nearly all eligible veterans had been served.[35] As the nation's largest retailer of VA loans, Home Savings could hardly have been pleased with the president's initiative. Fortunately for Home, neither was Congress.

These political and regulatory challenges did little to discourage Ahmanson's political enthusiasm. In March, Knight, Nixon, and Knowland announced the names of the California delegates to the Republican National Convention. Ahmanson was listed as one of Governor Knight's "delegates at large."[36]

Meanwhile, Home kept growing. In March, Howard announced that Home would acquire Pasadena Savings and Loan Association, with assets of more than $19 million, increasing Home's total portfolio to more than $395 million.[37] As he prepared for yet another sailboat race off the coast of California later that month, Howard must have felt that he was already in the race of his life and pulling far ahead of the competition. But the effort was taking a toll.

SPORT, HEALTH, AND HEART ATTACK

Ahmanson had fallen in love with the ocean soon after his arrival in Southern California. He bought his first racing sailboat in 1948. To be close to the water, Howard and Dottie looked for property near Newport Beach. Orange County's principal seaside resort, with its stucco Mediterranean-style villas, Newport had long been a weekend and summer destination for wealthy Angelenos. The most fashionable parts of the community were the islands—Balboa, Lido, and Harbor—in Newport Bay. On the western end of Harbor Island stood the house of the world-famous violinist Jascha Heifetz and his wife, Florence. Recently divorced from her husband, Florence wanted to sell the home.[38] In 1950, Howard and Dottie bought the property, added a large den and master bedroom, built a swimming pool, and constructed a two-story guest house on an adjoining lot.[39]

As his passion for sailing grew, Howard acquired a fifty-eight-foot vessel designed and built in 1933 by Johan Anker in Norway.[40] The boat had been owned by Roy Hegg, the president of San Diego Federal Savings and Loan. Hegg was indicted in 1952 along with twenty-three others for conspiracy to defraud the government using VA loans.[41] To pay for his defense, Hegg liquidated many of his assets.[42] He owed H. F. Ahmanson a considerable sum of money for insurance premiums. Howard agreed to take the boat instead. He renamed it *Sirius* after the "dog star," the brightest star in the night sky, named by the ancient Greeks, who associated it with the hot "dog days" of summer.

Whether the wind was howling or he was caught in the doldrums during a race, Howard enjoyed the company on his boat. The sun and the wind gave him a ruddy complexion with a barely noticeable tan. When he raced, he insisted on recruiting family, friends, business associates, or fellow sailing zealots from the Newport Harbor Yacht Club for his crew. "He did not want anyone saying that he bought victories," remembers TransAmerica Cup winner Bill Ficker.[43]

Given Ahmanson's competitive nature, it's not surprising that sailing precipitated a health crisis tied to the way he lived and worked. Four miles off the west end of Catalina Island in March 1956, Ahmanson's furious pace caught up with him. With ideal winds, thirty-five vessels had begun the

140-mile race from San Clemente more than twenty-four hours earlier. But then the winds died and the race became a "drifting match."[44] Through the night, the skippers tacked and turned trying to find some puff of breeze that would carry them forward. Taking the tiller in the morning, Howard had worked the boat forward, trying to build on *Sirius*'s lead. Suddenly, his left side went numb and he struggled for breath. He asked for a taste of scotch and then, in a semiconscious state from a mild heart attack, ordered the crew to keep going.[45] *Sirius* crossed the finish line shortly before 11:00 p.m. on Sunday night, the first of only six vessels to complete the race. Helped onto the dock, Ahmanson was quickly taken to a hospital.

For the next six weeks, he was under strict doctor's orders to minimize his activities.[46] He complained that "I have had, of course, endless hours of instructions about my future life," which all came down to the fact that he should work less.[47]

Begrudgingly, Ahmanson made a number of changes. He named Ken Childs president of Home Savings & Loan. As he explained to reporters, this was a move that was perhaps long overdue, since Childs had been effectively running the business on a day-to-day basis for years. Nonetheless, the gesture was appreciated. Childs's wife, Peg, wrote to Howard, "It was a generous gesture and a thoughtful one, too. Ken loves Home as if it was his own and, no matter how hard he works, I know that it will never hurt him because he takes such delight in what he is doing."[48]

Ahmanson then established himself in a home office so he could swim several times a day. He stayed away from yacht racing for a year. He stopped eating meat for a while, but he did not stop smoking or drinking pots of coffee and large amounts of liquor every day. Above all, the heart attack forced him to back away from politics.

KNIGHT, NIXON, AND SAN FRANCISCO

Although he remained on the delegate list and the host committee, Ahmanson's role in the Republican convention diminished. He chose Alphonzo Bell of Los Angeles to succeed him as chairman of the party.[49] Howard also passed some of his responsibilities to Charlie Fletcher, who served as treasurer for the California delegation.[50]

Despite his abdication of power, Howard attended the San Francisco convention as a delegate. Always quick to have his fill of crowds, he and Dottie rented a house in Atherton, a wealthy suburb south of San Francisco, for the week in addition to their hotel room in the city. In a characteristic display of sibling affection, Howard had invited his brother and sister-in-law, Hayden and Aimee, to come to San Francisco from Omaha and join the festivities.

Belying the lavish and elegant setting and the relative stability that should have been associated with the party's nomination of its sitting president, hostilities between factions in the California Republican Party continued to create drama at the convention. In the weeks leading up to the event, reporters pestered Knight to support Nixon's place on the ticket. Knight said only that the selection of a running mate was up to Eisenhower. No one was fooled. Less than two years into his tenure as governor, Knight clearly had ambitions to be president, and Nixon stood in his way.[51] When Eisenhower announced his support for Nixon at the last minute, the convention renominated the vice president. But long after the Republicans won in November, the enmity between Knight and Nixon would continue to play a critical role in the future of the party in California and would influence Howard Ahmanson's increasingly pragmatic approach to political power.

THE SWITCH

Although Ahmanson was quick to tell his friends that he had sworn off politics after 1956, in reality his businesses and personal relationships were too deeply intertwined with policy making for him to remain permanently on the sidelines. When the divisions in the Republican leadership fractured wide open in 1957 and Senator William Knowland decided to challenge Knight's bid for reelection, Ahmanson and Edgerton were drawn into an intramural fight to defend their longtime friend.

The events that became known as "the switch" began in stunning fashion even before Eisenhower's second inaugural in January 1957. In an interview with CBS, Knowland, the Republican leader in the Senate, impulsively revealed that he did not intend to run for reelection in 1958. The news shocked Washington and Sacramento and fueled speculation that Knowland might run for governor as a stepping-stone to the White House.[52] While Knight waited months for the senator to clarify his intentions, Knowland made several campaign-like tours through the state. Incensed, Knight announced in August that he would seek reelection and said he welcomed a primary race against the state's senior senator.[53]

The looming battle for governor was heavily influenced by the specter of the 1960 presidential race. Knowland, Knight, and Nixon were all obvious contenders. In the fall of 1957 it was widely rumored that Nixon intended to support Knowland for governor to get back at Knight for his efforts to dump Nixon from the ticket in 1956 and to make it difficult for Knowland, should he win the governorship, to break his faith with California to run for the presidency two years later.

There was also a deeper, more ideological quality to the looming battle. When Earl Warren was governor, many conservatives in the Republican Party were enthusiastic about Knight, thinking that he would be less amenable to New Deal–style approaches to government. As governor, however, Knight had been a disappointment to the conservatives. Knight built good relationships with labor and continued Warren's moderate, if not nonpartisan, approach. Knowland, on the other hand, was viewed as a strong fiscal conservative and an outspoken opponent of organized labor and communism. Some pundits predicted that a battle between the two of them would split the Republican Party and offer the Democrats their best chance to capture the governor's office in years.

Ahmanson proclaimed his full support for Knight. In a statement that was no doubt solicited by the governor's political team, Howard asserted that Knight's bid for reelection was "good news for Californians who place the welfare of our state above personal political aspirations." In the same story, Howard Edgerton said: "It was my pleasure to be one of Vice-President Nixon's supporters in the U.S. Senate campaign of 1950. It is now my pleasure to offer my support to another great Californian—Goodwin Knight."[54] Weeks later, still with no formal announcement of Knowland's candidacy, Knight was in Los Angeles and stayed with Howard and Dottie in their home. Writing his thank-you to Howard and Dottie on October 2, he noted sarcastically "how hard Bill is campaigning" despite his lack of an announcement.[55]

The following day, Knowland made his bid for governor official. He was unapologetic about challenging the party's sitting governor. "It is my belief that our citizens welcome the opportunity to nominate and elect their own public officials. The direct primary system has been in effect in California since 1910. I do not agree with those who say it is 'disruptive' or 'catastrophic' to have primary contests."[56]

Quickly it became apparent that Knowland had gathered the support of the party's leadership and primary voters. A year before the November 1958 election, polls showed Knight losing three-to-one. Through intermediaries, Nixon made it clear that if Knight ran for the Senate instead, he would find the financial support he needed; if he stayed in the race for governor, he wouldn't get any support. It's uncertain whether or how Ahmanson advised his friend at this critical moment in his political career, but Knight eventually caved to the pressure and announced that he would run for the Senate instead.[57]

The switch alienated many voters, who saw Knowland's run for governor as simply a self-serving step to the presidency. Knowland compounded his problems by alienating labor in a state where Democratic registrations outnumbered Republican. In the last months of the campaign, his organization fell apart.[58] Staffers quit. Funders closed their checkbooks. A month before election day, Goodwin Knight announced that he would not support Knowland for governor. On election day, Knowland lost by more than a million votes. Meanwhile, Democrat Claire Engle defeated Knight for the Senate and Democrats won a majority of the state's congressional seats.

Knight's defeat contributed to Ahmanson's retreat from active involvement in politics. He would later say, "I've never put in more time and done so little good."[59] But he was also clearly uncomfortable with the rough-and-tumble personal attacks. "I always felt like a Boy Scout," he told a reporter. "I was great at the all-citizens type of thing, but when it came to the backroom stuff, the pros had me over a barrel."[60] In reality, the Democratic victory began a new chapter in Ahmanson's political life.

The new Democratic governor, Edmund G. "Pat" Brown, had begun his political life in San Francisco as a Republican. After losing a race for the Assembly, he became a Democrat in 1934. He was elected district attorney ten years later. In 1950, he defeated Howard Ahmanson's longtime friend Edward Shattuck in the race for California attorney general. By 1958, however, Ahmanson had grown to like the gregarious attorney general, who seemed far more practical in his approach to government than Knowland and other conservatives in the Republican Party. Angry about Knowland's treatment of Knight, Ahmanson quietly provided financial support to Brown in the 1958 race. This support would open the door to a closer relationship with powerful Democrats in the years ahead.

Detractors suggested that Ahmanson's political activities and campaign contributions were simply aimed at protecting his own financial empire. Again they called him an octopus. Howard replied, with what one reporter called "mock horror," "Me an octopus? I'm more of the squirrel type." Indeed, Ahmanson seemed to be happiest quietly socking away cash like a squirrel storing acorns for the winter. "I'm so happy I'm rich," he said, "I'm willing to take all the consequences."[61] But success attracts attention, and by the mid-1950s other entrepreneurs were looking for ways to emulate Howard Ahmanson's success.

NINE

Big Business

HOME'S SUCCESS SPARKED a land rush of would-be entrepreneurs to Southern California's savings and loan business. At times, Commissioner Shaw and his staff were overwhelmed. Shaw complained that his Los Angeles office received an average of five phone calls a day from people who wanted to start new associations. He told Federal Home Loan Bank Board officials in Washington that he believed "promoters are moving into the field who are more interested in organization than they are in operation of an association." Speculators were filing applications with the intention of selling the licenses as soon as they obtained them.[1] Shaw suggested that the state and federal governments should jointly declare a moratorium on all new branches and charters. Inadvertently, he provided Ahmanson with an opportunity to solidify his first-mover advantages.

With $279 million in assets, Home dwarfed nearly every other thrift in the region. The company's nearest rival, Joe Crail's Coast Federal, had $202 million. Only three other thrifts had more than $100 million—Howard Edgerton's California Federal, Charles Wellman's Glendale Federal, and Adolph Slechta's Great Western.[2] Even more important, Home covered the broadest and richest geography. The company had nine branches in Long Beach, Highland Park, Huntington Park, Studio City, Arcadia, Glendale, Burbank, Lakewood, and Beverly Hills, in addition to its main office downtown at 800 South Spring Street. Other thrifts had only three or four offices at most.[3] Most of Home's branches had been acquired rather than started from scratch at a time when nobody wanted to buy a savings and loan. With Ahmanson's success, savings and loans were now valuable; any potential rival would have to pay a premium for an existing institution or be enormously successful in winning new licenses.

The FHLBB was reluctant to accept Shaw's proposal for a moratorium. Chairman Walter W. McAllister noted that the state had tried the same strategy sixteen months earlier. Since that ban had been lifted, the state had approved twenty new associations and eighteen branches. In the same period, the FHLBB had approved only one new federal association and seven branches. Given this track record, McAllister suggested, maybe the state ought to declare a unilateral moratorium.[4]

McAllister's criticisms were echoed by savings and loan executives operating with federal charters. Charles Wellman suggested that Shaw bore complete responsibility for the situation. If he was either unwilling or politically unable to stop approving new facilities, the FHLBB should draft standards for him that would preclude "overpopulating the industry." At a minimum, Wellman said, state and federal regulators should agree on "the simple principle of comity." Whenever multiple applications were pending for the same territory but in different regulatory jurisdictions, the state and the FHLBB ought to give preference to whichever application had been submitted first, regardless of whether it was from a state or federal association.[5] In Congress, Senator Estes Kefauver, who sat on the Judiciary Committee, expressed concern that a moratorium would raise antitrust issues.[6]

Shaw defended himself against this criticism. He pointed out that before approving an application his office required evidence that at least twenty-five thousand people in a community were not being served. Given Southern California's continued growth, additional savings and loan facilities were justified. He also noted that in the eighteen months elapsed since the lifting of the first ban, the state had processed seventy applications for Los Angeles and Orange Counties, forty of which had been denied. Seven of the approved facilities were not for new facilities but for the conversion of federally chartered institutions to state-chartered institutions (a further sign of the gold rush by individuals and executives who wanted an equity stake in the business).[7]

Ultimately, the FHLBB agreed to a one-year moratorium in the spirit of regulatory harmony.[8] With the announcement in June 1955, state and federal regulators also articulated a plan to survey the market in Los Angeles and Orange Counties in 1956 to determine the need for additional facilities and to develop new procedures and standards for future approvals.[9] A year later, however, the moratorium was extended for another six months.

With new competition prevented from entering the field, Home's growth in 1956 was spectacular. Its assets increased 41 percent, compared to a 25 percent increase for all savings and loans in California.[10] Savings deposits, the liquid cash that gave Home the ability to invest, rose 66 percent, from $217 million to more than $360 million. Meanwhile, other savings and loans in California grew their deposits by only 30.5 percent.[11] Acquisitions contributed to Home's growth, but most of these new deposits came from Ahmanson's continued marketing efforts to savers.

Never comfortable with the moratorium, the FHLBB finally made it clear to Shaw that the ban on new licenses in Los Angeles and Orange Counties should be lifted. Shaw reluctantly agreed. As he explained to the new FHLBB chairman, Albert Robertson, the situation in Southern California was unlike any other in the country. Already, there were ninety-six state and federal associations operating in these two counties, with an additional forty-eight branch locations. These thrifts had assets of $586 per person, compared to an average of $353 per person in savings and loans in the rest of the state. "The concentration of savings and loan facilities in the Los Angeles area is greater than in any other similar area in the United States," Shaw insisted, yet demand to enter the market continued to grow.[12]

This demand imposed a regulatory burden on Shaw's office and the state. During the previous eighteen months, the state had received requests from 215 individuals and groups that wanted to be advised when the ban was lifted. Shaw expected that as soon as the moratorium was lifted he would receive as many as a hundred applications for branches. "Unless some very rigid standards are adopted," he wrote, "it seems to me that the condition in the Los Angeles metropolitan area regarding approval of new facilities could become chaotic."[13] Ahmanson agreed. He expected incumbents to apply for new branches and "carpetbaggers" to seek charters.

While California and federal regulators debated new standards for license and branch approvals, some incumbents in the industry lobbied to restrict competition. They wanted new applicants to prove that a minimum of forty thousand people (rather than twenty-five thousand) were not being served by existing thrifts. Shaw and the FHLBB rejected this higher standard.

Indeed, within a week of the ending of the moratorium in January 1957, the commissioner's office received thirty applications for branches or charters, including four from Home Savings.[14] The pace of applications continued. From March through July, the commissioner's office held an extraordinary number of hearings but approved only a handful of new charters in the Southland.[15] It okayed nearly two dozen branches, including six for Home Savings.[16] The following year, Shaw also gave the green light to new facilities for Home in Santa Ana and Encino.[17]

Home continued to grow by acquisition and with the permission of the state. In April, having concluded negotiations with his longtime friend Mervyn Hope, who wanted to retire, Howard bought Hollywood Savings and Loan, including branches in the desert towns of Victorville and Barstow, east of Los Angeles. In June, the state also authorized a new branch in Compton.[18] But the pace of growth was slowing. In 1957, for the first time, Home Savings failed to keep pace with the field as a whole. The company's assets rose only 20 percent, compared to 21.5 percent for all state-chartered thrifts.[19]

As with all gold rushes, the arrival of so many new pilgrims seemed to coincide with the end of easy pickings and prompted some entrepreneurs to look for new ways to extract the gold. For thrifts, this meant adopting a new organizational structure.

HOLDING COMPANIES AND AN EFFORT TO MOVE NORTH

Holding companies offered two strategic advantages in the regulatory climate of the mid-1950s. First, they allowed investors to acquire existing savings and loans in different geographic areas without having to win permission from state or federal regulators for a new branch or charter. They also offered a structure conducive to the stock market, which gave these new companies greater access to capital and an easier way to realize gains from their investments. Critics suggested they simply provided speculators and stock promoters with a way to profit from the growing attention paid to the savings and loan industry.

The holding company movement in the thrift industry began in Southern California, the richest market in the country. In July 1955, a group of California investors working with Lehman Brothers organized the Great Western Corporation. With ten million dollars in private equity capital, the company acquired the assets of Great Western Savings and Loan and twenty-two escrow companies. The investors then filed a registration statement with the Securities and Exchange Commission for an initial public offering (IPO) of a half million shares of stock.[20]

Great Western's IPO sparked consternation in the industry. Smaller institutions feared that with massive infusions of capital from the stock market, speculative companies would begin aggressive efforts to open branches or acquire thrifts in an effort to increase their stock price. Members of the California and U.S. leagues suggested this would have a destabilizing effect on an industry that depended on depositors' trust to be successful. They called for legislation to ban the creation of savings and loan holding companies. Unfortunately for Ahmanson, the uproar came just as he was launching a major challenge to the traditional structure of the industry.

Localism was at the heart of the traditional savings and loan idea. In 1955, Ahmanson tried to acquire Home Mutual Savings and Loan of San Francisco and open offices in Oakland and Alameda. If approved by Milt Shaw and his staff, the deal would have marked the first time that state regulators allowed a savings and loan to operate in both Northern and Southern California.[21]

Ahmanson's proposal ignited a firestorm among competitors. Many felt that holding companies, including H. F. Ahmanson & Co., had already circumvented the regulators' efforts to confine savings and loan entrepreneurs to local communities. For example, Mark Taper's Los Angeles-based holding company, First Charter Financial Corp, had purchased Pioneer Savings in San Jose in 1955. The following year, H.F. Ahmanson & Co. paid $2.2 million for a 93 percent stake in Guaranty Savings and Loan of San Jose.[22] In each of these instances, because the holding company made the purchase and the acquired thrift was not legally integrated with either Taper's American Savings or Ahmanson's Home Savings in the Southland, regulators had no basis for denying the deal.[23] But competitors vowed to thwart any effort by Taper, Ahmanson, or anyone else to develop a statewide brand.

Dozens of rivals appeared at a hearing on December 28 to consider Home's San Francisco acquisition. Altogether, thirty-nine state-chartered savings and loan associations, representing 40 percent of the state's total, filed objections. With Home paying 3.5 percent on deposits in Los Angeles and most Bay Area companies paying only 3.0 percent, the protestors feared a rate war that they would lose. Elwood Hansen, the president of Bay View Federal Savings and Loan, told the commissioner that Bay Area companies maintained liquidity that was more than double the rate of Los Angeles associations. By implication, it was fine for Angelenos to take greater risks, but Bay Area depositors were more prudent and the state should protect them. Howard Stevens, who had served as president of the California Savings and Loan League, argued that if Home set up shop in San Francisco it would violate the FSLIC's rule that companies could not lend more than fifty miles away from their offices. Commissioner Shaw said he would consider these points.[24]

Politically, Ahmanson's expansion and the controversy over holding companies converged. In Washington, Henry Bubb, Ahmanson's friend from Kansas and the eloquent champion of small government, now led the U.S. league's efforts to seek protection from Congress. As chairman of the U.S. Savings and Loan League's legislative committee, he was preparing to announce that the league would ask Congress to outlaw holding companies in the savings and loan industry. By the nature of their service, Bubb told the press, "savings and loan associations are and should be locally owned, locally operated and locally managed institutions."[25]

Although H. F. Ahmanson & Company was not technically a holding company and Howard had no intention of taking the company public, he was clearly bent on geographic expansion that flew in the face of Bubb's sentiment. With the U.S. Savings and Loan League up in arms over the issue, neither California commissioner Milt Shaw nor FHLBB chairman Walter W. McAllister wanted to give Ahmanson what he wanted. They pressured him to withdraw his petition. Rather than jeopardize his relationships with these regulators, on January 25, 1956, the same day that Bubb offered the league's statement in Washington, Home withdrew its request and dropped its effort to move into Northern California.[26]

In Sacramento and Washington, the regulators were pleased and grateful. McAllister praised Shaw for the way he had handled the situation. He also took note that Ahmanson had "so graciously indicated an 'out' for the San Francisco situation." That out may have been regulatory approval for a deal closer to home—the acquisition of Pasadena Savings and Loan Association.[27] Regardless, Ahmanson's retreat reflected his continuing commitment to the basic concept of cooperation between regulated and regulator that permeated the managed economy.

Ahmanson's deal had little effect on the growing debate over localism in the banking and thrift industries. In 1958, bankers were able to persuade Congress to pass the Bank Holding Company Act, which limited the ability of holding companies to engage in interstate banking and extended many of the "compartmentalized" principles of Glass-Steagall to the holding company environment.[28] Meanwhile, in the thrift industry, the U.S. Savings and Loan League got a similar bill introduced in Congress. Considered a temporary measure until lawmakers could resolve issues facing the industry, the Spence Act was passed and signed by the president in 1959. It barred existing holding companies from acquiring additional savings institutions, and new holding companies were allowed to control only one savings and loan.[29]

Unfortunately for the industry's lobbyists, the law did not apply retroactively. Existing holding companies like H. F. Ahmanson & Co., Great Western, and First Charter were not forced to divest. As a result, early movers like Howard Ahmanson, Stuart Davis, and Mark Taper gained added protection from potential rivals and were free to continue to build personal financial empires with institutions that many people across the country still insisted should be communitarian or cooperative in nature.

The effort to block the development of holding companies in financial services evidenced all of the aspects of regulatory and political competition that were the hallmarks of the managed economy in the late 1950s and early 1960s. While consumers were largely ignored and played little role in the political debate, the trade associations battled on behalf of the many smaller, weaker thrifts that littered the competitive landscape while the larger companies, like Home Savings, employed their own lobbyists or made their case directly to elected officials. When legislative action finally came, it was too late to hinder the biggest players. Although Howard Ahmanson was forced to abandon his plans for statewide expansion, his graciousness in accommodating the government's interests resulted in other business opportunities.

FIGURE 1. Hayden Ahmanson was almost eight years older than his brother Howard. After Hayden left home to attend high school at the Kemper Military Academy and then enrolled at the University of Nebraska, Lincoln, Howard grew up as the only child in the house. Nevertheless, the brothers remained close and were deeply involved in National American Fire Insurance throughout their adult lives. (Photographer unknown. The Ahmanson Foundation Collection.)

FIGURE 2. Aimee, Florence, William, Hayden, and Howard Ahmanson (left to right) in Omaha. With Will's death in 1925, Howard moved himself and his mother to Los Angeles, where he finished college at the University of Southern California and launched his own insurance agency. Hayden and his wife, Aimee, remained in Omaha, and Hayden worked as an executive with the insurance company his father had founded in 1919. (Photographer unknown. The Ahmanson Foundation Collection.)

FIGURE 3. Omaha insurance executive William H. Ahmanson doted on his son Howard. After dinner, even when Howard was still in elementary school, father and son would discuss business and finance "as if I had the maturity and judgment of a man of 50," Howard recalled. When Will died suddenly in 1925, Howard was devastated. In part, his subsequent entrepreneurial drive was rooted in his desire to realize his father's ambitions. (Photographer unknown. The Ahmanson Foundation Collection.)

FIGURE 4. Howard Ahmanson launched his own insurance agency in August 1926 while he was still a student at the University of Southern California and just twenty years old. He was a persistent salesman and a shrewd judge of risk. Underwriters were astounded by the low loss rate on his fire insurance policies. With low losses, he earned high commissions and profits. During the worst years of the Depression, he made his first million dollars. (Photographer unknown. The Collection of Howard and Roberta Ahmanson.)

FIGURE 5. Glamorous and spirited, Dorothy "Dottie" Johnston Grannis worked as a social secretary for Paramount producer David O. Selznick and was a student at the University of California, Southern Branch (UCLA) in the late 1920s. She and Howard Ahmanson dated for more than six years before they were married in 1933. (Photographer unknown. The Collection of Howard and Roberta Ahmanson.)

FIGURE 6. Howard Ahmanson posed with the rest of his naval class at Quonset, Rhode Island, in 1943 (second row, second from the end on the right). They ranged from "excited kids to old time blasé naval officers." He was the "worst driller in the place," he wrote his wife, Dorothy. Though he was "lousy" at sports, he enjoyed the eight weeks of camaraderie. (Photographer unknown. The Collection of Howard and Roberta Ahmanson.)

FIGURE 7. Still eligible for the draft at the age of thirty-seven in 1943, Howard Ahmanson applied for a commission in the U.S. Navy. During the war, from his "foxhole at the Shoreham" Hotel in Washington, D.C., he was a chief expediter in the Aircraft Products Division at the Pentagon. His year in Washington deepened his political and business contacts and helped shape his perspective on the postwar economy. (Photo by John Engstead. The Collection of Howard and Roberta Ahmanson.)

FIGURE 8. Although his business empire was largely confined to Southern California, Howard Ahmanson traveled widely. Following a bout of ill health in 1951, he and his wife, Dorothy, took nephew Robert Ahmanson on a two-month trip to North Africa, Israel, and Europe. (Photographer unknown. The Collection of Howard and Roberta Ahmanson.)

FIGURE 9. Always the salesman, Howard Ahmanson sent stacks of postcards to his savings and loan customers when he traveled abroad. When copies of this image of Dorothy, Robert, and Howard Ahmanson in France in 1951 arrived in Southern California mail-boxes, *Los Angeles Times* society columnist James Copp noted the car and Dottie's leopard fur coat. (Photographer unknown. The Collection of Howard and Roberta Ahmanson.)

FIGURE 10. Howard Ahmanson and Goodwin Knight became friends in the mid-1930s when they both had offices in the same building in downtown Los Angeles. After Knight succeeded Earl Warren as governor of California in 1953, Ahmanson agreed to serve as the finance chairman of Knight's gubernatorial campaign. (Photographer unknown. The Collection of Howard and Roberta Ahmanson.)

FIGURE 11. Although they maintained a cordial relationship, Ahmanson was the victim of Richard Nixon's efforts to control the California Republican Party in 1954. After Goodwin Knight picked Ahmanson to serve as vice chairman of the party, Nixon's allies tried to block Ahmanson's election. Knight and Ahmanson prevailed, but the incident exacerbated growing tensions within the party. (Gift of the Rothschild Family; photograph by Otto Rothschild. UCLA Special Collections Library.)

FIGURE 12. In 1950, Howard and Dorothy Ahmanson bought the Lloyd Wright–designed home and property once owned by violinist Jascha Heifetz and his wife, actress Florence Vidor, on Harbor Island. With the help of Millard Sheets and another architect, the Ahmansons added a large den and master bedroom, built a swimming pool with a bridge over it that led to the front door, and constructed a two-story guest house on an adjoining lot. From this retreat, the family regularly set sail on the *Sirius* on weekends. (Photographer unknown. The Ahmanson Foundation Collection.)

FIGURE 13. Competitive by nature, Howard and Dorothy Ahmanson began racing sailboats with their nephews, William and Robert, soon after the end of the war. By the late 1950s, the couple spent most weekends with their son, Howard junior, on the boat or in their second home on Harbor Island in Newport Beach. (Photographer unknown. The Collection of Howard and Roberta Ahmanson.)

FIGURE 14. Evelyn Barty (right) managed the details of Howard Ahmanson's life for more than twenty-five years. A musician and singer, she had performed with her sister Dolores and brother Billy in the 1930s. While her brother went on to be a Hollywood star, Evelyn landed a job at H. F. Ahmanson & Co. She frequently accompanied the Ahmansons on their trips abroad and often performed with Howard during the voyage across the ocean. (Photographer unknown. Collection of Dolores Morse.)

FIGURE 15. After Home Savings & Loan surpassed all rivals in 1953, Ahmanson ran a series of ads associating the company with other American icons: Mt. Whitney, Hoover Dam, the Golden Gate Bridge, the Grand Canyon, Niagara Falls, the U.S.S. *Midway* aircraft carrier, the Los Angeles Coliseum, and the General Sherman giant sequoia—all the "largest in America." (JPMorgan Chase & Company.)

FIGURE 16. Howard Edgerton, the CEO of California Federal Savings & Loan (CalFed), was a close friend and competitor throughout Ahmanson's career. A pilot, Edgerton added a heliport to the top of the CalFed headquarters so he could commute by helicopter. (Photographer unknown. Courtesy of Beverly Adair.)

FIGURE 17. Overweight and bookish as a girl, Caroline Leonetti transformed her life through self-discipline and the study of charm and fashion. After winning a beauty contest at the 1939 World's Fair, she founded her own school and modeling agency in San Francisco. A single mother, she became a regular on Art Linkletter's radio program. When Linkletter moved to television and Los Angeles, Leonetti moved as well. Howard Ahmanson met her at a wedding shortly after he separated from his wife Dorothy. (Photographer unknown. Collection of Margo Leonetti O'Connell.)

FIGURE 18. Interpersonal tensions between Howard Ahmanson, Norton Simon, and Richard Brown were reflected in the inscription carved in stone in the new Los Angeles County Museum of Art. Simon and Brown were given credit for conceiving the museum. Ahmanson's lead gift provided the impetus for the project. Ahmanson's close ties to members of the Los Angeles County Board of Supervisors, including Ernest E. Debs (pictured here with Caroline Leonetti Ahmanson to his right and his wife, Lorene, to his left), played a key role in winning political support for the project. (Photographer unknown. Collection of Margo Leonetti O'Connell.)

FIGURE 19. Howard Ahmanson's nephews, William (left) and Robert (right), left Omaha as teens during the war. Both graduated from UCLA and went to work for their prosperous uncle. After Howard's death, William became CEO of H. F. Ahmanson & Co. and chairman of Home Savings & Loan. Robert became the president of the Ahmanson Foundation. (Photographer unknown. Collection of Margo Leonetti O'Connell.)

FIGURE 20. Howard Ahmanson and Caroline Leonetti were married in a simple ceremony at Robert and Kathleen Ahmanson's home on January 14, 1965. He was fifty-eight years old. She was forty-six. (Photographer unknown. Collection of Margo Leonetti O'Connell.)

FIGURE 21. University of Southern California president Norman Topping was a friend, neighbor, and sailing partner. Topping encouraged Ahmanson to join the university's board of trustees in 1961. The following year Ahmanson gave $1 million to help fund the development of a biosciences research center on campus. Designed by William Pereira, the center opened in April 1964. (SC Photo. Doheny Memorial Library. University of Southern California, on behalf of the USC Archives.)

FIGURE 22. Caroline Leonetti Ahmanson and architect William Pereira. Although one critic called him "Hollywood's idea of an architect," Pereira was one of the most prolific and influential architects in Southern California in the mid-1960s. With his space-age designs, he was the favorite of the region's aerospace industry. His master plans included the University of California campuses at Santa Barbara and Irvine. A close friend and business associate of Howard Ahmanson from the mid-1950s, Pereira developed plans for many of Home Savings & Loan's developments in the 1960s. (Photographer unknown. Collection of Margo Leonetti O'Connell.)

FIGURE 23. Howard Ahmanson had hoped that his son, Howard Fieldstad Ahmanson Jr., nicknamed "Steady" when he was young, would grow up to inherit his father's financial empire. Often cared for by his aunt Aimee (far right) when his parents were traveling, Howard junior coped with undiagnosed Tourette's syndrome. His parents enrolled him at Black-Foxe Military Institute, hoping it would provide structure. Howard junior loved the uniform and wore it constantly. (Photo by Irving L. Antler. The Collection of Howard and Roberta Ahmanson.)

FIGURE 24. When he announced plans to build the Ahmanson Center in October 1967, Howard Ahmanson envisioned a massive three-building office and commercial complex reminiscent of the Rockefeller Center in New York. Architect Edward Durrell Stone, designer of the Kennedy Center in Washington, planned a plaza in the tradition of the great cities of Europe that would serve as a public gathering place. Ahmanson died before the project broke ground. (Photographer unknown. Los Angeles Public Library Photo Collection.)

TEN

The Crest of a New Wave

IN JULY 1957, Howard and Dottie invited the Fletchers and the Edgertons to Harbor Island to catch up. "Put a couple of extra bolts in the diving board," Edgerton responded, "and practice up on your finest martinis."[1]

All three men had come a long way since 1941. After seventeen years of marriage, Howard and Dottie's home had been transformed when Dottie gave birth to a son on February 3, 1950. Howard senior spoiled Howard junior and pronounced him a genius, just as his father had done with him. The Edgertons' children, a daughter and a son, were grown and in college or graduated. Fletcher's children were also entering adulthood. Charlie's oldest son, Kim, had worked for H. F. Ahmanson & Co. at the age of fourteen. He spent the summer of 1942 as a "runner and sorter," picking up insurance contracts at one agency and delivering them to another.[2] After graduating from Stanford University in 1950, he went to work for his father, who was grooming him to become president of Home Federal. With seven-year-old Howard junior evidencing precocious intellectual abilities, Howard also imagined the day when his son would take over his empire.

All three men had benefited substantially from the growth of the savings and loan industry and the incredible expansion of home ownership in Southern California. By 1957, Home Savings and Loan was the largest in the country. Edgerton's California Federal ranked sixth. Charlie Fletcher's Home Federal was seventy-seventh.[3] But each approached business differently.

Edgerton had survived his prewar brush with the law to become a leader in the trade association. He served on committees and became president of the California Savings and Loan League in 1948. Seven years later, he was elected president of the U.S. Savings and Loan League.[4] He was also actively and visibly involved in public policy. On three occasions, Edgerton had tried to convert California Federal from a mutual to a stock company, a conversion that would have given him equity and a much greater stake in California Federal's growth. Each time, the government turned him down. "I wasn't smart enough to realize that I should have forgotten this little company and gone out and organized a new one," he later lamented.[5]

Charlie Fletcher had inherited money and position, and his intellect added to his good looks and charisma. He had failed to win reelection to Congress in 1948, but he stayed involved in federal policy making, especially on housing issues. "He thought private industry and home ownership were better than building big [public housing] edifices like they had in Chicago and New York," Kim Fletcher remembers. But he believed government had a role to play in housing. Home Federal underwrote the first VA tract in the San Diego area. As a lender and citizen, Fletcher also became active in antipoverty programs in San Diego. He and his wife, Jeannette, were both involved in the Urban League.[6]

Of the three, Howard alone never bore the industry's mantle of leadership. He appreciated and respected his competitors, who, like Edgerton and Fletcher, were often his friends, but he often went his own way. California Federal and Home Savings battled for customers in many of the same neighborhoods in Los Angeles and Orange Counties. That rivalry helped to keep Home strong. "The better your competition," Ahmanson once told a reporter, "the better it makes you."[7]

Ahmanson also had good reason to maintain his relationships with Edgerton, Fletcher, and potential savings and loan competitors. Despite the rivalry for market share and bragging rights in the industry, fire insurance was still important to all of them. In this arena, Ahmanson needed the political support of his longtime customers.

THE CONTINUED IMPORTANCE OF THE FIRE INSURANCE BUSINESS

The changing regulatory environment may have been one reason that Ahmanson got into the savings and loan business. It also offers a case study in the political competition associated with the managed economy. As Edgerton had warned Ahmanson and Fletcher in 1944, independent insurance agents were exerting increasing pressure on legislators to prevent mortgage lenders, especially savings and loans, and automobile financing companies, from tying insurance policies to loans. Savings and loans countered that revenues from writing insurance helped thrifts to attract and retain personnel. Mortgage lenders and auto dealers also asserted that they had a legitimate right to participate in the selection of the insurer. Their money was on the line.

Across the country, independent insurance agents were starting to score victories on this issue of "coercion." In 1944, the U.S. Supreme Court had broken with tradition and ruled that insurance companies were in fact engaged in interstate commerce and thus could be subjected to the federal anti-trust and fair trade practices acts.[8] The court's decision brought new pressure on tying relationships between lenders and insurance. It raised the specter of antitrust prosecution. It also put new pressure on state legislators to enact anticoercion laws.

State efforts to regulate these tying relationships gained momentum in 1941 when Nebraska passed a Small Loan Act that prohibited a lender from requiring the borrower to purchase insurance from the lender. Between 1947 and 1950, fourteen other states passed similar laws.[9] In California, state senator George Miller Jr. introduced an "anticoercion" bill in January 1949.

Economic interests rallied to support and oppose Miller's bill. Independent insurance agents and brokers sent more than sixty supportive letters and telegrams to the committee considering the measure, but lenders—especially savings and loans—along with contractors and nearly two dozen insurance agents opposed the bill.[10] Governor Earl Warren apparently sided with the independent insurance agents, but as one of Warren's chief deputies noted, "The Legislative branch has not been willing to join in taking this progressive step."[11]

The legislature did agree to study the issue.[12] The report issued by the Assembly Interim Committee on Finance and Insurance in 1950 suggested that changing the pervasive practice of tying insurance to mortgage loans would not be easy. Testimony from Commissioner Luke Kavanaugh of Colorado noted, "While I think our statute on unfair competition is a good one . . . it is practically impossible to enforce some of its provisions. For instance building and loan institutions, and others about to make a loan, want to write the insurance. If they cannot write the insurance they refuse to make the loan. If any insurance department attempted to stop this indirect coercion, it would have time for nothing else."[13] In Georgia, insurance commissioner Zack Cravey offered a similar perspective. Noting that the law passed by the state legislature included "no sanctions" against violators, he believed it would do little to deter lenders. "The procedure prescribed by the act is so extensive and its sanctions are so slight that I am disposed to believe it will not serve as a strong deterrent."[14] In Ohio, a subsidiary of General Motors went to court to block a similar law from taking effect.[15] With this kind of testimony, Ahmanson and the savings and loan industry were able to block new legislation in California through most of the 1950s.[16]

Meanwhile, H. F. Ahmanson & Co. continued to nurture its relationships with thrift managers.[17] Every issue of the *Savings and Loan Journal* published by the California Savings and Loan League featured a full-page, inside-cover ad for H. F. Ahmanson & Co. Every year at the state convention, H. F. Ahmanson & Co. sponsored the major cocktail party. But few people in the industry or the marketplace really knew how profitable the company was until one day in 1951 when a young man in Omaha paid Hayden Ahmanson a visit.

UPSTART IN OMAHA

Warren Buffett had never seen a cheaper stock. He was only twenty years old, but he had been picking stocks for years. Recently graduated from Columbia University, he was poring over the pages of *Moody's Bank and Finance Manual* "with the zest of a small boy reading comics," looking for good deals.[18] National American Fire Insurance shares were selling for an amount equal to the company's annual earnings. An investor could recoup the cost of investment with the earnings from a single year. Anything further would be gravy.[19] Most surprising, National American was headquartered a block and a half away from his father's investment management company's office.

Hayden Ahmanson undoubtedly recognized the name of the son of Omaha's former congressman and was friendly right from the beginning. He recounted the history of National American.[20] "He told me all about Howard, how he had gone west to California. He told me about his boys who were out there. He advised me to go there, saying that's where the real opportunity is." Buffett heard the awe in Hayden's voice.

He also realized that Howard Ahmanson was steering the best low-risk insurance business from Home Savings' mortgages to National American, ensuring that losses were remarkably low and National American was extremely profitable.[21] As Buffett later discovered, Howard had also enhanced National American's value by selling small portions of the equity of Home Savings and Loan and another thrift to National American.[22]

Howard didn't want anyone else in the market for National American's shares. He owned nearly 70 percent of the company's stock. The rest was still sitting in the drawers of Nebraska and Iowa farmers and small-town merchants who had bought the stock in 1919 and had little idea what it was worth. Hayden had given a local stockbroker a list of all of National American's shareholders. That broker quietly kept tabs and when someone was ready to sell, he bought the shares on behalf of H. F. Ahmanson & Co.

Buffett wanted in on this good deal and began looking for shares to buy. He was willing to pay thirty-five dollars a share, but finding stock was difficult. Hayden's broker "regarded me as a punk kid," Buffett recalls. He refused to sell shares to Buffett and wouldn't let him see the list of stockholders. When Buffett attended National American's annual meeting and asked to see the list, Hayden politely but firmly refused.[23] Then Buffett left Nebraska for Wall Street to work for his idol and mentor, the legendary investor Ben Graham. Over the next four years while he was in New York, he quietly continued to accumulate National American stock, but it was slow going.

Buffett returned to Omaha in 1956.[24] While establishing several investment partnerships that would eventually make him famous, he and his lawyer and friend Dan Monen decided to pursue National American's shares more aggressively. Buffett visited the office of the state insurance commissioner to research the history of the first directors of National American. He reasoned that these investors would have bought stock and encouraged their friends and neighbors to buy some as well. With Buffett's list, Monen barreled down two-lane highways in his red-and-white Chevrolet, pulling into small rural towns to track down the oldest residents. He asked about the former directors of National American and tried to discover what had happened to their stock.[25]

Word spread that there were buyers and the stock's price climbed. When it reached one hundred dollars a share, according to Buffett, "that was the magic number, because it was what they [the shareholders] had paid in the first place."[26] Suddenly lots of people wanted to sell. Monen found his biggest cache of stock in the small town of Eustis, the "sausage capital of Nebraska," where the original stock promoters had given a local banker a seat on the board of directors.

Not wanting to alert Howard and Hayden to the run they were making, Buffett and Monen left the shares in the names of the previous owners, using a power of attorney to exercise control. When they had accumulated nearly two thousand shares, or approximately 10 percent of the equity, Buffett walked into Hayden's office. "I plopped them all down and said I wanted to transfer them to my name."

"My brother's going to kill me," Hayden groaned.[27]

Buffett had never met Howard Ahmanson. "All I knew was that this guy was smart, and he was in a field that I was interested in—insurance," Buffett recalls.

Buffett held onto the stock for about a year. "I knew Howard would have liked to buy it," Buffett laughs, "but he wasn't going to pay some kid a big profit to get it."[28] Around the fall of 1958, Buffett sold his stock to a wealthy New York businessman who had made his money with Welch's Grape Juice, netting a profit of more than one hundred thousand dollars.[29] According to biographer Roger Lowenstein, this was "Buffett's first big strike."[30] To Ahmanson, it was a nuisance, but Howard had one reason to be grateful: Buffett had helped to redeem his father's legacy. At one hundred dollars a share, some shareholders felt that they had finally gotten their money back (though this ignored four decades of opportunity cost!).

POLITICAL PRESSURE ON INSURANCE

What Buffett saw in National American's stock became increasingly apparent to others. The synergy between Home Savings and National American Insurance was very profitable. By the beginning of 1957, H. F. Ahmanson & Co. was writing more than 50 percent of all the fire insurance on homes in Los Angeles and Orange Counties.[31] This accounted for 80 percent of National American's business.[32] For each of these policies, H. F. Ahmanson & Co. received a commission from National American. Since Howard owned most of the stock of National American, he also accumulated capital in the unpaid dividends that were held to bolster National American's reserves.

Independent insurance agents, who struggled to compete against Ahmanson's behemoth, continued to complain to regulators, legislators, and other elected officials. They suggested that Home Savings coerced builders seeking financing to buy fire insurance from National American. Home Savings & Loan's executives countered that borrowers could buy fire insurance from 135 highly rated capital-stock companies. Unsatisfied, the critics noted that the list didn't include any mutual or reciprocal companies, no matter how highly rated.[33] A U.S. Department of Justice investigation failed to reveal a case worth pursuing.

While one arm of the government looked at the growing market power of National American, another saw the advantages in the company's increasing scope and scale. In December 1960, H. F. Ahmanson & Co., representing National American, won an exclusive contract worth two million dollars a year in premiums from the California Department of Veterans Affairs to provide fire insurance on all CalVet-financed homes. The exclusive contract, negotiated by Robert DeKruif, brought cries of outrage from other insurance agents. Previously, nearly three hundred firms had been supplying fire insurance to the CalVet program. State Director for Veterans Affairs Joseph M. Farber, however, argued that the old system was inefficient and costly to the program's veteran home buyers. He estimated that the new agreement would save CalVet's 150,000 property owners $5.15 million a year. Moreover, H. F. Ahmanson had agreed to expand coverage under the agreement to include damage caused by landslides and other earth movement—a critical concern in many areas of the state.[34] With a deal that offered more coverage at a lower rate, Farby asked, how could the state go wrong?

With the CalVet deal, Ahmanson once again demonstrated how adept he and his organization were at aligning their business interests with the policy ambitions of government. Ahmanson also showed his continued ability to find profits in serving the financial needs of middle-income Californians. In the late 1950s, however, he began to shift his emphasis to focus on conventional home buyers who did not need government subsidies. He also looked for opportunities to broaden the scope of his business operations by launching businesses in related financial services.

CONTINUED DIVERSIFICATION
IN FINANCIAL SERVICES

Howard opened the Ahmanson Bank and Trust Company in 1958 in luxurious offices at 9145 Wilshire Boulevard. Advertisements in the *Los Angeles Times* made it clear that he did not intend to invade the field of general commercial banking. Instead, he proposed to "serve, and serve with exceptional facilities, the *forgotten area* of banking—the substantial personal account." The bank's slogan, "A Distinguished Bank for Distinguished People," said it all. Ahmanson promised that in his private bank, customers would not wait in line. "You will be served by the most highly paid staff per person in banking, and we hope the most competent." If customers couldn't come to the bank, an officer would come to them. To make sure that children would be discouraged from coming to the bank, Howard had the counters designed so that small children couldn't reach them with their jars of pennies.[35] "We do not propose to be all things to all men," Ahmanson continued, "but we do promise to put service above profit—to excel in the field we have chosen—to remain permanently a strong, conservative, independent bank."[36]

From some points of view, becoming a banker should have been easy for Howard Ahmanson and his organization. In reality, according to Robert DeKruif, "We were a horrible flop." Banks offered a much broader array of services than savings and loans and required different kinds of analytical skills to assess risk. After a number of years in the business, Howard conceded it wasn't going anywhere. "We're only good when we concentrate in home loans," he confessed.[37]

Ahmanson's recognition of the importance of focusing on homes was reflected in other conversations. As an aspiring young executive in Ahmanson's empire in the early 1960s, John Notter dreamed of a career in international finance. One day, he rode with Howard in his limousine to the Ahmanson house at La Quinta and told Howard about his ambitions. He pointed out that with Home's capital base there was nothing that would preclude it from getting into international markets. Howard responded, "I made my fortune here in California. There's no reason to go international. There's no reason to go to New York. I'm staying right here."[38] The lesson of the White Spot hamburger joint in Lincoln stayed with him—stick with what you know and what works.

ONE BILLION

In the summer of 1961, *Business Week* noted the emergence in Southern California of a new breed of millionaires who had "struck it rich in the fast-growing savings and loan industry, which is prospering most dramatically in California." Howard Ahmanson, "the richest of this new group," was profiled on the cover with Home's headquarters at Wilshire and Rexford rising behind him. With a white handkerchief folded neatly into his suit coat pocket, he gazed away from the camera, his thinning hair tousled by the wind. The caption noted that he "has been the fastest stepper in a trend that has reshaped mortgage lending."[39]

The magazine surveyed Ahmanson's empire: near-total control of Home Savings and Loan, majority control of National American Insurance Co., the Ahmanson Bank & Trust, and a "commanding stake" in two savings and loan holding companies: United Financial Corporation and First Surety Corporation (which was on the verge of going public). When asked how he had built his empire, Ahmanson gave the impression "that he has achieved his position more by accident than by design."[40] In fact, Howard had shrewdly ridden and driven the rise of the savings and loan industry along the crest of the great wave of postwar home building.

Two weeks before Christmas that year, Howard and Home Savings celebrated a milestone. The company had surpassed the billion-dollar mark for assets. Howard invited six hundred people to a luncheon celebration in the ballroom of the ornate Biltmore Hotel overlooking Pershing Square in downtown Los Angeles. The attendees included the mayors of Pasadena, Beverly Hills, and Los Angeles as well as several members of the Los Angeles County Board of Supervisors.[41] Art Linkletter served as the master of ceremonies. When it came time for Howard to speak, the audience rose for a standing ovation. He choked back the emotion, his blue eyes watering, his ruddy face flushing even more deeply. He abandoned his prepared speech. Instead, he began to name each of the executives who had played a key role in Home's success, summarizing their contributions.[42]

At times, the great success of Home Savings and the wealth that derived from all of his business activities seemed stunning even to Ahmanson. Like other American entrepreneurs who amassed great fortunes, he was increasingly besieged with requests for money for local charities and institutions. He and Dottie opened their checkbook to many requests. Their social life was set to the rhythm of charity events, but they were not big donors. As his health improved, Howard and Dottie returned to racing on the high seas and they continued to travel. But increasingly Ahmanson was thinking about aesthetics and the relationship of art to commerce and community.

ELEVEN

Southland Patrician

HOWARD AHMANSON SENT a cryptic letter to painter and sometime architect Millard Sheets in 1953. According to Sheets, it was almost like a telegram:[1]

> Dear Sheets. Saw photograph building you designed, L.A. Times. Liked it. I have two valuable properties, Wilshire Boulevard, need buildings. Have driven Wilshire Boulevard twenty-six years, know year every building built, names of most architects, bored. If interested in doing a building that will look good thirty-five or forty years from now when I'm not here, call me.

Sheets didn't know what to make of the letter or the sender. The two men had met on a number of occasions.[2] Sheets's wife, Mary Baskerville, who had studied art at UCLA, had been in the same sorority as Dottie, but the two had not remained close.[3] For several years, Home Savings and Loan had been a sponsor of the annual city art show, and Ahmanson had frequently presented the awards to the prize winners. Despite these connections, the letter came out of the blue.

When Sheets called the office, Ahmanson was characteristically abrupt. "Interested?" he asked.

"Well, it certainly sounds interesting," Sheets responded.

"Do you ever get hungry?"

"Well, yes, normally about noon."

"Lunch tomorrow?" Ahmanson asked.

Sheets agreed, but when he arrived at National American Fire Insurance's offices on South Spring Street, he briefly regretted his decision. He rode to the building's top floor in "the most rickety elevator I have ever seen." Stepping out, he faced "a sea of desks and confusion." It was "the worst sweatshop

I have ever seen in my life."[4] A woman led him weaving past desks, turning sideways at times to get through, to reach Howard's office.

Reclined in his chair with his feet up on the desk, Ahmanson was talking on the phone. With a cigarette between his fingers, he gestured for Sheets to sit on an old sofa. Sheets sank through the cushion and landed hard on the wood underneath. For thirty minutes, the artist waited as Ahmanson talked. In the meantime, he noted the unpainted sherbet-green plaster. "The lighting in the room was ghastly, and the drapes were terrible. . . . I thought, 'What kind of a gooney bird have I gotten myself with here?' "

Ahmanson talked on. When he finally hung up, he stood, reached back to an old coatrack, snagged his jacket, and put it on. Without greeting Sheets or shaking his hand, he said, "Let's go."

Sheets expected to walk to a lunch joint. Instead, Ahmanson led him through the parking lot to "the most beautiful, big, overgrown Cadillac I had ever seen," next to which a chauffeur stood waiting. The two men climbed into the back seat and the driver pulled away.

Howard had a table at the Beverly Hills Club, where TV host Ed Sullivan, famed newspaper columnist Walter Winchell, and other Hollywood stars and L.A. luminaries frequently dined on the patio amid a riot of flowers.[5] Over lunch, Sheets and Ahmanson engaged in an animated conversation. On the face of it, they were very different in temperament and background. Only a few months younger than Ahmanson, Sheets was a handsome, round-faced man with an open forehead, deep eyes, and big hands. He had been born in 1907 in Pomona. His mother had died as a result of the birth, and his father had given him to his maternal grandparents to raise. He grew up with four aunts for sisters. Like Ahmanson, he was spoiled by the man of the house. His grandfather raised, bred, and raced thoroughbreds. For years, Sheets rose at six in the morning to ride with his grandfather. He launched his art career at the age of sixteen when he had a painting accepted for a show at a gallery in Laguna Beach. After graduating from Pomona High School, he studied at the Chouinard Art Institute in Los Angeles and then traveled and painted in Europe. Returning to Los Angeles in 1929 to get married, he continued to paint and taught at Chouinard during the Depression. His regionalist paintings attracted national attention and he became a leader in the California Style watercolor movement. In 1932, he was hired as an art professor at Scripps College in Claremont. He also worked with the Public Works of Art Project. During the war, he was an artist-correspondent for *Life* and the U.S. Army Air Forces in India and Burma.[6]

.Over lunch, the conversation ranged widely. "It was like hundreds of conversations I had with Howard," Sheets later recalled. "He was one of the best-read men I've ever known. He read every night until two or three in the morning because he couldn't sleep." Sheets lost track of the time. When he looked at his watch, it was nearly five o'clock and he had completely missed a three o'clock appointment. As it turned out, Ahmanson had also missed an afternoon meeting. Still, Ahmanson had never once mentioned the projects he had in mind.

Back in the chauffeur-driven car headed east on Wilshire Boulevard, Ahmanson suddenly pointed to a block and said "That's one of them." Farther along Wilshire, he pointed again and said, "That's another one." That was all he said about the project until the Cadillac pulled into the parking lot off South Spring Street.

"Do you think you could put up with me?" Ahmanson asked.

"I don't know what you mean," Sheets responded.

"Well, do you think you could put up with me to do a building or two?"

Sheets said he didn't think it seemed like it would be that difficult.

"All right, that settles it." Ahmanson said. Then he proceeded to explain the ground rules. "I want you to understand something now: I don't want you to telephone me ever. I do not wish to discuss these buildings with you. I'm going to let you do one, and if it's right then we'll do the other."

Confused, Sheets responded, "Well, Mr. Ahmanson, we've got to discuss budgets. I haven't even discussed fees."

Ahmanson cut him short. "You'll be fair with me, and I'll be fair with you. The budget—that's up to what you build. You build it like you were building it for yourself."

"I can't take that responsibility," Sheets protested. "No way can I do that."

"Well then," Ahmanson responded, "you're not going to do the job."

"I don't even know anything about the function," Sheets said. "I don't even know what kind of a building it is."

"I have plenty of people who can give you that information," Ahmanson said dismissively. "But don't you let them tell you how to design this building. If you want to know how many bodies there have to be in the room and what they do, fine. But don't you talk design to anyone. I haven't got a guy in my organization that knows anything about this. And I don't. I want it done the way you would do it if you were doing it for yourself."

Driving back to Claremont, Sheets found himself trembling. "It was so utterly unusual," he confessed years later. "I'd done several buildings for commercial people, and we'd always set budgets. I'd studied the problems and presented the solutions, and then we discussed whether we could do what they wanted within the budget." Ahmanson didn't want any of that kind of conversation.

Yet, as Sheets discovered, Howard's attitude did not reflect a lack of interest. Asked by the press why he had chosen Sheets, known for watercolors rather than architecture, to design the new headquarters building for H. F. Ahmanson & Co., Ahmanson said he wanted a designer "who could combine the art and flavor of California with the utilitarian needs of a savings and loan association."[7] He pointed out that Sheets had designed other buildings, including the Beverly Hills Tennis Club, and that during the war he had worked with the Army Air Forces on the development of fifteen schools and airfields.[8] "When the building is completed and we have moved into our new quarters," Howard said, "we know the public will agree with us that no better designer could have been selected."[9]

To design the functional aspects of the building, Sheets met repeatedly with Ken Childs. When the drawings were ready, he offered to go over them with Ahmanson's chief lieutenant, but Childs demurred. "Don't you want to know anything about it?" Sheets asked.

"It wouldn't make any difference to me," Childs answered. "It's what the boss wants."[10]

Sheets took three sketches to Ahmanson. "I set them down on this god-awful floor in this god-awful office." Howard walked up and down the room for a long time looking over the drawings. Then, without a word, a frown, or a smile, he picked up the phone and called Dottie.

"I'm looking at the god-damnedest building," he told her. "It's just going to be great. I can't wait for you to see it. It's going to be just exactly what I wanted." While Sheets waited and listened, Howard gushed over the phone. When he finally hung up, he turned to Sheets and asked, "Well, could I borrow that sketch tonight, and I'll get it back to you tomorrow?"

Sheets had to ask which one he liked.

"That one," Ahmanson pointed.

It was just like him, Sheets says. "He never hesitated over what he wanted."

Art was a critical ingredient in Sheets's concept of the building. He wanted mosaics and sculpture done by local artists. But since the art was not a structural element of the project, he felt compelled to seek Ahmanson's specific approval for this portion of the project. When he called Ahmanson's office, Evelyn Barty put him through. Halfway into his conversation about the choices that needed to be made and the budget, however, Sheets heard the line go dead. He called back. Barty told him Ahmanson had hung up on him.

"Why the hell did he hang up?" Sheets asked.

"Because he told you it was your problem," Barty said.

Sheets organized a studio of artists and commissioned sculpture to complete the project. When the building was almost done, Sheets was surprised one day. Ahmanson announced that he was coming over. He was nearly silent as Sheets showed him through the building, including Ahmanson's office with its enormous desk and fireplace. Finally, Ahmanson pronounced the entire thing to be exactly what he wanted.

Critics also liked the building. Jarvis Barlow, the former director of the Pasadena Art Museum and an art critic for the *Pasadena Independent,* called it "by far and away the handsomest structure on Wilshire" and hoped it was indicative of a new trend in architecture "away from the post and pseudo Bauhaus, from the beehive and fishbowl cubicle, from the stark and stripped, or, again, away from the Hansel und Gretel cake-and-candy house." He praised Sheets's visual references to traditions in California architecture and history including the Mission, the Monterey style, and the Spanish California ranch. Barlow also grasped how important the client-designer relationship was to Sheets's work. He called the building "the most notable art achievement of the year."[11]

The roots of Ahmanson's aesthetic impulse and his delight in Sheets's designs were not clear. In part they derived from his travels abroad and from his reading. According to Sheets, Ahmanson believed that most American commercial buildings lacked the presence of art, "not merely in terms of pictures, but art that was integrated into the design of the building, both in sculpture and in murals of various kinds."[12]

With the H. F. Ahmanson & Company and National American Fire Insurance Company building done, Howard put Sheets to work on the second building—a new headquarters for Home Savings and Loan to be built at 9245 Wilshire Boulevard in Beverly Hills.[13] The architectural firm Cunneen Company of Philadelphia took Sheets's drawings and created the project's detailed plans. When the project broke ground in October 1954, it was expected to cost four hundred thousand dollars.[14] By the time it was finished seventeen months later, the cost had increased 500 percent to nearly two million dollars.[15] Ahmanson called it his Taj Mahal.

Like a modern Renaissance patron, Ahmanson again allowed the artist to realize his vision. Sheets again integrated art into the structure. Instead of leaving spaces for a mural or a mosaic, Sheets thought of "a form that required these arts."[16] At the entrance, a pair of sculptures by Renzo Fenci bracketed the walkway.[17] The huge bronze statues—eight feet tall, cast in Italy, and shipped to Los Angeles—represented a mother and daughter and a father and son. The statues were meant to suggest "the timelessness and indestructibility of the family group."[18]

Sheets's design emphasized the classical within a modern context. Roman travertine, "the stone of the Caesars," covered the exterior and much of the interior walls.[19] The floor of the lobby combined inlaid stone and cement blocks in actual terrazzo.[20] The renowned ceramics company Gladding McBean created a specially glazed ceramic veneer in a repeated pattern reading "H.S. & L."[21] The art in the project also incorporated mosaics designed by Jean and Arthur Ames of Claremont and fabricated in Italy.[22] Sheets and Margaret Montgomery designed a stained-glass mural depicting the history of trade, banking, and thrift that was created by Pasadena artist John Wallis.[23] It included images depicting the bartering of cows and conch shells, as well as the development of Chinese bronze coins and the modern buffalo nickel.[24] Altogether, the building felt as much like a museum as a financial institution.

"Deep in the inner core of man lies his strongest compulsion—the fierce and unswerving desire to protect his family," an elegant brochure reminded Home's visitors. Echoing patriarchal themes, the brochure likened the home to a primitive cave or a sturdy tree where a man shielded his woman and his children. "Primary is his love of family, and primary is his need for a home." Home Savings existed "to help man achieve his basic aim."[25] Thus, in structure and expression through its sculpture, mosaics, and stained glass, Home Savings offered a narrative of community and family that appealed to postwar Southern Californians who were bombarded with images and messages that idealized the nuclear family.

The opening of the Beverly Hills office in March 1956 signaled Home's arrival on the grand stage of Los Angeles commerce. Despite the Taj Mahal reference, Ahmanson was clearly proud of the building.[26] He invited the nearly six hundred craftsmen and laborers who had worked on the project, along with their wives, to a huge party. The group included representatives of twenty-five different unions along with Los Angeles mayor Norris Poulson, film stars like Audie Murphy, and others.[27] Ahmanson also invited many of the operative builders whose business had contributed to Home's success. They included seven of the nation's top twelve home builders. The four largest had started 13,405 homes in Southern California in 1955.[28]

Ahmanson was astonished to discover how profitable his investment in aesthetics could be. In the first place, it returned significant advertising value. Newspapers gushed over the new facility. As part of the Richfield *Success Story* series, KTTV featured Millard Sheets leading viewers on a behind-the-scenes tour of what the television station advertised as "America's most distinctive structure."[29] More important to Ahmanson, the building became a magnet for deposits. "In nine years the old building [across the street] had taken in approximately $11 million in deposits," Sheets later told an interviewer. "In the first ten days [after the new building was opened], $19 million walked in the front door."[30] Ahmanson concluded that, as a general principle, "business could do itself a great favor by placing a greater emphasis on the aesthetics of its buildings," including adding "good art."[31]

With this kind of incentive to invest in architecture and art, Home Savings & Loan commissioned Sheets to design a series of branches and remodels—all neoclassical marble buildings with iconic mosaics and sculpture that celebrated community, family, and home ownership. With each one, he repurposed the history of California and its abiding mythology—the missions, the ranchos, the gold rush, and the pioneers—to provide references to local history.[32] The murals and mosaics confirmed a regional mythology that appealed to the transplanted, middle-class customers of the region.

For the artist, however, success brought its own creative constraints. With later buildings, Sheets wanted to open up his basic design by adding more glass. He offered Ahmanson drawings that explored these new directions. Howard liked the concepts, but, he told Sheets, "I'm not willing to gamble, to change the image. . . . It's foolish for us to get off of something that we know is right. The image is established. Whether all people like it or not isn't the important thing." Resigned, Sheets acknowledged that the public "liked the sense of security that these buildings have had."[33]

Sheets was sensitive to some architectural critics who described the buildings as mausoleums, "but I think many of them wish that they could design a couple of mausoleums that would produce the incredible [return on investment], which is, after all, what an architect or a designer is supposed to do."[34] Lest he be accused of pandering, he asserted "unequivocally that I have never done one thing on those buildings to compromise my own personal understanding or taste."[35] He explained that "a good designer has always had to deal with real clients whether king, bishop or a commercial agency, satisfy their needs and never compromise his own aesthetic judgment. This requires an artist capable of living in his own times."[36]

Over time, Ahmanson's relationship with Sheets developed all of the complexities that infuse the interchange between rich patron and artist. With Sheets, however, Ahmanson clearly found a rich friendship. For one thing, Sheets was one of only a small number of people who had the courage to stand up to Ahmanson, and Howard seemed to appreciate his integrity. A thank-you note for a gift written in October 1960 turned into a much deeper expression of gratitude. "I know anybody's best friend is supposed to do whatever he can for the other guy," Howard wrote, "but somehow every time I see you, you raise me up another fifty miles and my horizons of interest and enthusiasm increase in geometric proportions. That you can do all these things and still be as cozy as an old high school chum and worry about my comb, tooth brushes, and all such trivia is really more than a guy can expect from one human being." Acknowledging his own tendency to be stingy with gratitude, Howard continued, "I am appreciative and grateful, even though I do not tell you so after each of your kind and thoughtful deeds—and that you cannot afford the time you waste on me makes these things even more eloquent." The letter suggested that Sheets also cultivated in Ahmanson new sensibilities. He thanked Sheets for "everything that I have begged, stolen, borrowed, and so gratefully accepted—but above all for learning a new way of life."[37]

Ahmanson did not detail what exactly he meant by the "new way of life," but the blossoming of his friendship with Sheets coincided with a new interest in the visual arts.[38] As the newest fad—painting by numbers—swept through "hobby-happy America" in the mid-1950s, Ahmanson began to collect old masters.[39] Sheets put him in touch with dealers and auction houses that helped Ahmanson begin building his collection.[40] Ahmanson also saw himself as "the great collector of Sheetses."[41] Under Ahmanson's direction, Home Savings also became a patron of community artists. The company provided funds for the acquisition of the best art pieces displayed each year at the county fair. For Los Angeles, this new passion would leave an important legacy as Sheets and then others leveraged Ahmanson's interest into a larger effort to build cultural institutions that reflected the civic elite's aspiration to make Los Angeles one of the world's great cultural cities. For Ahmanson, this process began when Sheets recruited him to the board of the Los Angeles County Art Institute.

Founded by *Los Angeles Times* publisher Harrison Gray Otis in 1918, the Los Angeles County Art Institute was housed in what had once been Otis's Westlake Park home. The school operated under the aegis of the art division of the Los Angeles County Museum of History, Science and Art for several decades. With enrollment booming after the war, the Board of Supervisors took control in 1947.[42] It then created a five-member advisory board to manage the institution.[43] At the same time, the institute was chartered as a college and incorporated as the Los Angeles County Art Institute, although it continued to be known informally as Otis.[44]

Struggles to define the institution and its governance in the postwar years shed light on cultural transitions taking place in Los Angeles. As artist Robert Irwin, who was a student there from 1948 to 1950, reports, the curriculum was very practical. "It was almost less of an education than it was preparing to be a plumber or something," he remembers. "I was learning techniques, I think, all the time I was in art school." The annual Los Angeles County Art Fair offered Irwin and other students an important showcase. The very first painting Irwin completed at Otis was accepted for the fair.[45]

Management of the institute had gone through a rocky period as artistic and political conservatism flourished in the cold war era. The 1947 County Art Fair ignited criticism from the "Sanity in Art" movement, which rejected modernism.[46] Actor Vincent Price, one of the judges for the show, said it was this kind of reactionary behavior that "consigned Los Angeles to a relatively unimportant place among the nation's art centers."[47] Price made little headway with the political elite. The Los Angeles City Council banned the public display of modern art in 1951, calling it communist propaganda.[48]

Despite the rebellion against modern art, as long as the GI Bill was available to pay the tuition of returning soldiers, enrollments grew. In August 1951, the institute broke ground for a new wing to accommodate the more than six hundred students who were attending classes. Following the trade school approach, the curriculum was expanded to address set design and lighting for motion pictures. Unfortunately, by the time the new wing was ready to be dedicated in October 1952, the institute's fortunes had turned. On the eve of the dedication, the director suddenly resigned. For the next two years, the board ran the day-to-day operations under the oversight of the vice chairwoman while it searched for a new director.

Millard Sheets was wrapped in bandages on the day the chairman of the Los Angeles County Board of Supervisors and the president of the institute's board arrived to visit. Thrown from a horse, he had cracked his skull and broken his nose in four places. The doctors told him he had to let his body heal for three months. In the middle of his recovery, Sheets agreed to talk about the institute's future.

The chairman and the president wanted him to suggest a new director. Characteristically blunt, Sheets told them he wouldn't do it. "I think it's such a lousy school that I wouldn't wish it on anybody," he said. "Unless you change your whole philosophy of why the school is being operated and get a staff that's competent, I wouldn't wish it on a dog." Taken aback, the chairman and the president asked Sheets if he would write a plan for them. Unable to paint because of his injuries, Sheets agreed.[49]

Weeks later, the Board of Supervisors and the institute's board invited Sheets to the California Club to present his ideas. He told them that if they wanted to turn the institute around, they would need to build new buildings and commit money for staff and operations. John Anson Ford, the chair of the Board of Supervisors, put Sheets on the spot. "If we support it in the way you've laid out, would you accept the position as director?" Sheets reminded Ford that he lived in Claremont and said he enjoyed teaching at Scripps. Nevertheless, "because I know you won't do it," he said, he would take the job. To his surprise, two weeks later the boards agreed to his terms.[50] On August 19, 1953, Sheets was officially appointed director.[51] In his letter to Ford accepting the position, Sheets stated that he would be committed to providing "a type of education in art that is deeper in significance, higher in its aesthetic aims, and demanding in unequivocal standards of discipline."[52]

Sheets set out to strengthen the curriculum, the faculty, and the institution's base of financial and political support.[53] He wanted to "stress solidity in the teaching of art so as to be equal with the best in the nation, in the world."[54] Under Sheets, the art institute developed a four-year curriculum and the school was accredited in the spring of 1956.[55] Part-time students were relegated to night classes only. Although Sheets said he would not favor fine arts—drawing, painting, sculpture, and design—over commercial arts, he decided that only fine arts would be taught in the day program. Sheets asserted that this curriculum would prepare students for their professional careers as effectively as the training required for careers in other professions.

Underlying these changes, Sheets said, was his belief that "the complex nature of our society demands a more complete and balanced curriculum of art study and work." A base of common knowledge was essential. "Special-ization without an adequate base of common culture and technical experi-ence, like an involved structure lacking a solid foundation, will not stand." Sheets also believed art needed to be mainstreamed into commercial cul-ture. He warned of the "dead end" of "art for art's sake."[56]

Sheets was culturally ambitious. He believed art would cure the sick-nesses of society that came with modern life, including a "maniacal pressure against a real show of feeling." To cure society, he told a group of Rotarians in 1956, "art appreciation and art experience should become a part of daily liv-ing."[57] Sheets also asserted that art appreciation belonged in a masculine world. A western outdoorsman who had braved combat during the war as a journalist, Sheets said men too often leave art to their wives. "Yet we gain great strength and courage in the study of art," he said.[58]

Sheets pushed to redesign the institute's campus. He razed old buildings on Wilshire Boulevard and designed a quadrangle to be constructed on the new site, including a new gallery to showcase students' work. Sheets also re-cruited a new generation of faculty. Applauding Sheets's work, the art critic for the *Los Angeles Times* wrote, "The tremendous growth of this area's popu-lation, industry and social life more than justifies the bold move the County Supervisors have taken to make a new, thorough and disciplined County Art Institute."[59]

Behind the scenes, Sheets also assembled a powerful board that could bring both political and financial capital to the institution. As part of his deal with the Board of Supervisors, Sheets had received their promise that Dorothy Buffum Chandler would be appointed to the art institute's board. Married to Norman Chandler, the publisher of the *Los Angeles Times*, "Buff" had become one of the region's most prominent and successful fund-raisers by the mid-1950s. Sheets believed she could provide critical connections to major donors.

In addition to Chandler, Sheets recruited his new client and patron, How-ard Ahmanson.[60] Howard's tenure on the art institute's board marked the beginning of his life as a cultural patron, and of the visual arts particularly. It was inspired by Sheets's evangelizing and integrated with a growing friendship that challenged Ahmanson on many levels. On the board, How-ard also began one of his first public collaborations with Dorothy Chandler, who impressed him with her leadership qualities and her ability to inspire the community to action.[61] Chandler's passionate efforts to promote the construction and development of major civic institutions rubbed off on Ahmanson, even as Sheets helped develop his sense of aesthetics.

LOS ANGELES COUNTY MUSEUM OF ART

Ahmanson's experience with Sheets, the County Art Institute, and the annual art fair helped him discover what others in the city were already discovering. In the postwar world, the city not only was burgeoning with new tract homes and factories but also was the center of a growing community of artists. Like New York after World War II or Paris after World War I, however, as Robert Wernick would later write, "Los Angeles had all the ingredients of a cultural explosion, but it had almost no cultural apparatus."[62] The city lacked a major art museum and, as late as 1960, could support only forty-one commercial galleries, including frame shops, art associations, and "vanity" shops devoted to the work of a single artist.[63]

For years the visual arts had been relegated to a portion of the Los Angeles County Museum of History, Science and Art, which had opened in Exposition Park near USC in November 1916.[64] Throughout the 1920s, the collection had grown with gifts and acquisitions. After a new wing opened in 1930, the museum received a gift of more than two hundred works of art that included paintings by Matisse, Segonzac, Rouault, Signac, Courbet, Modigliani, Vlaminck, Eakins, Bellow, Luks, Hassam, Henri, and Prendergast.[65] These additions finally gave the collection weight. Later, gifts of paintings by Renaissance artists including Titian, Rubens, Lotto, Bordone, Holbein, Petrus Christus, De Hooch, Ter Borch, van Orley, and Bouts added historical depth to the European collection.[66] As new donations arrived from William Randolph Hearst and George Gard DeSylva in the early postwar years, the Board of Governors began to consider the idea of establishing an independent art museum. In 1954, Arthur Millier, the art critic for the *Los Angeles Times,* offered a series of testimonials from leaders in the art community lobbying for a new and separate art museum, the Los Angeles County Museum of Art (LACMA). Many of these voices echoed architect Anthony Thormin, the president of the County Museum Association, who asserted, "We are no longer a pueblo in an unending mustard field."[67]

Real progress began after Richard "Ric" Fargo Brown arrived to become chief curator of art in 1953. The great-grandson of the founder of Wells Fargo,

Brown had a PhD from Harvard and came to Los Angeles from the Frick Gallery in Manhattan, where he had been a research scholar for five years.[68] With "his boyish face [and] his eloquent tongue," Brown quickly befriended the elite collectors in the community, including Norton Simon, a wealthy industrialist who owned Hunt's Foods.[69] A leading collector, Simon joined the Board of Governors of the County Museum in 1957 and agreed to help the fund-raising effort.[70]

At the time, Dorothy Chandler had already begun to raise money to erect a major concert hall downtown. Asked if she would lead the effort to build an art museum as well, she declined but recommended department store magnate Edward William Carter for the job. The president of the Broadway-Hale department stores, Carter was already chairman of the Southern California Symphony Association and the Board of Regents of the University of California. In 1958, he joined the museum's Board of Governors and became chair of the fund-raising committee.[71]

Fund-raising was key to winning political approval from the Los Angeles County Board of Supervisors. In the spring of 1958, Supervisor Kenneth Hahn declared that he would oppose any effort to build a separate county art museum because he feared that such a move would undermine the quality of the existing museum in Exposition Park (which was in his district). He also suggested that over the long run taxpayers should not have to pay for the maintenance of a second facility.[72] To counter Hahn's concerns, Carter told the board that the new facility would operate as a branch of the main museum and that it would offer the public an opportunity to view collections that had remained in storage because of a lack of exhibition space.

"Los Angeles is fast emerging as a world art center," Carter told the supervisors, "but we can never be great until we have quarters in which to house our cultural treasures." To seal the deal, Carter and Brown announced that they had already secured one-third of their three-million-dollar fund-raising goal by receiving a pledge from Norton Simon for one million dollars to help finance construction of the new facility.[73] Throughout the summer and fall of 1958, Carter courted other major donors.

Howard Ahmanson was among the most important of Carter's prospects. In the late summer of 1958, Ahmanson offered "to make available $2,000,000" to help build the new museum. The financing was "somewhat unusual" in character and came with "some very specific restrictions." As the Museum Associates attorney explained, Ahmanson's company would actually make a twenty-year, two-million-dollar loan to the board. No payments on principal would be due for ten years and Ahmanson's company would only charge a low 2 percent rate on the money. Meanwhile, Ahmanson would commit to donating stock in one of his corporations to Museum Associates. Over the course of seven years, the board would eventually own about 80 percent of this company, effectively becoming creditor and debtor on its own loan.[74]

The deal was also contingent on the Board of Supervisors agreeing to Ahmanson's terms and to a formal commitment on their part "to be responsible for the maintenance and operation expense of such a museum." At the same time, however, Ahmanson was convinced that the museum needed to be insulated from the political pressures that might be brought to bear on the Board of Supervisors; otherwise "there may be trouble in the future." To ensure that the Board of Supervisors would go along, Ahmanson personally presented his proposals to various individual supervisors and sought "to give Associates complete control over the building and as complete independence as possible from the Board of Supervisors."[75]

In exchange for his financial contribution and lobbying efforts, Ahmanson wanted changes in governance. He asked that the Museum Associates board be increased from fifteen to thirty members. Current members had officially been appointed by the Board of Supervisors, but Ahmanson wanted the new members to be appointed by the Museum Associates board itself, to make the board more independent of the politicians.[76] The proposed agreement also stipulated that "this building shall at all times be called the 'Ahmanson Gallery of Fine Arts'" and that this would be "the only name to appear on the building." Ahmanson also wanted to approve the location, the architect, and the builder.[77]

When Ahmanson's proposal was presented to the Museum Associates board in September 1958, the members were generally enthusiastic. Norton Simon said he would favor accepting the proposition but that if the plan went through he would like to modify the terms of his own one-million-dollar gift. There were people in the community who still questioned the quality of what the museum had to exhibit, Simon said, and he would like to work with Ric Brown to focus on building the collection.[78] The board's attorney agreed to work with Simon on a revised agreement, and the board accepted Ahmanson's concept with the details to be worked out by attorneys.

The donor agreement with Howard Ahmanson, according to writer Suzanne Muchnic, "was a bold move that signified Ahmanson's clout with the Board of Supervisors and Carter's political savvy." The supervisors were reportedly in debt to Ahmanson's bank, and Ahmanson chose this moment to call in his chits.[79] At Ahmanson's urging, the supervisors agreed to pay the salaries of the museum's employees and maintain the buildings and grounds at a level commensurate with that of major public cultural institutions in other cities.[80]

On December 2, 1958, Carter publicly revealed Ahmanson's pledge in a presentation to the Board of Supervisors.[81] Ahmanson's contribution, combined with the one-million-dollar pledge by Norton Simon and five hundred thousand dollars promised by dozens of other contributors, gave the Board of Supervisors enough confidence to enter into a contract on December 9 that would allow Museum Associates to build the museum on county-owned land in Hancock Park. Supervisor Hahn and Ed Carter reassured the public that no taxpayer dollars would be used for the actual construction. All of these dollars would be privately raised.[82] In fact, "the agreement was hailed as a blueprint for uniting public authority and private money in the field of culture."[83]

Although initially gracious and supportive, Norton Simon became increasingly frustrated with the Ahmanson plan. Even before it was revealed to the public, he asked for reassurance from Ed Carter that the agreement would not preclude naming other buildings for other people. Moreover, he hoped the initial building would be located on the site in such a way that it would not diminish other buildings that might be added in the future. He wanted to be clear that "the public should have a part in contributing to the present building fund so that it would not appear to be a private affair." He objected to the idea that this civic museum would seem to be a memorial to one individual. According to minutes of the board's November 18 meeting, Simon suggested: "If it were primarily the Ahmanson Gallery, no one would give to it." Carter and the museum's attorney reassured him that Ahmanson had no intention of binding the museum so tightly. Nevertheless, Simon "thought it was necessary to make it *very clear* that the Ahmanson gift is only *part* of the whole plan."[84]

Simon's objections remained private for a number of months.[85] When Carter held a press conference in April 1959, he told reporters that with the Ahmanson and Simon commitments, as well as one million dollars more pledged or given by fifty-five other donors, Museum Associates had four million dollars. Carter described the donors as "an excellent cross-section of the top leaders in our community." Before the end of the year, he expected to begin the first phase of construction of what would eventually be a $10.5 million facility that would open to the public in 1961.[86] But Carter's optimism and patience were tried over the next few months as the Board of Supervisors delayed formal approval of the site.

If Ahmanson had hoped that philanthropy would be less likely than politics to engender the slings and arrows of public opinion, he was sorely disappointed. In March 1960, the *Los Angeles Examiner* reported that a bitter debate had exploded over the plan to name the new museum after its largest contributor. A group known as the Los Angeles Art Committee asked the Board of Supervisors to reconsider the plan. They revealed that Norton Simon had already reduced his pledge from one million to one hundred thousand dollars because of his frustration with the idea.[87] Another donor, Judge and Mrs. Lucius Peyton Green, collectors of old masters, had decided to give their collection to the Fine Arts Museums of San Francisco rather than LACMA because of the naming plan. Art critic Jules Langsner, the chair of the Los Angeles Art Committee, reminded the supervisors that the National Gallery of Art in Washington, D.C., had successfully attracted major gifts and collections because its founding patron, Paul Mellon, had not insisted on putting his name on the institution.[88] After the Board of Supervisors ignored these protests and unanimously approved the Ahmanson name, another donor, art collector David E. Bright, announced that he would withdraw his fifty-thousand-dollar pledge if the board refused to reverse its decision.[89]

As the controversy continued, Ric Brown tried to find a compromise. He suggested that the new museum be designed as a series of structures, only one of which would carry Ahmanson's name. Howard and the other trustees agreed to this plan.[90] A delighted newspaper editorial celebrated this "happy compromise" that ended a controversy that had threatened either to diminish contributions to the project or to ignore the name of a generous donor.[91] Howard was not so pleased. "Now I know why people give their money away when they're dead, you can't argue about it then."[92]

Ahmanson's frustration with the controversy also affected his relationship with Brown. During the time that Carter was negotiating with Ahmanson over his gift, Brown had visited the Ahmanson house on South Hudson and seen Howard's growing collection of art. It included fifty paintings by old masters and others, including works by Jan Vermeer, Tintoretto, Pieter Brueghel, Titian, Claude Monet, Jean Francois Millet, Eugene Delacroix, Frans Hals, Rembrandt, David, Diego Velasquez, Gustave Courbet, and John Singer Sargent, as well as more modern works by contemporary Southern California artists.[93] The "Dutch school" was his favorite, but as he told a reporter, there was "no pattern" to his collecting. Every painting was an adventure. He just kept going to Europe and returning with art.[94] After looking over Howard's collection, Brown concluded that Ahmanson's casual approach had left him with several fakes. Ahmanson resented the idea that he might have been duped. "This led to very bad blood between Ric and Howard," according to one former board member.[95]

The tensions between Brown and Ahmanson increased when it came time to select an architect. Carter's original agreement had promised Ahmanson a significant voice in the selection process. Brown wanted a contemporary architect to design an iconic building that would be internationally recognized. He advanced the names of Ludwig Mies van der Rohe and Eero Saarinen.[96] Mies came to Los Angeles twice and was wined and dined at Perino's with board members.[97] Saarinen and architect Philip Johnson also met with Brown and the board. By September 1959, the board had accepted Brown's recommendation that Mies be chosen, but a final decision was dependent on Ahmanson's approval.[98]

Howard was not interested in the sober rationalism of Mies's architecture or the sweeping arcs and curves of Saarinen's style. By 1960, he was fiercely loyal to the region that had made him rich and keenly attached to the artistic and architectural vocabulary that Millard Sheets had established for Home Savings and other financial institutions in the region.[99] If Sheets wasn't acceptable and a nationally recognized architect was necessary, Ahmanson favored Edward Durrell Stone, whose clean white structures invoked a modern classicism. Ahmanson's preferences were reflected in a new list of architects submitted to the board in January 1960. Stone had been added, but local architect William Pereira was at the top of the list.[100]

Many of the major donors knew and admired Pereira, whose office was located two blocks from the proposed site for the museum. A Chicago native, Pereira was once dismissed by an architectural critic as "Hollywood's idea of an architect."[101] Fit and trim with thick wavy hair, deep-inset eyes, and a Roman profile, he had worked for the famed architectural firm Holabird & Root early in his career and had helped to design the 1933 World's Fair. He and his brother Hal had launched their own architectural firm focusing on movie theater design. In the late 1930s, the brothers moved to Los Angeles, where Bill worked in Hollywood as an art director and production designer. He became a professor of architecture at USC. In the 1950s, he formed a partnership with Charles Luckman. Together they designed commercial buildings, department stores, television stations, industrial facilities, banks, and hospitals. Fascinated with science fiction and the future, Pereira would become the architect of choice for Southern California's aerospace industry. With several collaborators, he and Luckman designed the Los Angeles International Airport and its iconic futuristic Theme Tower.[102] By 1960, he and Luckman had dissolved their partnership and Pereira had formed his own firm. His style appealed to Howard Ahmanson and other donors. In March 1960, he was awarded the design contract for the new art museum.[103]

At this same meeting, Ahmanson was elected to the Museum Associates board.[104] As Pereira submitted drawings and developed models, Ahmanson suggested changes.[105] As chairman of the Budget and Finance Committee, he clashed frequently with Simon and Brown, and sometimes with Ed Carter. It was all a personal battle of egos, according to Brown. "They all want power, and they all want their say." Howard understood the situation. He even made fun of himself. He told a reporter metaphorically, "I play several instruments, but what I love to play best is the organ because I can drown out any other instrument."[106]

CULTURE IN THE MANAGED ECONOMY

As Ahmanson transitioned from entrepreneur to cultural patron, others in the savings and loan industry in Southern California followed the same path, including Mark Taper and Bart Lytton. The localism at the heart of the industry's development, embedded in government policies that restricted operations to narrow geographic areas, reinforced the close relationship between local entrepreneurs and the community as a whole. This relationship in Los Angeles also reflected larger patterns in American society.

In 1962, historian Robert Wiebe traced the evolving relationship between business and government in the United States. He described the many ways in which government had become the arena for resolving once-bitter street fights among competitors and between shippers and producers, and labor and management in the American economy. Along the way, he said, the federal government had grown throughout the early twentieth century to rival business for national leadership. But in reality there was no rivalry, Wiebe concluded: "The great blend of our time has so intermixed business and government that a practical, precise separation of the two is no longer possible."[107]

Wiebe's observations were focused primarily on the regulatory environment, but they also carried over into cultural and social policy. By the early 1950s, presidents and governors regularly consulted business leaders on social issues. Increasingly, great entrepreneurial wealth in America was given to private philanthropy. Innovators like Andrew Carnegie and John D. Rockefeller had restructured the practice of the philanthropy to fund social innovation with an eye to transforming charity and government. These developments complemented the partnership between business and government in the regulatory environment and extended them into the social realm.

To a government entrepreneur like Howard Ahmanson this partnership between government and business in the cultural arena was totally appropriate. Ahmanson's gift to LACMA, for example, was one of many and in the end not the largest. Los Angeles County taxpayers, through the agency of their Board of Supervisors, made the biggest commitment by promising to fund the new museum's operations into the distant future. The project was conceived as a joint venture between the public and private sectors to promote civic culture. Given Ahmanson's apparent role in brokering this deal with the Board of Supervisors, it seems clear that he believed in the appropriateness, or at least the expediency, of this kind of partnership. Many business leaders did. It was simply another reflection of the cooperative relationship between business and government in the postwar economy.

Wiebe was impressed with this brilliant accommodation and suggested that it was responsible for the nation's prosperity and domestic tranquility. "With so few signs of domestic upheaval at the beginning of the 1960's," he wrote, "any elite would take pride in the record of America's durable business leadership."[108] Unfortunately for Wiebe, Howard Ahmanson, and the nation, the inherent and relentless destructive and creative forces of capitalism, combined with long-repressed resentment and dissatisfaction in the nation, opened a new era whose history would fade the brilliance of this great accommodation.

TWELVE

Influence

GOVERNOR PAT BROWN KNEW people in the savings and loan industry. He also had Democratic friends who weren't in the business but wanted to be. And why not? In 1959, when Brown took office, people like Howard Ahmanson were getting very rich. A state savings and loan charter seemed like a license to print money. With a Democrat in the governor's mansion, political insiders, including sitting legislators, lobbied to start new associations. If Republicans were awarded charters over Democrats, party loyalists accused Brown of being disloyal. If other Democrats emerged victorious from the state's hearing process, they accused Brown's former law partner Frank Mackin, the commissioner of savings and loans, of playing political favorites.[1] In 1959, Brown's staff concluded that trouble was brewing in the industry and that the governor needed to take action.

Brown wanted to protect consumers, avoid scandals, and ensure that no one was getting rich by taking advantage of the government. He had heard that some thrifts were coercing home buyers into buying high-priced insurance. He asked his advisors—including Los Angeles attorney Warren Christopher, a political confidant—to look into whether savings and loans should be prohibited from having tie-ins with insurance companies. Soon after the governor's inauguration, Brown's assistant Fred Dutton inaccurately wrote to Christopher, "I understand that in Ahmanson's case, for example, the fire insurance company he spun off from his savings and loan operations is actually now a greater moneymaking operation than the savings and loan business."[2] Without addressing Ahmanson's case, Christopher informed Dutton that the legislature, at long last, had recently added an "anticoercion" section to the insurance code. With proper enforcement, this new statute should alleviate any concerns.[3] Nonetheless, Brown and his staff weren't satisfied.

Brown was disturbed by the proliferation of holding companies. As Commissioner Mackin told the governor, these entities dodged the state's regulatory authority to block mergers and limit the geographic expansion of a company by putting separate savings institutions under the legal umbrella of a single holding company. Letters to the governor suggested that the holding companies were undermining the historic principles of the industry, which emphasized mutualism, localism, and thrift. Brown sided with these critics when he cabled California senator Clair Engle to support the Spence Act, suggesting that these companies were "dangerous to the stock buying public." If the "gold rush" of acquisitions was not stopped, he wrote, "it could lead to higher mortgage interest rates and greater risk taking by savings and loan associations," which would endanger the public's investment in these public companies.[4] In a follow-up letter, Brown underscored the speed with which holding companies were transforming the industry. In two years, the number of savings and loan holding companies in California had grown from one to fifteen, "most of them Delaware corporations." These companies controlled the stock of 50 of the state's 175 associations and operated 100 of the 315 state-licensed branches and offices.[5] From Brown's point of view, this kind of concentration was not healthy for the consumer.

Brown's concern for consumers belied the assertion that money bought influence. Some of Brown's biggest contributors were on the other side of the issue. Los Angeles oilman Ed Pauley, for example, one of Brown's most important financial and political backers, had formed a holding company to get into the savings and loan business. As Brown was lobbying Engel to pass the Spence Act, Pauley's representatives were in Washington testifying against the law. Savings and loan entrepreneur Bart Lytton, another key Democratic fund-raiser, called the governor to explain that the uproar against holding companies was all a conspiracy by the federal mutuals to repress the California capital stock companies, which had made enormous contributions to the California economy.[6] Howard Ahmanson, who owned several savings and loans under the umbrella of H. F. Ahmanson & Co., had provided significant help to Brown's campaign. Admittedly, Brown's courage on the issue was strengthened by the California Savings and Loan League's support for the Spence Act, but his fundamental concern was for the consumer.[7]

For Brown, passage of the Spence Act in 1959 did not solve the problem. Congress considered the law a temporary measure. It asked the Federal Home Loan Bank Board to study the issue and report back. Brown knew that regardless of what federal regulators learned, the situation in California would be different. In the Golden State, especially in Southern California, savings and loans were bigger and commanded a larger share of the mortgage market. And in California, savings and loans were tremendously profitable.

The governor's sense of urgency was apparent in a memo he wrote to Mackin and the state's new consumer watchdog, Helen Nelson, in October. He noted that savings and loans were charging high interest rates and "demanding from 7% to 10% of the loan as a consideration of making said loan." Reflecting an inaccurate view of the regulatory structure, he characterized thrifts as "monopolistic" because "only one to an area is allowed." Thus, he said, "there should be some restraint on the enormous profits made by loan societies." "They pay no taxes," he said, "and are merely enriching a few people."[8] Unwilling to wait for the FHLBB or Congress, he asked Mackin to commission an independent study that would set the stage for a legislative effort to win greater regulatory authority.

Ultimately, the investigation into all of these issues would lead to a broad analysis of the structure of the industry in California and a fundamental reevaluation of the state's approach to regulating savings and loans. It would also rupture the comfortable and cooperative relationship between industry and government that had characterized the managed economy of the postwar years.[9]

A THINK TANK'S REVIEW

Hired by the state to study the savings and loan industry, Stanford Research Institute (SRI) brought a new perspective to the regulatory process and reflected an important change in the way that policy makers searched for expertise.[10] Established in 1947 and governed by a board appointed by Stanford University's trustees, SRI operated as an independent think tank. It employed more than 1,550 people in 1958 to study problems ranging from weather data systems to thermal energy to cancer. By 1959, the *Los Angeles Times* described it as the leading independent applied research center in the West and an increasingly important adjunct of policy making by business and political leaders.[11]

Free of the vested interests of the industry or the political concerns of the regulator and armed with new economic theories, SRI highlighted in its study the ways in which the savings and loan industry had grown and changed in the previous ten years. While the state's population increased 42 percent, the number of thrift offices (headquarters and branches) had increased 159 percent. Meanwhile, mortgage loan balances held by savings and loans had increased 521 percent, and savings deposits had grown 532 percent. Given the scale of these increases, the authors wrote, the savings and loan had become "a major financial institution" in the state, especially in Southern California, where six out of ten California associations were located and where 80 percent of the California industry's total assets were held.[12]

SRI showed that California thrifts were, in fact, more profitable than their siblings across the country. In 1959, they earned almost 5.8 percent on their assets, while savings and loans in the rest of the nation earned nearly a full percentage point less.[13] But the difference in profitability did not necessarily reflect a conspiracy against the consumer. As SRI explained, California's relatively young and rapidly growing economy had a voracious appetite for capital. In an era when global financial markets were not well integrated, investment capital commanded a regional premium. As a result, interest rates in the Golden State were often higher than on the East Coast or in other parts of the nation.[14] California thrifts were also more profitable, SRI suggested, because they were larger and enjoyed economies of scale. Large state-chartered associations had lower expenses in proportion to their assets and higher income.[15]

SRI confirmed the governor's understanding that holding companies owned a growing share of the savings and loan business in California, including more than a third of all assets. H. F. Ahmanson & Co., the largest, controlled four savings and loan associations, with twenty-eight offices and assets of more than $764 million at the end of 1959.[16] Given the pace of mergers and acquisitions in the industry, the report noted, holding companies seemed destined to capture an even bigger share of the market.

The authors highlighted the positive and negative potential in holding company growth. On the one hand, holding companies could contribute to the development of regional and national markets for home loans and savings. They seemed to have lower operating costs. They also offered more financial security because they built large bad-debt reserves and diversified their risk across a broader geographic area. On the other hand, holding companies seemed to charge higher loan fees than the industry average, which was not good for the consumer. Concentration, SRI pointed out, might also lead to a reduction in competition.[17] The SRI report carefully steered clear of policy recommendations, but it gave Brown's staff a better understanding of the landscape. Most important for Brown, it gave the state a source of expertise outside of the industry itself.

As he approached the end of his first two years in office, with the presidential campaign over and fellow Democrat John Kennedy preparing for inauguration, Brown began to think seriously about his campaign for reelection in 1962. The politics of the savings and loan industry wasn't front-page news, but the deep pockets of savings and loan entrepreneurs were sure to play a role in the election. In the meantime, Brown's indispensable but sometimes combative ally in the California legislature had already figured out how to get help from Howard Ahmanson.

JESSE AND HOWARD

A cultural institution provided Howard Ahmanson the bridge he needed between the waning power of Republicans in California and the ascendant Democrats. It also created a personal relationship that would be at the heart of a "new politics" in California that reflected an important transition in the relationship between business and government.

While Republicans still held the governor's office, Howard Edgerton had launched an effort to transform the historic Exposition Building in Exposition Park into a museum of science and industry. After closing for renovations, the museum reopened in 1951 with major exhibit areas designated for agriculture, industry, minerals, and transportation. Three years later, the board of directors decided to launch a campaign to build a new museum with public and private funding. Edgerton asked Governor Knight to appoint Howard Ahmanson to a fifteen-member advisory committee for the museum.[18] He then enlisted Ahmanson's help to find a legislative champion to get state funding for the project.[19] Ahmanson sent his emissary Robert DeKruif to talk to a freshman legislator from Los Angeles who represented the district that included Exposition Park.

Jesse Marvin Unruh reflected the new face of the Democratic Party in California. For years, Republicans had taken advantage of an anomaly in California election law that allowed candidates to cross-file in the Democratic and Republican primaries without revealing their own party affiliation. Under this system, elections tended to be less partisan, but Democrats, who outnumbered Republicans by the early 1950s, were frustrated that their advantage in registrations failed to deliver victories at the ballot box. To abolish cross-filing, Democrats collected signatures for a ballot initiative in 1952. Republicans responded by qualifying another measure that simply required candidates to list their party affiliation. The Republican measure won. Nevertheless, the new truth-in-labeling law cost the Republicans State Senate and Assembly seats in 1954, and it led to the election of a new generation of Democrats, including Jesse Unruh.[20]

If Howard Ahmanson reflected the bourgeois midwestern immigrant to Los Angeles of the 1920s, Unruh epitomized the Dust Bowl migrant of the Depression and war years. The youngest of five children born to an illiterate but hardworking father, he had grown up on a series of farms in Kansas and Texas. By the time he reached high school, his parents had resorted to sharecropping cotton. Recognizing Jesse's intellectual gifts, his mother had taught him to read at an early age. Big and heavy, he played center for his high school football team but also graduated second in his class. After working briefly in an aircraft plant in Southern California, he returned to Texas and joined the army. He spent most of World War II in the heat of Corpus Christi and then the cold of the Aleutian Islands. In Corpus Christi he met and married Virginia June Lemon, a California girl. Returning to Los Angeles after the war, Jesse, along with hundreds of other veterans, enrolled at USC under the GI Bill. Active in campus politics, he ran for the California Assembly in 1948, during his senior year. He finished a distant fourth in the Democratic primary, but the experience whetted his political appetite. He threw himself into political organizing, struggling to make a living on the side. Virginia taught intermittently, and their family grew with the birth of four children. With the presidential contest between Dwight Eisenhower and Adlai Stevenson coloring the election of 1952, Unruh ran again for the Assembly. Short of money but bolstered by a strong political organization, he finished second to the cross-filing Republican incumbent. When the cross-filing rules changed in 1954, Unruh won the Democratic primary and the general election.[21]

DeKruif's visit came not long after Unruh arrived in Sacramento. As Howard had taught him to do when selling fire insurance, the gregarious DeKruif remained standing while he made his pitch. Unruh agreed to support the project.[22] After Democrats pulled even with Republicans in the California Senate in 1956 and increased their numbers to thirty-seven in the eighty-member Assembly, business interests feared that new social legislation would hurt their bottom line. They could no longer turn to the one-time "boss" of the legislature, lobbyist Artie Samish. Instead, the business community looked for a Democrat they could work with among the new generation of legislators, "someone they could trust, someone who had the trust of his fellow Democratic legislators." As the newly installed chairman of the Finance and Insurance Committee, Jesse Unruh filled that bill, and Ahmanson's relationship with Unruh, which began with the Museum of Science and Industry, was pivotal.[23]

The Ahmanson-Unruh connection was important because it coincided with a larger shift of political and economic power in California in the late 1950s. As Democratic assemblyman Thomas Rees described it, "The power was growing in LA when I was in office. This is where things were done. This is where the banks were moving. This is where foreign groups were locating. This is where major manufacturing was going. This is where UCLA was developing into a university supporting the engineering and technical businesses that we had in Southern California. There was this tremendous growth and everything was going the right way."[24]

Unruh worked to consolidate the power of the Democratic Party, power that he felt had been wrongfully denied the party for years. From Unruh's perspective, pragmatic business leaders should come to terms with the new political reality. Unruh stressed this point in an address to the California Savings and Loan League in 1961. "It is no secret that some businessmen regard the present Democratic administration as a temporary inconvenience at best and can hardly wait for the reestablishment of Republican control in Sacramento." But these businessmen would have to wait a long time to take control of the legislature. Unruh did the political math on registrations and showed that it would take "a revolution" to put the Republicans in control. In the meantime, members of the audience who were waiting for this revolution could choose to sit on the sidelines for what might turn out to be a long period of time, or "they can get in and cooperate with the party in power."[25]

Unruh was very creative in the way he leveraged the Democrats' growing political clout. Developing a strategy that has become commonplace today, he encouraged donors to give to candidates he was backing. He also created a campaign fund that he used to provide additional support. When elected, these legislators were beholden to Unruh, and these political debts had helped elect Unruh speaker of the Assembly in September 1961.

Ahmanson's money and influence played a big part in building Unruh's political power. In 1958, Unruh ran Pat Brown's campaign in Southern California. Officially, he received a ten-thousand-dollar salary for his work.

Unofficially, Howard Ahmanson contributed more than this amount to help Unruh do his work and ensure that Democrats loyal to Unruh got elected to the legislature.[26] After the election, Unruh became chairman of the powerful Ways and Means Committee in the Assembly. Every bill that needed funding passed through his hands.[27]

As Unruh deepened his base of financial backers in the Southland, Ahmanson connected the assemblyman to deep pockets. A new generation of political and economic elites in Southern California provided cash, including developers Mark and Lou Boyer, as well as savings and loan executives Bart Lytton, Manning Post, Gene Klein, and Charlie Wellman. This group became known to Rees, Unruh, and other Democratic legislators as the "Poker Club." Howard Ahmanson was "not part of the group," said Rees. "Ahmanson really was Jesse's private preserve," and he connected Unruh to the so-called Los Angeles establishment.[28]

For his support, Ahmanson enjoyed unparalleled access to Unruh and the legislative process. According to Rees, lobbyists would frequently go to Unruh and say, " 'We want to get this banking bill, [or] we want to get the savings and loan bill out.' And Jesse would make the deal. Then he would go to the chairman [of the committee] and say, 'Oh, by the way, we want this bill out, this bill that Ahmanson has.' That would more or less be the marching instructions."[29]

"Money is the mother's milk of politics," Unruh famously said, but Unruh also made clear his belief that this symbiotic relationship between politician and businessman did not make him captive to anyone's will. "If you can't eat their food, drink their booze, screw their women and then vote against them [lobbyists] you have no business being up here."[30] In fact, this famous quotation mischaracterizes Unruh's values. He was first and foremost a champion for his constituency, the working-class Democratic voters who shared his hardscrabble background. But he understood that, in the managed economy, business interests used the regulatory powers of the state to seek competitive advantage. In a battle between corporate interests that had little effect on his constituency, Unruh was happy to accommodate friends and allies like Ahmanson. According to Lou Cannon, who covered the legislature in these years, "Unruh and Ahmanson thought they could do things more efficiently. There was a good-government side to both of them."[31]

Unruh's political philosophy hardly warmed the hearts of the champions of Jefferson's virtuous democracy. But Ahmanson was equally pragmatic in his approach to politics. "The Right Wing calls me a pink Republican," he said,

"... too rich to be a Democrat and too liberal to be a Republican."[32] With his knowledge of the political system, he also understood, though it sometimes bothered him, that money did not always buy smooth sailing in the sea channels of government. In the office of the commissioner of savings and loans, a great deal had changed since Milton Shaw's tenure.

THE STATE FOCUSES ON THE STRUCTURE OF THE INDUSTRY

Pat Brown's sense that problems in the savings and loan industry could come back to haunt him grew as the election of 1962 loomed. Too many people were looking to get rich quick in the business. Howard Ahmanson called them "carpetbaggers." To Brown they were a political nuisance. To deal with the situation, he needed a stronger commissioner.

Preston Silbaugh, the forty-two-year-old deputy commissioner, succeeded Frank Mackin after Brown appointed Mackin to the bench.[33] A former professor and associate dean of the Stanford Law School, Silbaugh had run the commissioner's office in Los Angeles, the hotbed of the savings and loan industry, and he understood politics and the economics of the market.[34] Silbaugh knew that the governor's biggest problems in the thrift industry stemmed from the process of granting charters and branches, which had grown far too political and complicated.

By law, to grant a new license, the state required an applicant to demonstrate that an area was not adequately served by the existing institutions. The law also required that an applicant have a sound financial plan and that the new facility be in the interests of the association. In fact, these criteria were interpreted loosely, and the only rule that really mattered was that the population in the proposed facility's service territory should be at least twenty-five thousand per association office. Critics of this formula pointed out that the savings capacity of a given community of twenty-five thousand people could vary wildly. On a per capita basis, Beverly Hills, for example, could sock away more money for a rainy day than the working-class communities of South Gate or Compton. So Beverly Hills could benefit from much more competition.

Silbaugh recognized that the licensing process needed to change, but he needed time to develop a strategy. On February 2, 1962, he took a page from Milt Shaw's book and announced a moratorium on the approval of mergers in the savings and loan industry. During the period of the moratorium, the state would commission two studies. The first, led by Stanford University professor of business Edward S. Shaw, would build on SRI's research and look particularly at issues related to concentration and competition.[35] The second, undertaken by Fred Balderston, a professor at the University of California, Berkeley, would focus on the state's licensing criteria. Silbaugh told industry officials that both of these efforts were being made to determine "the optimal structure of the industry."[36]

The optimal structure of the savings and loan industry in California and especially in Southern California was not clear in 1962. With new market conditions and competitive forces at work, regulators and managers struggled to choose the right path forward. Increasingly, savings and loan executives lobbied for growth: by acquisition or geographical expansion, or by entry into new markets such as commercial lending or consumer credit. Regulators struggled to decide whether to allow further consolidation or force savings and loans to remain local and focused on the homebuyer market. Political conservatives in the industry predicted less entrepreneurial freedom and more regulation under Brown. Many hoped that the return of a vanquished but still powerful native son would restore their influence in Sacramento.

BROWN V. NIXON

When he left the governor's office in January 1959, Goodwin Knight told reporters: "I have no grudges, no regrets, no recriminations. I ain't mad at nobody."[37] Nevertheless, as the years of Pat Brown's first term passed, Howard Ahmanson's longtime friend was anxious to redeem himself. He believed that he would have won reelection if not for the interference of Knowland and Nixon.

Back in the private sector, Knight maintained his public profile in Los Angeles by serving as a political commentator on the independent television station KCOP.[38] In March 1961, after a series of political missteps, the California Poll showed that nearly one-third of Californians believed Governor Brown was doing a "poor" job. In a hypothetical matchup, Knight would win. The only other Republican who would do better was the party's 1960 presidential nominee, Richard Nixon.[39] With his eye still on the White House, Nixon told reporters in July 1961 that he did not want to be governor but that if the Republican Party "concludes that I am the only man who can save the state" he would run. He promised to announce his decision by the middle of September.[40]

Political commentators believed that Nixon wasn't just being coy. Traveling the country to make speeches, Nixon found that he was still very popular. If he ran for governor, he would be pressured to swear off running for president in 1964, and he wasn't ready to make that kind of commitment. With Nixon "apparently out of the picture," *Los Angeles Times* political analyst James Bassett concluded, "much of the talk now centers around former Gov. Goodwin J. Knight and San Francisco's Mayor George Christopher."[41]

Knight asked a reluctant Howard Edgerton to arrange a lunch with Nixon to confirm that the former vice president would not run for governor. Buoyed by Nixon's reassurances and press reports that suggested it would be a huge political gamble for Nixon to run for governor and risk undermining his presidential ambitions, Knight happily declared his candidacy on September 11. Vowing to be a full-time governor, he told reporters that "nothing will get me out of the race."[42] Others were not so sure. State Democratic chairman Roger Kent noted, "Knight makes brave statements now, but the noise of Republican check books snapping shut has always sounded like the clap of thunder in his ears. If Nixon runs, he'll hear that sound again."[43]

Two weeks later, Kent's forecast was put to the test when Nixon announced his own gubernatorial campaign.[44] Furious, Knight blasted Nixon and accused him of trying to bribe him to get out of the race, naming Edgerton as Nixon's emissary.[45] Edgerton was adamant that he had "never been an emissary of Nixon on any matter in my entire life."[46] The affair made headlines for several days. In an editorial full of tsk-tsking by the eastern establishment, the *Washington Post* concluded that no one except Pat Brown came out of the mess looking good. In fact, the affair reflected the rancorous state of the Republican Party in California. "Apparently Mr. Knight decided that he would rather pull the political temple down upon both himself and Mr. Nixon than to risk losing the Republican nomination. With this kind of bitterness in the campaign, the former Vice President may be facing one of the toughest campaigns in his political career."[47]

Knight campaigned hard over the next several months but withdrew from the race in February after he became ill.[48] Nixon then faced a challenge from the right wing of the Republican Party. On the eve of the June primary in 1962, writer Carey McWilliams suggested that the momentum was all going Brown's way. The only thing that might ruin his reelection bid was a scandal, and the place to look, he asserted, was in the regulation of the savings and loan industry. "Driving out Wilshire Boulevard today, one notices that almost every other corner is occupied by an ornate neo-Byzantine or equally ornate pseudo-Egyptian savings-and-loan building." Proportionately, "there are more 'S&L' institutions . . . in Los Angeles than there were saloons in Tombstone." The enormous success of the industry, he suggested, made it "a good inference that a major scandal lurks somewhere in the background of these burgeoning S&L institutions."[49]

Fortunately for Brown, McWilliams continued, any scandal tied to the growth of the savings and loans was likely to be bipartisan. "Every element in California politics has its special S&L tycoon as a patron: the far Right has Joe Crail, Nixon has Howard Edgerton, and former Governor Knight has Ahmanson . . . while the liberal Democrats have Bart Lytton."[50] If Brown's administration had been guilty of favoring political allies with charters and branches, his predecessors had done the same.[51]

After Nixon's victory in the primary, however, no scandal materialized. Brown won reelection in the fall with a margin of nearly three hundred thousand votes.[52] But once reelected, he seemed even more committed to a new order in the savings and loan industry.

THE STATE AND THE INDUSTRY GO TO WAR

In his second inaugural, Brown made it clear that he intended to rein in the growing power of the savings and loan tycoons. Among a list of regulatory reforms designed to protect consumers, Brown suggested: "We must apply greater control both to the issuance of charters and to the operating practices of savings and loan associations."[53] Brown's warning to the savings and loan industry was underscored days later when Commissioner Silbaugh released Edward Shaw's searing report on the structure of the savings and loan industry.

Shaw, a pillar of the economics department at Stanford, had been teaching on "the Farm" since 1929, with only a brief interlude during the war when he worked for the navy. He had a reputation as a tough and demanding professor. His report was characteristically blunt. He described what he saw as the growing concentration in the state-chartered savings and loan industry. Holding companies, in particular, were restraining competition. The state's regulatory system was "outmoded" and imbued with "the archaic principle that savings and loan associations are (or should be) neighborhood cooperatives for savers and home buyers, detached from the profit motivation of normal capital markets; that savings should be used locally; that management cannot accurately appraise property beyond easy travel limits of horse and buggy." In actuality, Shaw insisted, the industry was "mammoth" and served a "restless, urbanized population." It belonged in the mainstream of national capital markets "and should not be regulated on the joint principles of mutualism, atomism, and mercantilism."[54]

Shaw argued that misaligned incentives in the regulatory system, including tax breaks and competitive advantages over commercial banks, were preventing investment capital from going to its highest and best use. Instead, too much money was going into housing. The system, he wrote, "puts the mortgage on a pedestal." Shaw wasn't asked to recommend changes to federal policy, where many of these problems originated, but he suggested promoting competition in California by forbidding further mergers and giving a license to any entity that met minimal requirements.[55]

The savings and loan industry was furious about Shaw's report. Silbaugh tried to get the industry's leadership to allow the Stanford professor to speak at the industry's annual management conference, but they refused. Nine industry leaders boarded two airplanes and flew to Sacramento to take their complaints directly to the governor, boycotting an information session hosted by the commissioner.[56] After almost two hours of talk, Brown emerged from the meeting to tell reporters that he had agreed to mediate a conversation between the commissioner and industry representatives.[57]

While the press speculated that the savings and loan executives were engaged in a pure power play, others recognized that the nature of the industry's relationship with regulators was changing. The industry insisted it was not trying to censor reports commissioned by the state. It only wanted the right to have its perspective included. Silbaugh responded that academic experts wouldn't undertake the work if they thought their findings would be changed. Deputy Commissioner Kenneth Scott noted particularly that industry officials seemed to believe that if they were paying the costs of the commissioner's office, then the commissioner ought to act as an industry spokesman. "Those holding this view want us to reach all our decisions in joint industry-division [government] committee meetings. In truly technical matters this may be OK. But in basic matters of public policy, such as mergers or branch office permits, it seems to us this would be totally inappropriate."[58]

In essence, the debate went to the heart of a changing view of the nature of industry-based regulation. As Brown's staff recognized the political power of consumers, they pushed for a more arm's-length relationship between regulators and industry in the savings and loan business and elsewhere.[59] To respond to this new paradigm, the industry went in search of experts of its own.

RESPONDING TO EXPERTS WITH EXPERTS

The California Savings and Loan League commissioned its own academic study led by noted UCLA real estate economists Leo Grebler and Eugene F. Brigham. Grebler was a well-known figure in the field of policy making for mortgage finance. A German émigré who came to the United States in 1937, he had worked for the FHLBB during the war and had served as chief of housing finance for the FHA in Washington before becoming associate director of and research professor at Columbia University's Institute for Urban Land Use and Housing Studies. In 1958, he left New York for UCLA.[60] Brigham had served in the navy during the Korean War and had earned his PhD in finance at the University of California, Berkeley, before joining the faculty at UCLA. They were both serious students of urban economics.

Working quickly, Grebler and Brigham addressed what they believed was the fundamental weakness of the Shaw report: its narrow focus on only the savings and loan industry rather than the performance of the industry within the larger markets for savings and mortgage loans. As the authors pointed out, despite the best efforts of legislators, regulators, and industry lobbyists, financial services were not perfectly compartmentalized. Savers could choose among a variety of investment options. Home buyers could get loans from commercial banks and from mortgage brokers representing large insurance companies as well as from savings and loans. Shaw's narrow perspective on the industry, according to Grebler and Brigham, was "romantic" and out of touch with realities in the financial marketplace.[61]

In the managed economy of the early 1960s, financial institutions were "virtually creatures of society." As Grebler and Brigham pointed out, they were heavily imbued with the public interest and therefore highly regulated. This regulation was necessary because "credit is the lifeblood of the modern economy." But it could also be inefficient from a market point of view. "Resources may be misallocated, competition unduly restrained, credit costs unnecessarily increased, and inefficiencies perpetuated because of the ways in which financial intermediaries organize themselves and operate, or because of misdirected public policies or both."[62] These potential inefficiencies in regulation could be mitigated by smarter public policies, but they were also counterbalanced by the achievement of social goals embedded in the regulatory framework.

Despite the inherent inefficiencies of regulation, Grebler and Brigham concluded, the savings and mortgage markets in California were generally competitive, with a hint of oligopolistic behavior in some local areas. California thrifts were unquestionably "high-income, high-cost, and high-profit organizations," especially when compared to their peers in other states, but these factors could be explained by the higher cost of capital and operations, especially advertising, in the Golden State rather than inefficiency. Moreover, the industry's rapid growth had demanded a higher degree of investment in new facilities—another factor explaining the industry's high costs.

Grebler and Brigham offered suggestions for improving competition. Reflecting the basic assumptions of the managed economy, they addressed their recommendations to management and government. "Neither can alone move the markets or the industry perceptively closer to optimal efficiency. Governmental authorities can do so by revising the rules of the game, but it is management that plays the game, and management has considerable leeway in playing it within the rules."[63] The authors also noted that any move to greater competition would place a greater burden on regulators to "minimize the hazards to safety" that would come as managers were pressured to relax credit standards and reserve ratios in order to maximize profits.[64] In other words, deregulation would encourage greater risk taking. Greater risk taking might produce a market that was more efficient in the long term, but the social cost to depositors and home buyers might be higher.

The controversy sparked by these two economic studies commissioned by the state and the industry reflected a significant break in the relationship between regulator and regulated in the savings and loan industry. In the earlier postwar era, regulators like Milton Shaw had focused primarily on ensuring that savings and loans were prudently managed and that depositors were protected. Safety was their dominant concern. Markets were allocated among competitors on the basis of a relatively simple formula—twenty-five thousand unserved customers—because according to this paradigm, the industry performed an important public service.

The Shaw and Grebler-Brigham reports signaled that regulators in California, and later in Washington, now intended to emphasize competition and market efficiency. Competition was important to politicians, particularly Pat Brown, because it promised better prices and fairer treatment to consumers. It also removed the political liabilities stemming from scandals associated with the regulatory process when the government exercised a heavy hand in allocating markets among players in the industry. But as the competitive structure of the market became increasingly important, it diminished the fundamental basis on which the savings and loan industry had been created and then protected by government—to promote home ownership in the state and in the nation. This shift in philosophy would have enormous consequences for the savings and loan industry in California.

As the largest savings and loan in California and the nation in the mid-1960s, Home Savings was especially well positioned for a new and more competitive era in the industry. Although the Grebler and Brigham report supported the commissioner's view that there was little evidence that savings and loans above a certain threshold became more operationally efficient as they grew, Howard Ahmanson and Ken Childs undoubtedly chuckled when they read this conclusion.[65] On vacation in the Middle East when the report was released, Ahmanson knew that with its extremely low operating costs and enormous capital reserves, Home Savings could afford to take risks that others couldn't. Soon the importance of this ability would become all too clear in an increasingly competitive market. But in the meantime, he wasn't worried about the future of Home Savings. For the moment, he was more preoccupied with his son.

THIRTEEN

Short of Domestic Bliss

HOWARD AND DOTTIE'S MARRIAGE had never followed a standard script. Childless for seventeen years, the relationship was framed by social activities and trips around the globe. By the late 1940s, alcohol was affecting the health of their marriage. Dottie joined Alcoholics Anonymous and, coincident with her relative sobriety, surprised everyone when in 1949 she announced that she was pregnant.

The birth of a son changed everything for Howard. He now had an heir to what he called his "empire." Like his own father, he doted on his son. And Howard junior also turned out to be a precocious learner. Nicknamed "Steady" (a shortening of his grandmother's maiden name, Fieldstad), he was reading by age three.[1] Before the age of eight, he was quoted in a newspaper article explaining how a thermonuclear reaction took place.

Not surprisingly, given how late they had come to parenting and the fact that the boy was likely to be their only child, Howard and Dottie were extremely protective. The memory of the notorious kidnapping of aviator Charles Lindbergh's infant son in 1932 contributed to their concerns. Steady was not encouraged to run free in the neighborhood and play with other children. He never learned to ride a bike as a child.

In public, Howard senior liked to cultivate an image as the devoted and adoring father. He told *Fortune* in 1958 that he and his son were heavily involved in Cub Scouts. "This month it was jujitsu. Next month it's kites. I'm the oldest and lousiest father in the Pack." He and Dottie commiserated: "Dottie swears she'll be the only P.T.A. mother in school in a wheelchair."[2] In private, when he did have time to work on Scout projects with his son, the interaction was often one-sided. "One time I had to build a bird house," Howard junior remembers. "By the time he finished showing me how to do it, there was nothing left for me to do."[3] Sometimes the family went to a ranch they owned near San Bernardino. Howard and Steady would ride together, with Howard on a horse and Steady on a pony.[4] More often, Howard left parenting to Dottie; his trusted secretary, Evelyn Barty; or other members of his household staff.

The family spent many weekends on Harbor Island, eating and drinking at the Newport Yacht Club and sailing together. After Howard's heart attack in 1956, Dottie was usually the skipper when they raced. She took classes in piloting, seamanship, and advanced navigation.[5] Howard liked to brag that she had "probably sailed more tough races than any other woman" except Peggy Slatter, a famous yachtswoman of the era.[6]

Howard's nephews were frequent visitors to Harbor Island and the house on June Street in Hancock Park. In 1958, the *Los Angeles Times* published a photo of the extended family arranged around a French coffee table. Bill Ahmanson and his first wife, Patty, were arrayed with their five daughters: Mary Jane, Patty, Amy, Dorothy, and Joanne. Bob Ahmanson stood behind his wife, Kathy, who wrapped one arm around their little girl, Karen. Perched on a couch with his hands on his knees, eight-year-old Steady looked eagerly off camera while his proud parents, Howard and Dottie, stood beside the mantel on the hearth, Dottie with her arms crossed and her expression almost annoyed, and Howard, in a light suit with a white handkerchief in his breast pocket, smiling like the amused patriarch that he was.[7]

Among this group of girls and adults, Steady buried himself in reading books and volumes from the encyclopedia. With a crew cut and thick glasses at the age of eight, he was by turns excited and withdrawn. By his own admission, he was generally not introspective or self-conscious. Within the family, he later gravitated to his Aunt Kathy because he enjoyed her wit and she was emotionally "cool" in a family that tended toward what Steady perceived as sentimental and "gooshy" emotions, especially after the alcohol started to flow.[8]

After the heart attack, Howard worked from home. The swimming and yachting, combined with his natural ruddy complexion, left him looking "forever sunburned," yet not necessarily athletic.[9] With all his exercising he was down to 162 pounds, he wrote to Hayden. His tailor took in two inches at the waist of his suit pants. The jumpsuits he liked to wear when he was relaxing in Newport Beach or on the boat ballooned a little around him. But the new regimen had done nothing for his mental attitude. "I still have my same repulsive disposition," he joked.[10] In fact, his personality was so strong that, as Dottie put it, he could "change the spirit and conversational trend of a whole roomful of people merely by his mood." Sometimes that meant things became dour or serious. More often, he could turn a room of people "sitting around with their teeth in their mouth" into a party.[11]

Despite his desire to focus his business on Southern California, Ahmanson's interest in the wider world did not diminish. He and Dottie continued to travel. In April 1957, they invited Bill and Bob and their wives, along with the ever-present Evelyn Barty, to cruise the South Seas on the S.S. *Monterey*. Two years later, Howard planned a similar trip to Japan. In his usual glib and ironic style, he wrote a letter to a friend in Japan to make the arrangements. "I suppose we should see a Temple—good God, imagine coming home without one picture of a Temple, but I would prefer that it be close to the road and, as far as I am concerned, after you have seen one temple you have seen all of them. My compatriots are all of the same mood, believe me."[12] This trip had to be postponed, however, when Howard was hospitalized in May 1959 with an ulcer.[13]

By this time in his life, Ahmanson was pestered with health issues. In addition to his heart problems, he suffered from gout and lived on a fairly restricted, mostly vegetarian diet.[14] Under doctor's orders, he ate custards and pureed food.[15] He rarely slept well and often read or played the piano or organ late at night.[16] He drank heavily, though only the people closest to him could tell when he was really drunk. Even after he had been drinking, he had an uncanny ability to recall conversations and facts.[17] His doctors tried to get him to stop smoking and limit his drinking, but his lifestyle took a toll on his body.

When they returned from the Asia trip, the Ahmansons moved into a new home on South Hudson in Hancock Park, L.A.'s sanctuary for the very rich. The Tudor-style mansion had been built for Frederik S. Albertson, an automobile company executive, on the eve of the Great Depression in 1929. Designed by Alexander D. Chisholm, it was baronial in mass and tone.[18] From the flagstone walk, a carved door opened to admit guests to a spacious foyer with a thirty-foot domed ceiling. Golden oak-paneled walls set off paintings of the old masters. In the library, walnut paneling deepened the shadows in the room. The master bedroom featured seascapes by Millard Sheets hung on walls covered with a deep green Chinese silk. The window expanses were draped in gold and sand brocade.[19] Reflecting Ahmanson's eclecticism and deep-seated opposition to authority (unless he was in charge), a "Beatnik Alley" with chalk-white walls was splashed with what a society columnist called "vivid colors of the moderns." In the music room, Howard stashed and played his instruments, including his organ, accordion, banjo, vibraharp, ukulele, and clavietta.[20] Across the floors, the nails of Dottie's French poodles clicked as they followed her through the house, paying scant attention to her four cats.[21]

Despite the grandeur of the house, it was not especially ostentatious. It avoided nostalgia for the Spanish colonial era in California. It reflected the courtly life that Ahmanson imagined for himself, but it was a life that he wanted to live privately, not publicly. And it was the private life that was increasingly troubled. Alcohol and Dottie's "gremlins" fed a fundamental instability in the marriage, which Howard often tried to escape by sailing.

ESCAPE TO THE OCEAN

Ahmanson's attention to detail and strategy was especially obvious before a race. In 1961, for example, he badly wanted to win the Transpacific Yacht Race (the Transpac) from Los Angeles to Honolulu, so he bought a new boat. Built in the late 1920s, the eighty-one-foot sloop was named the *Barlovento*. It had won the Transpac before, finishing "first-in-fleet" in 1957, and had made the journey several times.[22] Howard rechristened it the *Sirius II*. When he bought it, the boat had a broken mast. After it was repaired, he had the mast and spinnaker pole x-rayed to identify any hairline fracture that might lead to another break.[23]

The race crew of fourteen included some of Ahmanson's closest associates: his nephews Robert and Bill Ahmanson, architect William Pereira, attorney Thomas Webster, and USC president Norman Topping. But there were also a couple of champion sailors: Fred Schenck, the 1957 national Snipe (a type of racing dinghy) sailing champion, as well as Bill Ficker.[24] Ahmanson offered his crew a one-page letter outlining his expectations. From the start, he insisted, all strategy would be delegated to the watch captain or his assistant. Yet he invited everyone to offer their best judgment and advice at all times. "There is almost no one aboard that is not fully competent to skipper a ship to Honolulu," he wrote, "so speak up. We would be fools to not beg for your suggestions about *anything at any time.* There is nothing that cannot be improved, and I've never seen such even-tempered sailing geniuses as you gents when it comes to taking suggestions from the other guy."[25]

On the day before the race, a reporter asked Ahmanson about his chances. "I'm always a pessimist," he confessed, "but the crew is always optimistic."[26] The crew's optimism seemed to be well placed the next day. *Sirius II* was extremely good off the start and was the first to reach the west end of Catalina. With the wind abeam, the crew covered a record distance on the first day.[27] That night the wind blew very hard, with water pouring over the deck.

There were all sorts of problems with provisions. Pereira was in charge of the menus. He had labeled cans and bags of food for each meal. But the first night, when Ficker went below deck, he discovered water everywhere. To lighten the boat, Howard had had the engine removed, but the underwater exhaust pipes had not been plugged. The whole crew worked the bilge pumps to empty the water. Then they discovered that the labels had been washed off all the food. "Everything was confused and the menu book was lost," remembers Ficker.

Howard's chauffeur, who was supposed to do the cooking, got sick and was incapacitated for the entire voyage. Topping, the president of USC, volunteered. Opening unlabeled cans and making the best of what he discovered, he prepared the meals and kept his assigned watch.[28] On board, by the skipper's rules, there was no drinking—except for beer and a Martini Night midway through the race.

After four days at sea, the crew discovered an imminent disaster. A crack had appeared in the bowsprit. If it grew worse, the boat would lose its jib. The crew immediately hove to and patched the crack as best they could. One of the professional sailors onboard, Roy Norr, said he was praying the high-masted boat wouldn't come apart in the race. "We were driving her hard to make her go as fast as possible." At some points, the boat ripped through the ocean at fourteen knots.[29]

Despite this speed, *Sirius II* swapped the lead back and forth with the *Ticonderoga,* a seventy-two-foot ketch owned and skippered by a Michigan native who had won twenty-two major events in the Atlantic. On the second-to-last day, the crew trailed the *Ticonderoga* by twenty-five miles on "dead reckoning" positions. But on the final day, over 226 miles, the *Sirius II* surged ahead. As they approached Hawaii after a 2,225-mile race from San Pedro, Ahmanson and his crew battled the *Ticonderoga* for position in the Molokai Channel. Spinnakers on both boats ballooned as the sun dropped below Diamond Head peak. Then suddenly, as they neared Koko Head, the spinnaker pole on *Sirius II* snapped. Thinking quickly, the crew cut the halyard, but they couldn't slice through the lines. With the sail dragging in the water behind her, the boat still made ten knots. As darkness gathered, the boat, thirty-seven minutes ahead of its rival, cut through the searchlight beaming across the water to mark the finish line with the crew assembled on the fantail. A flotilla of small boats packed with spectators swarmed around the ship with air horns blasting. At the time, it was the closest finish in the twenty-two-year history of the race.[30] Dottie sent Howard congratulations but she was not there when he celebrated.

LOSING BROTHER AND WIFE

Months earlier, in March 1960, Howard had returned to Los Angeles from a different sailing adventure to learn that his brother was gravely ill. Hayden died soon afterward of a cerebral hemorrhage.[31] At the funeral, Howard stood with Aimee, Bill, and Bob as his brother was buried in Omaha. It's unclear whether Dottie went with him, but six weeks later the couple separated.[32] Dottie remained in the house on Harbor Island. Howard stayed in the home in Hancock Park. With his usual wit, Howard explained to a reporter that of the couple's two dogs he had gotten "the one that bites."

Steady shuttled back and forth between houses and parents. Howard and Dottie wrote careful, even thoughtful notes to each other as they negotiated his schedule. Dottie explained to her son that Howard had not kept his wedding vows, but she did not elaborate.[33] She filed for divorce on May 6.[34]

Howard vacillated between trying to save the marriage and enjoying his new freedom to socialize without worrying about Dottie's drinking or reaction. At the same time, he continued to seek the fond and doting relationship with his son that his father had had with him. In August, he took the ten-year-old Steady on a tour of western national parks, including Yellowstone and the Grand Canyon.[35]

Throughout their separation, Howard and Dottie rehashed many of the deep tensions in their relationship. They tried counseling. Howard sometimes came to dinner at the house on Harbor Island. Sometimes they went out together. Dinner at La Scala. Dancing at the Grove. They went to parties with mutual friends. They attended community events, including a dinner at LACMA in April. Drinking led to fights in the car on the way home. Howard criticized Dottie's friends. They argued over whether Steady should attend public or private school. At times, Dottie wrote that Howard was "mad and bitchy."[36]

As the divorce trial loomed, Howard tried to convince Dottie to postpone. Alone, they talked over the terms of their settlement. Dottie did not keep a journal, but she sometimes jotted personal notes in her calendar. She wrote that Howard had agreed to a 50–50 split on everything.[37] But then they fought again. In letters to Dottie, Howard continued to call her "darling" and referred to himself as "yer ole man."[38]

Dottie and Howard worried that the divorce would cause Steady to retreat even further into himself. Howard insisted that Steady's problems all stemmed from the fact that he was brilliant.[39] As his father had done with him, Howard tried to include Steady in business meetings at the house, but the boy crawled under the table and showed little interest in the intricacies of mortgage lending and insurance. When Dottie wanted to send Steady to a psychiatrist, Howard resisted. Somewhat like his son, he tended to avoid introspection about his own emotions and hesitated to put his only son in a position where he would be expected to reveal himself. Eventually, however, he agreed.[40]

One night, when Dottie and Steady were eating dinner in the Harbor Island house, the eleven-year-old asked his mother how much the psychiatrist cost. When Dottie told him, he said he thought that "$30 an hour was pretty high to feed me cookies." Knowing that his father had gone to a psychiatrist, he asked his mother if she was going to one too. She had gone to one, and Howard had tried to get her to go back. Dottie asked her son if Howard still thought she was "nuts." Ever blunt, Steady replied, "Yes."[41]

Three weeks later, on the afternoon of October 23, Howard and Dottie appeared in court for the pretrial proceedings in their divorce.[42] Despite the looming finality of their break, Steady seemed to be doing fine in school. One Friday night when the boy was at Howard's home in Hancock Park, Dottie answered the phone. Steady reported that he was watching TV. His father had gone out and left him with the household staff.[43] Sunday morning, Dottie opened the *Los Angeles Times* to see a picture of Howard with the city's paragon of beauty and charm—Caroline Leonetti.[44]

CAROLINE LEONETTI

A charm, fashion, and beauty expert, Caroline Leonetti was a well-known television and radio personality in 1961. Twelve years younger than Ahmanson, she had been born in San Francisco in 1918 to first-generation Italian immigrants.[45] Her father was a wholesale tailor who worked for some of the city's leading haberdashers. Her mother was a seamstress who designed and made children's clothing. As a young teenager, she was anything but a modeling queen. At five foot five inches tall, she weighed 165 pounds. She read voraciously and avoided the social scene in junior high. Her mother got her interested in dancing, exercising, acting, and home economics. Driven by an inner discipline to transform herself, Leonetti lost weight. She was elected student body vice president in high school and was class valedictorian. A scholarship to the California School of Design helped to cultivate her eye for fashion and style. She took ballet to learn how to carry herself and move gracefully. She studied gymnastics to help build muscle.[46]

The 1939 World's Fair on Treasure Island in San Francisco opened a path to Leonetti's entrepreneurial future. As the winner of the city's Goddess of Beauty contest, Leonetti traveled the country inviting people to the fair. The experience further enhanced her self-confidence, brought modeling opportunities, and led to her decision to open her own school and modeling agency—the House of Charm—in San Francisco. Distilling the lessons she had learned, she taught her students to analyze and accept themselves, to make the most of their physical, mental, and spiritual qualities, and then to live gracefully.[47]

Leonetti's success attracted the attention of San Francisco radio host Art Linkletter. Every Wednesday she joined him in the studio for a segment called "What's Doing Ladies?" during which she provided tips on fashion and style to women in Linkletter's audience. With the advent of television after the war, Linkletter moved to Los Angeles, where his program was renamed *House Party* and was simulcast on both radio and TV. Leonetti stayed with the program, moving her House of Charm to Los Angeles.

Personally, the timing was good. An early marriage had ended in divorce, but not before the birth of her daughter, Margo. In Los Angeles as a single parent, Leonetti added a talent agency to her list of entrepreneurial initiatives. It was the first to be franchised by the Screen Actors Guild (SAG) and the American Federation of Television and Radio Artists (AFTRA). Her clients and students included Virginia Mayo, Mitzi Gaynor, Vicki Carr, Kim Novak, Angie Dickinson, and Jane Russell. Like Howard, Caroline was driven to succeed and worked sixteen hours a day.

Even before the end of the war, Leonetti had established a reputation as a fashion consultant and authority on "self-improvement for women." She spoke to women's groups. On Friday nights, she presided over fashion show dinners at Henri's on Sunset Boulevard.[48] She judged beauty contests. A leader in the mostly male Hollywood Advertising Club, she organized a fashion show in 1947 with gossip columnist Hedda Hopper as the featured speaker.[49] She was in the newspapers constantly from 1947 on. To combat juvenile delinquency, she founded the Los Angeles Charm Clinic for Under-privileged Girls, which, according to one newspaper report, spread to 135 cities in the United States and Canada.[50] As early as 1950, she became a regular on the local CBS affiliate offering hints on charm.[51] That year, she published a book, *24 Steps to Loveliness,* which launched yet another career as a syndicated newspaper columnist.[52]

Caroline was introduced to Howard by Art and Lois Linkletter at a wedding for a mutual friend. They sat together at dinner. Caroline had a broken arm and had covered the cast with gardenias. This elegant touch didn't solve the practical problem of cutting the meat they were served for dinner, so she asked for Howard's help. As the great financier, he expected to be held in awe and was dismayed that she knew nothing about the savings and loan business or his reputation.

Smitten, Howard invited Caroline out on a number of occasions. Caroline, however, had spent a lifetime fending off the advances of rich and powerful men. She was not about to rush into a serious relationship with a man who was technically still married to someone else. In the meantime, Howard adjusted to his life as a bachelor and to the camaraderie of his friends, including two university presidents.

UNIVERSITY PRESIDENTS

In March 1960, Howard had received a letter from his friend Henry A. Bubb, the president of Capital Federal Savings and Loan in Topeka, Kansas. According to Bubb, neither the worst snowstorm in sixty years nor its associated floods could compare with the disaster of losing the University of Kansas's chancellor, Franklin D. Murphy, to UCLA. As a member of the Kansas Board of Regents, Bubb had seen Murphy in action. "He is one of the most brilliant and most personable men I have ever known." Bubb credited Murphy with transforming the University of Kansas "into one of the top universities in the United States." "California's gain is Kansas' loss," Bubb wrote, "and it's a big loss."[53] Bubb hoped that Howard would "make a point to get acquainted" with Murphy and his wife, Judy, once they arrived in the Golden State.

Murphy was a brilliant, ambitious, and visionary man with "a gift for psychological insight into the intricacies of power and personality," according to his biographer, Margaret Leslie Davis.[54] Like Ahmanson, he had been born and raised in the Midwest, one of two sons of a prosperous father who died just as he was coming into adulthood. Like Ahmanson, Murphy had followed his father's career path, although into medicine rather than insurance, graduating first in his class at the University of Pennsylvania. Following a brilliant career as a doctor during the war, Murphy turned down an offer to join the medical faculty at Penn. Instead, he went to the University of Kansas to help build the institution that his father had started. He became dean of the medical school and in 1951, at the age of thirty-five, was appointed chancellor of the entire university. Enormously successful in this role, Murphy ran headlong into political conflicts when Kansas elected a mercurial populist as governor who was determined to demonize the "elitism" of the university system. In July 1960, Murphy left Kansas to become the chancellor of UCLA.[55] He told the guests assembled to witness his investiture that fall that he intended to transform what some considered a commuter college into a world-class university.[56]

As chancellor, Murphy understood that UCLA's future depended on the broader cultural and economic development of Los Angeles. He sensed that the city and the region were on the cusp of a cultural renaissance as millions of new residents sought to define their individual and collective relationships to place and as a new elite, enriched by the city's postwar growth, began to exercise its influence on the community's institutions. With remarkable acumen and alacrity, Murphy began to see himself as the culture broker who would manage big egos and guide the institution building that would make this vision possible.

Murphy met Howard Ahmanson, and they began to work together after Ed Carter asked both of them to serve on the newly reconstituted board of LACMA, with Murphy in charge of the building fund campaign. They soon became close friends and collaborators. The two men drank Scotch, chain-smoked, and talked about money, women, art, and the future of Los Angeles. According to Margaret Leslie Davis, "Murphy gave free rein to his bawdy Irish wit in competition with Ahmanson's droll observations."[57] At times, Ahmanson thought Murphy tended to be high-strung and Napoleonic.[58] But as Davis points out, they had much in common. "In their camaraderie they acknowledged a truth about themselves: they were not part and parcel of the ultrachic, sophisticated circle in which they functioned so well." They were midwesterners, deeply connected to what "Murphy insisted was the actual, beating heart of America."[59]

Howard also remained close to his own alma mater. When the university's board named Norman Topping president in 1958, Howard had his chauffeur drive him from Harbor Island to a reception for the new leader. When Howard was introduced to him, Topping was holding a martini glass. Howard was delighted to discover that he was not a teetotaler like the former president. Topping was also a transplant from the middle of the country and a medical doctor. Born and raised in Missouri, he had moved to Los Angeles with his parents at the age of fourteen and graduated from Los Angeles High School.[60] After Topping moved into a house a block away from Ahmanson, the two men saw more of each other. Topping became a member of Howard's racing crew because he could do double duty as Howard's personal physician.[61]

While Ahmanson recruited Topping to sail with him, Topping invited Howard to help him shape the future of his alma mater. In late 1960, Ahmanson joined USC's board.[62] He made several major gifts, including one million dollars in 1962 to help fund the development of a biosciences research center.[63] When the facility was complete, Howard brought Steady with him for a tour that included quarters for lab rats, mice, and monkeys. Steady dubbed the place "rat heaven."[64]

Howard's relationships with Murphy and Topping in the early 1960s were critical to the continued development of his vision for Los Angeles and his understanding of his potential role as a businessman and a philanthropist. As presidents of the region's two major universities, these men were keenly aware of how money, culture, and intellectual pursuits might shape the future of the region. With Millard Sheets, Ahmanson had married the essential localism of the savings and loan concept to collective images of community identity. In conversations with Murphy and Topping, however, Howard's cultural, commercial, and political vision was changing in 1963. Home Savings and Loan was more than a collection of neighborhood thrifts; it was a financial powerhouse in a city ready to take its place among the great cities of the world. From Ahmanson's point of view, the work of building that city was shared by private enterprise and public capital as a natural extension of the managed economy. Increasingly, however, the easy and comfortable relationship between government and private enterprise seemed to be coming apart as one era came to an end and another one began.

FOURTEEN

Breakdown of Consensus

PRESTON SILBAUGH HAD NEVER BEEN POPULAR with the savings and loan industry. In 1962, on the eve of the release of the Shaw report and in the midst of another good year for savings and loans, the commissioner seemed especially gloomy. "You are to be greatly commended for the role you have played in the 40s and 50s in home financing," he told executives at a thrift industry conference. But Silbaugh was worried about the future. "I do not think you can reasonably expect to grow at such a startling rate in the 1960s. The backlog need for simple shelter has been filled. Growth at such a rapid rate through the 60s might even imply a misallocation of national savings."[1]

Silbaugh's conclusions were echoed by New York University professor of finance Paul Nadler, who also declared that the "golden days" were coming to an end. Commercial banks, which had often ignored the savings and mortgage markets before 1957, were actively pursuing these customers. "From now on this industry will probably face the same competitive pressures that are now being experienced by the commercial banks and savings banks of the nation."[2]

Indeed, the political economy that had fueled the stratospheric growth of Home Savings was beginning to turn by the early 1960s. After growing at an average annual rate of 6.6 percent in the first decade after the war, the U.S. economy eased to a still strong pace of 5.5 percent between 1955 and 1965. Personal spending growth rates, which had averaged 8.1 percent in the first decade after the war, slowed to 5.9 percent as America's postwar demand for housing, automobiles, appliances, furniture, and a host of consumer goods was finally satiated.[3] Ups and downs in the business cycle reappeared. Three brief recessions in 1954, 1958, and 1961 contributed to an increase in the unemployment rate. California followed its own economic path, but it was not immune to national trends. Personal income rose far more quickly than income for the nation as a whole. But the rate of income growth, which had averaged nearly 9.4 percent between 1950 and 1956, slowed to 6.7 percent between 1956 and 1963.[4] Most important to entrepreneurs like Howard Ahmanson in financial services, debt increasingly paid for growth in the private and public sectors. Fearing inflation, the Federal Reserve began to raise interest rates in 1961, which had a major impact on the savings and loan industry.

The end of boom times fueled increased competition in nearly all sectors of the economy. With marketplace competition, political competition increased as well. California thrifts faced new challenges in Congress, in the state legislature, in the offices and hearing rooms of the Federal Home Loan Bank Board and the California Division of Savings and Loans, and in the chambers of local government as their interests collided with those of business rivals, increasingly vocal consumers, and minorities who had experienced discrimination. The politics of business were also influenced by changes in the market and consumer taste as the era of tract homes gave way to large-scale planned communities. Developers took advantage of new interstate highways to develop parcels of land far from the central city that included a mix of land uses for commercial and residential purposes. Under the weight of all these historical forces, a fundamental revision of the regulatory approach to the mortgage market posed major challenges for the savings and loan industry and marked the first signs of crisis in the managed economy.

Howard Ahmanson and Howard Edgerton faced these challenges from different perspectives. By 1963, the glad-handing Edgerton presided over the largest federally chartered savings and loan in the country, with more than a billion dollars in assets. Edgerton's California Federal paled by comparison to Ahmanson's nearly two-billion-dollar Home Savings and Loan, which was by far the largest savings and loan of any kind in the country. Edgerton supervised nearly two thousand employees soon to be located in a new twenty-eight-story corporate headquarters on Wilshire Boulevard, complete with a rooftop pad for Edgerton to land his two-seater Bell helicopter. Meanwhile, Ahmanson ran his empire from his home in Hancock Park.

Political fights over issues that affected California Federal's competitive opportunities took place in Washington. Not surprisingly, Edgerton, a former president of the U.S. Saving and Loan League, continued to be active at the national level and served as vice chairman of the League's Legislative Committee. Home Savings, which was primarily regulated by the Division of Savings and Loans in Sacramento, paid far more attention to politics in

Sacramento, though Ahmanson delegated most of this sensitive work to the lanky and affable Robert DeKruif.

Late at night, Edgerton often visited Ahmanson's home. The two men drank outside by the pool. Occasionally one or the other went for a swim. They talked about business. While Edgerton had shareholders and federal regulators to worry about, Ahmanson was smug in his relative freedom from these interlopers. After Edgerton provided Ahmanson with information on Washington politics, Ahmanson, full of alcohol, pontificated. Frequently they argued. Edgerton put up with Ahmanson's "egotistical" indulgences because, in the end, Ahmanson was "brilliant" and shed uncommon light on the market, the industry, and the politics.[5]

Through the 1950s, the friendship between the two men reflected a critical characteristic of the era of the managed economy—policy making built around personal relationships between competitors and regulators anchored in mutual systems of trust and obligation. In the 1960s, these relationships came under attack as consumers, minorities, journalists, and others who had been left outside the arenas of power challenged the status quo and as economic interests increasingly turned to the political arena to seek competitive advantage. Under the stress of this new era, the friendship between the two Howards would be tested, and in their response to crisis much of the future of the managed economy would be revealed.

COMPETITION

Threats to the savings and loan industry emerged first in the broader economy. At the beginning of the postwar era, most American families kept their nest eggs in savings accounts or invested in life insurance. Stocks were for the rich. Mutual funds, discredited by the Crash of 1929, had not yet come back into favor. Pension funds were just beginning to exercise influence on the investment community. While inflation was low, many investors who had lived through the Depression focused primarily on security and safety.

From Wall Street to Main Street, the lines within the carefully compartmentalized financial system began to blur by the early 1960s. Insurance companies developed policies to supplement Social Security or private pensions and moved into the market for the savings of the average household. After Congress established new rules that protected investors, Wall Street entrepreneurs proffered new mutual funds as an alternative to fixed-rate savings deposit accounts.[6] As early as 1950, the president of the California Savings and Loan League warned his peers: "The stock and bond houses are now after the man with $25 per month to invest in securities by offering him a systematic savings program for securities investment."[7] Meanwhile, commercial banks mounted a new assault on the savings and mortgage markets.

Political competition also posed a threat to the savings and loan industry. In the early 1960s, commercial banks gained a powerful ally when James J. Saxon, the former general counsel of the American Bankers Association, became U.S. comptroller of the currency. Saxon encouraged the Federal Reserve to let banks into a variety of businesses from which they had been barred, including insurance and credit cards.[8] He also pushed to level the playing field in the competition for savings deposits. Banks and other financial services institutions decided the time was ripe to challenge some of the competitive advantages given to thrifts by legislators in Sacramento and Congress.

As they rallied to resist the banks, some thrift executives were stunned to discover that politicians and the general public no longer associated them with the communitarian values celebrated in *It's a Wonderful Life*. After a trip to Washington in August 1961, Howard Edgerton's right-hand man, Oliver Chatburn, reported that "in the minds of some members of the Congress, there is no longer such a thing as a 'mutual' association. . . . Many of those to whom we talked stated frankly that they regarded us as an integral part of 'big business.'"[9] As some in the industry pressed politicians and regulators for opportunities to expand geographically and enter other lines of business, including commercial real estate and consumer loans, they reinforced this perception.

Consumers increasingly shared this perspective. According to one leading survey, the public now regarded savings and loan people as "shrewd businessmen out to make a profit" compared to other financial services companies, which were staffed with "serious, community-minded professionals devoting their lives to specialized training in banking and investment practices."[10]

Many people in the savings and loan industry blamed entrepreneurs like Ahmanson and the new holding companies for tarnishing the image of the thrift in America. These tensions led to political divisions within the industry. At odds with the majority in the U.S. League of Savings and Loans, several leading Los Angeles–based stock and holding companies joined together in 1963 and 1964 to hire law firms in Los Angeles and Washington to lobby for them in the legislature and Congress. In June 1965, they created their own trade association, the Council of Savings and Loan Financial Corporations, and hired former California assemblyman Tom Bane from the San Fernando Valley to represent them.[11]

Ahmanson resisted the direction of his peers. He proclaimed that he was "dead set" against the idea of savings and loans moving into the banking business. His primary objection went to the heart of his view of the managed economy. If thrifts tried to become banks, they would lose many of the competitive advantages provided to them by the legislature and Congress. Moreover, harkening back to the lessons learned from the White Spot hamburger joint in Lincoln, he argued that thrifts would lose focus if they tried to diversify their services. "We run a specialty shop and banks run a department store," he said. Diversification of services would lead to greater overhead and therefore more risk—something he didn't want.[12]

Ahmanson proved to be right. On the political front, thrifts were big losers in 1962 when Congress imposed new taxes that had a major effect on some California savings and loans. According to one investment advisor, they "wiped out most of the pre-tax gains in 1963" for publicly traded savings and loan holding companies.[13] Meanwhile, in the regulatory arena, the comfortable relationship with regulators that had been a hallmark of the golden era of the industry and of the managed economy became noticeably more uncomfortable.

VANGUARD OF A NEW POLICY ELITE

As thrifts and other financial institutions pushed for new opportunities, they were sometimes supported and sometimes inhibited by economists and other academics who began to question the fundamental compartmentalization of financial services embedded in the New Deal structure. These academics, including several based at the University of Chicago, asked questions about the impact of this regulatory system on the overall performance of the economy. Unlike their predecessors, who were primarily concerned with issues of stability and security, these new pundits focused on economic efficiency. They were also concerned that regulatory systems were too often "captured" to serve private, rather than public, interests.

As sociologist Marc Allen Eisner describes it, these new ideas established themselves broadly within the regulatory environment in the early 1960s and began to reshape the policy framework.[14] In 1961, for example, the Commission on Money and Credit suggested that "safeguarding small depositors and the money supply, until now a main objective of investment regulation, may be better accomplished in other ways."[15] The commission wanted to lower the burden of "a multitude of regulations promulgated by the states and the federal government." It also wanted to let commercial banks, savings banks, and savings and loan associations "direct their lending into areas and uses where more profitable opportunities exist."[16]

The regulation of the California savings and loan industry also reflected shifting ideologies. Governor Brown's appointment of the controversial Preston Silbaugh marked the beginning of this transition. When Silbaugh commissioned Professors Edward Shaw (Stanford University) and Frederick Balderston (University of California, Berkeley) to study the industry, he explicitly urged them to consider issues related to economic efficiency as well as security and stability.

The industry resisted this new theoretical approach to regulation and called for a return to the cooperative approach of the past. The CEO of one of the state's largest savings and loan holding companies wrote Silbaugh that he was "deeply concerned that the academic approach" would fail to produce the results the regulators were looking for. "As I ponder the problem," he wrote, "it seems that a new tack might be in order. We in the industry could continue to spend countless hours commenting on reports by college professors—or we could spend the time drawing on the best knowledge and experience available in the industry and put it to work, along with the help of your advisors and qualified research organizations, to engage in a cooperative effort which might more quickly and efficiently serve the public interest."[17]

Unfortunately for the thrifts, at the state level, regulators were no longer interested in cooperation. Politically they were suspicious of the savings and loan industry. Intellectually, they were focused on creating a regulatory system that would promote economic efficiency and let the marketplace do its work. Even when the thrifts scored an apparent victory, it only seemed to deepen the regulatory crisis.

Governor Brown, for example, had responded to the uproar over the Shaw Report by replacing Preston Silbaugh. The new commissioner, Frederick E. Balderston, was a tall, thin man with a long face and a big smile who often sported a bowtie. Raised in a suburb of Philadelphia with a passion for baseball and learning, he was the son of the dean of the Wharton School at the University of Pennsylvania. After attending a Quaker prep school, he had come to California in 1940 to attend Deep Springs College. Balderston served with his brother as a conscientious objector during the war, driving an ambulance with the British Eighth Army in North Africa and Italy. He had received a British medal for bravery. After the war, he completed his undergraduate education at Cornell and then earned a PhD in economics from Princeton. He joined the faculty of the University of California in 1953. Under contract with the Division of Savings and Loans, Balderston had played a substantial role in the revision of the state's rules regarding new charters and branches in 1963 before being tapped to become commissioner.

Under Balderston's leadership, the California Division of Savings and Loans worked to brighten the light on the industry and let the market discipline performance.[18] Like Silbaugh and others, Balderston believed the golden era of the savings and loan was over. Market conditions would put more pressure on management to manage risk and contain costs. "Price inflation no longer provides an automatic bail-out for over generous loans," he told industry leaders in a speech in San Diego shortly before Christmas in 1963.[19] To strengthen management decision making and to hold the industry more accountable to the public and policy makers, the Division of Savings and Loans collected and published more data. Balderston was in search of the Holy Grail for the industry—a way to assign ratings to mortgage risk that would be comparable to ratings used by analysts of corporate bonds and other debt securities. In this sense, he anticipated the rise of mortgage securitization, which would transform the industry in the 1980s.[20]

Balderston continued the department's unique practice of conducting a field reappraisal of 7 to 10 percent of the properties for which a thrift held loans.[21] As provided by state law, he forced lenders making risky loans to set aside greater reserves, which constrained a thrift's working capital and ability to grow. In 1964, he made it more difficult for thrifts to sell their loans, requiring that they retain half the value of the loan on their own books to ensure high-quality underwriting.[22] He worked with Governor Brown to write and pass the Savings & Loan Holding Company Disclosure Act, which required corporate and individual holders, like Ahmanson, of more than 10 percent control in savings and loan associations to report on their transactions with the affiliated associations. Balderston also announced that the department would conduct more surprise examinations of the books of the state's savings and loans. To accomplish this increased workload, commission staff increased dramatically, from 87 to 147 employees in three years, and the commission's budget rose to $1.5 million.[23] Because of Balderston's academic background and because the savings and loan industry was far more entrepreneurial and mattered more to the California economy than it did in any other state or even to the nation as a whole, it's not surprising that Balderston's approach to regulation differed significantly from that of his peers at the federal level.

Ironically, despite President Kennedy's support for the role of economic theory in macroeconomic policy making, the appointments he and President Johnson made to the Federal Home Loan Bank Board struggled to define their regulatory philosophy. Joseph P. McMurray and his successor John Horne were policy advocates but not academic theorists. Although McMurray had worked as an economist, he had spent most of his career as a housing advocate. Horne, an Alabama native, had worked for the Small Business Administration in the 1950s before joining the staff of Alabama senator John Sparkman. He became a political operative for the Kennedy campaign and was appointed head of the Small Business Administration in 1961 before succeeding McMurray at the FHLBB in 1963.[24] Both men were skeptical of the innovations introduced by California regulators in the savings and loan industry. They defended the traditional mutualist concept, and they remained committed to Herbert Hoover–style "associational" cooperation with business and the New Deal policy-making emphasis on stability and security over competition.

For academics and a growing crowd of consumer advocates, minority groups, and community organizers, the cooperative approach to regulation gave too much power to business leaders and industry insiders. Even if they were made with the public interest in mind, backroom deals corrupted the democratic process and paved the way for self-serving arrangements that betrayed the public trust. As the chorus of opposition to the practices of political entrepreneurs grew, Howard Ahmanson was once again drawn into the limelight he did not seek.

TWO CRISES OF THE OLD POLITICAL ORDER

In the 1950s, Ahmanson's success in the managed economy depended heavily on understanding the opportunities embedded in government programs and building a business that delivered on the government's goals. Relationships were at the heart of this kind of political entrepreneurship. Ahmanson's friendships with Commissioner Milton Shaw and Governor Goodwin Knight played an important part in the development of Home Savings, as well as the state's oversight of the savings and loan industry. In the political arena, in an era when campaign finance laws were weak, these personal relationships were often accompanied by direct infusions of cash for campaign support.

In May 1963, the *San Jose Evening News* ran a series of reports on money, power, and politics in California written by Harry Farrell. The series focused on the ways in which cash was funneled by various organizations to members of the legislature.[25] Farrell zeroed in on Ahmanson, showing how he had bankrolled Republican and Democratic legislators and governors.

"If the name means nothing to you," Farrell wrote to the reader, "you have plenty of company. In Northern California it is seldom heard, save in the worlds of finance, fine arts, and yacht racing and in the most informed circles of politics." The man himself was less known than his name, even in Sacramento, because, as Farrell pointed out, Ahmanson had visited the city only twice in his fifty-six years. Farrell suggested, however, that Ahmanson's influence with Unruh and his support for Governor Brown had helped to buy Home Savings and National American Fire Insurance many favors. An exclusive contract to provide fire insurance to veterans taking advantage of the state's Cal-Vet home-buying program seemed to reek of an insider deal.

When interviewed by Farrell, Ahmanson was characteristically nonchalant. He downplayed his role in politics. On the Cal-Vet program, he said H. F. Ahmanson & Co. simply offered the state a better deal. The company's Cal-Vet bid on a five-year renewal basis was $11.8 million, about $5 million less than the combined charges of roughly 238 companies serving the state at the time. According to Ahmanson, it was the other companies who "were caught with their hand in the cookie jar."[26] Farrell looked into it and agreed. So did a special investigation by the state legislature.[27]

Ahmanson also suggested that Governor Brown's administration had showed even less favor when it came to savings and loans. "I've been turned down on 34 consecutive applications for new branches," Howard said. "His commissioner doesn't believe in big companies."[28]

Despite Howard's protests, Farrell determined that Ahmanson had gained a great deal from his relationship with Unruh and other lawmakers. According to one state senator who had seen one of his bills killed by Ahmanson's opposition, he was "the top man of the three most politically powerful men in the state of California."[29] If Ahmanson needed a bill moved through the legislature, Unruh made sure that it happened.

Farrell's stories created a public relations crisis for Ahmanson and Unruh. According to longtime political reporter Lou Cannon, they were able to convince the *San Jose Evening News*'s editors to change the tone of the reporting. After Governor Brown offered a "purity of elections" bill to strengthen campaign finance laws, Unruh was able to kill the proposal. To repair the damage to his public image, Unruh embarked on a statewide speaking tour while Ahmanson retreated even further from the political limelight.

A second money and influence story that broke later that year in the nation's capital had a much greater impact on the comfortable relationships between lobbyists and legislators that characterized the managed economy. Once again, Howard Ahmanson was in the middle of it.

With Democrats in control of the U.S. Senate in 1962, Robert G. "Bobby" Baker was one of the most powerful staffers on Capitol Hill. Dubbed "Little Lyndon" by some Senate staffers, he had become Senate majority leader Lyndon Johnson's top aide by the age of thirty. Weighed down by personal debt, Baker decided to leverage his political position to pay his bills, and savings and loans were an easy target.[30] In September 1962, President Kennedy's tax reform bill would have ended the thrift industry's longtime exemptions from federal taxes. Ken Childs went to Washington to lobby against the bill on behalf of Home Savings and other large, state-chartered savings and loans. Baker suggested that Childs and his business allies should help their cause by raising $100,000 in cash for several key political races. Childs later passed on Baker's comments to Howard Ahmanson, who organized a meeting at his home that included Mark Taper and Charles Wellman, Taper's number two man. After the meeting, Childs discussed the request with Bill Ahmanson and Stuart Davis, a director with Great Western Financial Corporation. These executives and others in the industry in California gave the money to Baker in unmarked envelopes.[31]

The *Washington Post* revealed these transactions on September 12, 1963 (four months after Harry Farrell's series in the *San Jose Evening News*), and Baker resigned from the Senate staff soon afterwards.[32] Indicted by the federal government, Baker was able to delay his trial for years. Childs eventually testified and Baker was convicted of tax evasion, conspiracy, and larceny.[33] Howard Ahmanson was not drawn into the case, though his nephew Bill had played a key role in raising the money Baker wanted. Ken Childs, Mark Taper, Stuart Davis, and John Marten were all embarrassed by the headlines.[34]

The Baker case reopened a national debate over campaign finance that had been quiet since the muckraking days of the Progressive Era.[35] In the wake of the scandal, Congress established new financial disclosure requirements for people who worked for or served Congress. None of these reforms ended the influence of business money in government. In the years to come, personal lobbying by men like Ahmanson and Childs would certainly continue, but in the 1960s it became increasingly professionalized as large corporations and trade associations began to open Washington and Sacramento offices staffed with full-time lobbyists who institutionalized the processes of influence.

INSIDERS AND OUTSIDERS

Public outrage over the money spent by executives like Ahmanson to influence public policy grew in the 1960s and reached a peak in the Watergate era. Investigative news stories by reporters like Harry Farrell contributed to a sense that the interests of many Americans were not being represented in the hearing rooms, council meetings, and legislative chambers of government and coincided with the beginning of a significant drop in public trust in government. The growing civil rights movement furthered a national sense of unease, underscoring the idea that large segments of the American populace were excluded from the benefits of the managed economy.

By 1960 it was clear that U.S. Supreme Court decisions like *Shelley v. Kramer* and *Brown v. Board of Education* might have destroyed the legal basis for the separate-but-equal doctrine in housing and education but they had not ended discrimination. The results of the U.S. Census in 1960 showed that for many nonwhite citizens the American Dream was only a reverie. While nearly two-thirds of all white households in the United States owned their own homes in 1960, fewer than 40 percent of nonwhite households were home owners. When they did own their home, four in ten nonwhite households were living in substandard housing, compared to one in ten white home owners.[36]

Efforts by civil rights reformers to end housing discrimination waited first for basic civil rights legislation. In California, this effort moved forward dramatically in 1959, when Jesse Unruh and others pushed through the Civil Rights Act, a sweeping reform measure that barred discrimination in business. Courts later held that the law applied to real estate sales and development.[37] In 1963, Assemblyman Byron Rumford introduced a fair housing law to strengthen the rules against discrimination. With Unruh's support, the bill passed the legislature in June after bitter debate.[38] Opponents of the Rumford Act dubbed the measure "forced housing" instead of fair housing.

They argued that it interfered with the private property rights of owners. Led by the California Association of Real Estate, they qualified a referendum to overturn the Rumford Act. Voters approved the measure by a two-to-one margin in 1964.

At the national level, the struggle for equality, civil rights, and fair housing continued in the early 1960s. The U.S. Commission on Civil Rights issued a report in October 1961 asserting that mortgage credit was often denied to members of minority groups "for reasons unrelated to their individual characters or credit worthiness, but turning solely on race or color." It called on President Kennedy to issue an executive order requiring that all lenders participating in federal loan guarantee programs sign a statement that they did not discriminate on the basis of race, creed, or color. The commission was not unanimous in these recommendations. Vice Chairman Robert G. Storey objected to increasing federal control in the private sector.[39] The following year, President Kennedy issued Executive Order 11063, which prohibited lenders using federal guarantee programs from discriminating on the basis of race.[40]

In California, thrifts came under particular pressure in 1963 as the Congress for Racial Equality (CORE) took action against builders, developers, and lenders who they believed were discriminating. The California Savings and Loan League responded by adopting a policy encouraging members to make loans to qualified lenders regardless of race, color, or creed.

Meanwhile, ever sensitive to the signals coming from policy makers, Home Savings' leaders adjusted to the changing political winds, but not without difficulty. Early in the 1960s, the company tossed its redlined map. But in the summer of 1963, CORE accused Don Wilson, a major builder in the Torrance area and longtime customer of Home Savings, of refusing to sell a home in his Southwood Riviera Royale tract to Lloyd Ransom, an African American chemist. When CORE threatened to picket Home Savings' offices in Torrance, Ken Childs helped organize a meeting of the largest home builders in Los Angeles.[41] Childs understood that many builders believed if they opened up their developments to African Americans they would be competitively disadvantaged vis-à-vis builders who continued to discriminate. He believed the problem could be solved if he could convince the building community to end discrimination in unison. "The public would either have to accept this fact or not buy houses." But while Childs was able to get a handful of major builders to go along, he could not extract a similar pledge from enough small builders, so the effort collapsed.[42]

CORE continued to demand that Home Savings sever its relationship with Wilson, dubbed "Mr. Torrance" by the *Los Angeles Times* and others. Childs responded that Home could not unilaterally break its contracts. At an impasse, CORE began picketing, handing out leaflets in front of the company's Beverly Hills branch that encouraged customers to withdraw their accounts. Childs was clearly frustrated. He noted that CORE had never accused Home Savings of discriminating and that in fact Home was providing financing for a nearby tract development in Torrance that was "openly integrated." Privately, he complained that CORE's negotiators were "completely without logic and reason, or even common sense." He objected to the presumption that African Americans deserved "overpayment" to "balance the injustices of the past." But he was also clearly conflicted, confessing his sympathy for CORE's goal "to secure social and economic justice."[43]

Attorney General Stanley Mosk, who had issued a pathbreaking housing discrimination decision as a judge in 1947, eventually filed a suit against Wilson. And in the meantime, the Ransoms quietly bought the home they wanted through a third party and moved into the community without fanfare.[44] The entire episode signaled, however, that policy goals long neglected in the articulation of the American Dream would become increasingly important in the relationship between regulator and regulated in the housing and home mortgage industries.

RUNNING THE COMPANY AGAIN

Ken Childs may have been especially frustrated by the situation with CORE because while he responded to reporters and negotiated with the protest leaders, Howard Ahmanson was vacationing in the Middle East and Europe, touring with his son, Howard junior, and UCLA chancellor Franklin Murphy and his family. With the *San Jose Mercury* stories and the Bobby Baker scandal, it had been a tough year for Home Savings in the public eye. It's not clear from what little remains of Home Savings archives or Howard Ahmanson's personal papers how Ahmanson or Ken Childs personally reacted to the accumulation of this negative news, but in January 1964 Childs chose to leave Home Savings and seek his own fortune.

For nearly fifteen years, Childs had been the steady hand behind Home Savings' growth. He was the face of the company to the rest of the industry and often to the politicians. He was the executive who motivated employees and met with senior managers. Childs may have decided that he wanted to be an owner rather than an operator. Though he and Ahmanson remained friends, Childs left Home Savings and bought a major stake in Southern California Savings and Loan.[45]

Back in charge, Howard didn't change his routine or his decentralized style of management. Instead of going to Home Savings headquarters, he assembled his top executives in his home office on South Hudson. "It was the only time during the week that the men saw one another," says Richard Deihl. These were hardly team meetings. "He wanted to have you look at him and have allegiance to him, not to any group or any philosophy or anything else. He was a great believer in dealing with an individual."[46]

For the executives, these were tense encounters. They sat in Ahmanson's wood-paneled home office looking out through the leaded windows at the garden and the white balustrade in the distance. On the credenza behind his desk, Ahmanson's medley of framed pictures and yachting trophies offered the story of his life: his well-dressed, dignified, midwestern father; his wondering-eyed son; and his boat on a glassy sea. As Ahmanson reviewed the papers in front of him, they never knew what kind of a mood he would be in or whom he had decided to target. Alcohol was always served while they worked. "A clipboard was passed around," Richard Deihl remembers, "and we would mark our drinks and the waiter would go out and get them."

Ahmanson sometimes "laid a bear trap" for his managers. He studied some element of a manager's operations ahead of time and then would quiz him in detail, feigning innocence at first and then moving in with greater detail until the manager felt he was being interrogated. Sometimes, if someone rebelled or crumbled under the interrogation, Ahmanson would call Robert DeKruif or Bill Ahmanson to have the individual fired.

Ahmanson also communicated his values in these meetings. He expected loyalty and absolute attention to the competitive environment. Once, when one of his managers gave a speech at the annual meeting of the California Savings and Loan League, Ahmanson asked about it. With some measure of pride, the manager began to talk about the content of his speech. "Now let me make sure I understand," Ahmanson said. "These people are in the savings and loan business, the same business we're in." At that moment, according to Richard Deihl, the manager's expression began to change as he realized he'd stepped into a terrible trap. "You mean you spent time telling our competitors how we do business?" As the man's head hung lower and lower, Howard kept driving the point home. "He'd drive it through your heart," Deihl remembers. "He had a mean streak. On the other hand, he could make you feel so damn important."[47]

In many ways, the mean streak derived from Ahmanson's continuing need to feel like he was the most important person in the room, because in reality, he was a master delegator. Asked why his employees stayed loyal, Howard told a reporter in 1967: "They'd rather work for me because I don't get in their hair. They see me only if they come over to the house. I won't override an executive—even if he's wrong. But I may have a discussion with him later. You can't delegate authority with a string on it."[48]

Board meetings were also held at Ahmanson's house, but these events were largely social occasions, since the only real stockholder was Howard. The business meeting would be short and perfunctory. By the time the meeting was over, the coals on the built-in barbecue on the patio were glowing red and waiters were serving a fresh round of drinks.

Despite this socializing, Ahmanson and Home Savings remained in the vanguard of change with ever more ambitious projects. Yet at other times, the man and the company seemed blindsided by the cacophony of voices in city and county meeting rooms determined to disrupt the comfortable relationships between policy makers and private interests in the managed economy. As the policy environment began to shift away from the favorable framework that had allowed him to build his financial empire, Ahmanson was resolved that if he could not challenge the new generation of policy makers in their offices and hearing rooms, he would do so in the marketplace.

FIFTEEN

Crisis of the Managed Economy

SAVINGS AND LOANS in Los Angeles and across the country suffered their first serious downturn in the postwar era in the mid-1960s. Although the fourteen counties in Southern California had close to twelve million people—more than any state except California as a whole and New York—the region was finally saturated with housing. Immigration continued, but employment growth, especially in defense-oriented industries, slowed.[1]

As demand for housing softened, the savings and loan industry in Los Angeles entered a downward spiral.[2] When residential construction dropped sharply in January 1964, opportunities to make good investments in mortgages diminished. Without good opportunities to invest their capital, thrifts cut spending for advertising. Reduced advertising led to a reduction in savings deposits and assets. In 1964, for the first time in years, the overall annual rate of asset growth among California savings and loans fell to 18.2 percent, well below the average rate of 27.1 percent for the previous five years.[3]

The downturn deepened in 1965. During the first two months of the year, the net increase in savings for all California thrifts was $261.7 million, just over half the $514 million collected in the same period in 1964.[4] Meanwhile, residential construction in Los Angeles declined to the lowest level since the end of the war.[5] By the middle of 1965, foreclosures had begun to rise along with interest rates. By the end of the year, the growth of savings accounts was only 8.8 percent, the worst performance since the end of World War II.[6]

Unfortunately, savings and loans were not able to simply shutter their loan windows and wait for housing demand to return. They needed cash—and preferably income—to finance current operations and pay interest on the depositors' savings accounts. But as the drop in residential construction constrained profit opportunities, rising interest rates increased the cost of a lender's most basic resource—cash. Thrifts were suddenly squeezed on two sides. Holding large portfolios of loans written at lower rates, thrifts had to finance current operations with more expensive money provided by either savings depositors or loans from the Federal Home Loan Bank.[7]

For a while, most thrifts preferred to borrow from the FHLB. By June, the average thrift in California owed the FHLB an amount equal to nearly 14 percent of its assets. Since FHLB rules prevented new loans that would allow a thrift to exceed 17.5 percent, regulators were understandably worried about a liquidity crisis.[8] By the end of 1965, thrifts had no choice but to compete more aggressively in the market for savings deposits. To attract these deposits, they offered to pay higher interest rates and once again offered giveaways—from toasters to transistor radios—to bring new accounts in the door.

Like the industry he regulated, newly installed FHLBB chairman John Horne was trapped by conflicting policy initiatives and the changing economic landscape. On the one hand, he did not want to allow thrifts to become even more leveraged than they already were. At the same time, he berated them for aggressively raising the rates paid on savings deposits. Higher rates increased the cost of operations and increased the risk that a thrift might fail, leaving the taxpayer (through FSLIC deposit insurance) to pay the bill. Indeed, he suggested that providing loans to those institutions that were paying high dividend rates to savers would be a "betrayal of the public trust."[9] Horne wanted thrifts to finance operations the old-fashioned way—with earned revenues generated by lending. On the other hand, he and other FHLB officials worried that, given the soft housing market, thrifts might lower their credit standards just to keep their volume of loans up and that a wave of foreclosures would have an equally devastating impact on the government's insurance programs.

While regulators and industry leaders fretted publicly over the state of the industry, Ahmanson expressed confidence. "It has become fashionable to worry about the savings and loans," he told a reporter in June 1965, but the only savings and loans in trouble were "those growing too swiftly"—in other words, the companies trying to catch up to Home.[10]

Across town, Howard Edgerton didn't share his friend's point of view. As the competition for savings deposits intensified, he was continually frustrated by the misalignment between state and federal rules. In August 1965, Edgerton wrote to the head of the California Savings and Loan League, with a copy to FHLBB chairman Horne, to complain that since state thrifts had begun to advertise that they compounded interest daily on savings accounts, which the FHLBB didn't allow federals to do, the state-chartered thrifts had taken in twice as much in deposits as the federals in the first half of 1964, 50 percent more in the second half, and three times as much in the first half of 1965. Edgerton insisted that the playing field needed to be leveled. He suggested the need for a new law that would either force California-chartered thrifts to compute interest in the same way as the federals or restrict their ability to advertise anything but the basic rate.[11]

Fundamentally, Edgerton looked to the government to protect California Federal in the marketplace, but that didn't stop him or CalFed from exploiting their own position in California to the detriment of savings and loans in other parts of the country. For years, some California savings and loans had solicited so-called hot money from other parts of the country. As opposed to funds invested by local households and businesses, "hot money" came from individual and institutional investors, usually on the East Coast, who wanted to take advantage of higher interest rates in the West. In 1965, CalFed and Lytton Savings and Loan began advertising their deposit rates aggressively on national radio programs hosted by Arthur Godfrey and Don McNeill. When Edgerton and Lytton took to the airwaves, Henry Bubb was furious. The president of Capitol Savings and Loan in Kansas, Bubb complained and asked FHLBB chairman Horne to prevent this national competition for deposits.[12]

Climbing interest rates exacerbated these tensions. In December 1965, the Federal Reserve shocked the industry when it decided to allow banks to pay savers 5.5 percent on certificates of deposit (CDs) over five thousand dollars. The Fed was responding to a larger crisis in the banking industry and trying to ensure that banks would not lose corporate time deposits to other markets.[13] The Fed insisted that this decision would have little impact on the competition for regular passbook savings deposits (which were still capped at 4 percent).

Savings and loan officials weren't so sure. They described the Fed's action as "irresponsible" and "nothing short of incredible."[14] For the first time in postwar history, banks were able to pay more interest on some deposits than savings and loans. Thrifts were sure that banks would take advantage of the situation and create small-denomination CDs for household savers, siphoning the vital stream of deposits they needed to stay in business. Thrifts were also concerned that the Federal Reserve's decision to increase the federal funds rate would cause another spike in interest rates.

Savings and loan officials pleaded with legislators and regulators to do something. Shocked by the Fed's action, John Horne sent a telegram to the FHLB's twelve district banks acknowledging that the new rate would put pressure on thrifts already reeling from the credit crisis.[15] The FHLBB cautiously allowed thrifts to raise their premium rates to 4.75 percent, but this gesture was widely interpreted as too little, too late.[16]

Most thrift leaders believed a rate war was imminent. One savings and loan executive in Chicago told the *Wall Street Journal*. "We're all just sitting around hoping someone doesn't light the fuse."[17] In fact, the fuse was already sizzling. Bart Lytton announced that his savings and loans would begin offering a "bonus" payment of an extra half a percentage point on large savings accounts deposited for three years or more.[18]

The emerging rate war worried California and federal regulators. Residential construction lending in California virtually ground to a halt.[19] As the credit squeeze and housing slump continued into the first half of 1966, some thrifts reported losses on apartment developments that were failing and some associations seemed headed for trouble. For Howard Edgerton, the news was not good. CalFed lost savings deposits to other institutions at a disturbing rate. In the middle of a merger with First Federal Savings and Loan Association of Alhambra in the spring of 1966, the company was spending money faster than it was taking it in. Moreover, CalFed had promised money that it didn't have for loans and had to borrow nearly $71 million from the Federal Home Loan Bank between March and June 1966.[20] And FHLB officials were putting increasing pressure on Edgerton to improve his balance sheet.

In the middle of the crisis, Ahmanson seemed as cool as if he were steering the *Sirius* in the middle of a race. Planning a trip to Washington in February 1966, he asked to have lunch with Horne, describing himself as a "visiting fireman" with no particular mission. "In fact I am so happy about the types of things you folks have been doing in recent months I might go so far as to say I haven't even got any complaints." At lunch, he offered to help the chairman and FSLIC with the troubled Bellehurst subdivision in Buena Park—an offer right out of the Milton Shaw era of regulatory cooperation.[21] Ultimately, the project was taken over by another developer, but Ahmanson had made it clear that he was available to help the chairman if he could.

In the week or two following the lunch, Ahmanson appeared to be the FHLBB's number one cheerleader. In interviews with *American Banker*, the *San Francisco Chronicle Examiner*, and the *Los Angeles Times*, Ahmanson praised the FHLBB's efforts to hold down deposit savings rates and increase liquidity requirements. "The carpetbaggers almost ruined us in trying to make a quick buck," he said in reference to the fast-growing new entrants to the business, which, he believed, were taking too many risks in order to increase their share prices in the public markets.

"I'm not mad at the banks and I don't have any desire to enlarge our field," Ahmanson said.[22] In fact, he believed that banks and savings and loans competed intensely in only one arena—the market for savings accounts. He thought Home could beat the holding companies and the banks in this arena.[23] Chairman Horne wrote Ahmanson to praise his comments and to say that the members of the Federal Home Loan Bank Board agreed with him.[24] But this interlude of good feelings and collaboration would soon come to an end.

TAKING ON COMPETITORS AND REGULATORS

In many ways, Howard and Ken Childs had seen the crisis coming. As early as 1963, judging that the market for single-family homes in Southern California was on the verge of saturation, they had virtually stopped making tract loans. In the first quarter of 1966, loans for new construction accounted for only 3.2 percent of the company's nearly $83 million in new loans. Meanwhile, major competitors like Great Western and Gibraltar invested more than 9 percent of their loans for new construction, and at some smaller associations the number rose to 30 to 50 percent.[25] When housing sales slumped in the first half of 1966, these companies were hit hard. Home Savings didn't have unfinished housing projects, so it had very few troubled loans. It also had enough government bonds to be extremely liquid at a time when many savings and loans were borrowing heavily from the FHLB to meet their cash needs.

Home Savings' competitive advantages in the situation became dramatically apparent in the spring and summer of 1966. And Howard Ahmanson's unflinching willingness to press these advantages at a time when his competitors, including friends like Edgerton, were struggling desperately to stay afloat revealed much about his competitive and entrepreneurial instincts, as well as his changing attitudes toward regulators and the managed economy.

For months, Bank of America had remained above the fray over savings deposit rates while competitors waited to see what the giant would do. In the postwar years the bank had become the largest in the nation. By doubling the size of its branch system, pioneering the automation of transaction processing, and expanding its reach into consumer and mortgage credit markets, the bank enjoyed remarkable success in California's booming postwar economy.[26] But the company had also battled a series of antitrust suits that forced it to break off parts of A. P. Giannini's empire. By the mid-1960s, under the leadership of the politically savvy Rudolph Peterson, the company was reluctant to make competitive moves that would engender the wrath of regulators or lead others to complain about anticompetitive behavior.[27] Despite its size, Bank of America was not immune from the growing credit crisis, particularly as corporate customers turned to foreign capital markets, bonds, and equity to finance continued expansion.[28] At the end of March, Bank of America decided it had to take action to attract deposits. The bank announced that it would offer a 5 percent rate on CDs for five thousand dollars or more.[29]

Bank of America's action ignited a fusillade of responses. Within days, Gibraltar Savings declared that it would raise its dividend rates to 5 percent. A spokesperson for Home Savings said that the company had "no intention of not remaining competitive" and signaled that Home would raise rates to keep pace with the market.[30]

In Washington, John Horne was dismayed. Another round of rate hikes would further weaken thrifts that were already overextended. He warned the industry about "panicky" increases.[31] When the industry pushed back, the FHLBB allowed thrifts to offer CDs at a higher yield to customers who deposited more and kept their accounts intact for periods ranging from one to three years. Great Western and Mark Taper's First Charter quickly announced that they would offer these 5 percent certificates.[32] Home Savings said that it would do the same.[33] For a few days, an uneasy calm prevailed.

But Ahmanson was not happy to let the regulators dictate his relationship with customers. To follow the FHLBB's guidelines, Home Savings would have had to convert nearly three hundred thousand accounts, which would be "very costly." Moreover, customer surveys showed that eight out of ten people had no idea what CDs were. Ahmanson didn't see the point in a costly strategy to confuse his customers. He also recognized an opportunity to stay one step ahead of Bank of America. He chose simplicity instead, at the risk of angering the regulators.[34]

Howard announced that Home Savings would pay 5 percent on *all* of its deposit accounts, including the most simple passbook.[35] This was a clear violation of the FHLBB's guidelines. When reporters asked how Home could disobey the regulators, Ahmanson explained that the FHLBB's guidelines affected only a company's ability to borrow from the bank. Because Home Savings was so highly liquid and borrowed very little from the FHLB (4 percent), it could afford to lose this source of credit. Howard was willing to trade his borrowing privileges for the freedom to make his own entrepreneurial choices.

Ahmanson's bet was incredibly well timed. When the market price for three-month U.S. Treasury bonds surged past the prevailing rate of 4.85 percent on deposits, California thrifts suffered a massive $469 million outflow of funds in April.[36] Home Savings, however, experienced a $21.5 million increase.[37]

This newest round of rate wars set off alarm bells across town in both Sacramento and Washington. In May, Congress opened hearings to consider whether the government should control interest rates for savings and loans as it did for banks under Regulation Q.[38] In Sacramento, Fred Balderston's successor as commissioner of savings and loans, Gareth Sadler, wrote Governor Brown that a severe crisis was brewing that, though national and international in its origins, would hit California hard because the Golden State was still dependent on imported capital and because savings and loans were disproportionately important to the housing industry.[39]

In Washington, the FHLBB was stuck. Reluctant to allow thrifts to increase their costs of doing business in a fragile market, but unable to provide them the liquidity they needed by increasing FHLB lending, the bank was slow to react.[40] After some delay, the FHLB agreed not to penalize thrifts in California if they increased their savings deposit rates to 5 percent on CDs as low as one thousand dollars. And at the end of May, Ahmanson's leading competitors, including Mark Taper's First Charter, Great Western, and Edgerton's California Federal, matched Home Savings' rates. Regulators and executives at most of the other savings and loans hoped that the rate war would end with this increase.

Ahmanson thought differently. He believed that extreme measures were necessary to keep pace with the banks. He may have also sensed an extraordinary opportunity to take advantage of his competitors' weaknesses. For years he had supported the regulators in their efforts to manage the financial markets. When they blocked Home's move into Northern California in the 1950s, he had bowed out graciously and earned their gratitude. By 1966, however, he recognized that regulators in California had clearly signaled that they weren't going to allow Home to continue to grow by acquisition or through new branches, and Howard was determined to protect the market he had. He also believed that the FHLBB's efforts to control interest rates with brute force were misguided and could seriously injure Home Savings and the savings and loan industry.[41] As the sole owner of Home Savings, he was free to take an extraordinary entrepreneurial risk. In early June, he let it be known that he was thinking of raising Home Savings' deposit rates again—to 5.25 percent.[42] "A month ago I wanted to do it," he told a reporter. "I just haven't decided at what price this industry can compete for money."

With already weak balance sheets and higher operating costs, many of Ahmanson's competitors blanched at the idea of another increase. Regulators were furious. Ahmanson acknowledged their concerns. "I've been sitting here going out of my mind trying to decide what to do," he told a reporter in mid-June. He knew others were thinking of making the move. "One thing is for sure," he said, "we'll meet any competition. . . . We'll raise our rate in five seconds if anybody else goes up."[43]

Slouched in his high-backed leather chair with a cigarette in his left hand, a full ashtray on his desk, and a cup and saucer for coffee, he knew that Home Savings had a unique opportunity. As he bragged to a *Los Angeles Times* reporter, Home was in excellent shape because the company was so liquid. Real estate that had been acquired for $36 million was now worth close to $150 million. In addition, Home's operating costs continued to be incredibly low. While most of the larger associations and holding companies in California had an average overhead expense of 1.30 percent, Home's expense was 0.76 percent—almost half.[44] The company also had very little debt. "We don't borrow for expansion purposes from the Federal Home Loan Bank," Ahmanson explained. Nor did the company go after the hot money from the East. Thus, even if Home's cost of funds was slightly higher, "as long as we can prosper on what we've got," Ahmanson said, "I believe we should. I don't want to be subject to the whims of any other area, or any other money."[45]

Hoping to mollify the FHLBB chairman and underscore the point that Home Savings was financially secure enough to offer these new rates, Robert DeKruif sent a copy of the *Los Angeles Times* clipping to John Horne. Horne acknowledged that Ahmanson's "good judgment puts him in a very favorable position today," but—evidencing his continuing belief in the cooperative relationships between regulator and regulated that were at the heart of the managed economy—he told DeKruif that Ahmanson's good judgment "also imposes on him a responsibility not to act in a manner that will jeopardize his competition since to do so would jeopardize the industry generally and in the long run would even be harmful to Home Savings and Loan Association."[46]

Everyone waited for Ahmanson's decision. Late in June, he made it official—Home Savings would raise its rate to 5.25 percent. He told the press the move was necessary for the survival of the industry: "I hope the industry will join me in this move."[47] Wrapping his move in the traditional mantle of the industry, Ahmanson painted Home's decision as an effort to save the housing industry and to support the cause of home ownership. He was simply trying to "avert a near-catastrophe in the all-important housing industry and the allied trades that must rely upon it."[48]

In Washington, Horne politely told reporters that the FHLBB "regrets the decision" and warned that any association that tried to follow Home up to this higher interest rate "should be aware that it may very well be overreaching . . . and could therefore encounter difficulties further down the road."[49] Privately, Horne telegraphed Ahmanson to say, "I am disappointed in your decision and am in disagreement with it. I strongly feel that your action was not necessary and certainly is not in the best interests of the savings and loan industry."[50]

Ahmanson's decision strained personal, as well as political and professional, relationships. A number of savings and loan executives proposed that the California Savings and Loan League should support new legislation that would give the California commissioner of savings and loans the power to control the maximum rates thrifts could pay on deposits.[51] Mark Taper supported this effort. He called a news conference and made a direct appeal to savings and loans executives to "hold the line" against further "premature and inflationary interest rate increases." At the same time, Taper "lashed out at what he called 'the hysteria for growth' shown by 'one or two or three' associations."[52] When reporters asked him if he would favor direct control of interest rates by the government, Taper asserted: "For over 100 years the savings and loan industry has regulated itself [on interest rates]. But unless it shows responsibility, some form of regulation will have to be given to federal or state authorities."[53] A *New York Times* writer agreed: "In the long run the success of the California associations in overturning informal Federal rate control may backfire and lead to a fixed national ceiling set by statute."[54]

Even Bart Lytton looked to Congress to fix the crisis. He announced that his company would match whatever Home offered. He even raised the stakes by promising to compound interest daily, raising the effective yield to 5.39 percent.[55] "If this be a rate war," Lytton told the *Wall Street Journal,* "we're big, strong and ready." But Lytton also chastised Congress for not being willing to "put a ceiling on commercial-bank—or for that matter, savings-and-loan—interest rates."[56]

Howard Edgerton refused to follow his friend's lead, and the conflict strained their professional and personal relationship as they argued in the press. Edgerton called Home's decision "a direct violation of Federal Home Loan Bank Board regulation." He said it would be morally wrong to follow suit. If California Federal raised its savings interest rates, he said, it would have to raise mortgage rates as well. "We think those rates are just plain high enough already."[57]

While Edgerton cast his decision in a civic light and misrepresented the nature of the FHLBB's guidelines, the reality was that California Federal, the nation's largest federally chartered savings and loan, was in trouble. With its cash seriously depleted and its credit line with the FHLB at the limit, the company was unable to make new loans. Privately, Edgerton wrote to FHLB officials that he had even had to turn away the bishop of the Los Angeles Diocese of the Episcopal Church. He said other federal thrifts in Los Angeles were in the same position. If the FHLB didn't offer new loans to the industry, "public confidence in savings and loans in this area would deteriorate to the point where it would cause a tremendous strain on the liquidity of the bank system." In other words, there would be a run that might force some thrifts to close, leaving the FSLIC with huge liabilities to repay depositors.[58]

Edgerton pulled out all the stops to ensure that California Federal would survive the crisis. Enlisting many of the state assemblymen who had long been friends of the industry in Southern California, he organized a delegation to meet with members of the House Banking and Currency Committee in Washington. With Chairman Horne attending, Edgerton pressed the FHLBB to loosen restrictions on borrowing and reduce the amount of net income that had to go into reserves to free up cash for the associations. Horne again asked the thrifts to hold the line at 5 percent on savings rates, putting enormous pressure on Edgerton and the managers of other federal savings and loans.

For Edgerton, the situation was exasperating. Thrifts that cooperated with the federal regulators watched as money drained from their accounts.

California Federal lost more than $8.6 million in deposits. Gibraltar Savings complained that $4.78 million walked out the door in just five days. The company's chairman made it clear that his company had taken this hit in deference to the government's desire to hold the line on interest rates.[59] Still, regulators held back advances or loans as a way to keep thrifts in line. Without access to these government funds, some thrifts, including California Federal, faced dire circumstances. In a letter to the head of the Federal Home Loan Bank in San Francisco, Edgerton fairly shouted that his association had no money to lend.[60] It was like a store with overhead but no merchandise.

Some thrifts running out of cash threatened to take the government to court. Meanwhile, the FHLBB and FSLIC were forced to find a buyer for at least one savings and loan in serious trouble, and others seemed on the brink. California commissioner Gareth Sadler wrote to Horne expressing concern for the financial stability of several of the state's largest savings and loan holding companies.[61] When reporters tried to follow up on these stories, insiders at the FHLB were tight-lipped and intimated that their efforts "to resolve the 'California problem' [would] hinge on their ability to keep the California public in the dark about the true state of affairs in the California savings and loan industry."[62]

Under tremendous pressure, Ahmanson stood his ground. Unable to get regulators to fix the situation quickly, most of Howard's competitors were ultimately forced to follow his move. Great Western, United Financial Corp., and Mark Taper's First Charter Financial Corp. (owner of American Savings & Loan) all matched Home's rates by the beginning of July.[63] A deeply chagrined John Horne conceded that "events this week demonstrated that lacking specific statutory authority to control dividend rates," the FHLBB was powerless to control the industry.[64]

Over the next month, events proved that the FHLBB also was powerless to protect the industry. Ahmanson's insights into the threat posed by the credit crisis were borne out across the country as thrifts suffered a $1.5 billion outflow of deposits in July, the biggest one-month decline in the history of the industry. Meanwhile, Home enjoyed an enormous rush of new customers—16,805 new account holders by the time the July reinvestment period ended. The inflow of new money increased by 421 percent over the same period in the preceding year, for a total of $71.4 million.[65] "We're ecstatic," Robert DeKruif told reporters.[66] In large display advertisements in the *Los Angeles Times,* the company thanked the public: "You have honored us with the largest dollar growth in savings accounts ever received by any association in the world in ten working days."[67]

While Home Savings beamed with success, the crisis deepened for other savings and loans. By August, their situation, combined with a bank-led withdrawal from the bond markets, precipitated a crisis on Wall Street.[68] Under pressure from thrift managers, bankers, and others anxious to end the credit crisis, legislators in California and Washington sought to give regulators more power. In California, state senator Luther Gibson proposed legislation that would create a three-member commission to supervise the state's savings and loans. These steps sought to change the character of regulation, to make the new commission a rule-making body with greater control over the industry, as opposed to a line organization focused mainly on compliance.[69] They also sought to curb political influence on the savings and loan commissioner.[70]

Meanwhile, the federally chartered thrifts in Los Angeles turned to Congress. They found allies in the American Bankers Association, who were delighted to put thrifts on the same regulatory footing as commercial banks.[71] They also received support from the National Association of Home Builders, which hoped that the restrictions on bank CDs would help steer money back into the mortgage market.[72] Even President Johnson, who announced a sweeping effort to control inflation in August, encouraged Congress to pass a bill giving the government the power to set thrift interest rates.

In the face of this pressure, Ahmanson and the managers of other strong, independent savings and loans who did not want the government to control prices offered only weak resistance. Tom Bane, the former California assemblyman who had helped Ahmanson in political situations before, testified before a House committee as a lobbyist for state-chartered stock companies like Home Savings. He blasted the bill, blaming the FHLBB for the current predicament, and lauding the leadership of one or two thrifts (he did not name Ahmanson or Home but the reference was clear) for exercising good business sense.[73] Bane's testimony was to no avail. In September 1966, Congress passed the Interest Rate Adjustment Act, which gave the FHLBB the authority to cap deposit rates and thereby impose price controls.[74]

The new federal legislation turned out to be a disaster. During the entire postwar period, interest rates on Treasury bills had never risen above 4 percent and had provided a stable backdrop for interest rates in the savings and mortgage markets. After 1966, as the inflationary pressures of federal spending for the Vietnam War increased, rates on three-month Treasuries rose. "That really hurt us," Richard Deihl remembers, "when people started advertising T-Bill rates on television and telling investors how to buy them."[75]

With caps on deposit rates, savings and loans were forced to engage in nonrate competition, offering more valuable giveaways than before and providing depositors with other amenities. These efforts increased the average cost of each dollar deposited.[76] Even so, investors pulled their money out of savings and loans and invested elsewhere.[77] Because of its low cost structure, Home and other large thrifts continued to do well while others suffered.

Again and again in the ensuing years, savings and loans would ask the California legislature or Congress to fix a broken industry, but what they really wanted was a return to the protected markets that had characterized the golden era of the industry in the managed economy. In 1966, Howard Ahmanson recognized that regulators no longer had the capability to protect the industry and in some cases did not have the desire. The salvation for Home Savings and the industry in the new era lay in its ability to compete head-to-head for deposits and mortgages. Home could do that because it had sufficient scale, a strong balance sheet, and a marvelous track record of prudent lending.

Beyond what he said to the press, it's not clear how Howard felt about this crisis of the managed economy. As a businessman he had clearly resisted a policy that he felt to be wrongheaded, but his actions did not represent a fundamental shift in his perspective on the relationship between business and government. Indeed, as his empire increased beyond imagination, his view of the partnership between private wealth and public purpose expanded to include a major role for philanthropy.

SIXTEEN

A New Way of Life

LIKE MANY HIGHLY SUCCESSFUL ENTREPRENEURS, Howard Ahmanson did not set out to be a philanthropist. "He got the notion that a very successful businessman ought to have great art," Franklin Murphy explained. "From that point, he got interested in the possibility of a museum [LACMA]. Then he discovered a new dimension in life. That's when he started becoming charitable. In all fairness, when that door opened, he walked through it."[1]

Ahmanson was not sure this was a door he wanted to open in the late 1950s. Prior to 1958, he had made no major philanthropic gifts. With high federal income and estate tax rates in place for the wealthy, Ahmanson protected himself by letting his assets appreciate (Home Savings, for example) without liquidating them and thus realizing taxable gains. To permanently avoid a potentially huge tax liability, he created the Ahmanson Foundation in 1952 and began contributing shares of appreciated stock.[2] Following the path of a number of other very wealthy individuals, he put shares of Home Savings and Loan into the Ahmanson Foundation but stipulated that the shares could not be sold or transferred.[3] This way, he maintained control for corporate purposes, but earnings and dividends didn't flow to his personal tax return. They could be distributed to charity.[4]

To govern the Ahmanson Foundation, Ahmanson created a board that included his closest family and friends: Dottie, his nephews Bill and Bob, Gould Eddy, and attorney Thomas Webster. Prior to the divorce, Howard did not even serve on the foundation's board, and Dottie was president. After the divorce, Howard became president, but Dottie remained on the board.[5] The foundation was an extension of Ahmanson and his family.

Like most foundations established by very affluent Americans in the 1950s and early 1960s, the Ahmanson Foundation had no strategic framework for giving. Charitable organizations appealed directly to Howard, Dottie, or the nephews to support their annual giving or capital campaigns. The foundation gave modest amounts to nonprofits in Los Angeles and Omaha, including the Salvation Army, the Southern California Symphony Association, the Community Chest, and the UCLA Progress Fund, as well as the Dundee Presbyterian Church and other organizations in Omaha. The foundation also made contributions on behalf of Home's other executives. More focused giving was targeted toward medical research, often related to the conditions affecting Ahmanson's own health—gout and gout-related arthritis. He expressed interest in commissioning research on the purine content of foods, for example, since purine is a critical factor in gout.[6] None of the foundation's grants in the late 1950s was larger than $10,000. Most were below $1,000. The assets of the Ahmanson Foundation were only $370,810 at the end of October 1960.[7] As Ahmanson's wealth increased in the 1960s, however, he was incorporated into the circles of the civic elite in Los Angeles. And as in all major American cities, his philanthropy played a critical role in confirming his status.[8]

CULTURAL PATRON

Despite his late-night piano playing, Howard did not give generously to the performing arts prior to the 1960s. He once confessed to Los Angeles business leader John McCone that though he believed "opera is very, very important to culture, to be brutally honest, I find it far down on my list."[9] When Dorothy Chandler pressed him to contribute to the symphony, he responded: "I have been wrestling with my conscience. . . . My dilemma—to apportion my affections between the pleasure I get out of supporting any Buff Chandler enterprise and the vicarious thrill I get out of things well done—or to continue in my chosen path of supporting obscure medical research which basically thrills me more than culture."[10]

Ahmanson's reticence reflects one way in which he was still outside the circles of the civic elite in 1958, despite his growing wealth. In the immediate postwar era, key leaders had come together to create an organization called Greater Los Angeles Plans Incorporated (GLPI) with an explicit ambition to "recenter" the region and revitalize the city center. They called for the construction of an opera house on Bunker Hill as a way to renew the neighborhood and create a new cultural anchor for downtown. Over the next decade, these civic elites, overwhelming the resistance of the low-income ethnic

Mexican residents, sought to remake the neighborhoods of the Bunker Hill community into a modernist city center complete with high-rise corporate offices and monumental cultural institutions.[11]

There's no indication that Ahmanson had a strong connection to this effort. In fact, with the completion of Sheets's building for National American Fire Insurance, Ahmanson participated in the migration to Wilshire Boulevard, where a number of other savings and loan executives would establish their headquarters. But he remained close to many of the people playing a prominent role in this downtown project, including architect William Pereira, who had done some of the initial planning work for Bunker Hill's redevelopment.[12]

Like Howard, voters showed little interest in opera. They rejected a proposal for municipal financing of the opera house project three times between 1951 and 1954, even after backers enhanced the project's populist appeal by including an auditorium for sporting events and an exhibition hall for trade shows. Despite these losses at the polls, in February 1955, days after Howard Ahmanson helped convince the Republican National Committee to hold the 1956 convention in San Francisco, the Los Angeles Board of Supervisors revisited the idea of building a large auditorium downtown.[13] Fans of the opera and the symphony went back to the drawing board as well. Reframing their concept, the city's leaders offered a plan that involved a mix of public and private financing. Dorothy Chandler emerged as the project's spiritual leader and relentless fund-raiser.[14]

As writers Robert Gottlieb and Irene Wolt first pointed out, Chandler's efforts to fund the construction of Music Center represented an important turning point in the social dynamics of the civic elite in Los Angeles. Instead of relying on the city's long-established white Protestant families to provide the funds and the vision for the project, Chandler reached out to the growing community of affluent Jews, including Mark Taper, and to the nouveau riche, like Howard Ahmanson, to play a major role in sponsoring the Center.[15] Chandler's efforts helped forge a cohesive and powerful civic elite that shaped the development of leading cultural institutions like LACMA, the Music Center, and UCLA, as well as lesser entities like the Museum of Science and Industry and the County Art Institute.[16]

Led by this civic elite, the various campaigns to build or support these institutions were buoyed by a rising tide of cultural expression in postwar Los Angeles and America. The GI Bill helped to create a large, upwardly mobile, college-educated sector in society that had the time and money to appreciate the arts.[17] New cultural institutions also addressed cold war insecurities that suggested that Russia—with its classical composers, painters, and ballet—was more sophisticated and sensitive than the United States, where a crass materialism dominated the culture.[18] And, increasingly, performing arts centers and art museums became critical ingredients to urban renewal.

Ahmanson's role in this collective effort began with his relationship with Millard Sheets and his service on the board of the Los Angeles County Art Institute. Over time, his fellow board member Dorothy Chandler pressed him to take a bigger part and to open his checkbook to a grander vision of L.A.'s cultural life. Ahmanson's pivotal $2 million gift to LACMA in 1958 marked the beginning of this transition. Joining LACMA's board in March 1960 represented a next step. Months later he was elected to the USC Board of Trustees in December 1960.[19] He also became involved with the Music Center's Building Fund Committee.[20] All of these experiences strengthened his connections within the community of civic elites. Starting in 1963, however, he had the opportunity to consider the role of culture from a much larger vantage point.

NATIONAL CULTURAL CENTER

During the crisis of the Great Depression, Eleanor Roosevelt and others discussed the creation of a massive theater and arts complex on Capitol Hill in Washington. Congress held hearings, but nothing came of the plan until 1958, when it approved the creation of a National Cultural Center.

As supporters were quick to say, the project was not a local urban renewal project. It was intended to provide a venue for performances that would celebrate the artistry of the nation. Edward Durrell Stone was chosen to design the center. A board appointed by President Eisenhower set out to raise money to match a congressional appropriation, but over the next three years the board made little progress.

Following his inauguration in 1961, President Kennedy sought to reinvigorate the project. He recruited Roger L. Stevens to chair the board, and Stevens asked the first lady and former first lady Mamie Eisenhower to serve as honorary co-chairs. With the White House, Stevens recruited new board members, including Howard Ahmanson, the first trustee from California.[21]

For the announcement of his appointment on April 10, 1963, Howard and Steady flew to Washington. At the White House, Steady talked to the president about Civil War battles, and the president gave him a PT-109 pin to remember his visit.[22] Seven months later, the president was dead. Lyndon Johnson asked Congress to rename the cultural center as a memorial to Kennedy. To help ensure the completion of the project, he added more than a dozen new members, including members of the Kennedy family and some of the slain president's closest associates.[23]

On the board, Ahmanson once again witnessed the ways in which the development of a landmark public cultural institution could ignite controversy. The board proposed locating the Kennedy Center along the Potomac River. Urban planning advocates wanted a site on Pennsylvania Avenue closer to the heart of the city. Edward Durrell Stone defended the site on the river and compared it to London's Parliament on the Thames or Paris's Louvre on the Seine. In the end, the Potomac site won out.[24]

The argument over the site was also closely connected to the nature of the institution and a growing debate across the country. According to critics, the Kennedy Center, with its imposing white marble walls and expensive seats, would serve the elite rather than the ordinary citizens of Washington and the nation. Similar criticisms had been leveled in New York and Los Angeles, where urban redevelopment went hand in hand with the erection of downtown cultural facilities like Lincoln Center and the Music Center. Roger Stevens, the chairman of the Kennedy Center's board, pledged to address these concerns by keeping ticket prices affordable and promoting programming that would have a broad appeal.

By the end of June 1965, fund-raising for the Kennedy Center had topped the goal and Ahmanson and his fellow trustees voted to proceed with construction. In the meantime, the board's efforts to recruit an artistic director were protracted and highlighted the fears of many performing artists that politics would infect the programming of the Kennedy Center.

Ahmanson did not play a leading role on the board, which was dominated by insiders from the Kennedy circle and family, but he was exposed to the debate over the role of culture in representing the identity of a community and a people. He also grew comfortable with the idea of government involvement in the arts. "Thirty years ago, I would have been horrified," he told a reporter after President Johnson had signed the bill creating the National Endowment for the Arts and appointed Kennedy Center board chairman Roger Stevens to chair the new agency. "However, during the

Depression, the government supported hundreds of creative artists in all the crafts." No doubt remembering Millard Sheets's work with the Works Progress Administration, he continued, "Some marvelous things came out of those grey years, and subsequently some very fine, talented, useful people." Too much government interference could be extremely harmful, he conceded. "In Russia, the decline of contemporary art can be traced to excessive, totalitarian control. Properly administered this aid can be of great benefit to the cultural life of the nation."[25] It was obviously good for the metropolis as well.

LACMA REDUX

Just as the city of Los Angeles manifested the vitality of an America free from Depression and world war, the dedication of the new Los Angeles County Museum of Art on March 30, 1965, was a crowning cultural achievement in the postwar era. It was the largest museum of art to be built in the United States since construction of the National Gallery of Art on the eve of World War II.[26] It was absolutely the largest in existence west of Chicago.

As a major donor, Howard basked in the accolades of powerful friends. Ernest Debs, a member of the Board of Supervisors, congratulated everyone who had helped to make the museum a reality. "All of us and all our children and children's children will forever be in your debt for this magnificent achievement," he said to Ahmanson.[27]

After the opening, Howard embarked on a five-week summer tour of great cities of Europe, including cold war Moscow and Leningrad.[28] When he returned, tensions between Howard and LACMA's director Ric Brown grew worse. Throughout the process of construction, the board had exerted its authority and individual members had pushed their personal agendas. Plans for the theater were made, revised, and revised again because board members argued over the size. Bart Lytton wanted a second story for the gallery to be named in his honor.[29] David Bright "rode herd on contractors, subcontractors, carpenters, locksmiths, guards, everybody."[30] As director, Ric Brown tried to assert his leadership. Ahmanson felt he was in over his head. Brown said later he was increasingly at odds with board members, particularly Ahmanson, who wanted him to exhibit the pictures they owned, whether or not they were genuine.

Others on the board felt Brown did not have the interpersonal skills to build and lead a team. Meanwhile board and director continued to struggle over the boundaries of their respective roles.[31] In the months that followed the opening, despite the obvious success of the museum, people sensed "administrative chaos and impending doom." Some members of the board wanted to hire an administrator to lead the institution and supervise Brown.[32] Brown resisted this plan. When Brown was offered a position at the new Kimbell Art Foundation in Fort Worth, the board suggested he should take the job.[33]

The announcement of Brown's departure in November 1965 sparked an uproar in Los Angeles. Bitter over the way he had been treated, Brown issued a public statement criticizing the board's constant interference in the day-to-day activities of the museum. In an editorial, the *Los Angeles Times* sided with Brown. In a public rebuttal, Ed Carter noted that "the Museum's trustees are among the most experienced and successful managers of both profit and non-profit enterprises in the west." They were devoted to Los Angeles and had spent hundreds of hours on the museum's management issues. "I respectfully suggest, therefore, that they are in a better position to make judgment of Dr. Brown's adequacy than the editorial writers of the *Los Angeles Times*."[34]

Among the cultural cognoscenti in Los Angeles and across the country, Ahmanson's role in pushing Brown out reinforced a popular narrative that businessmen didn't know anything about art or about running arts institutions. The *Nation* magazine editorialized that Howard was still angry that his name hadn't been affixed to the entire museum complex, that Brown had resisted "Mr. Ahmanson's pet architect (a man noted for gold-leaf bank facades) and had refused to hang in the museum Mr. Ahmanson's collection of dubious old masters." The editorial went on to suggest that Brown and the people of Los Angeles were "victims of cultural 'explosion.' Culture has become 'big league,' 'big money,' a bandwagon phenomenon. And men who have prospered by grabbing front seats on bandwagons are jumping aboard the art wagon." The editors concluded with the hope that rich men in America would eventually learn "to support creative excellence without assuming that they can buy it."[35]

The criticisms that followed Brown's dismissal failed to dissuade Ahmanson from continuing his civic patronage. In December 1965, Dorothy Chandler announced that the Ahmanson Foundation would give $1 million to fund completion of the Center Theater at the Music Center complex. The gift raised Ahmanson's total contribution to the project to $1.5 million.[36] And shortly after making his gift, Ahmanson joined the Music Center board, where he was once again teamed up with Dorothy Chandler and Franklin Murphy, as well as Walt Disney and nine other Los Angeles power brokers.[37]

The Los Angeles County Board of Supervisors named the facility the Ahmanson Theater. When Ahmanson wrote to Supervisor Kenneth Hahn to express his gratitude, he also noted "the 'explosion' in cultural affairs in Los Angeles County" and suggested that it was due, to a great extent, "to the benevolent county government under which we live." He affirmed his sense that government and elected leaders had played a key role in the development of L.A.'s cultural landscape. LACMA and the Music Center embodied a partnership between private philanthropy and public works. This shared responsibility was a familiar concept to an entrepreneur like Ahmanson whose great wealth derived from the social contract implicit in the managed economy. "When all other things are forgotten," he wrote to Hahn, "it is probable that history will record that five wise and farsighted public servants were the major force in making all these things possible in our time. I think this has occurred no place else in America."[38]

With the completion of the Ahmanson Theater and the Mark Taper Forum in the spring of 1967, the Music Center scheduled a weeklong celebration of performances and speechmaking. Zubin Mehta conducted the Los Angeles Philharmonic. The Metropolitan Opera National Company sprinted through performances of *La Traviata, La Boheme, Marriage of Figaro,* and *Rape of Lucretia* on successive nights. The Center Theater Group staged the West Coast premiere of *The Devils,* a play by John Whiting based on the book by Aldous Huxley, in the Mark Taper Forum.[39]

Unintentionally, the Los Angeles Civic Light Opera Association chose an appropriate script to open the Ahmanson Theater. Based on the classic novel by Miguel de Cervantes, *Man of La Mancha* showed Don Quixote pursuing an impossible romantic dream. Colored by his delusions, his chivalrous actions and strategies made audiences laugh. At the end of the play, Don Quixote awakes from his insanity only to realize the nobility of the dream. Though he drew no allusions to the play, Ahmanson often liked to portray himself in a similar way, as a bemused and lucky businessman who had happened into a great fortune.

The opening of LACMA and the Music Center reflected a remarkable development in the cultural life of Los Angeles and the pattern of philanthropy among the city's wealthiest individuals. Bringing the region's old money and its new tycoons to the table, Dorothy Chandler and Ed Carter, working with Howard Ahmanson as a leading donor, managed to make philanthropy "a sport," in Ahmanson's words, and in the process transformed a community that until the mid-1950s, according to the *New York Times,* had been "distinguished mainly for its cultural miserliness."[40]

LACMA and the Music Center grabbed headlines, but myriad other cultural institutions were blossoming as well. Fund-raising was under way for a projected $80 million CalArts campus. The Los Angeles Opera Company had presented its first two performances at the Music Center. Chamber music had blossomed to the point where more than five hundred concerts were performed annually. Private collections of art were growing and becoming more well known, chief among them the collection amassed by Norton Simon. The commerce of culture was growing as well. In the mid-1960s, Los Angeles surpassed Chicago as the nation's second-largest book market. Commercial art galleries were expanding.[41]

With all of this expansion, Ahmanson talked about the need for a cultural plan for the city and the region. "I've been thinking of having [the Ahmanson Foundation] join with other foundations to sponsor an objective inventory of cultural needs," he said. This survey would be analogous to work done by health care leaders to determine where hospitals and other medical facilities needed to be located. "In the same way, we have to find out how many art galleries we're going to need," he said, "how many symphony orchestras and theaters." Ahmanson was politically sensitive enough to suggest that this should be a collaborative effort but said it should be centrally coordinated. Done community by community, "local pride may cause us to waste a lot of time, energy and money."[42]

This idea of cultural leadership had become so important to Ahmanson that he urged civic leaders in Omaha to undertake a similar effort. Noting that in Los Angeles "we just sat around out there for 25 years" before civic leaders began an aggressive campaign to build a major art museum, concert hall, and zoo, Ahmanson said during a visit to his hometown in 1961, "You have the means now to start the next step in the town's growth—a step toward the cultural life."[43]

Without a doubt, when Ahmanson talked about nurturing cultural expression, he focused on elite institutions that would bring prestige—major museums, symphony halls, and the like. With ethnic and racial pride movements developing around the city in the late 1960s, he paid no particular attention to this kind of culture. Yet his long association with Sheets and Home's support for the annual county art show also reflected an old-fashioned populist sensibility that transcended his integration into the region's civic elite. Asked to comment on the propriety of exhibiting Ed Kienholz's controversial *Back Seat Dodge '38* at LACMA in 1966, for example, he said the work was clever but didn't rise to the level of great art. "But it doesn't really make any difference whether I fancy it or not. A public institution should have something for everybody."[44]

A VISION FOR LOS ANGELES

By the mid-1960s, with Ahmanson's name etched in several major cultural institutions, journalists began to wonder about the man and whether he had a plan for the future of Los Angeles. "Let's start with the idea that we are building a new way of life out here," Howard told a reporter in January 1967.[45] He didn't describe this new way of life. No doubt he felt he didn't have to. The idealized view was everywhere in magazine ads, billboards, and the movies. A temperate climate combined with mountain and seaside living enabled a casual indoor-outdoor lifestyle focused on swimming pools, tennis courts, golf courses, and beach clubs. To cover the distances between these outdoor destinations, "mobility" was central—thus the need for automobiles and freeways.[46] Market forces ensured that real estate agents, architects, furniture companies, clothing designers, moneylenders, and hundreds of other entrepreneurs responded to and cultivated the demand for the goods and services associated with this Southern California way of life.

To be sure there was a dark side to this dream. An epidemic of personal bankruptcies seemed to suggest that the region's reputation for crass materialism and self-indulgence had a social cost.[47] Riots in Watts and growing unrest in the Hispanic neighborhoods in East L.A. drew attention to the fact that employers, lenders, and real estate companies had long excluded many people from these material dreams. Exhaust from automobiles and factories fouled the air, and rampant development left little room for parks and other public amenities. Meanwhile, a heightened desire for privacy, which *Los Angeles Times* columnist Art Seidenbaum said was at the heart of Southern California culture, seemed to undermine a sense of community and inhibit collective action.[48]

Ahmanson's philanthropic investments reflected a desire to cultivate a greater sense of community through art. This was, after all, the "new way of life" that Millard Sheets had given him in the 1950s. At the same time, he and Home Savings increasingly searched for ways to develop community from the ground up.

By the mid-1960s, Ahmanson believed the era of inexpensive, mass production housing was over. "I don't like tracts," he told a reporter.[49] He was not alone. Despite the popularity of television shows anchored in the suburban ideal like *Donna Reed, Leave it to Beaver* and *Father Knows Best,* a broad critique of mass-production postwar housing tracts was under way. Critics charged they were ugly, promoted cultural conformity, led to social isolation, and degraded the environment.[50]

Several market forces combined to respond to this criticism and led to the development of a new kind of builder. The introduction of mass-production techniques into the residential construction market inevitably led to the development of larger firms. These firms needed greater management capacity to organize a larger workforce and investments in materials and land. Increases in the scale of the business also increased the need for working capital. Some companies relied on credit relationships with companies like Home Savings; others increasingly turned to the equity markets, and in the mid-1950s a growing number of residential construction companies began selling stock in the equities markets. With more capital and management talent in areas like marketing and planning, as well as basic construction, these large companies were able to look at the development process more comprehensively.[51]

These new building and development companies were uniquely positioned to respond to market conditions in the 1960s.[52] After fifteen years of postwar construction in the suburbs surrounding America's largest cities, large tracts of land were less available, and they were expensive. The government's construction of interstate highways opened new tracts to development, but to induce central city workers to make the long commute, developers had to offer lifestyle amenities that went beyond those that could be incorporated into the individual home. Buyers wanted environmental amenities and a sense of community.[53]

Community builders responded to these challenges. Borrowing from European and especially British new town traditions, a new group of developers in the United States planned on a much larger scale—ten thousand acres, for example, with housing and employment opportunities for communities of fifty thousand to one hundred thousand people—far beyond the scale of the operative builder erecting seven hundred to one thousand homes in a single year. These developers built on earlier traditions, the New Deal projects of the Resettlement Administration in Greenbelt, Maryland; Greenhills near Cincinnati; and Greendale in Milwaukee, for example. They also extended the strategies of postwar developers like Burns and Kaiser who sought to create new decentralized, regional cities that included a mix of land uses, were close to emerging regional employment centers, and incorporated rationalized community building amenities like schools, churches, and recreation facilities.[54] As one writer put it, this new breed of community builder "fastens his eyes on the social objective of a self-sufficient community, and hopes that good planning will make good money."[55]

In new towns like Columbia, Maryland, or Reston, Virginia, these developers experimented with a new paradigm. They planned for open space, employment centers, retail, schools, and public services. They included walking paths to separate pedestrians from vehicular traffic. In Columbia, developer James Rouse, like Ahmanson, believed that capitalism could respond to meet the consumer or home buyer's need for more than shelter and build successful communities.[56] Rouse aspired to create an inclusive community that would include African Americans as well as whites, and low-income as well as middle- and upper-middle-income residents.

Ahmanson evidenced no desire to shape the market to similar social objectives, but he did want to build whole communities complete with parks, shopping, and cultural amenities.[57] In many ways, his embrace of community development supplanted his earlier focus on home ownership. But it also reflected his famous ability to read the market.

Ahmanson's friendship with architect William Pereira was critical to this transition. In addition to his architectural practice, Pereira had developed a strong reputation for master planning in the 1950s. He and his partner Charles Luckman created the master plans for Cape Canaveral and the campus at the University of California, Santa Barbara, in addition to the work they did on urban renewal in the Bunker Hill neighborhood.[58] The opportunity to build on this practice area increased after 1954 when Congress added a provision to the National Housing Act allocating substantial grants to cities and counties that prepared general plans for future development.[59] By the late 1950s, when he and Ahmanson were serving on the Art Institute board, Pereira had become Southern California's leading master planner.[60]

Developers hired Pereira to transform vast tracts of land into entirely new cities. "The resulting scale of Los Angeles in the 1960s was so staggering and unprecedented," writes planning historian William Fulton, "that distinguished urban planners were left speechless."[61] By 1961, a number of Southern California projects reflected the scale of these new initiatives. Century

City, a $500 million development on the west side of Los Angeles, was developed on what had once been the back lot of the 20th Century-Fox Film Corporation. Laguna Niguel, a seven-thousand-acre planned community in Orange County, included plans for single-family homes, apartments, a shopping center, industrial parks, a research center, and recreational facilities. In the Conejo Valley, the Janns Investment Company was developing ten thousand acres near Thousand Oaks. On the Irvine Ranch, Pereira was working on a massive community to be developed around a new campus for the University of California. But the largest development was California City, with nine thousand acres located twelve miles from Mojave in Kern County.

The scale of these projects often engendered resistance. Ahmanson acquired 260 acres owned by the Fox Hills Country Club near Culver City, for example, and hired Pereira to develop a master plan to include homes, apartments, office buildings, and shopping.[62] The project was expected to provide housing for eight thousand people along with a hotel and other businesses. Howard grandly asserted that he planned to build the largest single apartment complex "anybody has ever had." He envisioned moderately priced garden apartments surrounded by green areas with recreational space including swimming pools.[63] Home Savings representatives said the development would surpass Century City in quality and character.[64] But residents of the area complained that the project would result in less open space and would eliminate one of the few public golf courses from the area. The County Parks and Recreation Commission agreed and recommended that the Board of Supervisors buy the property for recreational use. The project was further delayed when the California State College system expressed an interest in locating a proposed "South Bay State College" on a one-hundred-acre portion of the site.[65] For years the project was tied up in a series of hearings and quasi-judicial proceedings.

Meanwhile, Ahmanson and Home Savings ran into neighborhood resistance in other areas. When the company sought permission for a 670-unit development in Laurel Canyon in 1962, neighbors on Mulholland Drive protested plans to create a 110-foot hill of dirt that would obstruct their views.[66] Home also proposed to develop an 824-acre tract, part of the Morrison Ranch in Agoura, to accommodate eight hundred new homes and a shopping center.[67] In the Baldwin Hills area, Home planned to build a 3,500-unit residential project around a 120-acre, eighteen-hole golf course between Slauson and Centinela Avenues. On this project opponents included neighbors and Howard Hughes, who feared that twenty-two-story apartment buildings would create a hazard for aircraft approaching or taking off from Hughes Airport.[68]

In West Covina, where Ahmanson had acquired four thousand acres, he proposed to build moderately priced homes with architectural variety, clustered units, roads that followed the contours of the land, playgrounds for children, and open space. Ahmanson hoped to offer all of these community amenities to buyers of homes priced between $17,500 and $20,000, well below the usual market price for this kind of development.[69] Here again neighbors resisted and delayed construction for years.

All of these projects suddenly paled when Home Savings announced in June 1963 that it planned to develop the 6,300-acre Crummer Ranch on the border of Ventura and Los Angeles Counties into a community for fifty-three thousand people. Once again, Pereira was hired to develop the master plan, which would include homes, shopping, and a golf course.[70] "I imagine this is part of the fulfillment of the prediction that some day all the area from Santa Barbara to San Diego will be one big city," commented the head of the Valleywide Better Government Committee. The mayor of Hidden Hills, adjacent to the Crummer Ranch, bemoaned the fact that he would lose his pastoral view of cattle grazing peacefully on the hillsides. "But this is progress," he said, "and how are you going to stop progress even if you're against it—which I am."[71]

In fact, citizens were increasingly successful when it came to blocking large-scale developments, and many of the new communities envisioned by Ahmanson were never built because new voices challenged the old pattern of local land use decision making. Home Savings struggled to accommodate the new voices entering the conversation—local property owners who resisted development in their backyard, consumers who were increasingly concerned about the quality of the homes and communities that were being built, and people of color who insisted that with this next chapter of the American Dream they should not be left out.

COMMUNITY AND GOVERNMENT

Ahmanson's experiences from the late 1950s to the mid-1960s no doubt gave him confidence that a power elite existed to constructively guide civic change in Los Angeles if others would simply get out of the way. But others were not so sure. Francis Carney, a professor of political science at University of California–Riverside noted in 1964 that Los Angeles suffered from "the absence of a subjectively coherent upper class. There are 'old families' and the 'very rich' and a world of 'celebrities,' and their bazaars, cotillions, balls, hunts, and betrothals are duly chronicled on the society pages, most especially of the *Times.* But nobody really cares what this stratum does and no one is under the illusion that it constitutes a powerful class." Most important to Carney, there was no evidence that the city's rich and famous "provide Los Angeles with a corps of disinterested leadership dedicated to civic betterment and the common interests."[72] Arguably, one could look at LACMA, the Music Center, or a dozen other institutions in Los Angeles and suggest that Carney was wrong.

Carney's description of the new business elite, however, shed light on changing attitudes among the power elite. At its base, much of the new great wealth in Los Angeles was dependent on the federal government. In industries ranging from aerospace to savings and loans, federal contracts or insurance guarantees played a critical role in economic success. As a result, the leaders of these new industries were far less parochial than earlier generations. "[They] look outward, to Washington and New York for capital, for ideas, for stimuli," Carney wrote.[73] Republican or Democrat, these leaders tended to be pragmatists who believed in the role of experts and expressed a basic faith in the managed economy.[74] But as Carney suggested, their local leadership was diffused. They acted in civic arenas in ways that appealed to them personally, but rarely in a coordinated fashion, leaving a power vacuum at the heart of the region.[75]

Ahmanson sensed this vacuum. Moreover, he had grown increasingly frustrated with the parochialism of local government, Ahmanson favored a time-honored tradition in American business—elevate planning and rule making to the federal government and give greater power to elite experts and power brokers. "Federalism in urban affairs is a necessary evil," he said. "Local government simply doesn't have the tools to supply all the services people need."[76] Ahmanson talked of the need for a super-regional government that would address problems at a system level. Although local governments had banded together in 1965 to create the Southern California Association of Governments, this was not what he had in mind. He believed local elected officials, protecting their parochial interests, would block the path to a more rational planning system. To bring about change, "We have to take the initiative out of political hands," he said, "and not be afraid to step on some political toes."[77]

Working with the federal government, smart, powerful elites were the key to making good public policy, Howard suggested.[78] In his mind, "We'll only get [a regional government] when a strong bunch of civic leaders sits down around a table and says, this has got to be done."[79] Franklin Murphy agreed. "It doesn't take a lot of people to trigger citizen action," Murphy told *Los Angeles Magazine* in 1966, "just three or four knowledgeable, visible people who make a commitment."[80] In this sense, Ahmanson's ideology did not differ dramatically from the elitist Progressive framework that he had grown up with in the 1910s and 1920s. In an era dominated by large-scale corporations, big government, and the military, he believed, the power elite naturally coordinated the resources of civil society.[81] To a longtime political entrepreneur like Howard Ahmanson, this made infinite sense. To those outside the networks of power, it undermined the promise of American democracy.

Although he said that Los Angeles could not look to older cities in the East to model the new way of life under construction in the West, Ahmanson personally looked to New York for role models. The Rockefeller family in particular evidenced the ways in which great wealth and the power elite could work with government and the people to foster the civic culture of a great city. In October 1967, Ahmanson announced that he would tear down the first building that Millard Sheets had built for him. In its place, he would develop a massive $75 million office and commercial complex to be known as the Ahmanson Center that would occupy the entire 3700 block on Wilshire Boulevard. Ahmanson directed that this new structure, like Rockefeller Center in New York, would include a great plaza with fountains and sculptures. According to architect Edward Durrell Stone, Ahmanson wanted this space to be "in the tradition of some of the great plazas of Europe" and serve as a public gathering space.[82] Undoubtedly, it would also be a monument to all that he had accomplished.

SEVENTEEN

A Personal Epic

IN THE SUMMER OF 1965 writer Stewart Alsop introduced readers of the *Saturday Evening Post* to "America's New Big Rich." They were all men. All had made their big money since the end of World War II. Alsop described them as "a different breed from the old big rich—Astors, Vanderbilts, Morgans, Rockefellers, Mellons, Harrimans, du Ponts, Carnegies, and the like." They were not conspicuous consumers, at least not on the scale of their predecessors. Most did not seek the fame of being rich. Some even seemed to be embarrassed by their great wealth.

Howard Ahmanson alone seemed to genuinely enjoy being rich, Alsop wrote. "Perhaps being rich gives him a sense of fulfillment. For he has magnificently fulfilled the mission for which the father he worshiped trained him—the mission of making money."[1]

Unquestionably, Ahmanson had succeeded at this mission. When asked by reporters how much he was worth, he refused to answer, often saying he hadn't ever totaled it up. Some reporters tried to do it for him. In January 1966, it was estimated that his equity in Home Savings alone was worth $700 million. National American Insurance accounted for another $23 million and the Ahmanson Bank and Trust $35 million. In addition, he held a "commanding" interest in two other financial companies: United Financial Corp. and First Surety Corp. The latter business was a $40 million concern. This article didn't even include his real estate holdings, but it concluded that Ahmanson was the wealthiest man in California.[2]

Like his father before him, Howard Ahmanson dreamed of turning his business over to his son and of his son carrying the empire to greater heights. At an even deeper level, he wanted the same kind of relationship with Steady that he had had with his father. For his part, at a young age, Steady discerned the respect and even obsequiousness that people displayed around his father. In small ways, he aligned himself with his father's greatness, saving newspaper clippings that profiled his father's business and sailing triumphs. He even named his own small sailboat after the *Sirius II*.

As Steady entered his teenage years, however, the relationship between father and son became strained. When Howard told his son about how his own father had trusted him implicitly, Steady became anxious. Increasingly he feared that he would not be able to live up to the example his father had set or that he would be suffocated inside such a relationship.[3]

Steady's withdrawal reflected more than the epic story of a son in the shadow of a powerful father. Never an athlete and often bookish to the point of caricature, Steady was intellectually brilliant but prone to explosive emotional outbursts. Outsiders who watched him concluded that he was spoiled and undisciplined. Under stress, he exhibited compulsive behavior and physical tics. He mumbled to himself. When they were together, Howard sometimes put an arm around Steady to try and calm him. Sometimes the boy took comfort in this gesture.[4] Other times he resisted this intimacy.

Years later, Steady's condition would be diagnosed as Tourette's syndrome, a neurological disorder that presents itself in adolescence and occurs most frequently in boys. Associated with involuntary tics and vocalizations, the condition was first medically described in 1885 by the pioneering French neurologist Dr. Georges Gilles de la Tourette. In the 1960s, however, it was often considered a psychiatric disorder because psychological stress tended to exacerbate the symptoms and researchers could find no physiological cause for Tourette's various behaviors.[5] Most practicing physicians were unfamiliar with Tourette's and often missed its diagnosis.

Without medical insight, Howard held onto the idea that he could resolve Steady's anxieties and mentor his son as his father had mentored him. At an early age he tried to teach his son to read financial statements, but Howard junior had no schema for many of the concepts. Howard also wanted to train Steady to be decisive, but by nature Steady was often indifferent to things.

Years later, Howard junior looked back on these interactions and realized, "He was trying to train me in the habit of mind that even if you don't care, one alternative has to be selected when you're in charge." Howard also tried to train his son to be aggressive about answers and solutions. "'I don't know' is not an answer," he often reminded Steady. For Steady, however, "I don't know" was the obvious answer when, in fact, he did not have the information his father wanted.[6]

Striving to sustain Steady's remarkable cognitive abilities, Howard and Dottie pushed the boy far ahead of his age peers in school. He spent only half a year in each of second, third, fourth, and fifth grades, entering junior high school sixth grade at the age of ten. But the experience was so emotionally trying that after one month in seventh grade he was moved back to sixth.[7] When Steady reached high school, Howard thought he needed a highly structured environment to monitor his emotional behavior. He convinced Dottie that they should send him to Black-Foxe Military Institute, an elite prep school for boys founded by Charlie Fletcher's father-in-law, Charles E. Toberman, in 1928.[8]

Howard shared his concerns with Franklin Murphy. They were both ambitious men who had been mentored by their fathers and hoped to similarly mentor their only sons. Murphy suggested that Howard should look at the example of Paul Mellon, who had rejected a career in the Mellon family's banking and financial companies but had collaborated with his father on the creation of the National Gallery of Art in Washington. Murphy suggested that Howard junior might develop a similar passion for nonprofit work. Howard embraced this idea and appointed Howard junior to the board of the Ahmanson Foundation when he was still only seventeen.[9]

Often after the scotch-infused grand planning was over and Murphy or some other drinking companion had left, Howard wandered into Steady's room to talk. Through the gush of an alcoholic cloud, he tried to bolster his son's confidence by telling him how great he was. Steady hated these "lectures." "He was able to print praise like presses mint money and devalue it," he says.[10] On other occasions, Howard turned nasty and cruel, especially if he thought Steady was being obstinate. Like many divorced children and especially only children, Steady felt trapped in what he would later describe as a pair of emotionally incestuous relationships where Howard and Dottie relied on him to meet their needs.

Howard referred to Steady's condition as a problem of "nerves" and often gave him lectures on how to control himself.[11] At the same time, Howard's concern and embarrassment over Steady's tics reinforced his latent desire to protect his son or keep him in what Howard junior calls "my golden cage."[12] Increasingly, Howard's bewilderment in the face of Steady's condition and his growing realization that the young man might never mature into an adult capable of running Howard's vast financial empire took its toll. Driving across Los Angeles with Richard Deihl in 1967, Howard confessed his fears and broke down.[13]

MARRIAGE TO CAROLINE

Steady had hoped that if his father remarried it would diminish the emotional pressure. Howard dated a number of women after his divorce was finalized in 1962. There was a notable fling with film star Rhonda Fleming, who accompanied Howard and Steady on a trip to Hawaii. But Howard remained fascinated with Caroline Leonetti.

Although she found him interesting, Caroline was initially skeptical about a long-term relationship with Ahmanson. She was put off by his imperious nature and occasional verbal cruelty—especially when he had been drinking too much. He was always remorseful afterwards, but several times she decided she'd had enough. Once, she told him, "Please don't bother me anymore." She put pillows over the phone to ignore his calls. But when she went to Europe, he got her itinerary from her secretary and sent a rose a day to the various hotels where she was staying.[14]

With time, the many fights they had during this off-and-on courtship helped Caroline understand Howard better and led her to establish ground rules that made the relationship work. She admired him for many reasons. His strengths as a businessman were evident. He had a quick mind. When he sat down to the piano, the joyful and creative aspects of his character played through the keys. "I may not play good," he said with a smile, "but I can sure play loud."

Howard hinted at marriage, but Caroline felt Steady didn't want her for a stepmother. After a while, however, the teenage Steady looked at the prospect of his father's remarriage as a way to get out from under the pressure he felt from his parents. Finally, late in 1964, Howard called Caroline while she was in Vienna to formally propose. With fourteen-year-old Steady sitting beside him, he told her, "Howard junior is here, and we want to marry you."[15]

They were married on January 14, 1965, in a simple ceremony at Bob Ahmanson's home. Just weeks from her forty-seventh birthday, Caroline posed with Howard in front of the mantel. In a sweet ivory knee-length sheath dress with drape sleeves and a scoop neck, she looked very mod. A long single strand of pearls hung around her neck and down to her waist. With a pillbox hat, she seemed to emulate the Audrey Hepburn blend of sophisticated naïveté. With his arm around her, a white carnation in his lapel and his thinning gray hair swept back from his temples, fifty-eight-year-old Howard beamed so that his sunburned apple cheeks swelled beneath his pale blue eyes.

Caroline was effusive and charming but hardly naive. Howard told a reporter from *Newsweek:* "She's a terrific businesswoman. I married her for security."[16] Howard admired her ability to make quick business decisions. Her style contrasted so sharply from his own careful and deep ruminations.[17] Others saw the same thing Howard did. Richard Deihl remembered: "She brought to Howard a business acumen; not that he did n't have it, but she brought to him and to their union a tremendous amount of energy, experience and intellect."[18]

Caroline seemed to pivot to her new role. At home in Hancock Park, she quickly took control of the household. The men's club atmosphere with long nights of drinking and poker with Franklin Murphy, Norman Topping, and others came to an end.[19] Believing that she could not run her business and embrace the challenges and opportunities opened by her marriage, she talked to Howard about closing her modeling agency and charm school. Ultimately, her daughter Margo, who had grown up in the business, became the leader of Caroline Leonetti, Ltd., while Caroline devoted herself to the roles of wife and civic leader.[20]

CANDOR BETWEEN FATHER AND SON

To some extent, Steady's strategy worked. While Howard and Caroline entertained and traveled, his friendships at Black-Foxe deepened. After graduating at the age of seventeen, he enrolled at Occidental College in Los Angeles in the fall. But having a stepmother, especially one with so much presence in the world, created its own challenges.

Caroline tried to exercise discretion in her relationship with Steady. She encouraged Howard junior and showed him affection, but it was hard because he was usually stiff and emotionally distant. Dressed in his Black Foxe military academy uniform, with his hair loosely combed over from the side, he looked at her through thick glasses with eyes that seemed to focus inward rather than out. Like her new husband, she worried about how he would transition to life as an adult.

Hoping to find some way to ease his son's anxieties, Howard asked Steady to travel with him and Caroline to Europe in the summer of 1968. Steady resisted. Howard had a tradition of going to Europe every other year to celebrate his birthday. Steady had been expected to travel with him. But he was eighteen now and in college. Why didn't his father expect him to get a summer job like other college students? That spring, Howard wrote Steady a note acknowledging that they had grown apart. He again asked Steady to come to Europe to see if time together would help improve their relationship. Steady reluctantly agreed.

Two days before the Ahmansons were scheduled to leave for Europe, Howard was expected to preside over the grand opening of the new Hollywood branch at Sunset and Vine. The location had magic in Hollywood lore. Cecil B. DeMille had directed the first full-length film, *The Squaw Man,* on the site. In designing the facility, Millard Sheets and the artists associated with his studio had chosen to celebrate the golden age of Hollywood.[21] Expansive mosaics, framed almost like a film screen, overshadowed the main entrance depicting twenty of Hollywood's legendary stars. In a plaza in front of the bank, Paul Manship's sculpture *The Flight of Europa* hovered on a pedestal surrounded by a fountain.

Several of Hollywood's most famous stars, including Charleton Heston and Elsa Lanchester, were scheduled to appear at the opening on Saturday, June 8. But on Tuesday night, June 4, moments after celebrating his victory in the California primary, Senator Robert Kennedy was gunned down as he passed through the kitchen of the Ambassador Hotel in Los Angeles. Kennedy's assassination cast a pall over the city. Governor Ronald Reagan proclaimed a state of mourning throughout California to last until after Kennedy's funeral.[22] With the funeral slated for the same day as the Hollywood branch opening, Home Savings postponed its celebration. Booked to depart for Europe on June 10, Howard handed the baton to the man he had picked to succeed Ken Childs as president of Home Savings and Loan.

Howard was never comfortable with the day-to-day job of running an organization, but it took him a while to decide who should lead the company after Childs left. Although he was close to his two nephews Bob and Bill Ahmanson, whose family loyalty mattered a great deal, he did not see either as a
candidate to lead Home.[23] As his friendship and civic collaboration with
Franklin Murphy deepened, Howard talked to Murphy about leaving his
job as chancellor of UCLA to become chairman of Home Savings & Loan.
Recognizing that Ahmanson was too tough and strong-willed to really share
leadership with anyone, Murphy politely turned him down.[24] "The day I became an associate of yours would be the day our friendship would end," he told
Howard. Ahmanson said Murphy was exaggerating, but Murphy insisted.[25]

With Murphy's rejection, Ahmanson looked to Home's executives. Richard Deihl had grown up in the business. His father Victor, a professor at
Whittier College in the 1920s, had managed the Pico Building and Loan and
kept it alive through the Depression. Deihl remembered watching him work
at night in the den, calculating and then recording the interest on people's
savings accounts on index cards. Like other savings and loan managers, Victor Deihl ran an insurance agency on the side and placed accounts with
H. F. Ahmanson & Co.

The younger Deihl graduated from Whittier College and completed all of
his coursework for an MBA at UC Berkeley, but with the outbreak of war in
Korea he enlisted in the air force. He spent ten months flying close support
for infantry in combat. Out of the service, he worked for National Cash Reg-
ister in Pomona. Deihl met Ahmanson in 1960 at a party for his father's sixtieth birthday. "He asked me who I worked for," Deihl remembers, "and then
says, 'Oh, yes, one of those very big giant corporations that squeeze everything out and then discard you.'" Turned off by Ahmanson's arrogance,
Deihl was surprised when Evelyn Barty called later and told him that Ahmanson would like to meet with him. This time Ahmanson was affable and
warm. "When he wanted to be, Howard was probably as charming as any guy
I ever met." The two men talked for two hours, Deihl remembers. "I tried to
impress him with how bright I was. He tried to get through the veneer to see
who I really was."[26] Afterward, Robert DeKruif called and offered a job.

Deihl worked for Ahmanson first at South Gate Savings and Loan. In
this largely blue-collar neighborhood on the south side of Los Angeles, he
swept the sidewalks, read the machine totals at night, kept the books by hand,

and became the loan service manager. He was also in charge of the radios, silverware, and teapots that the association gave away as premiums to customers with larger accounts. After six months at South Gate, Howard Ahmanson offered him a choice between a job in the controller's office and a sales job. Deihl took the one that made more money—sales.

"I didn't talk to [Ahmanson] again for four years," Deihl remembers.

After Ken Childs left the company in 1964, three men jockeyed to become the next president. Ahmanson had reservations about all of them. Deihl's big opportunity came when the Federal Home Loan Bank began to have problems with Home Savings' loan portfolio. The company had tried to centralize its loan management operations, but the effort created considerable confusion. According to Deihl, the regulators declared that Home was unauditable. Deihl found out about the problem one day in an executive staff meeting. When one of the senior executives announced that the company had lost yet another manager of loan servicing, Ahmanson asked who was going to fill the slot.

When the executive hesitated, Ahmanson turned to Deihl and asked, "What do you know about loan servicing?"

"Not a lot," Deihl responded, "but I can learn."

"Okay, you're the new head of loan service," Ahmanson decreed.

Deihl took over the management of a staff of nearly two hundred demoralized employees. "You can't imagine the chaos," Deihl remembers. Immediately, he began offering prizes, "a belt, a blouse, or a pair of hose," to whoever could post the most payments in a week. He paid for the prizes from his own pocket. Almost overnight, the number of postings per day doubled. He also reorganized the staff into teams that included a poster, a collections person, and an insurance person. These teams were responsible for a certain number of specific accounts. This way, the risk that someone would get multiple calls on the same issue was greatly reduced. Customers could build relationships with individuals who were managing their accounts. With these reorganizations of the work flow, Home's books were back in order within months.

Ahmanson appreciated Deihl's work and the fact that he wasn't afraid of Ahmanson or any job he might give him. After becoming disenchanted with and firing his head of Lending, Ahmanson looked for a replacement. This was one of the most important roles in the organization. This time, the executive meeting at Ahmanson's house went into the wee hours of the morning. Still the scotch flowed. Finally, near six in the morning, Ahmanson looked at the group and said, "Deihl is going to be the head of Lending."

Ahmanson's decision reflected his growing confidence that Deihl was the one man who could run all parts of the organization. Ten months later, at lunch in his regular booth at Perino's in October 1967, Ahmanson gathered Deihl, DeKruif, and Bill Ahmanson. Deihl sat to Howard's right. They were in the middle of a conversation where Howard was "chewing out" Bill Ahmanson for something related to the insurance business, when Howard turned and said, "Deihl, you're the new president of Home Savings."

The announcement silenced the table. Almost impulsively, Ahmanson had picked his new Ken Childs, and it was not his nephew or one of his longtime associates. Still in his thirties, Deihl would be the backbone behind Home Savings operations.

But if Deihl thought that as president he would finally get to know Howard Ahmanson and understand what made him tick, he was disappointed. Most interactions continued to take place during Ahmanson's weekly meetings with the executives. Occasionally, he would get a call from Evelyn Barty relaying a question. Once or twice a complaint letter sent to Ahmanson would land on Deihl's desk. Occasionally, if Ahmanson had to duck out of some public appearance, Deihl would stand in for him. On June 7, 1968, Ahmanson told Deihl he would have to run the show at the Hollywood opening because Howard, Caroline, and Howard junior had a plane to catch. It would be the last assignment that Ahmanson would give to his new president.

BELGIUM

Howard's good friend Maurizio Bufalini chartered a boat for Howard and his friends. They anticipated that they would traverse the Rhine between Amsterdam and Frankfurt. The entourage included a host of Southern California friends.[27] When they arrived in Amsterdam, however, Bufalini looked at the boat and deemed it unacceptable. Instead, he hired drivers and a blue bus, and the party drove down to Frankfurt and then up to Luxembourg. Howard planned to highlight the trip with a birthday celebration in Oslo at the home of world champion ice skater Sonja (Henie) and her husband Niels Onstad.

The motorcade was on its way to Brussels and nearing the city of Marche in Belgium on June 17. Riding in the back seat of his chauffeur-driven car, Howard suddenly felt ill.

Turning to look at him, Caroline said: "You aren't feeling very well."

"No," he answered, "I'm not feeling very well."

She found a nitroglycerine pill and put it under his tongue, but it didn't seem to help. She put another one there.

He kept patting her hand. At one point, he said, "You're a very good wife."

Then it got quiet in the vehicle. Suddenly Caroline realized that Howard had stopped breathing. She screamed, "Stop! Stop!"

The driver pulled to the side of the road.

Steady tried to revive his father with rescue breathing, but Howard didn't respond.

Someone called the closest hospital for an ambulance. At the hospital, they happened to find a surgeon from Boston who attended to Howard, but according to Caroline, "it was no use." Although Howard had attended a Methodist church on occasion, Caroline, a strong Catholic, asked a priest to administer the last rites.[28]

A CIVIC FUNERAL

A wildfire raged on Bald Mountain in the Angeles National Forest through the night before Howard Ahmanson's funeral. It was the worst of a half-dozen fires burning in the Southland as temperatures soared to unseasonable highs. At dawn, a blood-red sun rose through the heavy smoke and smog that hung over the Los Angeles basin.[29] Across the city, in Howard's honor, flags flew at half mast in front of Los Angeles County buildings by order of the Board of Supervisors.[30]

As the lavish service started, Howard's rose- and carnation-draped casket lay in state beneath the vaulted Gothic ceiling of the Wilshire United Methodist Church.[31] Before this same altar, a number of Hollywood stars had been married, including seventeen-year-old actress Shirley Temple in 1945. For Howard's funeral the mood of the more than five hundred mourners in the congregation was more sober. When Roger Wagner introduced his Chorale and announced that they would perform the old cowboy song "Curtains of the Night," to honor Ahmanson's "love for the great out-of-doors," it brought a smile to the faces of some in attendance who remembered Howard's sunburned face as he worked the tiller of his boat.[32]

The congregation included more than fifty honorary pallbearers who represented much of the power elite of Los Angeles: Supervisors Burton W. Chace and Kenneth Hahn, Assembly Speaker Jesse M. Unruh, Sheriff Peter

J. Pitchess, Councilman John Ferraro, former Governor Goodwin Knight, *Los Angeles Times* publisher Otis Chandler, savings and loan owner Bart Lytton, and television personality Art Linkletter.[33] An honorary pallbearer, Richard Deihl couldn't help but think that Howard had organized the event himself, since the speakers included a rabbi, a Catholic priest, and a Protestant minister. "He was covering his bases."[34]

Norman Topping and Franklin Murphy, the presidents of L.A.'s two great universities, delivered eulogies. Topping described Howard as "a friend we loved for his dedication to living graciously, giving wisely and loving deeply." Murphy said Howard was "a complex man; a restive, creative, loyal man who wedded his energy and genius to the dynamics of the West, here in Southern California, and created not only a financial empire, but also a community rich in cultural and spiritual values."[35]

Steady sat watching the service, seemingly impassive. He was overwhelmed by a sense of the public significance of his father's demise, as if his father was more historical figure than parent. "I had this feeling that a great personality had been lost," he recalls. During the service he started to cry. "For the first time and only time," he remembers. "I'm not sure why. I didn't feel a great sense of personal loss. It was just the grandeur of the whole thing."

With the service over, Howard junior joined his father's closest friends and collaborators as they lifted the casket. Edward Boland, Maurizio Bufalini, Hernando Courtright, Franklin Murphy, William Pereira, Millard Sheets, Norman Topping, Thomas Webster, and J. Howard Edgerton, along with his nephews Bill and Bob, helped carry Howard's casket out of the church, past an honor guard of sheriff's deputies and to the waiting hearse.[36]

DISSOLUTION OF THE EMPIRE

Shortly before his death, Ahmanson had been working on estate planning and the future of H. F. Ahmanson & Co. Long talks with Thomas Webster were focused on two primary goals: preserving control of the Ahmanson empire within the family and ensuring that Ahmanson's family and certain friends would benefit from his estate. These conversations resulted in the creation of a testamentary trust and a new will, which Ahmanson signed two weeks before his death. The plan was one of the most complicated in U.S tax history. Ahmanson did not want his death to lead to a breakup of his empire. And even in death, he wanted to prevent others from gaining control of his companies. As a result, the bulk of the value of the estate, appraised at $105.4 million ($681.6 million in 2011 dollars) passed to the Ahmanson Foundation.[37] Control of the empire was less clear.[38]

Prior to his death, Ahmanson had created a master holding company—Ahmanco Inc. Nearly all of the shares in this company were given to the Ahmanson Foundation, but these were nonvoting shares. The one voting share was awarded to Howard junior. Trust 28, the instrument that controlled most of his estate, gave Howard junior the sole right to vote this share once he reached the age of twenty-eight. From the time he was twenty-one until he was twenty-eight, he would share this right with the Ahmanson Bank & Trust, which acted as the executor for Howard senior's estate.[39] But in 1968, Howard junior was not even twenty-one.

Unlike his father, who at the age of nineteen aspired to carry forward his father's legacy, Steady was mentally, emotionally, and developmentally in no position to direct his father's empire. Still struggling to deal with his undiagnosed Tourette's and suffering from grief, he seemed lost. Years later, Steady compared his reaction to a diver who comes up from the deep too quickly. "They get the 'bends' when nitrogen bubbles form in the blood vessels which can be extremely painful." He thought now he had to straighten himself out. Sharing the house on South Hudson with Caroline, he went to work for Home Savings in Beverly Hills, hoping to work his way up to be a teller. But Caroline and Bob Ahmanson felt that he was not coping. After seeing a psychiatrist at UCLA, Steady was misdiagnosed as schizophrenic. He was told he couldn't be treated on an outpatient basis. At Franklin Murphy's suggestion, Robert Ahmanson and Howard's driver, Conway, flew halfway across the country to Kansas City. On the night of July 14, less than a month after his father's death and five months after Howard junior turned eighteen, someone other than Steady filled out the voluntary admission form to the Menninger Memorial Hospital, the world-famous psychiatric clinic, and signed Howard junior's name, authorizing the clinic to perform diagnostic and therapeutic procedures as determined by the hospital.[40] Howard junior remained in Kansas for months, eventually taking classes at nearby Washburn University so he could continue his schooling while the psychiatric staff at Menninger monitored his condition.[41]

With Steady too young and incapacitated by his affliction, the future of the Ahmanson empire seemed uncertain. In many ways, Bill and Bob Ahmanson saw themselves as inheritors of their uncle's business empire, if not literally, at least operationally. Caroline believed that she had better insight into Howard's desires and sought to prevent Bill from taking control. She organized a meeting that included Howard's closest business associates and excluded Bill and Bob. She sought to persuade Howard's loyalists to side with her in a struggle for control. Everything turned on the single voting share of Ahmanco, which would be voted by the board of the Ahmanson Bank & Trust. Although they were torn, most of these leaders chose to follow Bill and Bob. Bill became the CEO of H. F. Ahmanson & Co, and in January 1969 was elected chairman of Home Savings & Loan.[42]

Caroline sought to have the final will overturned in court. Under the terms of the estate, she received $5 million as her share of community property. Taking advantage of a provision of California law that allowed for challenges when a will left gifts to charity and was signed within thirty days of the testator's death, she sought to invalidate the will and at least two of the trusts that Ahmanson and Webster had established.[43] Eventually, the foundation settled with her and paid her an additional $750,000 from the funds included in the gross estate.[44] Everything that was left went to the Ahmanson Foundation.

The complexity of Ahmanson's estate was also magnified when the tax laws were rewritten in 1969. The Tax Reform Act required private foundations with a controlling share of the ownership of for-profit companies to divest their majority stake. The law essentially forced Ahmanson's heirs and the Ahmanson Foundation to take H. F. Ahmanson & Co. public. When stock in H. F. Ahmanson & Co. was sold on the open market for the first time on October 17, 1972, it was one of the largest initial public offerings in history.[45] It also established the Ahmanson Foundation as one of the largest and richest in Southern California.

The foundation board appointed Bob Ahmanson as president. It developed a set of informal giving guidelines to reflect the board's best understanding of Ahmanson's intent: giving would be primarily in Southern California and Omaha. Giving would also follow Ahmanson's historic lead, focusing on institutions like LACMA, the Music Center, and others that he had supported.[46] Under Franklin Murphy's influence, the foundation also provided substantial support to academic and private libraries in the region.[47] It continued to support medical research and hospitals.[48] In 1992, Murphy claimed that the Ahmanson Foundation had played "a greater role in the cultural life of Southern California than any other single force."[49]

Charlie Fletcher and Howard Edgerton both lived for many years after Ahmanson's death. For competitive men, it was a lousy way to end the race.

Edgerton remained with CalFed for many years. In public, he sometimes rued the fact that he had not acquired his own state-chartered savings and loan like his friend Howard Ahmanson and built it into a financial empire. When he died in 1999 at the age of ninety-one, he was remembered for his long history of service to the community and the thrift industry. Charlie Fletcher turned over the leadership of Home Federal Savings and Loan to his son Kim and moved to Hawaii. Described as a "perpetual motion machine," he was hardly comfortable in retirement. He went to work for Pioneer Federal Savings and Loan in Hawaii and soon became its president and chairman. He continued to swim nearly every day until three weeks before his death in the fall of 1985.[50] In 1991, during the savings and loan crisis and after operating for more than half a century, Home Federal was seized by federal regulators.[51] Several years later, Cal Fed and Home Savings disappeared as well in a wave of corporate mergers that came with banking deregulation. The end of these three major Southern California thrifts signaled the end of an era just as the deaths of these three men marked the passing of a generation in the savings and loan industry and in America.

Conclusion

HOME OWNERS HAD TAKEN THE PLACE of yeoman farmers as the virtuous citizens of America's increasingly urban democracy by the early 1960s. The rhetoric of the building and loan industry of the late nineteenth century had been translated into government policies. As the yeoman farmer rose early in the morning to tend the fields and the livestock to put food on his family's table, the suburban home owner, as Walter Russell Mead has pointed out, got in his car and went to work to pay the mortgage on his house. The mortgage and property taxes forced the citizen and taxpayer to weigh the value of government services against the cost to his pocketbook, and these considerations kept him or her engaged in the processes of governance.[1]

In the postwar era, these federal and state policies that favored home ownership framed the market for home loans. Undoubtedly, the historical moment for home buyers, builders, lenders, and policy makers in Los Angeles and across the country was extraordinary. Unprecedented and widespread prosperity and the mass production of homes and loans contributed substantially to the increase in home ownership. To be sure, not everyone realized the dream. Systemic racism, sexism, and poverty prevented many people from owning a home. But the partnership between government and private enterprise at the heart of the managed economy had incorporated huge numbers of Americans into the property-owning ideal at the heart of the nation's democracy.

In the years that followed Howard Ahmanson's death, the challenges to the savings and loan industry were greater. The pent-up middle-class demand created by depression and war had been satisfied. Increasingly inflation, declining productivity, and global competition threatened the basis of

American prosperity. To continue to raise the rate of home ownership, builders and lenders needed to innovate to reach further down the economic ladder. Policy makers created new subsidies to encourage these innovations and in some cases make them possible. Along the way, many of these innovations undermined the institutional basis for the savings and loan.

Increasingly, savings and loans struggled with a fundamental structural problem. They depended on two kinds of customers: savers and borrowers. Savers wanted access to their cash on demand. Borrowers wanted long-term mortgages. The creation of the Federal Home Loan Bank had provided a way for thrifts to borrow when the balance between savers and borrowers tipped too far one way or another, but the FHLB was not designed to be the fundamental source of mortgage capital. As savings and loans struggled to compete for deposits, regulators and industry leaders clung to the old regime. Widespread failure to adapt is not unusual, but then thrifts were hit from another direction.

A second wave of financial innovations affected the lending side of the savings and loan concept. The sellers of mortgage-backed securities bypassed the traditional savings and loan depositor and went straight to Wall Street to raise mortgage capital. Low-overhead mortgage brokers operating out of small offices in suburban strip malls didn't need the expensive infrastructure of Millard Sheets buildings and faux vault doors to attract capital. Borrowers cared more about low mortgage rates. In Southern California in the 1980s Angelo Mozilo, the co-founder of Countrywide Home Loans, represented the most successful entrepreneur of the new regime.

With increased competition for savers and borrowers, savings and loans struggled to redefine their role in the financial system. They joined with other financial services industries to lobby for an end to their historic place in the compartmentalized system of financial services. Some survived and thrived. Others collapsed. The growing disconnect between the regulatory regime and the market misaligned incentives and created fertile opportunities for bad behavior. In the aftermath of the federal bailout and crisis, the institution of the savings and loan became stigmatized. No longer associated with Jimmy Stewart's George Bailey and *It's a Wonderful Life,* the trade association known since Seymour Dexter's days as the U.S. League of Savings and Loans became America's Community Bankers. The Federal Home Loan Bank was renamed the Office of Thrift Supervision.

Home survived and thrived despite the turmoil, though it shortened its name to Home Savings of America. While other thrifts sought to succeed by taking greater risks and entering new markets, Richard Deihl, like Ahmanson, was an innovator, but he also maintained Home's conservative lending practices. He was so successful at managing operations that *Time* suggested Howard Ahmanson was still running the company from the grave. As regulators opened the door for interstate expansion, Deihl moved aggressively into twenty states. The company's assets grew from $2.5 billion at the time of Ahmanson's death to $54 billion in 1994. By then, Home was lending more than $1 billion a month to home buyers across the country.[2] Deihl retired at the mandatory age of sixty-five. Soon afterwards, Home was swept up in a wave of consolidations that anticipated the repeal of Glass-Steagall and was sold to Washington Mutual in 1998. The deal helped create one of the largest banks in the country.

In 2008, the real estate bubble that helped fuel the growth of Washington Mutual burst. Overwhelmed by falling asset values, Washington Mutual was acquired by JPMorgan Chase. Journalists, politicians, and academics searched for the cause of the financial disaster. Some blamed the Federal Reserve for monetary policies that had fueled asset inflation. Others argued that federal policy makers, in their effort to extend home ownership to lower-income Americans, had pressured banks to weaken their underwriting standards. The rating agencies were criticized for failing to recognize the weaknesses of complicated mortgage-backed securities tied to subprime mortgages. Others asserted that the success of "the quants," highly mathematical approaches to investment and risk analysis, had lulled Wall Street into a belief that the risks in lending, no matter what the borrower's credit profile, had been eliminated by the creation of credit default swaps and collateralized debt obligations. In their elaborate algorithms, however, the quants had ignored the kinds of risks that Howard Ahmanson's insurance executive father had understood—the tornado that appeared suddenly on a cloudless spring day.

In the financial crisis that followed, home values fell across the country for the first time since the Depression. Widespread foreclosures in some parts of the country, including the more recently developed suburbs of the Los Angeles megalopolis, recalled the days when Howard Ahmanson had gotten rich as the undertaker at a plague. For the first time in generations, many people questioned the essential virtue and wisdom of buying a home.

Policy makers confronted the reality that the mortgage market had changed dramatically. The ethos of home ownership was so deeply embedded in the American psyche that most people still believed in the American Dream, and so did the politicians who represented them, but there was no clear consensus, as there had been in the 1930s, on government's role in supporting private efforts to sustain this American ideal.

Howard Ahmanson, Howard Edgerton, and Charlie Fletcher had played a pivotal role in the transformation of the local mutual savings and loan into a highly profitable corporate entity. Despite the success of their endeavors, they were always profoundly influenced by the history of their industry and the legacies of the Great Depression and World War II on their generation. They leveraged the opportunities that government had created for home owners to reap rich rewards for themselves, but they understood their relationship with government to be a kind of partnership where each side knew and understood its role.

Ahmanson did not agree with every law or regulation that was adopted in Sacramento or Washington. Nor did he gladly hand over his wealth to the State of California or the federal treasury. Risking his own capital over and over during the course of his career, he deserved to think of himself as an entrepreneur—albeit the kind of political entrepreneur who succeeds by fulfilling the ambitions of the nation as represented by his elected officials.

Ahmanson died just as this grand partnership between business and government was beginning to break down. A series of cultural, political, and economic forces combined to recharacterize the managed economy as an era in which the state was corrupted by big business and government ultimately overreached in its efforts to make the American Dream possible for everyone. As men in uniform in the World War II era, Ahmanson, Edgerton, and Fletcher were as cynical as any other GI about the wisdom of the bureaucracy, but they never doubted the goal. A democratic government working hand in hand with the free enterprise system could realize national dreams as well as private ambitions.

ABBREVIATIONS USED IN NOTES

AAA	Archives of American Art, Smithsonian Institution, Washington, DC
BL	Bancroft Library, University of California–Berkeley
CSA	California State Archives, Sacramento, CA
CSLJ	*California Savings and Loan Journal*
FA	Fieldstead Archive, Fieldstead, Inc., Irvine, CA
FHA	Federal Housing Administration
FHLB	Federal Home Loan Bank
FHLBB	Federal Home Loan Bank Board
FNMA	Federal National Mortgage Association
FSLIC	Federal Savings and Loan Insurance Corporation
JPMCA	JPMorgan Chase Archives, New York, NY
LACMA	Los Angeles County Museum of Art
LAT	*Los Angeles Times*
LH files	Lisa Hausdorfer files, Fieldstead Archive
NAHB	National Association of Home Builders, Washington, DC
NARA-CP	National Archives and Records Administration—College Park, MD
NARA-DC	National Archives and Records Administration—Washington, DC
NYT	*New York Times*
OCCJ	*Omaha Council Chamber Journal*

RG	Record Group (in NARA)
TAFA	The Ahmanson Foundation Archives, Beverly Hills, CA
WP	*Washington Post*
WSJ	*Wall Street Journal*

NOTES

INTRODUCTION

1. Josephine Hedges Ewalt, *A Business Reborn: The Savings and Loan Story, 1930–1960* (Chicago: American Savings and Loan Institute Press, 1962), 203.

2. Clark H. Woodward, "Admiral Woodward Notes: Japan Marks Time, Watches Russian War," *WP,* December 7, 1941, B1.

3. San Diego Hall of Champions, "Charles Fletcher," n.d., www.sdhoc.com/sport /diving-and-swimming/charles-fletcher (accessed October 7, 2009).

4. "Hostess at Hollywood Home," *LAT,* October 31, 1926, C2; Elizabeth Goodland, "Kim Fletcher to Claim Bride," *LAT,* August 15, 1954, C3.

5. Daniel M. Weintraub, "Charles Fletcher, 82, Dies; Founder of Home Federal," *LAT,* October 1, 1985.

6. Howard Edgerton to Mr. and Mrs. Charles K. Fletcher and Mr. and Mrs. Howard Ahmanson, November 26, 1943, in accordion file, box 23AV: World War II Era, FA.

7. "Meet Mr. Edgerton," *Savings and Loan News,* December 1954, 15–18. See also J. Howard Edgerton, *The Story of California Federal Savings* (New York: Newcomen Society in North America, 1969), 5.

8. Edgerton, *Story of California Federal Savings,* 5.

9. "J. Howard Edgerton, 91, Official in S&L Industry in California," *NYT,* October 30, 1999.

10. Edgerton to Mr. and Mrs. Charles K. Fletcher and Mr. and Mrs. Howard Ahmanson, November 26, 1943.

11. Caroline Leonetti Ahmanson, interview by Roberta Green Ahmanson and Marc Nurre, notes, August 23, 1993, in FA; Richard H. Deihl, interview by author, September 25, 2009.

12. "Mr. and Mrs. H.F. Ahmanson," *Japan News-Week,* June 1, 1940, 7.

13. Edgerton to Mr. and Mrs. Charles K. Fletcher and Mr. and Mrs. Howard Ahmanson, November 26, 1943.

14. Franklin Delano Roosevelt, "Proposed Message to Congress," December 7, 1941, www.archives.gov/education/lessons/day-of-infamy/images/infamy-address-1.gif.

15. Robert C. Albright, "Calm Congress Accepts Challenge with But One Dissenting Vote; Long Ovation Given President; Packed Galleries Applaud Speech," *WP*, December 9, 1941, 1.

16. For background on the evolution of the managed economy, see Louis Galambos and Joseph Pratt, *The Rise of the Corporate Commonwealth: United States Business and Public Policy in the 20th Century* (New York: Basic Books, 1988). See also Martin J. Sklar, *The Corporate Reconstruction of American Capitalism, 1890–1916: The Market, the Law and Politics* (New York: Cambridge University Press, 1988), and William G. Scott, *Chester I. Barnard and the Guardians of the Managerial State* (Lawrence: University of Kansas Press, 1992).

17. Leo Grebler, David M. Blank, and Louis Winnick, *Capital Formation in Residential Real Estate: Trends and Prospects* (Princeton: Princeton University Press, 1956), 238–60. See also David L. Mason, *From Buildings and Loans to Bail-Outs: A History of the American Savings and Loan Industry, 1831–1995* (Cambridge: Cambridge University Press, 2004), 140–53.

18. Only a limited number of business biographies or corporate histories have explored the theme of the government or political entrepreneur, although examples permeate the history of the American economy. Successful business leaders in this arena leverage government contracts to build market power or use legislative, legal, or regulatory processes to reshape markets to gain competitive advantage. See, for example, Stephen B. Adams, *Mr. Kaiser Goes to Washington: The Rise of a Government Entrepreneur* (Chapel Hill: University of North Carolina Press, 1997).

19. Between 1951 and 1962, savings and loans increased their share of the residential nonfarm mortgage market from 33.9 percent to 58.2 percent in Southern California, compared to an increase from 38.2 percent to 49.4 percent for the nation as a whole. In Los Angeles County, they accounted for 70.1 percent of all mortgage recordings by 1961. Federal Home Loan Bank data in Leo Grebler and Eugene F. Brigham, *Savings and Mortgage Markets in California* (Pasadena: California Savings and Loan League, 1963), 33, 41.

20. Data developed by the University of Michigan Survey Research Center (also Center for Political Studies) reflect Americans' relative confidence in government's efficacy and its ability to serve the interests of all. In 1964, for example, 76 percent of those surveyed said they trusted government to "do what's right" always or most of the time. By 1970, that number had declined to 53.5 percent. In 1964, 64 percent said government was run for the benefit of all, rather than a few big interests. By 1970, that percentage had fallen to 40.6 percent. In 1964, 68.2 percent believed that government officials were smart people who knew what they were doing. By 1970, only a slight majority—51.2 percent—held that view. Arthur H. Miller, "Political Issues and Trust in Government, 1964–1970," *American Political Science Review* 64, no. 3 (September 1974): 953. For a discussion of World War II's influence on attitudes toward government and civic engagement, see Robert D. Putnam,

Bowling Alone: The Collapse and Revival of American Community (New York: Simon and Schuster, 2000), 268–72. For an overview of the scholarly literature on the public's trust in government, see Luke Keele, "Social Capital and the Dynamics of Trust in Government," *American Journal of Political Science* 51, no. 2 (April 2007): 241–54.

21. David Vogel highlights the impact of growing consumerism on business regulation in *Fluctuating Fortunes: The Political Power of Business in America* (New York: Basic Books, 1989), 37–59.

22. Neoclassical economics explains regulation as a result of market failure. Theorists associated with the University of Chicago (George Stigler, Richard Posner, and Sam Peltzman) have emphasized regulation as the product of political bargaining by interest groups seeking economic advantage from the state. For a review of regulatory history emphasizing the latter approach, see Claudia Goldin and Gary D. Libecap, *The Regulated Economy: A Historical Approach to Political Economy* (Chicago: University of Chicago Press, 1994). For a more contingent historical view, see Thomas K. McCraw, "Regulation in America: A Review Article," *Business History Review* 49 (Summer 1975): 162–83. See also Thomas K. McCraw, *Prophets of Regulation* (Cambridge, MA: Harvard University Press, 1984), 216–21.

23. Richard H. Vietor, *Contrived Competition: Regulation and Deregulation in America* (Cambridge, MA: Harvard University Press, 1994).

24. See, for example, S. Liebowitz, "The Real Scandal, How Feds Invited the Mortgage Mess," *New York Post,* February 5, 2008, cited in Manuel B. Aalbers, "Why the Community Reinvestment Act Cannot Be Blamed for the Subprime Crisis," *City and Community* 8, no. 3 (2009): 346–50.

25. See, for example, Andrew Ross Sorkin, *Too Big to Fail* (New York: Viking, 2009); Scott Patterson, *The Quants* (New York: Crown Business, 2010); Bethany McLean and Joe Nocera, *All the Devils Are Here* (New York: Portfolio/Penguin, 2010); and Roger Lowenstein, *The End of Wall Street* (New York: Penguin Press, 2010).

26. Richard A. Posner, *The Crisis of Capitalist Democracy* (Cambridge, MA: Harvard University Press, 2010); and Joseph E. Stiglitz, *Freefall* (New York: Norton, 2010).

27. Kevin Fox Gotham, "Racialization and the State: The Housing Act of 1934 and the Creation of the Federal Housing Administration," *Sociological Perspectives* 43, no. 2 (Summer 2000): 291–317.

1. FATHER AS MENTOR

1. Landmarks Heritage Preservation Commission, "Calvin Memorial Presbyterian Church," n.d., www.co.douglas.ne.us/omaha/planning/landmarks/alphabetical -listing/calvin-memorial-presbyterian-church (accessed October 3, 2009).

2. U.S. Bureau of the Census, 1910 U.S. Census, Douglas County, NE, www .census.gov/prod/www/abs/decennial/1910.html.

3. "The Track of the Tornado," *Omaha Bee,* special issue, n.d., www.memorial library.com/NE/Tornados/Track/story.htm (accessed September 30, 2009).

4. "How Omaha Was Stricken," *NYT,* March 25, 1913, n.p.

5. Amazingly, none of the patrons were killed as they took refuge on the floor, and the seats kept the roof from falling on them. People then crawled to escape. Travis Sing, *Omaha's Easter Tornado of 1913* (Charleston, SC: Arcadia, 2003), 82.

6. The estimated death toll in Omaha from the tornado differs from source to source. This number is taken from ibid., 7.

7. Andrew Jenson, *Church Chronology: A Record of Important Events Pertaining to the History of the Church of Jesus Christ of Latter Day Saints* (Salt Lake City, UT: Deseret News, 1914), 47.

8. Fieldstad was also sometimes spelled Fjeldstad. George T. Flom, "The Danish Contingent in the Population of Early Iowa," *Iowa Journal of History and Politics,* January 1906, 239.

9. [Chris Bone], "Partial History/Chronology Howard Ahmanson," typescript from the files of Home Savings of America, [1988], copy provided by Robert DeKruif.

10. Ibid.

11. William Harvey King, *History of Homeopathy* (New York: Lewis, 1905), 399.

12. U.S. Bureau of the Census, 1880 U.S. Census, Douglas County, NE, www .census.gov/prod/www/abs/decennial/1880.html.

13. See W. H. Ahmanson's World War I draft registration listing at Nebraska State Historical Society, "Nebraska WWI Draft Cards Index Search Result," http://nshs.hallcountyne.gov/cgi-bin/WWIdraft_search.cgi?co=Omaha (accessed October 3, 2009).

14. "W. H. Ahmanson Dead; Was Ill One Year," *OCCJ,* June 6, 1925, 7.

15. "Application for Commission or Warrant, U.S. Naval Reserve," in file: H. F. Ahmanson–Navy, box 23AV, FA.

16. "Mortality Statistics," *Omaha Daily Bee,* April 4, 1899, 12.

17. Harold Tucker, "It's Not All Finance with L.A. Financier," *LAT,* June 11, 1961, J1.

18. Seymour Freedgood et al., "Croesus at Home," first draft typescript, March 17, 1958, in FA.

19. Norris Leap, "H. F. Ahmanson, 'Spoiled Boy,' Becomes Financial Genius," *LAT,* December 28, 1958, part IV, 1.

20. Freedgood et al., "Croesus at Home."

21. Leap, "H. F. Ahmanson."

22. Ibid.

23. Ibid.

24. Seymour Freedgood, "Emperor Howard Ahmanson of S&L," *Fortune,* May 1958, 150.

25. Stewart Alsop, "Multi-Millionaires: How America's New Rich Made Their Vast Fortunes," *Saturday Evening Post,* July 17, 1965, 42.

26. "The Hot Rodder," *Omaha World Herald*, May 14, 1980, n.p., clipping provided by Mary Jane Bettefreund.

27. Leap, "H. F. Ahmanson."

28. Freedgood et al., "Croesus at Home."

29. Leap, "H. F. Ahmanson."

30. "Application for Commission."

31. Certificate awarded to Howard Ahmanson by International YMCA Bible Study, 1919, in FA.

32. Mrs. Aimee Ahmanson and Florence Hoffman, interview by Howard F. Ahmanson Jr., August 21, 1993, 1, in FA.

33. Ibid.

34. The foreign born and their children accounted for nearly half of the city's population in 1920. For population numbers, see Lawrence H. Larsen et al., *Upstream Metropolis: An Urban Biography of Omaha and Council Bluffs* (Lincoln: University of Nebraska Press, 2007), 205.

35. In 1918 alone, bank clearings increased by 50 percent, the fastest growth in the financial sector of any leading city in the nation. "Omaha's Phenomenal Growth in Bank Clearings," *OCCJ*, January 11, 1919, 1.

36. "Nebraska in Banking," *OCCJ*, February 8, 1919, 2.

37. Lawrence H. Larsen and Barbara J. Cottrell, *The Gate City: A History of Omaha* (Lincoln: University of Nebraska Press, 1997), 183–84.

38. Larsen et al., *Upstream Metropolis*, 214–15.

39. Henry Fonda was a little more than a year older than Howard and apparently lived next door to the Ahmansons' house in Dundee at one time. See Omaha City Directories; "Henry, Too," *Omaha World-Herald*, May 14, 1980, n.p., clipping provided by Mary Jane Bettefreund; and Dan Rock, *Dundee, Neb.: A Pictorial History* (Omaha, NE: Shurson, 2000).

40. Larsen et al., *Upstream Metropolis*, 218.

41. Alsop, "Multi-Millionaires," 42.

42. Naomi R. Lamoreaux, *The Great Merger Movement in American Business, 1895–1904* (Cambridge: Cambridge University Press, 1985).

43. Martin J. Sklar, *The Corporate Reconstruction of American Capitalism, 1890–1916: The Market, the Law and Politics* (New York: Cambridge University Press, 1988). See also James Willard Hurst, *Law and Social Order in the United States* (Ithaca, NY: Cornell University Press, 1977).

44. Dalit Baranoff, "Shaped by Risk: Fire Insurance in America, 1790–1920" (PhD diss., Johns Hopkins University, 2003).

45. The Woodmen of the World, established in Omaha in 1895, was already one of the largest fraternal insurance organizations in the United States. Mutual of Omaha, started in 1909 as the Mutual Benefit Health and Accident Association, was growing rapidly. Larsen and Cottrell, *Gate City*, 214–15. On Woodmen of the World, see also "Facts Every Omahan Should Know about Omaha," *OCCJ*, January 22, 1921, 6–7.

46. Insurance Department, State of Nebraska, *Summary of Insurance Business in Nebraska for the Year 1913* (Fremont, NE: Hammond Printing Co./State Insurance Board, 1914), 116, Nebraska State Historical Society, RG 008, Dept. of Insurance, Summaries of Insurance Business, 188–1928, box 1 of 3. They earned just over $4.4 million in insurance premiums, while paying out a little more than $2.7 million in claims. "Nebraska Fire Business," *Weekly Underwriter,* September 12, 1914, in *The Weekly Underwriter, Volume 91* (New York: Underwriter Printing, 1914), 280.

47. "Omaha, Insurance Center," *OCCJ,* February 8, 1919, 3.

48. "C.C. Leaders Know Budgets," *Omaha World-Herald,* May 28, 1952, n.p.

49. *Omaha City Directory,* 1914, http://distantcousin.com/directories/ne/omaha /1914/.

50. For more on the history of regulation in this context, see Thomas K. McCraw, "Regulation in America: A Review Article," *Business History Review* 49 (Summer 1975): 162–83. See also Thomas K. McCraw, *Prophets of Regulation* (Cambridge, MA: Harvard University Press, 1984), 216–21.

51. H. Roger Grant, *Insurance Reform: Consumer Action in the Progressive Era* (Ames: Iowa State University Press, 1979).

52. Baranoff, "Shaped by Risk," 163, 178.

53. Harry Chase Brearley, *The History of the National Board of Fire Underwriters: Fifty Years a Civilizing Force* (New York: Frederick A. Stokes, 1916).

54. Guy Ashton Brown and Hiland Hill Wheeler, *Compiled Statutes of the State of Nebraska, 1881: With Amendments, 1882–1901* (Lincoln, NE: State Journal Company, 1901), 1182.

55. Baranoff, "Shaped by Risk," 195.

56. Tim Bartley and Marc Schneiberg, "Rationality and Institutional Contingency: The Varying Politics of Economic Regulation in the Fire Insurance Industry," *Sociological Perspectives* 45, no. 1 (Spring 2002): 58. See also, Grant *Insurance Reform,* 100–107.

57. Sklar, *Corporate Reconstruction,* 433.

58. The company was initially organized as the American National Fire Insurance Company, but shortly after it was launched the name was changed to National American Fire Insurance.

59. Display advertisement, *Evening World Herald,* August 28, 1919, 13.

60. Foster joined the Aetna Company at the age of fifteen and stayed for twelve years, working the last six years as auditor. He had managed a local agency and then served as Nebraska state agent for the Sioux Fire Insurance Company before going to work for Columbia. Display advertisement, *Evening World-Herald,* August 28, 1919, 13. See "J.E. Foster Succeeds to Presidency," *OCCJ,* June 6, 1925, 9.

61. Display advertisement, *Evening World-Herald,* August 28, 1919, 13.

62. "Men Who Are Making Omaha: W.H. Ahmanson," *Omaha Bee,* May 22, 1924, clipping in biography file at Omaha Public Library; "W.H. Ahmanson Dead."

63. Hayden's testimony comes from Warren Buffett, who knew him in Omaha. Alice Schroeder, *The Snowball: Warren Buffett and the Business of Life* (New York: Bantam Books, 2008), 210, 860 n. 23.

64. A. M. Best Company, *Best's Insurance Reports: Fire and Marine, 1920–1921* (New York: Alfred M. Best Company, 1920), 261.

65. Ibid.

66. *OCCJ*, November 19, 1919, 3.

67. Meanwhile, as of the end of 1919, the company had nearly $628,450 invested in certificates of deposit, another $334,194 in stocks and bonds, and $150,483 in real estate mortgages. A. M. Best Company, *Best's Insurance Reports*, 261.

68. "Home Patronage for Fire Insurance," *OCCJ*, February 19, 1921, 14–15.

69. Freedgood et al., "Croesus at Home."

70. Rock, *Dundee, Neb.*, 12.

71. Ibid., 2.

72. Ibid., 41.

73. Ibid.

74. Howard P. Chudacoff, *Mobile Americans: Residential and Social Mobility in Omaha, 1880–1920* (New York: Oxford University Press, 1972), 122.

75. Freedgood et al., "Croesus at Home."

76. Howard Buffett, Warren Buffett's father, was also a student at the University of Nebraska in these years, a couple of years older than Howard Ahmanson. Warren Buffett guesses that the two men knew each other, but he does not know how well. Warren Buffett, interview by author, December 9, 2010.

77. Unattributed notes in file: Howard F. Ahmanson Sr., box: TAF History, TAFA.

78. Alfred D. Chandler Jr., *The Visible Hand: The Managerial Revolution in American Business* (Cambridge, MA: Harvard University Press, 1977).

79. Samuel Haber, *Efficiency and Uplift: Scientific Management in the Progressive Era, 1890–1920* (Chicago: University of Chicago Press, 1964); Robert H. Wiebe, *The Search for Order, 1877–1920* (New York: Hill and Wang, 1967); Robert Wiebe, *Businessmen and Reform: A Study of the Progressive Movement* (Chicago: Quadrangle Books, 1968).

80. "Secretary of Commerce," *OCCJ*, April 16, 1921, 8.

81. Ellis W. Hawley, "Herbert Hoover, the Commerce Secretariat, and the Vision of an 'Associative State,' 1921–1928," *Journal of American History* 61, no. 1 (1974): 116–40.

82. Quoted in William E. Leuchtenburg, *Herbert Hoover* (New York: Times Books, 2009), 64.

83. Wiebe, *Businessmen and Reform*, 222.

84. "Purely Personal," *Underwriters' Report*, February 17, 1944, n.p., clipping in FA.

85. John Taliaferro, *Charles M. Russell: The Life and Legend of America's Cowboy Artist* (Boston: Little, Brown, 1996). Russell had goiter surgery at the Mayo Clinic in 1926 and survived.

86. "Jaycees Right on Prediction," *Omaha World-Herald*, February 5, 1952, n.p. See also Aimee Ahmanson and Florence Hoffman, interview by Howard F. Ahmanson Jr., August 21, 1983.

87. "Chamber Gossip," *OCCJ*, December 20, 1924, 9.

88. Aimee Ahmanson and Florence Hoffman, interview by Howard F. Ahmanson Jr., August 21, 1983.

89. Freedgood et al., "Croesus at Home."

90. Freedgood, "Emperor Howard Ahmanson," 150.

91. Foster had been secretary and treasurer of the company since it was organized in 1919. See "J. E. Foster Succeeds."

92. Freedgood et al., "Croesus at Home."

93. Freedgood, "Emperor Howard Ahmanson."

94. In an article in *Forbes* in 1965, Ahmanson deadpanned that after the stockholders at National American gained control of the company following his father's death, "My inheritance shrank to a measly half a million dollars. That's why mine is a rags-to-riches story." He did not detail the specific assets he received. "Faces behind the Figures," *Forbes*, July 1, 1965, 26.

95. Freedgood, "Emperor Howard Ahmanson."

96. Freedgood et al., "Croesus at Home."

97. Alsop, "Multi-Millionaires," 39.

98. Freedgood, "Emperor Howard Ahmanson," 150–51.

2. AMONG THE LOTUS EATERS

1. Carey McWilliams, *Southern California: An Island on the Land* (1946; repr., Salt Lake City, UT: Peregrine Smith Books, 1985), 165.

2. Midwestern immigrants romanticized California's Hispanic past but isolated the large Hispanic and Asian minority groups, as well as the smaller communities of African Americans living in Los Angeles. By 1930, minority groups accounted for the following shares of the 1.2 million people living in Los Angeles: Asian American, 2.2 percent (27,838); Hispanic, 7.8 percent (97,116); African American, 3.1 percent (38,894). See table 5, "California—Race and Hispanic Origin for Selected Large Cities and Other Places: Earliest Census to 1990," www.census.gov/population/www/documentation/twps0076/CAtab.pdf; U.S. Bureau of the Census, *Fifteenth Census of the United States: 1930: Metropolitan Districts, Population and Area*, 9, www2.census.gov/prod2/decennial/documents/03450421_TOC.pdf (accessed March 8, 2011).

3. Carey McWilliams, "I'm a Stranger Here Myself," in *Southern California*, 178–80.

4. "Looking Again into the Future," advertisement, *LAT*, October 5, 1925, 7.

5. "—The Second Million," advertisement, *LAT*, October 5, 1925, A6.

6. "Automobiles as Indicators," *OCCJ*, March 19, 1921, 9.

7. "Omaha Leads World in Telephones," *OCCJ*, January 3, 1925, 13.

8. Omaha led all other cities in the nation except Des Moines, Grand Rapids, and Toledo. "Many Omahans Own Homes," *OCCJ*, November 12, 1921, 8. Nationally, the rate of home ownership was 45.6 percent in 1920. See "Historical Census

of Housing Tables: Homeownership," October 2011, www.census.gov/hhes/www /housing/census/historic/owner.html.

9. "Facts Every Omahan Should Know about Omaha," *OCCJ*, January 22, 1921, 6–7.

10. Robert M. Fogelson, *The Fragmented Metropolis: Los Angeles, 1850–1930* (Berkeley: University of California Press, 1993).

11. Industrial Department, Los Angeles Area Chamber of Commerce, *Special Report to Henry M. Robinson, Chairman of the Board, Security-First National Bank of Los Angeles, California,* 2 vols. (Los Angeles: Industrial Department, 1930), cited in Greg Hise, "Industry and Imaginative Geographies," in *Metropolis in the Making: Los Angeles in the 1920s,* ed. Tom Sitton and William Deverell (Berkeley: University of California Press, 2001), 19.

12. Fogelson, *Fragmented Metropolis.*

13. Clark Davis, "The View from Spring Street: White-Collar Men in the City of Angels," in Sitton and Deverell, *Metropolis in the Making,* 185.

14. Howard Ahmanson Jr., interview by author, May 27, 2009.

15. Kevin Starr, *Material Dreams: Southern California through the 1920s* (New York: Oxford University Press, 1990), 153.

16. "Many Enter for Course at College," *LAT,* October 28, 1925, 14.

17. "Thurston Ross; Property Appraiser and Economist," *LAT,* November 16, 1990.

18. Ross was invited to Washington in 1926 to meet with commerce secretary Herbert Hoover to help arrange the program for national management week. "Goes to Meet Hoover," *LAT,* October 1, 1926, A22.

19. Seymour Freedgood et al., "Croesus at Home," first draft typescript, March 17, 1958, in FA.

20. David S. Hannah, interview by Marc Nurre, [1994], in FA.

21. Frank Grannis was the vice president and general manager of the Southern California Music Company in 1927. "School Children to Receive Free Music Lessons," *LAT,* March 4, 1927, A4.

22. Freedgood et al., "Croesus at Home."

23. Howard F. Ahmanson to Dorothy Grannis, June 8, 1927, in FA.

24. Howard F. Ahmanson to Dorothy Grannis, July 30, 1927, in FA.

25. Ibid.

26. Freedgood et al., "Croesus at Home."

27. "Pending Changes in Insurance," *Pacific Underwriter and Banker,* January 25, 1926, n.p.

28. [Chris Bone], "Partial History/Chronology Howard Ahmanson," typescript from the files of Home Savings of America, [1988], copy provided by Robert DeKruif. Ahmanson was also appointed as general agent for National American Fire Insurance on August 23, 1926. See James E. Foster, "To Whom It May Concern," March 20, 1943, in file: H.F. Ahmanson–Navy, box 23AV, FA. For the company's founding date, see "Natl. American Shows Steady Growth," *Underwriter's Report,* August 8, 1929, 11.

29. "Permits Issued," *LAT,* June 3, 1928, C12. For the office location, see "Natl. American Shows Steady Growth."

30. National American Fire Insurance did not have deep connections in California. In 1925, the company reached an agreement with A.J. Baldwin to act as its agent but reported no business activity that year. "Pacific Coast Fire Business for 1925," *Pacific Underwriter and Banker,* January 25, 1926, 111. The following year, the trade journal reported that National American had premiums of $5,071 and a loss ratio of only 2.7 percent, but no agent was listed for the company. *Pacific Underwriter and Banker,* March 25, 1927, 87.

31. Robert DeKruif, interview by Margaret Bach, [1992], in TAFA.

32. Freedgood et al., "Croesus at Home."

33. "Application for Commission or Warrant, U.S. Naval Reserve," in file: H.F. Ahmanson–Navy, box 23AV, FA.

34. Freedgood et al., "Croesus at Home."

35. "Natl. American Shows Steady Growth."

36. "Agency Supt. Named," loose clipping, September 22, 1927, in FA.

37. Ahmanson's relationship to Garrigue must have been meaningful to him because after Garrigue's arrest he clipped a series of articles related to the case and saved them. See FA.

38. For his quote, see Margaret Bach, "The Ahmanson Foundation," June 1993, 11–12, in TAFA.

39. Howard Ahmanson told different versions of this story to a number of reporters over the years, and it was referenced in an oral history with Aimee Ahmanson as well. I conclude that the man was Morgan Adams. In press accounts of these stories, Howard does not mention Morgan Adams by name. In an oral history, Howard Ahmanson Jr. asked Aimee Ahmanson if the individual in the story was Morgan Adams and she seemed to affirm that it was. The transcript is somewhat ambiguous on this point. In a different interview, David Hannah, who worked for Ahmanson starting in the early 1940s, says that Ahmanson and Adams were partners. He is the source for the partnership part of this story. David S. Hannah, interview by Mark Nurre, [1994]; see also Aimee Ahmanson and Florence Hoffman, interview by Howard F. Ahmanson Jr., August 21, 1993; Robert Ahmanson, interview by unknown interviewer, October 11, 1993; all in the FA.

40. Stewart Alsop, "Multi-Millionaires: How America's New Rich Made Their Vast Fortunes," *Saturday Evening Post,* July 17, 1965, 39. A different version of this story is offered by David Hannah. Hannah says that Ahmanson and Adams agreed to become partners. Adams convinced Metropolitan Life to provide underwriting for the policies, but when it became clear that the business was highly profitable he tried to buy Ahmanson out. Ahmanson bought Adams out instead, turning to the bank that was next door to Mortgage Guarantee to borrow the funds. David S. Hannah, interview by Mark Nurre, [1994], in FA.

41. Seymour Freedgood, "Emperor Howard Ahmanson of S&L," *Fortune,* May 1958, 150.

42. Ibid., 151.

43. Alsop, "Multi-Millionaires," 39.

44. Freedgood, "Emperor Howard Ahmanson," 150.

45. David S. Hannah, interview by Mark Nurre, [1994], in FA.

46. Robert DeKruif, interview by Margaret Bach, [1992], in TAFA.

47. This story was told to Warren Buffett by Hayden Ahmanson. See Warren Buffett, interview by author, December 9, 2010.

48. Richard Deihl, interview by author, September 25, 2009.

49. Howard Ahmanson Jr., interview by author, December 15, 2010.

50. Aimee Ahmanson, interview by unknown interviewer, August 20, 1993, in FA.

51. Alan Teck, *Mutual Savings Banks and Savings and Loan Associations: Aspects of Growth* (New York: Columbia University Press, 1968).

52. John Lintner, *Mutual Savings Banks in the Savings and Mortgage Markets* (Boston: Division of Research, Graduate School of Business, Harvard University, 1948).

53. During this period, savings banks expanded into the mortgage market as well (restrictions were lifted in the 1830s in New York). Between 1875 and 1890, mortgages as a percentage of total assets at savings banks rose from 20 to 40 percent. Teck, *Mutual Savings Banks,* 45.

54. Kenneth A. Snowden, "The Evolution of Interregional Mortgage Lending Channels, 1870–1940: The Life Insurance—Mortgage Company Connection," in *Coordination and Information: Historical Perspectives on the Organization of Enterprise,* ed. Naomi Lamoreaux and Daniel M. G. Raff (Chicago: University of Chicago Press, 1995), 216–18.

55. Ibid., 220. Noninstitutional lenders—families, estates, trust funds, individuals and business firms—continued to extend more than half of all mortgage loans made at the turn of the century. Leo Grebler, David M. Blank, and Louis Winnick, *Capital Formation in Residential Real Estate: Trends and Prospects* (Princeton: Princeton University Press, 1956), ch. 13.

56. Robert H. Wiebe, *The Search for Order, 1877–1920* (New York: Hill and Wang, 1967), 67–68; Jerry Voorhis, *American Cooperatives* (New York: Harper and Row, 1961).

57. For a valuable analysis of the importance of personal connections and information networks in nineteenth-century banking, see Naomi R. Lamoreaux and National Bureau of Economic Research, *Insider Lending: Banks, Personal Connections, and Economic Development in Industrial New England,* NBER Series on Long-Term Factors in Economic Development (New York: Cambridge University Press, 1994).

58. David L. Mason, *From Buildings and Loans to Bail-Outs: A History of the American Savings and Loan Industry, 1831–1995* (Cambridge: Cambridge University Press, 2004), 32–39.

59. All quotes from Dexter's speech come from Seymour Dexter, "President's Address," in U.S. League of Local Building and Loan Associations, *Proceedings of the First Annual Meeting* (Chicago: Financial Review and American Building Association News, 1893), 38–43.

60. The linkage between the home and the Republican ideal has deep roots in American history. Looking at the home as a symbol in the United States, Jan Cohn points out that smaller homes—log cabins and cottages—have been symbols of both individual independence and successful egalitarian communities. Jan Cohn, *The Palace or the Poorhouse: The American House as a Cultural Symbol* (East Lansing: Michigan State University Press, 1979).

61. Jackson Lears, *Fables of Abundance: A Cultural History of Advertising in America* (New York: Basic Books, 1994); Roland Marchand, *Advertising the American Dream: Making Way for Modernity, 1920–1940* (Berkeley: University of California Press, 1985); Susan Strasser, *Satisfaction Guaranteed: The Making of the American Mass Market* (New York: Pantheon Books, 1989); Richard Tedlow, *New and Improved: The Story of Mass Marketing in America* (New York: Basic Books, 1990).

62. Lendol Calder, *Financing the American Dream: A Cultural History of Consumer Credit* (Princeton: Princeton University Press, 1999), 20.

63. K. V. Haymaker, in U.S. League of Local Building and Loan Associations, *Proceedings of the Twenty-Fourth Annual Meeting* (Chicago: American Building Association News, 1916), 144. Haymaker would later play a leading role in the "Own Your Own Home" campaign launched in 1918. Karen Dunn-Haley, "The House That Uncle Sam Built: The Political Culture of Federal Housing Policy, 1919–1932" (PhD diss., Stanford University, 1996).

64. Oliver E. Connor, "Home-Owning Halted," *American Building Association News,* July 1923, 310.

65. "'Homes First,' Should Be the Goal," *American Building Association News,* December 1923, 552.

66. In a number of places throughout this book I refer to economies of scale and scope in the mortgage business. For many years, scholars generally believed that beyond a certain minimum size banking yielded very few economies of scale. This was especially true in a predigital era before computerization allowed for the aggregation of transaction-processing systems on a single platform. These earlier studies, however, rarely accounted for the ways in which scale could affect levels of risk—a key cost for anyone in financial services. More recent studies suggest that larger banking organizations achieve significant economies of scale by reducing the cost of risk taking (better credit information systems) and risk management (greater diversification). For an overview of studies related to scale economies in banking, see Loretta J. Master, "Scale Economies in Banking and Financial Regulatory Reform," *The Region* (Federal Reserve Bank of Minneapolis), September 2010, 10–15.

67. L. L. Rankin, "Building and Loan Growth: Its Benefits, How Obtained," in U.S. League of Local Building and Loan Associations, *Proceedings of the Thirteenth Annual Meeting* (Chicago: American Building Association News, 1905), 66.

68. Ibid., 68.

69. Other cooperatives also made this turn from local mutualism to aggressive market competition at the turn of the twentieth century. Agricultural producer

cooperatives like Sunkist adopted "hardheaded" marketing strategies. As Robert Wiebe has described it, "Where the earlier cooperatives had dreamed of surmounting the profit system or returning business from evil men to the people, these [new cooperatives] sought a lucrative place, often a monopoly, within the existing system." Wiebe, *Search for Order, 1877–1920,* 127.

70. These contracts represented only one-third of the total value of all residential mortgages in the United States, underscoring the fact that building and loans were still focused on working- and middle-class families. Morton Bodfish, "The Depression Experience of Savings and Loan Associations in the United States," address given to the Fifth International Congress of Savings, Building and Loan Associations, Building Societies and Similar Thrift and Home Financing Institutions, Salzburg, Austria, September 1935, 1.

71. "Home Building Looms Strong," *LAT,* February 17, 1929, E2.

72. State Mutual Building and Loan granted 1,013 mortgages to home owners in the first six months of 1928. "Record Volume Announced in Month's Loans," *LAT,* July 8, 1928, E4.

73. Independent insurance agents included building and loans in their ban, but their primary concern was the Bank of Italy. To quell growing criticism, the bank pledged in 1927 that it would not offer insurance in markets where there were established agents (leaving open the question of serving rural communities). The industry's trade journal welcomed this gesture, but some wanted the legislature to license only individuals who made placing insurance their sole business. *Pacific Underwriter and Banker,* November 25, 1927, 341, 344. The industry's trade journal asserted that such a rigid approach would affect a wide range of industries including, for example, railroad ticket agents who sold travelers' insurance. *Pacific Underwriter and Banker,* January 25, 1928, n.p. In the fall of 1928, the California attorney general ruled that it was legal for lenders to also sell insurance as long as they did not "coerce" their customers. *Pacific Underwriter and Banker,* May 10, 1928, 136.

74. Robert DeKruif, interview by author, May 1, 2009.

75. David S. Hannah, interview by Marc Nurre, [1994], in FA. In a study of management incentives in the mutual savings and loan industry, Alfred Nicols looked at the use of management-owned affiliated businesses, like insurance agencies, as a way for savings and loan executives to increase the rewards from the success of building their organizations. Nicols noted that these businesses were highly profitable because the insurance agency (owned by the savings and loan manager) incurred almost no solicitation costs and there were opportunities to cross-sell insurance for auto, life, etc. Moreover, the due diligence required to qualify the borrower and the property had already been done by the savings and loan in the context of making the loan. Alfred Nicols, *Management and Control in the Mutual Savings and Loan Association* (Toronto: Lexington Books, 1972), 27–28.

76. "Ex-Omahan Is a Giant in the Loan Industry," *Omaha World-Herald,* June 6, 1965, n.p. See also Alsop, "Multi-Millionaires," 42.

77. Alsop, "Multi-Millionaires," 39.

78. Freedgood, "Emperor Howard Ahmanson," 150.

79. "Howard Ahmanson—Biographical Information," in file: Howard F. Ahmanson, box: TAF History, TAFA.

80. The foray into the petroleum industry may not have been very successful. In 1944, when a friend offered him a similar opportunity to get into the mining business, Howard quickly said no. "I've always been afraid that I would get greedy and try to make money in somebody else's racket," he wrote. "I have a deep-seated and childish mental picture in my mind of how awfully silly a miner would be if he opened offices across from mine and started running fire insurance companies.... I think I might look the same way going into the mining business." Howard F. Ahmanson to Gosta Guston, January 10, 1944, in accordion file, box 23AV, FA.

81. "Application for Commission."

82. "June Bride Will Motor Home," *LAT,* July 14, 1933, A6.

83. Freedgood et al., "Croesus at Home."

3. UNDERTAKER AT A PLAGUE

1. James L. Davis, "Survey Shows Realty Status," *LAT,* July 5, 1931, D11.

2. "Home Seizure Relief Urged," *LAT,* July 20, 1931, A8.

3. "The Special Session," *LAT,* July 13, 1932, A4.

4. "New Loan Plan Details Told," *LAT,* April 6, 1932, A1.

5. "Ex-Omahan Is a Giant in the Loan Industry," *Omaha World-Herald,* June 6, 1965, n.p.

6. Susan Hoffmann and Mark K. Cassell, *Mission Expansion in the Federal Home Loan Bank System* (Albany: State University of New York Press, 2010), 30.

7. Kyle D. Palmer, "Millions Hear Hoover Accept His Nomination," *LAT,* August 12, 1928, 1.

8. Quoted in William Greider, *Secrets of the Temple: How the Federal Reserve Runs the Country* (New York: Touchstone Books, 1987), 300–302. Economic historians still debate the cause or causes of the Great Depression. For one overview, see Ben Bernanke, *Essays on the Great Depression* (Princeton: Princeton University Press, 2000).

9. William E. Leuchtenburg, *Herbert Hoover* (New York: Times Books, 2009), 105–7.

10. Ibid., 129.

11. Ibid., 130.

12. Leon T. Kendall, *The Savings and Loan Business: Its Purpose, Functions, and Economic Justification* (Englewood Cliffs, NJ: Prentice-Hall, 1962), 7.

13. William Bartlett, *The Valuation of Mortgage-Backed Securities* (New York: McGraw-Hill, 1993), 480.

14. Many building and loans relied on commercial banks for lines of credit collateralized with home loans. As banks struggled, they called in these loans, putting additional pressure on building and loan liquidity and working capital. Viewers of

It's a Wonderful Life will remember George Bailey's efforts to get the banker Mr. Potter to extend credit to the building and loan. Hoffmann and Cassell, *Mission Expansion,* 31.

15. Between 1930 and 1935, real estate as a percentage of the total assets of savings and loans in the United States rose from 2.8 percent to 20.2 percent. Josephine Hedges Ewalt, *A Business Reborn: The Savings and Loan Story, 1930–1960* (Chicago: American Savings and Loan Institute Press, 1962), 21, table 1.

16. Herbert Hoover, "Address to the White House Conference on Home Building and Home Ownership," December 2, 1931, www.presidency.ucsb.edu/ws/index.php?pid=22927#axzz1G9hjfrZE.

17. Quoted in Greider, *Secrets of the Temple,* 299.

18. R. Dan Brumbaugh, *Thrifts under Siege: Restoring Order to American Banking* (Cambridge, MA: Ballinger, 1988), 25.

19. Hoffmann and Cassell, *Mission Expansion,* 29.

20. Ibid., 34.

21. Ibid., 35.

22. Political scientists Susan Hoffman and Mark K. Cassell raise two possible theoretical explanations for passage of the act. First, public choice theory suggests that public policy reflects the triumph of particular interests—in this case, the building and loans. But Hoffmann and Cassell argue for a second, more nuanced, behavioral perspective. In this theoretical framework, solutions to public policy problems emerge from the interaction of facts and values and the availability of alternative policy models. In this case, the building and loans had pioneered the long-term, self-amortizing mortgage and Europeans had successfully used the bond markets to provide mortgage capital. The availability of these models, combined with genuine public concern for the problem of mortgage finance, provided the support necessary to pass the act. Ibid.

23. David L. Mason, *From Buildings and Loans to Bail-Outs: A History of the American Savings and Loan Industry, 1831–1995* (Cambridge: Cambridge University Press, 2004), 78–86. For Hoover's comment on the passing of the credit crisis, see "The Home Loan Bank," *LAT,* August 30, 1932, A4.

24. Scholars have debated the extent to which Hoover had already moved away from cooperation to regulation and whether Roosevelt took credit for the implementation of Hoover's initiatives. R. Gordon Hoxie, for example, argues that with his decision to promote the government-controlled Reconstruction Finance Corporation over a National Credit Corporation organized voluntarily by banks, Hoover "rejected volunteerism" as a way to reform the banking system. His support for the Glass-Steagall Act of 1932 and the creation of the Federal Home Loan Bank provide further evidence of his new thinking. R. Gordon Hoxie, "Hoover and the Banking Crisis," *Presidential Studies Quarterly* 4, nos. 3/4–5, no. 1 (Summer/Fall 1974–Winter 1975): 25–28.

25. Herbert Hoover, speech in Des Moines, October 4, 1932, reprinted in "Hoover Tells Inside Story of Battle Which Prevented Economic Disaster in America," *LAT,* October 5, 1932, 6.

26. Franklin Roosevelt, quoted in Constance Perin, *Everything in Its Place: Social Order and Land Use in America* (Princeton: Princeton University Press, 1977), 72.

27. Franklin D. Roosevelt, "Campaign Address on the Eight Great Credit Groups of the Nation," St. Louis, MO, October 21, 1932, www.presidency.ucsb.edu /ws/index.php?pid=88401#axzz1kmBiWOsl.

28. "Bank Use Urged by Realty Head," *LAT,* February 10, 1933, A8.

29. Hoxie, "Hoover and the Banking Crisis."

30. Richard H. K. Vietor, *Contrived Competition: Regulation and Deregulation in America* (Cambridge, MA: Harvard University Press, 1994), 239.

31. Vincent Carosso, "Washington and Wall Street: The New Deal and Investment Bankers, 1933–1940," *Business History Review* 44, no. 4 (1970): 425.

32. "Farmers' Army at State House," *LAT,* February 17, 1933, 7.

33. For "suffocated with foreclosed property," see Harry Carr, "The Lancer," *LAT,* January 21, 1933, A1. See also Mason, *From Buildings and Loans,* 89.

34. Franklin Delano Roosevelt, First Inaugural Address, in "Text of New President's Address at Inauguration," *LAT,* March 5, 1933, 5.

35. Kendall, *Savings and Loan Business,* 7.

36. Thrifts lobbied hard for FSLIC, in part because earlier legislation had provided deposit insurance to banks through the newly created Federal Deposit Insurance Corporation (FDIC). Savings and loans felt they also needed deposit insurance or banks would have a competitive advantage. Ewalt, *Business Reborn,* 95.

37. FNMA has been characterized as a more permanent successor to the Home Owners Loan Corporation, which also provided a secondary market for loans. Authors Richard K. Green and Susan M. Wachter also assert that "the invention of the fixed-rate, self-amortizing, long-term mortgage was, above all else, a response to a general financial crisis, as opposed to a design for the promotion of homeownership per se." I argue that the crisis provided the moment for crystallizing the basic mortgage and a policy framework suggested by various reform movements that championed homeownership, including the building and loans. Richard K. Green and Susan M. Wachter, "The American Mortgage in Historical and International Context," *Journal of Economic Perspectives* 19, no. 4 (2005): 95.

38. With the enthusiasm for deregulation in full swing in the early 1990s, historian Richard Vietor concluded that "noncompetitive and inefficient markets were the result" of these new laws. Vietor, *Contrived Competition,* 246–47.

39. Louis Galambos and Joseph Pratt, *The Rise of the Corporate Commonwealth: United States Business and Public Policy in the 20th Century* (New York: Basic Books, 1988), 126.

40. Dennis McDougal, *Privileged Son: Otis Chandler and the Rise and Fall of the L.A. Times Dynasty* (Cambridge, MA: Perseus, 2001), 115.

41. Howard F. Ahmanson, "Buyer Beware," speech presented to the Economic Round Table of Los Angeles, 1933, in FA.

42. For background on why the savings and loan executives supported these arrangements, see Robert DeKruif, interview by author, May 1, 2009. For efforts to

kill reform efforts in the legislature, see Howard Edgerton, "Memorandum to the Two Prides of the Navy," December 1, 1944, in box: World War II Era, FA.

43. Robert DeKruif, interview by author, May 1, 2009.

44. David S. Hannah, interview by Marc Nurre, [1994], in FA.

45. "Aunt Lottie" to Aimee Ahmanson, September 16, 1940, in Robert Ahmanson Files, TAFA.

46. Robert DeKruif, interview by author, May 1, 2009.

47. Juana Neal Levy, "Ahmansons Give Gay Grid Party," *LAT,* December 7, 1937, A5.

48. See "Application for Commission or Warrant, U.S. Naval Reserve," file: H. F. Ahmanson–Navy, box 23AV, FA; and "They Leave for Europe Today," *LAT,* July 3, 1938, D4.

49. "Mr. and Mrs. H. F. Ahmanson," *Japan News-Week.* June 1, 1940, 7, clipping in file: DGA—Japan—1940, in DGA 002, FA.

50. See Howard F. Ahmanson and Dorothy Grannis Ahmanson to Robert Ahmanson, December 21, 1943, in box 23AV, FA.

51. "Suspects Put Up Mail Fraud Bonds," *LAT,* June 20, 1941, A11.

52. "J. Howard Edgerton," n.d. (ca. 1956), unattributed memorandum, in folder: Edgerton, J. Howard, box 18, Correspondence of Chairman Joseph P. McMurray, Records of the Federal Home Loan Bank, RG 195, NARA-CP.

53. "Mail Fraud Trial of Seven Starts," *LAT,* February 19, 1942, 11.

54. "Jury Convicts Two Attorneys," *LAT,* April 6, 1942, A8.

55. "Convicted Lawyer Gets Prison Term," *LAT,* April 28, 1942, A3.

56. "Twombly Allowed Prison Probation," *LAT,* May 19, 1942, A2.

57. "Local Loans of Prudential Told," *LAT,* June 11, 1932, 9.

58. "New Insurance Chief Named," *LAT,* June 21, 1939, 6.

59. "Insurance Merger Hit," *LAT,* January 12, 1943, A2.

60. Howard F. Ahmanson to H. B. Thomas, January 7, 1944, in accordion file, box 23AV, FA.

61. "Post Will Go to Attorney," *LAT,* September 4, 1943, A1.

62. H. B. Thomas to Howard F. Ahmanson, October 26, 1943, in accordion file, box 23AV, FA.

63. One letter refers to "Joe's actions." This may have been Joe Hoeft. Hoeft worked for Glendale Federal Savings and Loan, was chairman of the Glendale Selective Service Board in 1943, and was also a friend and customer of H. F. Ahmanson & Co. "Glendale Draft Official Quits over Father Call," *LAT,* November 2, 1943, A3.

64. Howard F. Ahmanson to H. B. Thomas, January 7, 1944.

65. J. Howard Edgerton to Mr. and Mrs. Charles K. Fletcher and Mr. and Mrs. Howard Ahmanson, November 26, 1943, in accordion file, box 23AV: World War II Era, FA.

66. Ibid.

67. See "Application for Commission."

68. For Ahmanson's acquisition of the Mayan Theater, see interview with [Robert] Bob Ahmanson, October 11, 1993, in LH files, FA. For an overview of the shows appearing at the Mayan in 1942–43, see *LAT*.

69. Howard F. Ahmanson to Al Butler, February 7, 1944, in accordion file, box 23AV, FA. See also David S. Hannah, interview by Marc Nurre, [1994], in FA.

4. THE COMMON EXPERIENCE

1. For an analysis of how the war transformed American attitudes toward government through a host of experiences, including military service, see James T. Sparrow, *Warfare State: World War II Americans and the Age of Big Government* (New York: Oxford University Press, 2011).

2. Lucy Quirk, in *LAT*, August 24, 1943.

3. "Savings, Loan League Elects," *LAT*, June 7, 1942, A3. See also "Loan League Boosts War Bond Sales," *LAT*, August 16, 1942, A14.

4. Quonset Air Museum, "History," n.d., www.quonsetairmuseum.com/history.html. For information on Nixon's experience at OCS Quonset, see Jonathan Aitken, *Nixon: A Life* (London: Weidenfeld and Nicolson, 1993), 98–99.

5. Howard F. Ahmanson to Dorothy G. Ahmanson, September 24, 1943, in FA.

6. Howard F. Ahmanson to Dorothy G. Ahmanson, n.d., in FA.

7. For example, see Gould Eddy to Howard F. Ahmanson, November 15, 1943, in accordion file, box 23AV: World War II Era, FA.

8. Howard F. Ahmanson to Dorothy G. Ahmanson, n.d., in HFA letters from Quonset, 1943, box 23AV: World War II Era, FA.

9. "R. F. Gross, Ex-Financier, Dies at 78," *LAT*, January 26, 1963, 5.

10. Howard F. Ahmanson to H. B. Thomas, January 7, 1944, in accordion file, box 23AV: World War II Era, FA.

11. Howard F. Ahmanson to N. V. Alison, December 8, 1943, in accordion file, box 23AV: World War II Era, FA.

12. Howard F. Ahmanson to G. L. Eddy, January 6, 1944, in accordion file, box 23AV: World War II Era, FA.

13. Howard F. Ahmanson to R. F. Gross, January 3, 1944, and R. F. Gross to Howard F. Ahmanson, January 24, 1944, both in accordion file, box 23AV: World War II Era, FA.

14. Howard F. Ahmanson to R. F. Gross, January 3, 1944.

15. Howard F. Ahmanson to National American Fire Insurance Co., December 21, 1943, in accordion file, box 23AV: World War II Era, FA.

16. Howard F. Ahmanson to Joe Crail, February 4, 1944, in accordion file, box 23AV: World War II Era, FA.

17. Kim Fletcher, interview by author, December 8, 2009.

18. Mark J. Denger, Norman S. Marshall, and John R. Justice, "Lieutenant Commander Morgan Adams," n.d., www.militarymuseum.org/Adams.html (accessed October 8, 2009).

19. Howard F. Ahmanson to Dorothy Grannis Ahmanson, postcard, June 1[3], 1944; see also Howard F. Ahmanson to Dorothy Grannis Ahmanson, [received June 18, 1944], both in FA.

20. Howard F. Ahmanson to Dorothy Grannis Ahmanson, [received June 3, 1944], in FA.

21. Melinda Hurst, interview by author, December 12, 2009.

22. State of Nebraska, Department of Insurance, "Report of Examination of the National American Fire Insurance Company as of June 30, 1943," October 1, 1943, 4, Nebraska State Archives.

23. Total net assets increased from $1.884 million to $1.967 million. Ibid., 39.

24. Ibid., 5.

25. Ibid.

26. Howard F. Ahmanson to Dorothy Grannis Ahmanson, February 4, 1943, in FA.

27. Iowa's loss ratio averaged 40 percent. State of Nebraska, Department of Insurance, "Report of Examination of the National American Fire Insurance Company as of June 30, 1943," 6.

28. Ibid., 7.

29. The state suspended its examination of the company in the fall of 1941 but resumed two years later. When it submitted its report, the total accounting adjustments and analysis of net income for the fiscal year ended June 30, 1943, led to a drop in capital of $50,470. Ibid., 18, 36.

30. Ibid., 17–18.

31. Ted Crane to Howard F. Ahmanson, n.d. [1943], in accordion file, box 23AV: World War II Era, FA.

32. Howard F. Ahmanson to Dorothy Grannis Ahmanson, February 4, 1943.

33. Howard F. Ahmanson to Dorothy Grannis Ahmanson, February 14, 1943, in FA.

34. On Stryker's role, see Ted Crane to Howard F. Ahmanson, n.d. [1943].

35. Howard F. Ahmanson to G. L. Eddy, January 6, 1944, in accordion file, box 23AV: World War II era, FA.

36. Ted Crane to Howard F. Ahmanson, n.d. [1943].

37. Ibid.

38. Seymour Freedgood et al., "Croesus at Home," first draft typescript, March 17, 1958, in FA.

39. Stewart Alsop, "Multi-Millionaires: How America's New Rich Made Their Vast Fortunes," *Saturday Evening Post*, July 17, 1965, 39.

40. Howard F. Ahmanson to G. L. Eddy, January 6, 1944. One source put National American's total value at about $1.6 million. See Freedgood et al., "Croesus at Home."

41. Hayden W. Ahmanson to Howard F. Ahmanson, January 14, 1944, in accordion file, box 23AV: World War II Era, FA.

42. Howard F. Ahmanson to B. K. Richardson, February 3, 1944, in accordion file, box 23AV: World War II Era, FA.

43. Ibid.

44. Howard F. Ahmanson to Hayden W. Ahmanson, February 15, 1944, in accordion file, box 23AV: World War II Era, FA.

45. Hayden W. Ahmanson to Howard F. Ahmanson, handwritten note, n.d., in accordion file, box 23AV: World War II Era, FA.

46. Howard F. Ahmanson to G. L. Eddy, January 6, 1944.

47. Howard F. Ahmanson to Dorothy Grannis Ahmanson, [received September 9, 1944], in FA.

48. Howard F. Ahmanson to Dorothy Grannis Ahmanson, [received August 23, 1944], in FA.

49. Howard F. Ahmanson to Dorothy Grannis Ahmanson, [received July 27, 1944], in FA.

50. Howard F. Ahmanson to Dorothy Grannis Ahmanson, [received August 3, 1944], in FA.

51. Ibid.

52. Howard F. Ahmanson to Dorothy Grannis Ahmanson, [received August 19, 1944], in FA.

53. Howard F. Ahmanson to Dorothy Grannis Ahmanson, [received August 14, 1944], in FA.

54. "J. Howard Edgerton," n.d. [ca. 1956], unattributed memorandum, in folder: Edgerton, J. Howard, box 18, Correspondence of Chairman Joseph P. Mc-Murray, Records of the Federal Home Loan Bank, RG 195, NARA-CP.

55. Howard Edgerton to Lieutenant Charles K. Fletcher and Lieutenant Howard Ahmanson, October 31, 1944, in box: World War II Era, FA.

56. Ibid.

57. Quoted in J. Howard Edgerton, *The Story of California Federal Savings* (New York: Newcomen Society, 1969), 13.

58. Howard Edgerton, "Memorandum to the Two Prides of the Navy," December 1, 1944, in box: World War II Era, FA.

59. Howard F. Ahmanson to Dorothy Grannis Ahmanson, [received September 1, 1944], in FA.

60. Howard F. Ahmanson to George Davis, February 10, 1944, in accordion file, box 23AV: World War II Era, FA.

61. H.F. Ahmanson to H.W. Ahmanson, Western Union, January 8, 1944, in accordion file, box 23AV: World War II Era, FA.

62. Sparrow, *Warfare State*, 7.

5. BUILDING HOME

Portions of this chapter appeared in Eric John Abrahamson, "One after Another: Building Homes and Making Loans," in *Carefree California: Cliff May and the Romance of the Ranch House,* ed. Jocelyn Gibbs and Nicholas Olsberg (Santa Barbara:

Art, Design and Architecture Museum, University of California, Santa Barbara; New York: Rizzoli, 2012). I am grateful to the Regents of the University of California for permission to use this material.

1. Hernando Courtright to H.F. Ahmanson, December 15, 1944, in FA. See also photo and caption, clipping, n.d., "Social" folder; Lucille Leimert, "Confidentially," *LAT,* January 18, 1945, both in box 23AV, FA; and Jessie Jean Marsh, "Fetes Given by West Side and Bay Sets," *LAT,* February 4, 1945, C2.

2. "The Beverly Hills Hotel: History," n.d., www.beverlyhillshotel.com/history #30 (accessed November 1, 2010).

3. "Leniency on Midnight Curfew Here Indicated," *LAT,* February 23, 1945, 1.

4. "Eviction of 10 Families Halted," *LAT,* March 6, 1945, A1.

5. "Mayor Asks F.D.R. Action on Housing," *LAT,* March 6, 1945, A1.

6. Roger W. Lotchin, *Fortress California, 1910–1961: From Warfare to Welfare* (New York: Oxford University Press, 1992), 131–69. See also Gerald D. Nash, *The American West Transformed: The Impact of the Second World War* (Bloomington: Indiana University Press, 1985), 62–63.

7. John Lawrence, "The Master Builders of Savings & Loan," *Los Angeles West Magazine,* June 15, 1969, 8–11.

8. Quoted in J. Howard Edgerton, *The Story of California Federal Savings* (New York: Newcomen Society, 1969), 13.

9. Edgerton, *Story of California Federal Savings,* 13.

10. Richard Deihl, interview by author, September 25, 2009, 19.

11. Nash, *American West Transformed,* 62–63.

12. Ahmanson was an extremely successful "place entrepreneur," a category described by Harvey Molotch as including "land speculators, bankers, newspaper publishers, politicians, and public utilities who all had a stake in the economic growth of [a region.]" Harvey Molotch, "The City as a Growth Machine: Toward a Political Economy of Place," *American Journal of Sociology* 82, no. 2 (1976): 309–32. For the application of Molotch's concept to the Los Angeles area, see William Fulton, *The Reluctant Metropolis: The Politics of Urban Growth in Los Angeles* (Baltimore: Johns Hopkins University Press, 2001), 7.

13. The population would increase another 16 percent in the years between 1946 and 1951, with two-thirds of this growth coming from continued immigration. James Gillies and Clayton Curtis, *Institutional Residential Mortgage Lending in Los Angeles County, 1946–1951* (Los Angeles: Real Estate Research Program, Bureau of Business and Economic Research, University of California, Los Angeles, 1956), 8.

14. Robert M. Williams, "The Southern California Economy in Perspective," in *Planning for the Economic Growth of Southern California,* ed. Ernest A. Engelbert (Berkeley: University Extension/University of California, 1955), 7–8.

15. Adjusted for inflation, incomes doubled rather than tripled. Gillies and Curtis, *Institutional Residential Mortgage Lending,* 8–9.

16. Median family income in Los Angeles was $3,669 (equivalent to $31,167 in 2011). The national median was $3,073. Ibid.

17. Nationally, income payments rose 75 percent between 1940 and 1945. Donald S. Thompson, "What Is the Position of the Mortgage Lender Today?" *CSLJ*, May 1947, 9.

18. California State Chamber of Commerce, *Economic Survey of California* (San Francisco: California State Printing Office, 1950), 23, cited in Gillies and Curtis, *Institutional Residential Mortgage Lending*, 8.

19. "Stork Flaps Oftener Than in World War I," *LAT*, February 4, 1945, 4.

20. "Births Gain Steadily; Death Rate Decreases," *LAT*, October 10, 1951, 19.

21. "More of Almost Everything in L.A., Census Discloses," *LAT*, June 8, 1951, A1.

22. "Postwar Housing Boom Predicted," *LAT*, February 15, 1945, 4.

23. At the end of his book on mass production in America, David Hounshell notes that Lewis Mumford recognized in 1934 that war was the ultimate consumer for systems of mass production because "quantity production must rely for its success upon quantity consumption; and nothing ensures replacement like organized destruction." The war, according to Hounshell, ended an era of debate over the ethos of mass production in America but served to solidify its presence in American society. David A. Hounshell, *From the American System to Mass Production, 1800–1932* (Baltimore: Johns Hopkins University Press, 1984), 330.

24. Lizabeth Cohen, *A Consumers' Republic: The Politics of Mass Consumption in Postwar America* (New York: Vintage Books, 2003), 306.

25. Michael Kazin, *Barons of Labor: The San Francisco Building Trades and Union Power in the Progressive Era* (Urbana: University of Illinois Press, 1987).

26. Ibid.

27. Lester Walker, *American Shelter* (Woodstock, NY: Overlook Press, 1981), 242.

28. Sweat equity played a crucial role in the rise of homeownership in working-class suburbs prior to World War II. See Becky M. Nicolaides, *My Blue Heaven: Life and Politics in the Working-Class Suburbs of Los Angeles, 1920–1965* (Chicago: University of Chicago Press, 2002). For the number of homes constructed per year by the average builder, see James Thomas Keane, *Fritz B. Burns and the Development of Los Angeles* (Los Angeles: Loyola Marymount University and the Historical Society of Southern California, 2001), 93.

29. Hounshell, *From the American System*, 314. On stressed-skin plywood, see David L. Lutin, "The Factors Impeding the Mass Production of Prefabricated Homes" (MBA thesis, Syracuse University, 1949), 3. Copy in box 7, Collection 1582, Department of Special Collections, UCLA.

30. Joseph E. Stevens, *Hoover Dam: An American Adventure* (Norman: University of Oklahoma Press, 1988); Donald E. Wolf, *Big Dams and Other Dreams: The Six Companies Story* (Norman: University of Oklahoma Press, 1996).

31. Greg Hise, *Magnetic Los Angeles: Planning the Twentieth Century Metropolis* (Baltimore: Johns Hopkins University Press, 1997), 86–116.

32. The Lanham Act of 1940.

33. Keane, *Fritz B. Burns*, 79.

34. Apparently, the idea of the NAHB had been formulated in 1940 by leadership in the National Association of Real Estate Boards (Herbert Nelson) and leading builders. See Herbert U. Nelson to Fritz B. Burns, February 17, 1943, in box 04–005, F-2, NAHB Archives. For background on the impact of Title VI, see Nicolaides, *My Blue Heaven*, 191; and Keane, *Fritz B. Burns*, 93–94.

35. Nicolaides, *My Blue Heaven*, 191.

36. Lutin, "Factors Impeding the Mass Production," 1.

37. "Vast Kaiser Home Building Plans for Coast Disclosed," *LAT*, May 10, 1945, A1.

38. Across the country, the early exclusive ranks of this new group included W. J. Levitt of Long Island, David Bohannon in the Bay Area, and John E. Byrne in Baltimore. In Los Angeles, they included men like Milton J. Brock, Spiros G. Ponty, and Walter Bollenbacher. Milton J. Brock, "Private Builder Is Solving the Housing Shortage," *CSLJ*, April 1948, 9.

39. "Housing: Puny Giant," *WSJ*, October 21, 1947, 1.

40. Ibid.

41. Ibid.

42. Ibid.

43. Keane, *Fritz B. Burns*, 121.

44. Ibid., 131.

45. Ibid., 132.

46. Martin J. Schiesl, "The Politics of Contracting: Los Angeles and the Lakewood Plan, 1954–1962," *Huntington Library Quarterly* 45, no. 3 (1982): 227.

47. Robert Fishman, "Review," *Journal of the Society of Architectural Historians* 64, no. 4 (2005): 563.

48. County of Los Angeles Public Library, "Lakewood Community History," n.d., www.colapublib.org/history/lakewood/ (accessed March 17, 2011).

49. U.S. Bureau of the Census, *Seventeenth Census of the United States, 1950: Population and Housing, 1950*, vol. 1, *General Characteristics, Part 2* (Washington, DC: Government Printing Office, 1952), 5–92, building permit data, cited in Gillies and Curtis, *Institutional Residential Mortgage Lending*, 8.

50. Keane, *Fritz B. Burns*, 75. Unfortunately, Keane does not say who the lender was.

51. After selling out, Tomlinson entered into a partnership with one of his sons, Lloyd W. Tomlinson, in a real estate and insurance agency in Highland Park. "Loan Firm Founder Tomlinson Dies," *LAT*, August 6, 1953, A12. At the end of 1946, North American Savings and Loan Association had nearly $1.75 million in assets. Undoubtedly, this was more than it had when Ahmanson purchased it. State of California, Division of Building and Loan, *Fifty-Third Annual Report* (Sacramento: California State Printing Office, 1947), 26, CSA.

52. Howard undoubtedly recognized this second name. The original North American had been seized by the California Building and Loan commissioner in 1932 after the manager confessed to embezzling. When the state proposed to liquidate the building and loan, the directors and some of the more than 22,600 investors

protested. Their protests gained traction when newspapers reported that after the seizure California governor Rolph's former insurance partners and his son received all the fire insurance business associated with the company's outstanding loans. This was not the first time that Governor Rolph had been accused of steering insurance business to his former partners and sons. When the state took over the Pacific Coast Building-Loan Association, the company of Rolph, Landis & Ellis had received a "binder" to cover fire insurance while the association's affairs were resolved. "Rolph Group Gets Plums Via State Department," *LAT,* April 3, 1932, A1. For the specific claims related to North American, see "Loan Company Row Continues," *LAT,* October 27, 1932, A8; and "Loan Company Theft Related," *LAT,* October 26, 1932, A10. Ahmanson would have paid attention to this story in 1932. It was associated with names that would become all too familiar to him. The investigator for the California Building and Loan Commission was Milton Shaw, who would become deputy commissioner for Los Angeles by 1945. Meanwhile, the deputy commissioner who handled the proceedings in 1932 was a San Francisco attorney who was a relative of one of Howard's best friends.

53. This story and the dialogue appear in Lawrence, "Master Builders." See also Kim Fletcher, interview by author, December 8, 2009.

54. David S. Hannah, interview by Marc Nurre, [1994], in FA.

55. Hollywood Savings & Loan was run by Howard's friend Mervyn Hope. It had just over $5.2 million in assets in 1945. The *Los Angeles Times* said Ahmanson bought Hollywood in 1942. "I remember the price, $60,000." Elsewhere, Ahmanson says he owned 28 percent of the stock of a savings and loan at this time but doesn't specify which one. For Hollywood's assets in 1945, see State of California, Division of Building and Loan, *Fifty-Second Annual Report* (Sacramento: California State Printing Office, 1946).

56. By the end of 1952, the company carried more than 50 percent of all the fire insurance written on homes in the region. Bob Bergen, "'Specialist' Turns Hobby into Profit," *Los Angeles Mirror,* January 20, 1953, 46.

57. State of California, Division of Building and Loan, *Fifty-Fifth Annual Report* (Sacramento: California State Printing Office, 1949), 18–19, in CSA.

58. Ibid., 4.

59. "Consolidated Statement of Number and Amount of New Loans by California Associations—Members of Federal Home Loan Bank of San Francisco," *CSLJ,* April 1948, 16–17.

60. Crail came from Iowa. In 1946, he was elected president of the Iowa Association of California, a group with more than one hundred thousand members. That same year, Crail served as chairman of the Bill of Rights Commemoration Committee. "Iowans Headed by Joe Crail," *LAT,* November 15, 1946, A1. For Crail as a classmate of Ahmanson's, see Seymour Freedgood et al., "Croesus at Home," first draft typescript, March 17, 1958, in FA.

61. "Savings, Loan Assets Climb," *LAT,* August 7, 1945, 9.

62. Lawrence, "Master Builders," 10.

63. Marquis James and Bessie Rowland James, *Biography of a Bank: The Story of Bank of America* (New York: Harper and Brothers, 1954), 475. See also Williams, "Southern California Economy," 8.

64. In 1958, only seventeen states, mostly in the East, allowed for mutual savings banks. Albert L. Kraus, "Savings Bankers Eye U.S. Charters," *NYT,* May 4, 1958, F1.

65. Policy makers had long expressed reservations about the development of branch banking in the United States. This antagonism traced its roots to democratic opposition to state-run or national banks that concentrated economic power and were susceptible to manipulation by powerful groups of political insiders. By the early twentieth century, advocates suggested that branch banking offered a way to provide service to rural communities. Opponents believed they undermined local control. The California Bank Act (1909) allowed branch banking, subject to the approval of the state superintendent of banks, upon a finding that it served "public need and convenience." Richard H. K. Vietor, *Contrived Competition: Regulation and Deregulation in America* (Cambridge, MA: Harvard University Press, 1994), 242–43.

66. Albert H. Schaaf, "The Savings Function and Mortgage Investment by California Banks and Financial Institutions," in *California Banking in a Growing Economy: 1946–1975,* ed. Hyman P. Minsky (Berkeley: Institute of Business and Economic Research, University of California, 1965), 252.

67. In 1951, Congress passed a new law subjecting savings and loans and mutual savings banks to federal taxation, but the law allowed savings and loans to avoid income taxes on up to 12 percent of net income by diverting this cash into capital reserves, where it could be reinvested in new loans. J. Richard Elliott Jr., "Savings and Loans: Rapid Growth Can Be Risky Even in Thrift," *Barron's,* February 13, 1956, 20, clipping in box 4, Correspondence of Chairman Walter W. McAllister, 1952–1956, RG 195, NARA-CP. See also State of California, Division of Building and Loan, *Fifty-Seventh Annual Report* (Sacramento: California State Printing Office, 1951), 10, in CSA.

68. David S. Hannah, interview by Marc Nurre, [1994].

69. Elliott, "Savings and Loans."

70. Among the states that did allow stock companies organized to benefit a separate group of equity holders, activity was greatest in California, Ohio, and Texas. C. Joseph Clawson et al., *The Savings and Loan Industry in California* (South Pasadena, CA: Stanford Research Institute, 1960), III-1.

71. David L. Mason, *From Building and Loans to Bail-Outs: A History of the American Savings and Loan Industry, 1831–1995* (Cambridge: Cambridge University Press, 2004), 176.

72. In a mutual association, net income after the payment of dividends to depositors was often held as retained earnings in the association's capital reserve. These retained earnings belonged to the association and not to the depositors. For decades courts wrestled with the question of whether depositors were entitled to a share of the surplus upon the dissolution or merger of the thrift. See Dwight C.

Smith and James H. Underwood, "Mutual Savings Associations and Conversion to Stock Form," Business Transactions Division Memorandum, Office of Thrift Supervision, May 1997, http://files.ots.treas.gov/48801.pdf.

73. Initially, the VA was authorized to guarantee up to 50 percent of the principal amount of the loan up to a maximum guarantee of two thousand dollars. To ensure affordability, the government capped the interest rate a lender could charge at 4 percent and guaranteed loans for terms up to twenty years. Leon T. Kendall, *The Savings and Loan Business: Its Purpose, Functions, and Economic Justification* (Englewood Cliffs, NJ: Prentice-Hall, 1962), 8.

74. "Straight GI" loans relied on only the VA for the loan guarantee, but a lender could also write a loan insured by the FHA and then use the VA to guarantee a second mortgage for up to 20 percent of the total purchase price. These "FHA-GI combination" loans further lowered the barriers to home ownership. Mason, *From Building and Loans,* 143.

75. Stephen B. Adams, *Mr. Kaiser Goes to Washington: The Rise of a Government Entrepreneur* (Chapel Hill: University of North Carolina Press, 1997), 8.

76. State of California, Division of Building and Loan, *Fifty-Third Annual Report,* 8, CSA.

77. State of California, Division of Building and Loan, *Fifty-Fourth Annual Report* (Sacramento: California State Printing Office, 1948), 28, CSA.

78. Ibid.

79. "Savings-Loan Assets Climb," A7.

80. The June purchase date comes from "Home Is Biggest in U.S. in Its Field," *Los Angeles Herald Express,* September 10, 1956, clipping in Home Clipping File, 1956, FA.

81. At the time of the sale, the company's offices were located at 115 West Ninth Street in Los Angeles. Two months later, the company leased a "storeroom" at 812 S. Spring Street and relocated. See Board of Directors, Home Building and Loan, "Minutes: January 14, 1947—March 15, 1950," in box: Home Savings & Loan Board of Directors Minutes, JPMCA; Robert E. Nichols, "No. 5 Joins the Select Ranks of Area's Billion-Dollar Firms," *LAT,* December 3, 1961, I1.

82. By April 1947, Ahmanson had become the majority shareholder. Elected to the board in January 1948, he became chairman and president soon afterward. Nevertheless, when he attended the board of directors meeting in December 1947, the corporate secretary described him in the minutes as an "invited guest." In formal documents later in its history, H. F. Ahmanson & Company used 1948 as the year of acquisition. See, for example, H. F. Ahmanson & Company, "Preliminary Prospectus," October 13, 1972, 3. According to the minutes, he was not elected president of the company until November 17, 1948. Home Savings of America, FSB Minute Book Highlights, 1948–1968, in file: "Minutes," in LH files, FA; "L.A. Group Elects Two New Officers," *LAT,* March 28, 1948, 20.

83. Richard Deihl, interview by author, December 19, 2009, 19.

84. "L.A. Insurance Men in Housing Syndicate," *Insurance Journal,* April 1947, clipping in FA.

85. Harold Tucker, "It's Not All Finance with L.A. Financier," *LAT,* June 11, 1961, J1; Nichols, "No. 5 Joins"; Robert DeKruif to Howard Ahmanson, January 1, 1959, in file "To HFA," LH files, FA.

86. Home offered 2.5 percent, compared to the going rate of 2.0. By the end of 1948, Ahmanson had increased the association's assets to $15.4 million. "Home Savings Slates Preview of New Building," *Los Angeles Examiner,* February 28, 1956, clipping in Home Clippings File, 1956, FA.

87. Lawrence, "Master Builders." In another article, Ahmanson says they raised four million dollars in a month. "Howard F. Ahmanson," *Finance,* February 1966, 10. The friend was J. E. Hoeft, the founder and chairman of Glendale Federal. The campaign was most likely executed by the Elwood J. Robinson Agency. See Board of Directors, Home Building and Loan, "Minutes: January 14, 1947–March 15, 1950," in box: Home Savings & Loan Board of Directors Minutes, JPMCA.

88. See, for example, Board of Directors, Home Building and Loan, "Minutes: January 14, 1947–March 15, 1950," 160 and 189, in box: Home Savings & Loan Board of Directors Minutes, JPMCA.

89. Regulators were apparently critical of Home Building & Loan's rapid growth, noting particularly in the fall of 1948 that 96 percent of the association's loans had been made in the previous eighteen months. Ahmanson was flummoxed by this criticism. During a board meeting he said "he knew of no other alternative to making new loans in the face of the heavy increase in share accounts." Board of Directors, Home Building and Loan, "Minutes: January 14, 1947–March 15, 1950," 189, in box: Home Savings & Loan Board of Directors Minutes, JPMCA.

90. Freedgood et al., "Croesus at Home." See also David S. Hannah, interview by Marc Nurre, [1994].

91. Regulators later changed the accounting rules to force lenders to take profits over the life of the loan. David S. Hannah, interview by Marc Nurre, [1994], in FA.

92. Freedgood et al., "Croesus at Home."

93. "Richest of the Rich S&Ls," *Business Week,* July 1, 1961, 80. Also referred to in Seymour Freedgood, "Emperor Howard Ahmanson of S&L," *Fortune,* May 1958, 152.

94. Freedgood et al., "Croesus at Home."

95. "Richest of the Rich S&Ls." See also Freedgood, "Emperor Howard Ahmanson," 150.

96. Freedgood et al., "Croesus at Home."

97. Ibid.

98. "Elect Childs Home S&L President," *Los Angeles Herald Express,* January 24, 1957, D11. For biographical information on Childs, see Millard Sheets, "Kenneth D. Childs," on reel 5704, in Millard Sheets Papers, AAA; and David S. Hannah, interview by Marc Nurre, [1994], in FA.

99. Richard Deihl, interview by author, September 25, 2009, 20.

100. See Board of Directors, Home Building and Loan, "Minutes: January 14, 1947–March 15, 1950," 187, in box: Home Savings & Loan Board of Directors Minutes, JPMCA.

101. "Richest of the Rich S&Ls." See also Freedgood, "Emperor Howard," 152.

102. Board of Directors, Home Building and Loan, "Minutes: January 14, 1947–March 15, 1950," 197–98, in box: Home Savings & Loan Board of Directors Minutes, JPMCA.

103. Board of Directors, Home Building and Loan, "Minutes: January 14, 1947–March 15, 1950," 214, in box: Home Savings & Loan Board of Directors Minutes, JPMCA.

104. "Richest of the Rich S&Ls."

105. Freedgood, "Emperor Howard Ahmanson," 152.

106. David S. Hannah, interview by Marc Nurre, [1994], in FA. See also Freedgood, "Emperor Howard Ahmanson," 152.

107. "Richest of the Rich S&Ls."

108. Freedgood et al., "Croesus at Home."

109. Ibid.

110. Banks were also unsettled by the prospect of a lack of liquidity in the secondary market, especially after the Reconstruction Finance Corporation was dissolved in 1953 and strict limits were placed on FNMA's ability to purchase mortgages. Lynne Pierson Doti and Larry Schweikart, *Banking in the West: From the Gold Rush to Deregulation* (Norman: University of Oklahoma Press, 1991), 161.

6. SCALING UP

1. Robert DeKruif, interview by Margaret Bach, [1992], in TAFA.

2. Richard Deihl, interview by author, September 25, 2009.

3. This process was somewhat analogous to the method used by A. P. Giannini in the 1910s, when California law prohibited a bank from buying the stock of another bank but allowed for the transfer of assets belonging to the bank. When Giannini wanted to acquire a bank, a group of individuals representing the Bank of Italy (Bank of America's predecessor) would buy the stock of the target bank. The target bank would then transfer its assets (deposits, loans, real estate, etc.) to the acquiring bank. Bank of Italy would then pay the individuals for the value of their shares in the target bank. Marquis James and Bessie Rowland James, *Biography of a Bank: The Story of Bank of America* (New York: Harper and Brothers, 1954), 75.

4. "Home Building & Loan Buys Long Beach Unit," *LAT,* January 17, 1951, B4.

5. "Savings Group Resources Jump," *LAT,* July 7, 1951, 8. See also display advertisement, *LAT,* January 5, 1952, 9.

6. State of California, Building and Loan Commissioner, "Fifty-Seventh Annual Report," 1950, 27, 39, in CSA. One source says that Ahmanson made these moves for tax reasons. See Seymour Freedgood et al., "Croesus at Home," first draft typescript, March 17, 1958, in FA.

7. "Top-Ranking United States League Members," *Savings and Loan News,* March 1952, 40.

8. Home Savings of America, FSB Minute Book Highlights, 1948–1968, in file: "Minutes," LH files, FA. See also "Merger Forms Huge Southland Savings-Loan," *LAT,* July 1, 1952, 16.

9. "Merger Forms Huge Southland Savings-Loan."

10. "Home Savings Resources Pass $100 Million Mark," *Los Angeles Herald Express,* January 6, 1953, clipping in Home Clippings File, 1953, FA.

11. "Top-Ranking United States League Members," *Savings and Loan News,* March 1953, 20.

12. "Home Savings in Acquisition," *LAT,* February 9, 1954. 18. For population data on the San Fernando Valley, see Max Lupul and Paul B. Blomgren, "The Current Status and Outlook of the Real Estate Business in the San Fernando Valley," Bureau of Business Services and Research, School of Business Administration and Economics, San Fernando Valley State College, 1967, 6.

13. S. Oliver Goodman, "Investment Analysts Here Form Society," *WP,* February 11, 1954, 16; Robert E. Nichols, "No. 5 Joins the Select Ranks of Area's Billion-Dollar Firms," *LAT,* December 3, 1961, I1. "Home Savings Expansion Set," *LAT,* February 18, 1954, A10.

14. David S. Hannah, interview by Marc Nurre, [1994], in FA.

15. Robert DeKruif, interview by Margaret Bach, [1992], in TAFA.

16. John Notter, interview by author, August 20, 2009.

17. Robert DeKruif, interview by Margaret Bach, [1992], TAFA.

18. John Notter, interview by author, August 20, 2009; see also David S. Hannah, interview by Marc Nurre, [1994], in FA.

19. Richard Diehl, interview by author, September 25, 2009.

20. Freedgood et al., "Croesus at Home."

21. "On Coronado Program: Dr. Thurston H. Ross," *CSLJ,* May 1948, 13.

22. Richard Deihl, interview by author, December 19, 2009.

23. [Chris Bone],"Partial History/Chronology of H.F. Ahmanson & Company," [1988], in TAF History files, TAFA.

24. In 1952, 80 percent of National American Insurance Company's total premium volume came from H.F. Ahmanson & Company, Inc. Alfred M. Best Company, *Best's Insurance Reports* (New York: Alfred M. Best Company, 1953), 663.

25. Aimee Ahmanson to Howard F. Ahmanson, [February 1952], FA.

26. Bill was born October 12, 1925. See his obituary, "William Hayden Ahmanson," *LAT,* October 17, 2008. See also Hayden Ahmanson to Mrs. H.F. Ahmanson, September 14, 1943, in file: "Gould," box 23AV, FA.

27. M. Hahn to W.H. Ahmanson, January 17, 1949, in "Correspondence," USC folder, LH files, FA.

28. Eddy is referred to as president of the North American Savings and Loan Association in "North American Occupies New Home," *CSLJ,* October 1948, 21.

29. Wesley Morse, "Eulogy," December 27, 2000, www.billybartyandfriends.com/eulogy.html.

30. Robert DeKruif, interview by author, May 1, 2009.

31. Charles T. Munger, interview by author, January 13, 2011.

32. It also allowed him to become more and more involved with yachting and socializing. Almost every day, Ahmanson ate lunch at Perinos, where he had a regular booth and held court. Robert DeKruif, interview by author, May 1, 2009.

33. Robert Ahmanson to Aimee and Hayden Ahmanson, various letters, 1951, in Aimee Ahmanson records, TAFA. See also Kenneth Childs to Howard F. Ahmanson, April 19, 1941 [1951], in FA.

34. "Richest of the Rich S&Ls," *Business Week,* July 1, 1961, 80.

35. John Notter, interview by author, August 20, 2009.

36. Richard Deihl, interview by author, September 25, 2009.

37. Ibid.

38. Ibid.

39. Alfred Nicols, *Management and Control in the Mutual Savings and Loan Association* (Toronto: Lexington Books, 1972), 247.

40. Richard Deihl, interview by author, September 25, 2009.

41. "New Money Merchants: Saving & Loan Men Teach Bankers Lesson," *Time,* November 29, 1954, 92.

42. Life insurance's share of all savings rose from 27.5 to 31.4 percent. Edwin L. Dale, "Our Saving Ways," *NYT,* March 15, 1956, 56.

43. Leo Grebler and Eugene F. Brigham, *Savings and Mortgage Markets in California* (Pasadena: California Savings and Loan League, 1963), 70.

44. Ibid., 80.

45. Howard Ahmanson, "Some Bosses Forget Customer Is King," *Los Angeles Examiner,* October 21, 1956, 10.

46. "Richest of the Rich S&Ls."

47. This was part of a series of ads featuring historic photos of Los Angeles with copy focused on the same theme. Display advertisement, *LAT,* January 2, 1951, A7.

48. Display advertisement, *LAT,* January 9, 1950, 27.

49. Display advertisement, *LAT,* January 4, 1952, 16.

50. Display advertisement, *LAT,* July 29, 1952, 6.

51. David Rees, "Home S&L's Ahmanson to Become Banker," *Los Angeles Mirror-News,* January 23, 1957, pt. 3, 5.

52. Robert DeKruif, interview by author, May 1, 2009.

53. David S. Hannah, interview by Marc Nurre, [1994], in FA.

54. Richard Deihl, interview by author, September 25, 2009.

55. Display advertisement, *LAT,* July 6, 1954, 12; display advertisement, *LAT,* September 7, 1954, 20.

56. Display advertisement, *LAT,* July 5, 1955, B10.

57. Richard Deihl, interview by author, September 25, 2009.

58. Ibid.

59. Ibid.

60. Rufus Turner, interview by Adam Arenson and author, October 7, 2010.

61. Alfred D. Chandler Jr., *The Visible Hand: The Managerial Revolution in American Business* (Cambridge, MA: Harvard University Press, 1977), 290–99. See

also Roland Marchand, *Advertising the American Dream: Making Way for Modernity, 1920–1940* (Berkeley: University of California Press, 1985).

62. Good data for this argument are hard to come by. As standardization and government guarantees lowered the cost of lending related to risks and due diligence on the loan, profitability should have risen. In a competitive market, however, these excess profits should have disappeared and the ultimate reward should have been passed on to borrowers, making home loans generally more affordable regardless of interest rate conditions.

63. Freedgood et al., "Croesus at Home."

64. The difference in attitudes between Edgerton and Ahmanson may also have derived from the difference in corporate form. Officers of federal savings and loans had no equity stake in the business. As a result, they tended to divert some profits to nonsalary forms of compensation. Nicols, *Management and Control,* 27–28. For Ahmanson's quote, see Seymour Freedgood, "Emperor Howard Ahmanson of S&L," *Fortune,* May 1958, 149–50. See also Freedgood et al., "Croesus at Home."

65. Warren Buffett, interview by author, December 9, 2010.

66. "Ahmanson Cut Nice Figures In Savings, Loan Business" *[Omaha World-Herald],* June 19, 1968, n.p., clipping provided by Mary Jane Bettefreund.

67. Robert DeKruif, interview by author, May 1, 2009.

68. John Notter, interview by author, August 20, 2009.

69. "Home Savings Loans Reach All-Time High," *Los Angeles Mirror and Daily News,* January 20, 1956, clipping in Home Clipping Files, 1956, FA.

70. Robert DeKruif, interview by author, May 1, 2009.

71. Richard Deihl, interview by author, September 25, 2009.

72. "Old Home Town Look . . . ," *[Omaha World Herald],* March 19, 1958, n.p., clipping provided by Mary Jane Bettefreund.

73. "Howard F. Ahmanson," *Finance,* February 1966, 21.

74. Richard Deihl, interview by author, December 19, 2009.

75. Guy Stuart, *Discriminating Risk: The U.S. Mortgage Lending Industry in the Twentieth Century* (Ithaca: Cornell University Press, 2003), 29–69.

76. Raymond M. Foley to Community Homes, July 3, 1947, in Helen Gahagan Douglas Collection, Carl Albert Center, Norman, OK, cited in Anthony Denzer, "Community Homes: Race, Politics and Architecture in Postwar Los Angeles," *Southern California Quarterly* 87, no. 3 (Fall 2005): 281.

77. "Negroes to Get 1200 Houses," *LAT,* January 3, 1945, 11.

78. Josh Sides, " 'You Understand My Condition': The Civil Rights Congress in the Los Angeles African-American Community, 1946–1952," *Pacific Historical Review* 67, no. 2 (May 1998): 236. See also Lawrence B. De Graaf, "The City of Black Angels: Emergence of the Los Angeles Ghetto, 1890–1930," *Pacific Historical Review* 39 (1970):323–52.

79. U.S. Bureau of the Census, *Sixteenth Census,* 629; *Seventeen Decennial Census,* 1:5–100, and *Seventeenth Decennial Census,* 2/5:100, all cited in Shana Bernstein, "Interracial Activism in the Los Angeles Community Service Organization:

Linking the World War II and Civil Rights Eras," *Pacific Historical Review* 80, no. 2 (May 2011): 231–67.

80. Sides, "'You Understand My Condition,'" 237.

81. Clement E. Vose, *Caucasians Only: The Supreme Court, the NAACP, and the Restrictive Covenant Cases* (1959; repr., Berkeley: University of California Press, 1973).

82. Quoted in Bill Boyarsky, *Big Daddy: Jesse Unruh and the Art of Power Politics* (Berkeley: University of California Press, 2008), 81.

83. For years, realtors and property owners had asserted that the Fourteenth Amendment banned only discrimination by the government. Private property owners were free to reach binding agreements with one another, including racial covenants. In the case of *Shelley v. Kraemer,* they argued that government enforcement of these private contracts did not constitute state action. Arguing on behalf of a black couple named Shelley, who had purchased a home in a racially restricted neighborhood in Missouri and were denied the right to occupy that property by the Missouri Supreme Court, Thurgood Marshall insisted that state action, even in the context of enforcing private agreements, remained a violation of the Fourteenth Amendment, and the court agreed. See *Shelley v. Kraemer* (334 U.S. 1, 1948); *Hurd v. Hodge* (334 U.S. 24, 1948). For background on how cases in California helped provide the foundation for Marshall's argument, see Mark Brilliant, *The Color of America Has Changed: How Racial Diversity Shaped Civil Rights Reform in California, 1941–1978* (New York: Oxford University Press, 2010),ch. 4.

84. "Jim Crow Is Dying," *Los Angeles Sentinel,* October 7, 1948, cited in Daniel Wei HoSang, "Racial Propositions: 'Genteel Apartheid' in Postwar California" (PhD diss., University of Southern California, 2007), 12.

85. Brilliant, *Color of America*, 123. See also Kevin Roderick, *Wilshire Boulevard: Grand Concourse of Los Angeles* (Santa Monica, CA: Angel City Books, 2005), 9.

86. At the end of 1957, the combined assets of these four institutions equaled nearly $50 million. See "Negro Operated Savings, Building and Loan Associations that are Members of the FHLB System," December 31, 1957, in box 8, Correspondence of Chairman Robertson, Records of the Federal Home Loan Bank, RG 195, NARA-CP. See also Josh Sides, "Straight into Compton: American Dreams, Urban Nightmares, and the Metamorphosis of a Black Suburb," *American Quarterly* 56, no. 3 (2004): 583–605.

87. D. A. Squire to Dean Chamberlin, May 21, 1963, in box 58, files of FHLBB Chairman McMurray, RG 195, NARA-CP.

88. A. V. Ammann to William K. Divers, October 13, 1953, in folder: California Federal Savings & Loan, Branch Applications, 1953, box 4, Correspondence of Chairman William W. McAllister, 1952–1956, Records of the Federal Home Loan Bank, RG 195, NARA-CP.

89. Robert DeKruif, interview by Margaret Bach, [1992], in TAFA.

90. Freedgood, "Emperor Howard Ahmanson," 148.

91. Ibid.

92. Albert H. Schaaf, "The Savings Function and Mortgage Investment by California Banks and Financial Institutions," in *California Banking in a Growing Economy: 1946–1975,* ed. Hyman P. Minsky (Berkeley: Institute of Business and Economic Research, University of California, 1965), 249.

93. Ibid.

94. Refers to nonfarm mortgages valued at less than twenty thousand dollars. See ibid., 258.

95. By comparison, home ownership rose from 39.4 percent to 61.3 percent in New Jersey, 45.9 percent to 68.3 percent in Pennsylvania, and 40.5 percent to 61.9 percent in Connecticut in the same period. See U.S. Census Bureau, "Historical Census of Housing Tables: Home Ownership," n.d., www.census.gov/hhes/www /housing/census/historic/owner.html (accessed September 18, 2011).

96. The home ownership rate in the Los Angeles–Long Beach SMSA was higher than that in the San Francisco–Oakland SMSA (54.5 percent). See U.S. Census, 1960, reported in Leo Grebler, *Metropolitan Contrasts: Profile of the Los Angeles Metropolis, Its People and Its Homes,* Research Report no. 3, Real Estate Program, Division of Research (Los Angeles: Graduate School of Business Administration, University of California, 1963), 34–35.

7. HOME AND THE STATE

1. Scholars have also described this system as "segmented and sedated." Louis Galambos and Joseph Pratt, *The Rise of the Corporate Commonwealth: U.S. Business and Public Policy in the Twentieth Century* (New York: Basic Books, 1988), 105–6.

2. I'm grateful to Zachary Abrahamson for this analogy.

3. For "interventionist state," see Theodore Levitt, "The Johnson Treatment," *Harvard Business Review* 45 (January–February 1967): 114, cited in David Vogel, *Fluctuating Fortunes: The Political Power of Business in America* (New York: Basic Books, 1989), 24. For "corporate commonwealth," see Galambos and Pratt, *Rise of the Corporate Commonwealth.*

4. Stephen B. Adams, *Mr. Kaiser Goes to Washington: The Rise of a Government Entrepreneur* (Chapel Hill: University of North Carolina Press, 1997), 11.

5. The commissioner could require a savings and loan to submit its advertising at least five days prior to publication. In general, the commissioner required this only of new associations "until they become familiar with the rules and ethics of advertising savings and loans." He could also bar an association from using a particular advertisement. Milton O. Shaw, "Commissioner Launches Course in Savings and Loan Law," *CSLJ,* March 1955, 7.

6. Ibid., 5.

7. California, Division of Building and Loan, *Fifty-Fifth Annual Report* (Sacramento: California State Printing Office, 1949), 12, in CSA.

8. Howard P. Stevens, "President's Message," *CSLJ,* June 1950, 6.

9. Ibid.

10. LeRoy Hunt to Earl Warren, March 10, 1953, in folder F3640:2525, box 1 (2515–31), Earl Warren Papers, Administrative Files, Department of Investment, Building and Loan, 1949–1953, CSA.

11. Hunt to Warren, March 10, 1953. See also California, Division of Savings and Loan, *Sixty-First Annual Report* (Sacramento: California State Printing Office, 1955), 12.

12. On the national context for state regulation of building and loans, see David L. Mason, *From Building and Loans to Bail-Outs: A History of the American Savings and Loan Industry, 1831–1995* (Cambridge: Cambridge University Press, 2004), 69–74. For industry efforts to seek regulation as a way to standardize services and products and temper competition, see the discussion of the fire insurance industry in chapter 1.

13. When Frank Mortimer left his position as commissioner after eight years, he became executive vice president of Pioneer Savings and Loan in Los Angeles. California, Division of Savings and Loan, *Sixty-Third Annual Report* (Sacramento: California State Printing Office, 1957), 41. After Milton Shaw retired in 1958, he became a consultant to the industry.

14. Home also purchased the troubled Burbank Savings and Loan under similar circumstances. Home Savings of America, FSB Minute Book Highlights, 1948–1968, in file: "Minutes," LH files, FA.

15. J. Howard Edgerton to Goodwin J. Knight, January 4, 1954, in Goodwin J. Knight—Administrative Files, Department of Investment, Division of Savings and Loan, box 35/8–35/9, C114.106-E5990 b2, folder 35/8, CSA.

16. "Typortraits: Milton Otis Shaw," *CSLJ,* March 1950, 21. See also California, Division of Savings and Loan, *Sixty-Third Annual Report* (Sacramento: State of California, 1957), 10.

17. Seymour Freedgood, "Emperor Howard Ahmanson of S&L," *Fortune,* May 1958, 149.

18. California, Division of Savings and Loan, *Sixtieth Annual Report* (Sacramento: State of California, 1954), 20.

19. "Savings, Loan Firm of L.A. Drops S.F. Bid," *San Francisco Call-Bulletin,* January 25, 1956, 39.

20. Anonymous to Earl Warren, January 26, 1952, in folder F3640:2525, box 1 (2515–31), Earl Warren Papers, Administrative Files, Department of Investment, Building and Loan, 1949–1953, CSA.

21. Milton O. Shaw to M. F. Small, February 26, 1952, in folder F3640:2525, box 1 (2515–31), Earl Warren Papers, Administrative Files, Department of Investment, Building and Loan, 1949–1953, CSA.

22. M. F. Small to Milton O. Shaw, April 7, 1952, in folder F3640:2525, box 1 (2515–31), Earl Warren Papers, Administrative Files, Department of Investment, Building and Loan, 1949–1953, CSA.

23. A. T. Purtell to Earl Warren, June 8, in folder F3640:2525, box 1 (2515–31), Earl Warren Papers, Administrative Files, Department of Investment, Building and Loan, 1949–1953, CSA.

24. Milton O. Shaw to M. F. Small, April 23, 1952, in folder F3640:2525, box 1 (2515–31), Earl Warren Papers, Administrative Files, Department of Investment, Building and Loan, 1949–53, CSA.

25. J. Howard Edgerton to Walter W. McAllister, September 27, 1954, in folder: California Savings and Loan Association, box 4, Correspondence of Chairman Walter W. McAllister, 1952–1956, RG 195, NARA-CP.

26. Ibid.

27. Federal Home Loan Bank Board, *Savings and Home Financing Chart Book: No. 5* (1960), in box 7, Correspondence of Chairman Robertson, Records of the Federal Home Loan Bank, RG 195, NARA-CP.

28. Josephine Hedges Ewalt, *A Business Reborn: The Savings and Loan Story, 1930–1960* (Chicago: American Savings and Loan Institute Press, 1962), 104–8.

29. J. Howard Edgerton, *The Story of California Federal Savings* (New York: Newcomen Society in North America, 1969).

30. Walter McAllister, Dwight Eisenhower's first chairman of the FHLBB, had been active in the U.S. Savings and Loan League and, like Edgerton, served a term as president. Like Edgerton, he was a hunter, and their letters back and forth kept each other informed of various hunting trips.

31. Walter W. McAllister to J. Howard Edgerton, September 24, 1954, in folder: California Federal Savings and Loan Association, box 4, Correspondence of Chairman Walter W. McAllister, 1952–1956, RG 195, NARA-CP.

32. Ibid.

33. All this correspondence is summarized in Walter W. McAllister to J. Howard Edgerton, November 4, 1954, in folder: California Federal Savings and Loan Association, box 4, Correspondence of Chairman Walter W. McAllister, 1952–1956, RG 195, NARA-CP.

34. Walter W. McAllister, [speech text for California Savings and Loan League conference], Los Angeles, 1953, in folder: California Savings and Loan Association, box: 5, Correspondence of Chairman Walter W. McAllister, 1952–1956, RG 195, NARA-CP.

35. Kevin Starr, foreword to *Making a Better World: Public Housing, the Red Scare and the Direction of Modern Los Angeles,* by Don Parson (Minneapolis: University of Minnesota Press, 2005).

36. Gayle B. Montgomery and James W. Johnson, *One Step from the White House: The Rise and Fall of Senator William F. Knowland* (Berkeley: University of California Press, 1998), 63.

37. "U.S. Housing Plan Hit as Leading to Socialism," *LAT,* November 13, 1947, 10.

38. Kim Fletcher, interview by author, December 8, 2009.

39. Dan Normark, *Chávez Ravine, 1949: A Los Angeles Story* (San Francisco: Chronicle Books, 1999), 18.

40. A number of scholars have written about the fight over public housing in Chávez Ravine. See Parson, *Making a Better World;* Scott Kurashige, *The Shifting Grounds of Race: Black and Japanese Americans in the Making of Multiethnic Los Angeles* (New Jersey: Princeton University Press, 2008).

41. Ibid.

42. Charles G. Mayo, "The 1961 Mayoralty Election in Los Angeles: The Political Party in a Nonpartisan Election," *Western Political Quarterly* 17, no. 2 (1964): 325–37.

43. Normark, *Chávez Ravine, 1949.*

44. Edwin M. Eaton, "It's Time to Do Something about It," *CSLJ,* April 1950, 13.

45. Stevens, "President's Message," 6.

46. "Capitol Federal History," n.d., www.capfed.com/site/en/home/about /history.html (accessed August 8, 2011).

47. Henry A. Bubb, "Our Role in the 1952 Elections," *CSLJ,* March 1952, 9–10.

48. Mason, *From Building and Loans,* 144. Leon Kendall says that in 1946, "the first year of substantial volume," savings and loans accounted for $1.25 billion of the $2.3 billion loaned to GIs. Leon T. Kendall, *The Savings and Loan Business: Its Purpose, Functions, and Economic Justification* (Englewood Cliffs, NJ: Prentice-Hall, 1962), 8.

49. C.J. Burns, "We Don't Make Veterans' Loans OR We *Won't* Make Them," *CSLJ,* April 1947, 29.

50. "Brief Chronology of the Loan Guaranty Program and Related Statutory Functions," 3, in file: Loan Guaranty Service: Benefits: Appraisal History, re: Servicemen's Readjustment Act, box 33, RG 15: A1.1017, NARA-DC.

51. Donald S. Thompson, "What Is the Position of the Mortgage Lender Today?" *CSLJ,* May 1947, 11.

52. Edgerton, *Story of California Federal Savings,* 14.

53. Walter J. Ray, "Home Building and Financing in a Mobilized Economy," *CSLJ,* September 1951, 7–8.

54. NAHB, *Washington Letter,* March 10, 1954, 3. NAHB Archives.

55. Burns, "We Don't Make Veterans' Loans," 28. The NAHB criticized lenders who refused to make VA loans because the interest rates weren't high enough. After Congress passed the Housing Act of 1950, which authorized the VA to make direct loans to borrowers, the NAHB noted, "It would appear that the time has come for somewhat less concern by lending institutions with ¼ of 1% interest and somewhat greater concern for this dangerous encroachment by government in the field of private mortgage lending." "Direct Federal Lending for G.I. Home Loans," *Washington Letter,* June 29, 1951, 4.

56. Mason, *From Building and Loans,* 144–45.

57. J. Richard Elliott Jr., "Savings and Loans: Rapid Growth Can Be Risky Even in Thrift," *Barron's,* February 13, 1956, 20.

58. Sterling W. Ellis and Harold F. Dunton, *The Big Promise* (Altadena, CA: Veteran's Organizations Council of Altadena, [1950]), in John Anson Ford Papers, box 65, folder B III, 14.d.cc, Huntington Library, San Marino, CA.

59. Ibid.

60. "Action Taken to Spur GI Loans," *LAT,* May 27, 1953, 21.

61. "L.A. County Leads U.S. in V.A. Volume of Loans," *LAT,* November 14, 1954, E5. For national statistics, see Veterans Administration, *GI Loans: The First 10*

Years (Washington, DC: Veterans Administration, 1954), in folder: Loans to Veterans, box: 19, Correspondence of Chairman Walter W. McAllister, 1952–1956, RG 195, NARA-CP.

62. "Home Savings Loans Reach All-Time High," *Los Angeles Mirror and Daily News,* January 20, 1956, clipping in Home Clippings File, 1956, FA. It's also interesting to note that in 1959 only 16 percent of the total mortgage loan balances held by thrifts were insured by either the FHA or the VA. C. Joseph Clawson et al., *The Savings and Loan Industry in California* (South Pasadena, CA: Stanford Research Institute, 1960), II-15.

63. "Home Savings Assets Show Jump in '56," *Highland Park News Herald,* December 27, 1956, clipping in Home Clippings File, 1956, FA.

64. Home's VA loan strategy stood in sharp contrast to its participation in the FHA-insured loan program. Like many other savings and loans, Home wrote very few FHA loans in the 1950s (less than 2 percent). Savings and loans generally paid more than commercial banks to acquire loanable funds (reflected in the higher interest rates they paid to savers). With their higher cost of capital, the FHA insurance program simply didn't pay. The VA program would have been the same, except that profits could be enhanced by charging fees, which builders were happy to pay because the VA loan program was more attractive to borrowers and the cost of the fees could be included in the total purchase price of the home.

65. Freedgood, "Emperor Howard Ahmanson."

66. Warren Buffett, interview by author, December 9, 2010.

67. Kenneth Childs to Howard Ahmanson, April 19, 1941 [1951], in FA.

68. The first building codes and standards were adopted by the State of California in 1909 and 1911. Statewide regulation began with the establishment of the Commission (later Division) of Housing and Immigration in 1913 along with the first state and local "planning stimulation" laws that same year. Gerald N. Hill, "A History of Housing Law in California," in Governor's Advisory Commission on Housing Problems, State of California, appendix to the *Report on Housing in California,* April 1963, 3.

69. Hill, "History of Housing Law," 13.

70. Ibid., 4.

71. During the war, standards for war housing were so low that, according to builder Fritz Burns, they were rejected by the public and lending institutions. Fritz Burns, "Article on New Revised War Housing Standards," ms., in file 19: 1943–1944 Speech Material, box 1, series 1, CSLA-4, Burns Collection, Special Collections, Loyola Marymount University, Los Angeles.

72. Carl F. Boester, "The Home of Tomorrow," *CSLJ,* February 1947, 5.

8. POLITICAL ECONOMY

1. Al Morch, "GOP's Ahmanson Topped Heap on 'Chicken Feed,'" *NewsLife,* August 19, 1954.

2. Jeff Crawford, "Inventory of the Goodwin J. Knight Papers," 2, Collection No. C114, CSA.

3. "Goodwin J. Knight, a Biographical Sketch," February 23, 1954, in 1954 Campaign Scrapbook, Goodwin J. Knight Papers, Special Collections, Stanford University Library.

4. Howard F. Ahmanson to Goodwin J. Knight, n.d., and Goodwin J. Knight to Howard F. Ahmanson, April 25, 1951, both in folder 201, box 30, Goodwin J. Knight Papers, Special Collections, Stanford University Library.

5. Howard F. Ahmanson to Goodwin Knight, July 3, 1951, folder 201, box 30, Goodwin J. Knight Papers, Special Collections, Stanford University Library.

6. "New Savings, Loan Head Lauds Group," *LAT*, February 28, 1953, 10.

7. Verne Scoggins to Milton O. Shaw, December 17, 1952, in folder F3640:2525, box 1 (2515–31), Earl Warren Papers: Administrative Files, Department of Investment, Building & Loan, 1949–1953, CSA.

8. "Merger Forms Huge Southland Savings-Loan," *LAT,* July 1, 1952, 16.

9. For background on the politics that led to Earl Warren's nomination to the U.S. Supreme Court, see Jim Newton, *Justice for All: Earl Warren and the Nation He Made* (New York: Riverhead Books, 2006) and Gayle B. Montgomery and James W. Johnson, *One Step from the White House: The Rise and Fall of Senator William F. Knowland* (Berkeley: University of California Press, 1998), 123.

10. Harry Farrell, *San Jose—And Other Famous Places* (San Jose, CA: San Jose Historical Museum Association, 1983), 12.

11. Knight for Governor, press release, March 22, 1954, in folder 28.47—Southern California Primary, box 28, Whitaker-Baxter Collection, CSA.

12. Quoted in Peter Lyon, *Eisenhower: Portrait of a Hero* (Boston: Little, Brown, 1974), 586, and cited in Montgomery and Johnson, *One Step,* 188.

13. Arthur Krock, "The Knight-Nixon Feud," *NYT,* August 22, 1956, 14.

14. Montgomery and Johnson, *One Step,* 162–63.

15. Clint Mosher, "Caldecott Choice of Gov. Knight for State GOP Leader," *San Francisco Examiner,* July 24, 1954. See also C. Lyn Fox, "Knight Explains Stand in GOP State Control Bill," *San Francisco Call Bulletin,* August 11, 1954.

16. "Goodwin J. Knight, 1954 Campaign Scrapbook," in Goodwin J. Knight Collection, Special Collections, Stanford University Library.

17. Jackson Doyle, "Knight and Powers Differ on GOP Post," *San Francisco Chronicle,* July 24, 1954.

18. "Skirmishes Seen in Two Party State Committees," *LAT,* July 16, 1954. See also "Knight Backs Caldecott as State GOP Head," *LAT,* July 24, 1954.

19. Earl C. Behrens, "Knowland for Caldecott as GOP Leader," *San Francisco Chronicle,* July 28, 1954.

20. Vernon O'Reilly, "Knight Takes Party Control Battle to Ike," *San Francisco News,* August 6, 1954.

21. Clint Mosher, "Knight Wins GOP Battle; Demos in Rebuff to Graves," *San Francisco Examiner,* August 9, 1954.

22. Fox, "Knight Explains Stand."

23. Mosher, "Knight Wins GOP Battle."

24. Earl C. Behrens, "Knight Ready to Forget GOP Row," *San Francisco Chronicle,* August 11, 1954.

25. Clem Whitaker and Leone Baxter to Howard Ahmanson, August 12, 1954, in folder 28.48, box 28, Whitaker-Baxter Collection, CSA.

26. "Itinerary," in folder 25.24—Governor's Itineraries, box 25, Whitaker-Baxter Collection, CSA.

27. Knight for Governor, press release, September 10, 1954, in folder 28.48, box 28, Whitaker-Baxter Collection, CSA.

28. Montgomery and Johnson, *One Step,* 164.

29. Nathan L. Fairbairn to Clem Whitaker Sr., September 16, 1954, in folder 24.15, box 24, Whitaker-Baxter Collection, CSA; Howard Ahmanson to Clem Whitaker and Leone Baxter, August 27, 1954, in folder 31.1, box 31, Whitaker-Baxter Collection, CSA.

30. Ibid.

31. "Itinerary," in folder 25.24—Governor's Itineraries, box 25, Whitaker-Baxter Collection, CSA.

32. "U.S. League Convention Events," *Savings and Loan News,* October 1954, 22–23.

33. "Howard Ahmanson—Biographical Information," in file: Howard F. Ahmanson, box: TAF History, TAFA.

34. Don Shannon, "Californians Hail GOP Choice for Convention," *LAT,* February 17, 1955, 19.

35. NAHB, *Washington Letter,* January 17, 1956, 2, NAHB Archives.

36. Press release, source unknown, March 7, 1956, in folder 398, box 56, Goodwin J. Knight Papers, Special Collections, Stanford University Library.

37. "Home Acquires Pasadena Loan," *LAT,* March 13, 1956, 22.

38. The house had been designed by Lloyd Wright, son of the architect Frank Lloyd Wright, in 1937. Seymour Freedgood et al., "Croesus at Home," first draft typescript, March 17, 1958, in FA.

39. Howard F. Ahmanson Jr. to author, e-mail, March 19, 2012. See also "Beach House History," *Newport Beach/Costa Mesa Daily Pilot,* April 24, 1995.

40. In a letter to Howard written October 21, 1943, Hegg mentions that he just bought a new sailboat: sixteen meters (fifty-eight feet long), draws eight feet, twenty thousand pounds of lead in the keel, with an eighty-foot mast, "and does she sail." Hegg was eager to enter this boat in "the Honolulu race." He mentions that the boat was getting "a complete going over." Roy E. Hegg to Howard F. Ahmanson, October 21, 1943, in FA.

41. Executives at San Diego Federal made side deals with builders that guaranteed them a share of the profits on housing developments in violation of Federal Home Loan Bank regulations that barred lenders from having an interest in a construction company. After he was indicted, Hegg resigned as president and chairman of the company. "Attorney Faces Housing Charges at San Diego," *LAT,* June 24, 1952, 19. See also "Deal for $111,000 Profit Cited in Housing Inquiry," *LAT,* December 5, 1951, A11.

42. The conspirators bribed VA appraisers, bought loan qualifying certificates from veterans, and then used them fraudulently to help nonveteran borrowers get GI loans. "Chairman Resigns," *LAT,* March 4, 1953, 18.

43. William P. Ficker, interview by Howard F. Ahmanson Jr., Frank Trane, and Steven Ferguson, August 24, 2009, in FA.

44. Bob Ruskauff, "Compete Today on Newport Bay," *LAT,* April 14, 1956, pt. III-3. See also "Boats Will Sail Today in Pt. Fermin Regatta," *LAT,* April 15, 1956, pt. II-2.

45. Miscellaneous notes in "Stories of HFA" file, TAFA.

46. Seymour Freedgood, "Emperor Howard Ahmanson of S&L.," *Fortune,* May 1958, 148–152.

47. Howard F. Ahmanson to Lawrence Cooper, May 14, 1956, in HFA files, LH files, FA.

48. Peg Childs to Howard Ahmanson, January 27, 1957, in LH files, HFA Correspondence, FA.

49. Alphonzo Bell with Mark L. Webert, *The Bel Air Kid: An Autobiography of a Life in California* (Victoria, Canada: Trafford, 2002), 82–83; Sydney Kossen, "Labor behind Knight's Dim View of Nixon," *San Francisco News,* August 6, 1956.

50. Correspondence in folder 404, box 57, series 1—Correspondence, Goodwin J. Knight Papers, Special Collections, Stanford University Library.

51. Krock, "Knight-Nixon Feud," 14.

52. Montgomery and Johnson, *One Step,* 228–30.

53. Ibid., 235.

54. Carl Greenberg, "Knight Gains Ex-Backers of Knowland; Will Crossfile," *Los Angeles Examiner,* August 21, 1957, n.p. Clipping in FA.

55. Goodwin Knight to Howard and Dorothy Ahmanson, October 2, 1957, in FA.

56. Quoted in Montgomery and Johnson, *One Step,* 239.

57. Ethan Rarick, *California Rising: The Life and Times of Pat Brown* (Berkeley: University of California Press, 2005), 93–97; and Montgomery and Johnson, *One Step,* 238–43.

58. Rarick, *California Rising,* 106–10.

59. "Howard F. Ahmanson," *Finance,* February 1966, 21.

60. Freedgood et al., "Croesus at Home."

61. Freedgood, "Emperor Howard Ahmanson," 149.

9. BIG BUSINESS

1. Milton O. Shaw to J. Alston Adams, April 26, 1955, in box 7, Correspondence of Chairman Robertson, Records of the Federal Home Loan Bank, RG 195, NARA-CP.

2. "California Savings and Loan Associations, Assets as of June 30, 1955," *CSLJ,* September 1955, 42–43.

3. J. Alston Adams to Walter W. McAllister, May 12, 1955, with attachments, in box 7, Correspondence of Chairman Robertson, Records of the Federal Home Loan Bank, RG 195, NARA-CP.

4. Walter W. McAllister to J. Alston Adams, May 23, 1955, in box 7, Correspondence of Chairman Robertson, Records of the Federal Home Loan Bank, RG 195, NARA-CP.

5. Charles Wellman to Walter W. McAllister, June 20, 1955, in box 7, Correspondence of Chairman Robertson, Records of the Federal Home Loan Bank, RG 195, NARA-CP.

6. Estes Kefauver to Walter W. McAllister, November 17, 1956, in box 7, Correspondence of Chairman Robertson, Records of the Federal Home Loan Bank, RG 195, NARA-CP.

7. State-chartered thrifts had rushed to convert to federal charters in the New Deal years, but federal thrifts were required to be mutuals. By the 1950s, as entrepreneurs realized how profitable thrifts could be, many managers of federal thrifts sought to convert back to state charters and then transform themselves from mutuals to guaranteed stock companies. Milton O. Shaw to A. C. Newell, August 9, 1955, in box 7, Correspondence of Chairman Robertson, Records of the Federal Home Loan Bank, RG 195, NARA-CP.

8. The meaning of the "moratorium" is a little unclear. According to the 1956 annual report of the California Division of Savings and Loan, the state licensed ten new associations in 1956 and approved thirty new branches statewide, including several in Los Angeles and Orange Counties. California, Division of Savings and Loan, *Sixty-Third Annual Report* (Sacramento: State of California, 1957), 8–9.

9. The moratorium is referred to extensively in the papers of Albert Robertson. Curiously, it is not mentioned in the annual reports of the California Division of Savings and Loan for 1955 and 1956. Albert J. Robertson to Estes Kefauver, December 28, 1956, in box 7, Correspondence of Chairman Robertson, Records of the Federal Home Loan Bank, RG 195, NARA-CP.

10. Percentage calculated using figures reported in the annual reports of the California Division of Savings and Loan. In February 1957, the *LAT* reported that the company's loan portfolio had increased 36.7 percent in 1956. "Home Savings Loans Up 36.7%," *LAT,* February 10, 1957, A17.

11. California, Division of Savings and Loan, *Sixty-Third Annual Report,* 1957, 6–7, 50; California, Division of Savings and Loan, *Sixty-Second Annual Report* (Sacramento: State of California, 1956), 50.

12. Milton O. Shaw to Albert J. Robertson, December 5, 1956, in box 7, Correspondence of Chairman Robertson, Records of the Federal Home Loan Bank, RG 195, NARA-CP.

13. Ibid.

14. David Rees, "Gold Rush On for S&L Offices," *Los Angeles Mirror-News,* January 31, 1957, n.p., in box 7, Correspondence of Chairman Robertson, Records of the Federal Home Loan Bank, RG 195, NARA-CP.

15. Keystone S&L (Anaheim), Lifetime S&L (Granada Hills), Baldwin Park S&L (Baldwin Park), Harbor S&L (Redondo Beach), Sherman Oaks S&L (Los Angeles), Victory S&L (Los Angeles). California, Division of Savings and Loan, *Sixty-Fourth Annual Report* (Sacramento: State of California, 1958), 7, 21–22.

16. Ibid.

17. "Home Savings Gets Approval for New Offices," *Los Angeles Herald Express,* March 15, 1957, clipping in Home Clippings File, January–March 1957, FA.

18. California, Division of Savings and Loan, *Sixty-Fourth Annual Report,* 7, 21–22.

19. California, Division of Savings and Loan, *Sixty-Third Annual Report,* 5, 57.

20. "Stock Offering Is Filed," *NYT,* August 2, 1955, 33. See also *House and Home,* March 1956, 74–75, cited in James Gillies and Frank G. Mittelbach, *Mergers of Savings and Loan Associations in California,* Research Report no. 1, Real Estate Research Program, Division of Research (Los Angeles: Graduate School of Business Administration, University of California, Los Angeles, 1959), 26.

21. "Savings, Loan Firm of L.A. Drops S.F. Bid," *San Francisco Call-Bulletin,* January 25, 1956, 39.

22. Guaranty was an attractive target because the thrift had made loans in fifty-four counties in California before laws had been passed restricting the geographic territory of state savings and loans. Seymour Freedgood et al., "Croesus at Home," first draft typescript, March 17, 1958, in FA. In 1958, Ahmanson sold his substantial interest in Guaranty Savings and Loan Association of San Jose to Great Western. "California Savings, Loan Sold," *NYT,* October 30, 1958, 45.

23. John Lawrence, "The Master Builders of Savings & Loan," *Los Angeles West Magazine,* June 15, 1969, 10. American became the fifth-largest thrift in the country when it merged with Inter-Valley Savings and Loan the following year. Gillies and Mittelbach, *Mergers of Savings and Loan Associations,* 26.

24. Alfred J. Schneider, "Svgs.-Loan Merger Protested," *San Francisco Examiner,* December 29, 1955, clipping in Home Clippings File, 1955, FA. See also California, Division of Savings and Loan, *Sixty-First Annual Report* (Sacramento: State of California, 1955), 22.

25. "Saving-Loan Unit Urges Home Rule," *NYT,* January 26, 1956, 41.

26. The FHLBB apparently had some concerns about this issue. After learning that Ahmanson had agreed to withdraw his application, Chairman Walter McAllister, wrote Howard: "I personally appreciate very much your graciousness and cooperation under the circumstances." He did not elaborate on how he viewed the circumstances. Walter W. McAllister to Howard Ahmanson, January 10, 1956, in file: "A," box 1, Records of the Office of the Chairman of the Federal Home Loan Bank Board, Correspondence of Chairman Walter W. McAllister, 1952–56, RG 195, NARA-CP. See also "Savings, Loan Firm of L.A. Drops S.F. Bid."

27. Walter W. McAllister to Milton O. Shaw, January 5, 1956, in folder: California, State of—1953, box 5, Correspondence of Chairman Walter W. McAllister, 1952–1956, RG 195, NARA-CP.

28. Sarkis J. Khoury, *The Deregulation of the World Financial Markets: Myths, Realities, and Impact* (New York: Quorum Books, 1990), 69.

29. "Bill to Regulate Savings-Loan Holding Units," *LAT,* March 22, 1957, C8.

10. THE CREST OF A NEW WAVE

1. Howard Edgerton to Howard F. Ahmanson, July 1, 1957, in HFA files, in LH files, FA.

2. Kim Fletcher, interview by author, December 8, 2009.

3. "Home Savings & Loan Largest in Nation," *LAT,* February 24, 1959, G7.

4. "U.S. League Convention Events," *Savings and Loan News,* October 1954, 22–23.

5. Howard Edgerton, interview by Marc Nurre, September 7, 1993, notes, in FA.

6. Kim Fletcher, interview by author, December 8, 2009.

7. "Prosperous Omaha Should Turn to Culture—Ahmanson," *[Omaha World-Herald],* February 11, 1961, n.p., clipping from Mary Jane Bettefreund.

8. U.S. Supreme Court, *United States v. South-Eastern Underwriters,* 322 U.S. 533 (1944).

9. California Legislature, "A Preliminary Report on Alleged Coercive Insurance Practices," Assembly of the State of California, 1950, 15–16.

10. Ibid., 42.

11. M. F. Small to Clark F. Waite, November 3, 1949, in box 1 (2515–31), folder F3640:2525, Earl Warren Papers, Administrative Files, Department of Investment, Building and Loan, 1949–1953, CSA.

12. California Legislature, "Preliminary Report," 5.

13. Ibid., 17.

14. Ibid., 36.

15. Ibid., 60–61.

16. Rex W. Hendrix, "Revolutionary Changes in Insurance Regulations," *CSLJ,* June 1948, 19.

17. At the end of 1949, the company became the Southern California agent for Pacific National Fire Insurance Company, based in San Francisco (owned by Transamerica). With the addition of Pacific National, H. F. Ahmanson's combined underwriting facilities swelled to more than three hundred million dollars. "Ahmanson and Co. Expands Insurance Facilities," *CSLJ,* February 1950, 16.

18. Roger Lowenstein, *Buffett: The Making of an American Capitalist* (New York: Broadway Books, 1995), 49.

19. Lowenstein tells this story without putting a specific date on it, though it's set in the context of the narrative in 1957 or 1958. Lowenstein says the Ahmansons were offering $50 a share for National American Fire Insurance. Lowenstein, *Buffett,* 65. See also Warren Buffett, interview by author, December 9, 2010.

20. Warren Buffett, interview by author, December 9, 2010.

21. Alice Schroeder, *The Snowball: Warren Buffett and the Business of Life* (New York: Bantam Books, 2008), 211.

22. Warren Buffett, interview by author, December 9, 2010.

23. Lowenstein, *Buffett,* 65.

24. Ibid., 58–59.

25. Warren Buffett, interview by author, December 9, 2010. See also Lowenstein, *Buffett,* 65.

26. Lowenstein, *Buffett,* 65. See also Schroeder, *Snowball,* 210–12. Schroeder points out that "under the Williams Act, passed in 1968, one could not do this today, nor could Howard Ahmanson buy back the stock piecemeal. The act requires buyers to make a 'tender offer' that puts all sellers on a level playing field under the same price and terms" (861 n. 27).

27. Warren Buffett, interview by author, December 9, 2010.

28. Ibid.

29. Howard was negotiating with Jack M. Kaplan in March 1959. The negotiations began with Kaplan claiming that Howard had "absconded with five or six million dollars." The conversation improved and Kaplan asked Ahmanson to help him buy a savings and loan. See Howard Ahmanson to Hayden Ahmanson, March 13, 1959, in file: Howard F. Ahmanson Sr., box: TAF History, TAFA.

30. Lowenstein, *Buffett,* 65.

31. David Rees, "More on Plans of Financier Ahmanson," *Los Angeles Mirror-News,* January 24, 1957, pt. 3, 5.

32. Alfred M. Best Company, *Best's Insurance Reports—Fire and Casualty* (New York: Alfred M. Best Company, 1957), 698.

33. Seymour Freedgood, "Emperor Howard Ahmanson of S&L," *Fortune,* May 1958, 150.

34. "One Firm to Handle Cal Vet Insurance," no source, December 3, 1960, clipping in file: "Articles and Abstracts," folder "Articles," LH files, FA.

35. Robert DeKruif, interview by Margaret Bach, [1992], in TAFA.

36. Ahmanson Bank and Trust Company display advertisement, *LAT,* January 1, 1960, 20.

37. Robert DeKruif, interview by Margaret Bach, [1992], in TAFA. Actually, Ahmanson realized, Home did well in financial services that related to the process of buying a home, so in 1958 he launched Southern Counties Title Company. Three years later, he diversified the insurance business by creating National American Life Insurance Company of California. This business specialized in selling mortgage term life insurance to customers of savings and loans and mortgage bankers. Chris Bone, "A Chronology of Home Savings of America, F.A., the First 100 Years—1889 to 1989," [1989], JPMCA.

38. John Notter, interview by author, August 20, 2009.

39. Cover, *Business Week,* July 1, 1961.

40. "Richest of the Rich S&Ls," *Business Week,* July 1, 1961, 80.

41. "Home Savings and Loan Celebrates," *CSLJ,* January 1962, n.p.

42. "Howard Ahmanson,". notes compiled in file: Howard F. Ahmanson Sr., box: TAF History, TAFA.

11. SOUTHLAND PATRICIAN

1. Millard Sheets, interview by George M. Goodwin, in "Los Angeles Art Community: Group Portrait," by UCLA Oral History Program, 1977, copy in folder: Howard F. Ahmanson Sr., box: The Ahmanson Foundation, TAFA.

2. Robert DeKruif mentions that Ahmanson and Sheets both attended a Friday morning breakfast club (the Economic Round Table) and had gotten to know each other a little this way, though the timing is unclear. Robert DeKruif, interview by Margaret Bach, [1992], in TAFA.

3. Carolyn Sheets Owen-Toole, *Damngorgeous: A Daughter's Memoir of Millard Owen Sheets* (Oceanside, CA: Oceanside Museum of Art, 2008), 95.

4. Millard Sheets, interview by George Goodwin, 1977, in TAFA.

5. Christy Fox, "Face-Lift for Beverly Club," *LAT,* June 11, 1972, E3.

6. Patricia K. Craig, "A Finding Aid to the Millard Sheets Papers, 1907–1990," in AAA.

7. "Office Building Project Is Set," *LAT,* January 10, 1954, clipping in Home Clippings File, 1954, FA.

8. "Home Savings Name Millard Sheets to Design New Bldg.," *Los Angeles Herald Express,* January 5, 1954, clipping in Home Clippings File, 1954, FA.

9. "Office Building Project Is Set," F2.

10. Millard Sheets, interview by George Goodwin, 1977, in TAFA.

11. Jarvis Barlow, "Art Matters," *LAT,* undated clipping [1954], in FA. For information on Barlow, see "Jarvis Barlow Institute Aide," *LAT,* July 24, 2954, 16.

12. Millard Sheets, interview by George Goodwin, 1977, 384, in TAFA.

13. Chris Bone, "A Chronology of Home Savings of America, F.A., the First 100 Years—1889 to 1989," [1989], JPMCA.

14. "Home Savings New Beverly Hills Bldg. under Construction," *Los Angeles Herald & Express,* October 27, 1954, clipping in Home Clippings File, 1954, FA.

15. "New $2,000,000 Savings Loan Unit Completed," *LAT,* March 4, 1956, F21.

16. Millard Sheets, interview by George Goodwin, 1977, 385, in TAFA.

17. Jarvis Barlow, "Art Matters," *Pasadena Independent,* April 10, 1955, clipping in Home Clippings File, 1955, FA.

18. "Family Group Statues Adorn Wilshire Blvd.," *Los Angeles Herald-Express,* February 24, 1956, clipping in Home Clippings File, 1956, FA.

19. Home Savings & Loan brochure, Beverly Hills Branch, on reel 5692, in Millard Sheets Papers, AAA.

20. "Home Savings & Loan Dedication," *Los Angeles Building News,* April 5, 1956, clipping in Home Clippings File, 1956, FA.

21. Home Savings & Loan brochure, Beverly Hills Branch.

22. "News, Views of Art," *LAT,* November 18, 1956, clipping in Home Clippings File, 1956, FA.

23. Several of the artists who worked with Sheets on this first Home Savings project became part of a studio group that continued to work on Home Savings and other commercial building projects. See Adam Arenson, "Marketing Banks by Telling History: Howard Ahmanson, Millard Sheets, and the Art and Architecture of Home Savings Banks," paper presented at the 2011 Business History Conference, St. Louis, MO. See also "'New Look' Boom in Stained Glass," *North Hollywood Valley Times,* November 6, 1956; "New Edifice Hailed for Decorative Features," *LAT,* February 26, 1956, clippings in Home Clippings, file 1956, FA.

24. Home Savings & Loan brochure, Beverly Hills Branch.

25. Ibid.

26. Howard F. Ahmanson to Lawrence Cooper, May 14, 1956, in HFA files, LH files, FA.

27. "600 Workers Guests at Home Savings Fete," *Los Angeles Examiner,* March 15, 1956, clipping in Home Clippings File, 1956, FA.

28. The builders included Adrian Wilber of McDonald Brothers, Walter Bollenbacher, Louis Kelton, Don Metz of Aldon Construction Co. (eighth in the country), Max Levine of Midwood Homes (rated twelfth), Don Wilson of Kauffman-Wilson (rated fourth), and Richard Diller (rated seventh). Photo caption, *Los Angeles Mirror and Daily News,* March 16, 1956, clipping in Home Clippings File, 1956, FA.

29. Display advertisement, *LAT,* March 9, 1956, B9.

30. Millard Sheets, interview by George Goodwin, 386, in TAFA.

31. "Howard Ahmanson," *Valuator,* fall 1966, 12, clipping in FA.

32. "New Outside for Building," *Long Beach Independent Press Telegram,* March 15, 1957, clipping in Home Clippings File, January–March 1957, FA.

33. Millard Sheets, interview by George Goodwin, 388.

34. Ibid.

35. Ibid.

36. Millard Sheets, "Art Must Serve Two Masters," *LAT,* September 4, 1955, C5.

37. Howard Ahmanson to Millard Sheets, October 8, 1960, on reel 5676, in Millard Sheets Papers, AAA.

38. "Ex-Omahan Is a Giant in the Loan Industry," *Omaha World-Herald,* June 6, 1965, n.p.

39. Arthur Millier, "Painting-by-Numbers Craze Sweeps Hobby-Happy America," *LAT,* April 4, 1954, D7.

40. Howard F. Ahmanson Jr., interview by author, December 15, 2010.

41. Howard Ahmanson to Millard Sheets, October 8, 1960.

42. "Art Institute Board Shifted," *LAT,* January 1, 1947, A2.

43. "County Art Institute Advisory Board Named," *LAT,* January 24, 1947, A3.

44. Suzanne Muchnic, "Art; Pay Attention, Class; Otis Chief Samuel Hoi Has Big Ideas for the Reinvigorated Art School," *LAT,* September 23, 2001, F4.

45. Robert Irwin, interview by Frederick S. Wight, UCLA Oral History Program, 1977, 7–9, in Department of Special Collections, Charles E. Young Research Library, UCLA.

46. Arthur Millier, "Plan to Move Art Shows Climaxes Row at Museum," *LAT,* June 1, 1947, C1.

47. "Art Tempest Brings Shift," *LAT,* May 28, 1947, A1.

48. "Los Angeles Art History: A Timeline," *Los Angeles Times,* October 26, 2008.

49. Millard Sheets, interviews by Paul Karlstrom, October 1986–July 1988, in AAA.

50. Ibid.

51. "Millard Sheets Named Art Institute Director," *LAT,* August 20, 1953, A1.

52. Millard Sheets to John Anson Ford, August 25, 1953, in box 38 / B III 9 a cc (8), John Anson Ford Papers, Huntington Library, San Marino, CA.

53. New faculty recruited by Sheets included ceramicist Peter Voulkos, who inspired a generation of artists in the Los Angeles area. See Andrew J. Perchuk, "From Otis to Ferus: Robert Irwin, Ed Ruscha, and Peter Voulkos in Los Angeles, 1954–1975" (PhD diss., Yale University, 2006), 51 and 169.

54. "Millard Sheets Named Art Institute Director."

55. "Accreditation Granted to County Art Institute," *LAT,* April 2, 1956, 5.

56. Sheets, "Art Must Serve Two Masters."

57. "Rediscovery of World of Mind Urged," *LAT,* April 21, 1956, A1.

58. Ibid.

59. Arthur Millier, "Institute Making Impressive Gains," *LAT,* July 25, 1954, D7.

60. Margaret Bach, "The Ahmanson Foundation," June 1993, 16. TAFA.

61. Norma H. Goodhue, "Mrs. Chandler Tells of Life in Russia," *LAT,* December 16, 1955, B1.

62. Robert Wernick, "Wars of the Instant Medicis," *LIFE,* October 26, 1966, 102.

63. Perchuk, "From Otis to Ferus," 9.

64. Richard Brown, "The Art Division," photocopy from LACMA, no source, 14. See also "Exposition Park Called Plague Spot Years Ago," *LAT,* October 23, 1955, A2.

65. The donors were Mr. and Mrs. William Preston Harrison.

66. Brown, "Art Division," 17.

67. Arthur Millier, "L.A. Museum Future Aired," *LAT,* April 3, 1955, E6.

68. Caroline E. Liebig, "The Past Twenty Years," unpublished manuscript, library of the Los Angeles County Museum of Art, n.d., 10; Norris Leap, "Curator's Love of Art Began at Age of 3," *LAT,* August 19, 1958, A1. See also Wernick, "Wars of the Instant Medicis," 105; and Kevin Starr, *Golden Dreams: California in an Age of Abundance, 1950–1963* (New York: Oxford University Press, 2009), 164.

69. Wernick, "Wars of the Instant Medicis," 105.

70. Suzanne Muchnic, *Odd Man In: Norton Simon and the Pursuit of Culture* (Berkeley: University of California Press, 1998), 51–53.

71. Ibid., 48–51.

72. "Board Delays Action on New Art Museum," *LAT,* April 2, 1958, 2.

73. "$1,000,000 Gift Planned for Museum," *LAT,* April 16, 1958, B1.

74. Museum Associates, Board Minutes, September 16, 1958. Photocopy provided by TAFA.

75. Ibid.

76. Ahmanson's legal team cited a law passed in the mid-1950s that allowed the San Francisco Board of Supervisors to contract with a donor of a building to entrust its administration to a special, nonappointed body. This model would allow Museum Associates to oversee the day-to-day management of the building. Ibid.

77. Ibid.

78. Ibid.

79. Several sources make reference to this point, but no one elaborates. Given Ahmanson's tendency to do favors for state and federal regulators in the savings and loan business, it wouldn't be surprising if he or Home had done the same for the County of Los Angeles. It's also unclear as to whether these sources are suggesting that some of the supervisors were personally in debt to Ahmanson for some reason.

80. Muchnic, *Odd Man In,* 53. See also "He Gives $2 Million for New Gallery," *Los Angeles Examiner,* December 9, 1958, n.p., clipping in FA.

81. Ahmanson proposed a complicated structure for his gift. The funds would be provided as a loan extended by one of Ahmanson's corporate entities. Ahmanson would then make seven annual gifts of stock in the company, which would eventually equal about four-fifths of the equity in the business. "Excerpts from Meeting of Museum Associates, September 16, 1958," in file: LACMA, box: TAF History, TAFA. See also "County Receives Offer of Gallery of Fine Arts," *LAT,* December 3, 1958, 5.

82. "Ahmansons Identified as Art Museum Donors," *Los Angeles Evening Mirror News,* December 9, 1958, n.p., clipping in FA. See also Suzanne Muchnic, "A Little Historical Context Please: It's Never Been Easy," *LAT,* October 3, 1993, calendar section, 7.

83. Wernick, "Wars of the Instant Medicis," 106.

84. Museum Associates, Board Minutes, November 18, 1958, [2].

85. Months after the announcement of Ahmanson's gift, the *Los Angeles Times* was still reporting Simon's gift as one million dollars. See, for example, "Fund 80% Raised for Art Museum," *LAT,* April 15, 1959, B1. For information on Simon's decision to reduce his gift, see Muchnic, *Odd Man In,* 53.

86. "County: Work May Start by Year's End," *Los Angeles Examiner,* April 15, 1959.

87. "Name for Museum Rends Art Circles," *Los Angeles Examiner,* March 1, 1960, 12.

88. Muchnic, *Odd Man In,* 53.

89. This article pointed out that the Fine Arts Museums of San Francisco included the De Young Museum, which had been named for a generous donor. "Park Museum Named Ahmanson Gallery," [no publication identified], March 2, 1960, n.p., clipping in FA. See also "Ahmanson Chosen as Museum Name," *Los Angeles Evening Herald Express,* March 2, 1960, n.p., clipping in FA. On Bright, see "Row Flares on Naming of Museum," [no publication identified], March 3, 1960, n.p., clipping in FA. Meanwhile, the concept for the museum expanded to include two additional buildings, each to be named for a major donor who would contribute at least half of the cost of the building, although the board also considered naming one of the buildings after Captain George Allan Hancock, who had donated the land. Museum Associates, Board Minutes, March 8, 1960, 2–3.

90. Muchnic, *Odd Man In,* 54.

91. "Gallery Name," no publication, March 3, 1960, n.p., clipping in FA.

92. "Giving Money Away," *Newsweek,* March 21, 1960, n.p., clipping in TAFA.

93. Harold Tucker, "Outlook Profile: It's Not All Finance with L.A. Financier," *LAT,* June 11, 1961, J1.

94. Photograph and caption, clipped from *Los Angeles Herald Examiner,* May 29, 1966, n.p.

95. Los Angeles was full of dubious old masters in the 1950s, some of which were in the collections of the County Museum. Often a masterpiece attributed to Rubens or some other old master was in fact done by "the workshop of" or "the school of" the artist. Or in Ahmanson's case, a painting attributed to Breughel was actually done by the master's son. For background on art collecting in Los Angeles, see Winifred Haines Higgins, "Art Collecting in the Los Angeles Area, 1910–1960" (PhD diss., University of California, Los Angeles, 1963), 440–42. On Breughel, see Howard F. Ahmanson Jr., interview by author, December 15, 2010. After Ahmanson's death, Franklin Murphy persuaded the board of the Ahmanson Foundation to help finance the acquisition of "absolutely first-grade works of art that will honor the Ahmanson name and erase forever this blemish that had spread upon him." Franklin D. Murphy, interview by Margaret Bach, November 16, 1992, in TAFA.

96. Starr, *Golden Dreams,* 165.

97. John Dreyfuss, "New LACMA Building: Orchid or Daisy," *LAT,* August 17, 1979, IV:19.

98. Ibid.

99. Franklin D. Murphy, interview by Margaret Bach, November 16, 1992, 14, in TAFA.

100. Ahmanson had also been given veto power over the location and the builder. "Excerpts from meeting of Museum Associates, September 16, 1958," in file: LACMA, box: TAF History, TAFA. See also Dreyfuss, "New LACMA Building."

101. Allen Temko, quoted in Scott Johnson, "William Pereira," Forum Issue 7, January 7, 2010, Los Angeles Forum for Architecture and Urban Design, www .laforum.org/content/online-articles/william-pereira-by-scott-johnson. For more on Pereira, see James Steele, ed., *William Pereira* (Los Angeles: Architectural Guild Press, 2002).

102. Starr, *Golden Dreams,* 164.

103. Richard F. Brown, "Progress Report on the Los Angeles County Museum of Art," *Quarterly of the Los Angeles County Museum,* Summer 1961, 7. LACMA's trustees apparently approved the award on February 16, 1960. Dreyfuss, "New LACMA Building."

104. "Art Leaders Appointed to Museum Associates," *Quarterly of the Los Angeles County Museum,* summer 1960, 44–45. Ric Brown, Vincent Price, and Mrs. Stuart E. Weaver Jr. were also added at this time. Museum Associates, Board Minutes, March 8, 1960, 3.

105. Museum Associates, Board Minutes, January 17, 1961, 2.

106. Wernick, "Wars of the Instant Medicis," 107.

107. Robert Wiebe, *Businessmen and Reform: A Study of the Progressive Movement* (Chicago: Quadrangle Books, 1968), 223–24.

108. Ibid.

12. INFLUENCE

1. Mackin coordinated Brown's campaigns for state attorney general and became one of Brown's top deputies after the first victory in 1946. After he was elected governor in 1958, Brown named Mackin commissioner of savings and loans. "Municipal Judge Named to Fill Court Vacancy," *LAT,* December 30, 1960, B12.

2. Fred Dutton to Warren M. Christopher, January 21, 1959. See also Hale Champion to Warren M. Christopher, May 30, 1959. Both in file: Savings & Loans, Sept–Dec., 1959, carton 321—Investment, Department of, Edmund G. Brown Papers, BL.

3. Warren M. Christopher to Fred Dutton, January 26, 1959, in file: Savings & Loans, Sept–Dec., 1959, carton 321—Investment, Department of, Edmund G. Brown Papers, BL.

4. Edmund G. Brown to Clair Engle, August 29, 1959, in file: Savings & Loans, Sept–Dec., 1959, carton 321—Investment, Department of, Edmund G. Brown Papers, BL.

5. Edmund G. Brown to Clair Engle, September 4, 1959, in file: Savings & Loans, Sept–Dec., 1959, carton 321—Investment, Department of, Edmund G. Brown Papers, BL.

6. In his testimony before the Senate, Charles Hughes argued that holding companies offered an important path for smaller, local entities to raise the capital needed to compete against the dominant players in the savings and loan industry in Los Angeles, including Home Savings, California Federal, Coast Federal, and Glendale Federal Savings and Loan. Charles M. Hughes to Edmund G. Brown, August 28, 1959, in file: Savings & Loans, Sept–Dec., 1959, carton 321—Investment, Department of, Edmund G. Brown Papers, BL. For Pauley's relationship to Brown, see

Ethan Rarick, *California Rising: The Life and Times of Pat Brown* (Berkeley: University of California Press, 2005), 46–47, 93–95.

7. Rarick, *California Rising,* 115.

8. Edmund G. Brown to Frank Mackin and Helen Nelson, October 13, 1959, in file: Savings & Loans, Sept–Dec., 1959, carton 321—Investment, Department of, Edmund G. Brown Papers, BL.

9. Frederick G. Dutton to Frank J. Mackin, August 26, 1959, in file: Savings & Loans, Sept–Dec., 1959, carton 321—Investment, Department of, Edmund G. Brown Papers, BL.

10. James Allen Smith, *The Idea Brokers: Think Tanks and the Rise of the New Policy Elite* (New York: Free Press, 1991), 113–21.

11. "Stanford Research Institute Worked on 30 Programs in 1958," *LAT,* February 9, 1959, B3.

12. Los Angeles County alone was home to more than a third of all associations and 65 percent of assets. C. Joseph Clawson et al., *The Savings and Loan Industry in California* (South Pasadena, CA: Stanford Research Institute, 1960), II-2–3.

13. Ibid., II-6.

14. Some California thrifts actively solicited deposits by investors in other parts of the country and hired brokers to pursue these investors. According to SRI, "broker savings" in California thrifts accounted for about 6 percent of all assets. Ibid., II-12.

15. Curiously, federally chartered associations "showed no consistent relationship" between their size and relative efficiency. Ibid., II-6–7.

16. Ibid., VI-4.

17. Ibid., II-8.

18. "15 Named to State Museum Committee," *Los Angeles Mirror News,* May 18, 1956.

19. University of Southern California, "The Story of the California Museum of Science and Industry," n.d., www.usc.edu/CSSF/History/CMSI_History.html (accessed October 31, 2010).

20. Bill Boyarsky, *Big Daddy: Jesse Unruh and the Art of Power Politics* (Berkeley: University of California Press, 2008), 54.

21. Lou Cannon, *Ronnie and Jesse: A Political Odyssey* (New York: Doubleday, 1969), 9–13, 20–26, 58–67.

22. Boyarsky, *Big Daddy,* 72–73.

23. Cannon, *Ronnie and Jesse,* 98.

24. Thomas M. Rees, oral history interview by Carlos Vasquez, December 9 and 11, 1987, Oral History Program, University of California, Los Angeles, 239–40, in Department of Special Collections, Charles E. Young Research Library, UCLA.

25. Jesse M. Unruh, "California's Fiscal and Legislative Future," *CSLJ,* November 1961, 21.

26. Cannon, *Ronnie and Jesse,* 99.

27. Boyarsky, *Big Daddy,* 84.

28. For example, Ahmanson connected Unruh to the Chandlers and the Carters. Thomas M. Rees, interview by Carlos Vasquez, December 9 and 11, 1987, 242, in Department of Special Collections, Charles E. Young Research Library, UCLA.

29. Ibid.

30. Several authors have searched for the source for this quote famously attributed to Unruh, but none have been successful. For a discussion, see Jackson K. Putnam, *Jess: The Political Career of Jesse Marvin Unruh* (Lanham, MD: University Press of America, 2005), 21.

31. Lou Cannon, interview by author, March 3, 2011.

32. Harry Farrell, "Political 'Angel' Plays Dual Role," *San Jose Evening News,* May 16, 1963, 1.

33. To open the commissioner's position, Brown appointed Mackin to a municipal judgeship. "Municipal Judge-Named," B12.

34. California, Division of Savings and Loan, *Sixty-Ninth Annual Report* (Sacramento: California State Printing Office, 1963), 17. See also "Municipal Judge Named."

35. California, Division of Savings and Loan, *Sixty-Ninth Annual Report,* 10.

36. Preston N. Silbaugh, "Supervision, Safety and Sustained Growth," *CSLJ* 35, no. 11 (November 1962): n.p.

37. James Bassett, "Nixon-Knight Feud Born of Old Rivalry," *LAT,* November 5, 1961, G2.

38. Gladwin Hill, "Coast G.O.P. Fight Could Be Costly," October 8, 1941, 58.

39. Rarick, *California Rising,* 230; see also 427 n. 3.

40. James Bassett, "Nixon Will Tell Plans in 60 Days," *LAT,* July 12, 1961, 1.

41. James Bassett, "Nixon Firmly Refuses to Declare Himself Now," *LAT,* July 14, 1961, B4.

42. "Goodwin Knight," *LAT,* September 12, 1961, 13.

43. "Nixon View," *LAT,* September 13, 1961, 25.

44. James Bassett, "Brown and Knight Ask Equal Time with Nixon," *LAT,* September 25, 1961, 1.

45. Drew Pearson, "Press Balked at Nixon's Demand," *Washington Post-Times Herald,* October 29, 1961, E5.

46. Seymour Korman, "Knight Names Banker as Nixon 'Voice,'" *Chicago Daily Tribune,* October 5, 1961, 3.

47. "California Imbroglio," *Washington Post–Times Herald,* October 6, 1961, A16.

48. Richard Bergholz, "Knight to Stay Clear of GOP Endorsement," *LAT,* January 18, 1962, 2.

49. Carey McWilliams, "Has Success Spoiled Dick Nixon?" *Nation,* June 2, 1962, 491.

50. Ibid.

51. Ibid.

52. Rarick, *California Rising,* 246.

53. Edmund G. "Pat" Brown, "Second Inaugural Address," January 7, 1963, http://governors.library.ca.gov/addresses/32-Pbrown02.html.

54. Edward S. Shaw, *Savings and Loan Market Structure: A Study of California State-Licensed Savings and Loan Associations* ([Sacramento]: California Savings and Loan Commissioner, 1962).

55. Ibid.

56. Jack Searles, "S&L's," *LAT,* February 20, 1963, C8.

57. Jerry Gillam, "S&Ls Win Round in Shaw Dispute," *LAT,* February 20, 1963, C8.

58. Jack Searles, "Key to S&L Dispute: The Role of the Commissioner," *LAT,* February 24, 1963, M1.

59. The political power of the growing consumer movement became especially apparent in Washington in the late 1960s. David Vogel suggests that a "decline in the relative political influence of business" began in 1966 with the passage of new federal laws regulating corporate social conduct. These new laws undermined the concept of the managed economy, or what Vogel calls "creative federalism," and tended to increase the power of both business and government. David Vogel, *Fluctuating Fortunes: The Political Power of Business in America* (New York: Basic Books, 1989), 37–58.

60. "Leo Grebler, 90, Dies; Authority on Land Use," *NYT,* April 5, 1991.

61. Leo Grebler and Eugene F. Brigham, *Savings and Mortgage Markets in California* (Pasadena: California Savings and Loan League, 1963), 8.

62. Ibid., 9.

63. Ibid., 13.

64. Ibid., 181.

65. Ibid., 14.

13. SHORT OF DOMESTIC BLISS

1. Norris Leap, "H.F. Ahmanson, 'Spoiled Boy,' Becomes Financial Genius," *LAT,* December 28, 1958, pt. IV, 1.

2. Seymour Freedgood, "Emperor Howard Ahmanson of S&L," *Fortune,* May 1958.

3. Howard F. Ahmanson Jr., interview by author, December 15, 2010.

4. Ahmanson's property near San Bernardino was bounded by Barton, Waterman, Hunt and the railroad, just north of Montecito Memorial Park cemetery. Ibid.

5. [Dorothy Grannis Ahmanson], [unsourced notes for introduction of Howard Fieldstad Ahmanson], March 22, 1954, in FA.

6. Leap, "H.F. Ahmanson."

7. Ibid.

8. Howard F. Ahmanson Jr., interview by author, December 15, 2010.

9. Leap, "H.F. Ahmanson."

10. Howard F. Ahmanson to Hayden Ahmanson, March 13, 1959, in FA.

11. [Dorothy Grannis Ahmanson], [unsourced notes for introduction of Howard Fieldstad Ahmanson], March 22, 1954, in FA.

12. Howard F. Ahmanson to A. J. McIntyre, March 26, 1959, in file: Steady, box HFA 10, FA.

13. Howard Ahmanson to Giuliana Liquori, April 16, 1959, and June 24, 1959, in Foster Parents' Plan file, TAFA.

14. Norman Topping, interview by Marc Nurre, November 1, 1993, in FA.

15. Howard F. Ahmanson Jr., interview by Marc Nurre, [1993], in FA.

16. David S. Hannah, interview by Marc Nurre, [1994], in FA.

17. Ibid.

18. Diane Wedner, "Real Estate: Home of the Week," *LAT,* September 28, 2008, C12.

19. Howard and Dottie actually maintained separate bedrooms—as did many wealthy couples in this era. Howard F. Ahmanson Jr., interview by author, December 15, 2010.

20. Instruments are listed in "Howard Ahmanson: Biographical Information," in file: Howard F. Ahmanson Sr., box: TAF History, TAFA.

21. Howard Ahmanson Jr. says the dogs were always French poodles. See Wanda Henderson, "Confetti," *Los Angeles Examiner,* November 2, 1959, which says that they included a German Shepherd and a Pomeranian.

22. Ferd Borsch, "Sirius II Is First in Trans-Pac," *Honolulu Advertiser,* July 1, 1961, 1.

23. But Howard did nothing to enhance the boat's competitive capabilities. "He didn't even add new or larger winches," remembers crew member Bill Ficker. Bill Ficker, interview by Howard F. Ahmanson Jr., Frank Trane, and Steve Ferguson, August 24, 2009; Norman Topping, interview by Marc Nurre, November 1, 1993, both in FA.

24. See crew list, FA. For information on Schenck, see Thomas Atkinson, "For Hustle and Plain Fun," *Sports Illustrated,* August 3, 1959.

25. Howard Ahmanson, "The First and Last Profound Words from the Skipper," June 29, 1961, in FA.

26. "Art First Love for Ahmanson," *Los Angeles Mirror,* July 3, 1961, n.p.

27. Bill Ficker, interview by Howard F. Ahmanson Jr., Frank Trane, and Steve Ferguson, August 24, 2009.

28. Ibid.

29. Borsch, "Sirius II Is First."

30. Bill Ficker, interview by Howard F. Ahmanson Jr., Frank Trane, and Steve Ferguson, August 24, 2009. See also W. Bradley Avery, "Commodore's Column," *Hard on the Wind,* March 2010, 2; and Borsch, "Sirius II Is."

31. "Ahmanson Kin Dies in Omaha," *LAT,* March 9, 1960, B30.

32. Aimee Ahmanson and Florence Hoffman, interview by Howard F. Ahmanson Jr., August 21, 1993, in FA.

33. Several people told me of Ahmanson's affair with actress and singer Rhonda Fleming in 1962. Fleming got her first big break in Alfred Hitchcock's *Spellbound*

(1945) and was a major box office attraction for the next ten years. Married six times, Fleming was single from 1958 to 1960 and again from 1962 to 1966. See "Rhonda Fleming," n.d., http://en.wikipedia.org/wiki/Rhonda_Fleming.

34. "Wife Suing to Divorce Ahmanson," *LAT,* May 7, 1960, 6. See also Howard F. Ahmanson Jr., interview by author, December 15, 2010.

35. Howard Ahmanson to Giuliana Liquori, September 26, 1960, in Foster Parents' Plan file, TAFA.

36. Dorothy Grannis Ahmanson calendar, 1961, in FA. See entries for March 11, April 7, and September 5.

37. Ibid. See entry for March 18.

38. Howard F. Ahmanson to Dorothy Grannis Ahmanson, [August 1961], in FA.

39. Franklin D. Murphy, interview by Margaret Bach, November 16, 1992, 10, in TAFA.

40. Howard F. Ahmanson Jr., interview by author, December 15, 2010.

41. Dorothy Grannis Ahmanson calendar, 1961. See entry for October 2.

42. Ibid. See entry for October 23.

43. Ibid. See entry for November 24.

44. Ibid. See entry for November 25.

45. Paul Ditzel, "Special People: Caroline Leonetti Ahmanson," clipping, no source, [1983], in FA.

46. Ibid.

47. "Nonnie Book," unpublished manuscript provided by Margo Leonetti O'Connell.

48. Display advertisement, *LAT,* February 14, 1947, 7.

49. "Hedda Hopper Denounces Long Skirts in Ad Club Talk," *LAT,* September 9, 1947, A1.

50. Marie McNair, "Will Cupid Disturb Singing Jim's Date with Fifth Avenue?" *WP,* September 16, 1952, 21.

51. "TV Tidbits," *LAT,* October 12, 1950, 26.

52. For the Linkletter show, Leonetti created the "Cinderella Story" segment. Each week she chose three women from the audience. Over the next week, these women took daily classes at her school and received a clothing allowance to purchase a new outfit. When the contestants returned to the show a week later, dressed and styled for glamour, one was named the "Cinderella" of the week.

53. Henry A. Bubb to Howard F. Ahmanson, March 17, 1960, in box 4, file 18, collection 363, Franklin D. Murphy Papers, UCLA Special Collections.

54. Margaret Leslie Davis, *The Culture Broker: Franklin D. Murphy and the Transformation of Los Angeles* (Berkeley: University of California Press, 2007), xii.

55. Ibid., 1–17.

56. Ibid., 47.

57. Ibid., 59.

58. Howard F. Ahmanson Jr., interview by author, December 15, 2008, Los Angeles County Museum of Art Oral History project.

59. Davis, *Culture Broker,* 59.

60. Norman Topping, interview by Marc Nurre, November 1, 1993, in FA.

61. Ibid.

62. "Ahmanson Named SC Trustee," *Los Angeles Mirror,* December 15, 1960, n.p., clipping in FA.

63. Dick Turpin, "$1 Million Given to USC by Howard Ahmanson," *LAT,* May 17, 1962, A1.

64. Norman Topping, interview by Marc Nurre, November 1, 1993, in FA.

14. BREAKDOWN OF CONSENSUS

1. Preston N. Silbaugh, "Supervision, Safety and Sustained Growth," *CSLJ,* November 1962, n.p.

2. Paul S. Nadler, "A Look at Future Competition," *CSLJ,* November 1962, n.p.

3. David L. Mason, *From Buildings and Loans to Bail-Outs: A History of the American Savings and Loan Industry, 1831–1995* (Cambridge: Cambridge University Press, 2004), 159–60.

4. Hyman P. Minsky, "Commercial Banking and Rapid Economic Growth in California," in *California Banking in a Growing Economy: 1946–1975,* ed. Hyman P. Minsky (Berkeley, CA: Institute of Business and Economic Research, 1963), 87. To some extent, thrifts were protected from this slowing economy because the average annual rate of personal savings in the United States continued to rise through the 1950s, reaching 5.7 percent by the end of the decade. But thrifts were increasingly challenged to find places to invest this cash, given the slowing demand in the mortgage market. Mason, *From Buildings and Loans,* 159–60.

5. Howard Edgerton, interview by Marc Nurre, September 7, 1993, in FA.

6. By 1948, there were approximately one hundred different mutual funds companies managing approximately $1.5 billion in assets. Mary Rowland, *A Common Sense Guide to Mutual Funds* (Princeton, NJ: Bloomberg Press, 1996), 142. By 1965, mutual fund assets had risen to $17 billion. Mason, *From Buildings and Loans,* 162.

7. Howard P. Stevens, "President's Message," *CSLJ,* June 1950, 6.

8. While savings and loans faced increasing competition on the savings side of their business, they were squeezed on the lending side as well. By 1963, thrifts accounted for 73 percent of California's new loan volume for residential construction. F. E. Balderston, "A New Service Program of the Division of Savings and Loan: Comprehensive Market Reports for the Savings and Loan Industry," speech to the California Savings and Loan League Convention, September 16, 1964, 5, in folder: California State 1964, July–December, box 10, Correspondence of the Office of the Chairman, Joseph McMurray, RG 195, NARA-CP. See also Mason, *From Buildings and Loans,* 183.

9. Oliver M. Chatburn, "The President's Message," *CSLJ,* October 1961, 10.

10. Ibid., 12.

11. "Sixteen Holding Firms in Savings-Loan Field Form Trade Association," *WSJ*, June 14, 1965, 11.

12. Jack Miller, "S&L's in Banking—A Mistake," *San Francisco News-Call Bulletin*, September 21, 1962, n.p.

13. Richard L. Vanderveld, "Money: An Embarrassment of Riches in '63," *LAT*, January 7, 1964, E2; Robert T. Allen, "Current Outlook for the California Savings and Loan Stock: A Special Institutional Report" (Shearson-Hammill & Co., March 1964), 2, in folder: California State-1964, box 10, in Correspondence of the Office of the Chairman, Joseph McMurray, 1965–1968, RG 195, NARA-CP.

14. See Marc Allen Eisner, *Regulatory Politics in Transition* (Baltimore: Johns Hopkins University Press, 1993); and Marc Allen Eisner, *Antitrust and the Triumph of Economics: Institutions, Expertise and Policy Change* (Chapel Hill: University of North Carolina Press, 1991), 19.

15. "Report on 4-Year Study of Money and Credit," *CSLJ*, August 1961, 15.

16. Ibid.

17. Edward L. Johnson to Preston N. Silbaugh, April 9, 1963, in folder: Balderston Report-1962 *[sic]*, box 11, in Correspondence of the Office of the Chairman, Joseph McMurray, 1965–1968, RG 195, NARA-CP.

18. Balderston noted that during the heyday of its loan program the VA was able to manage the overall supply of new residential construction in a market through its approval process. As conventional loans dominated the market in the early 1960s, the government (through the FHLB, for example) was less able to manage this overall supply, and booms and busts from uncoordinated market activity were more likely. Balderston pointed out that the commissioner of savings and loans had legal authority to force savings and loans to stop making loans and that in an extreme situation this authority could be used to avoid oversupply, but he said this was not something he wanted to do. "If it is at all possible to do so," he said, "it is far better to leave the flow of individual business decisions in the hands of operating managers." Balderston, "New Service Program," 2–3.

19. Ronald J. Ostrow, "S&L Loan Risk Policies Draw Eye of State," *LAT*, December 18, 1963, part III, 9.

20. Balderston, "New Service Program."

21. Balderston acknowledged that "state regulation in California has gone farther in policing lender's risks than is generally characteristic of savings and loan regulation." This was in part because of the size and importance of the industry within California's markets and thus the need to manage the risk that thrifts might pose to the state's financial system. F. E. Balderston, "Financial Regulation as a Control System Problem: The Case of the Savings and Loan Industry," *Management Science* 12 (1966): B-418.

22. "Half of Loan Must Be Held, State Rules," *LAT*, July 14, 1964, B7.

23. Balderston, "Financial Regulation," B-418. For data on employees in 1962, see California, Division of Savings and Loan, *Sixty-Eighth Annual Report* (Sacramento: California State Printing Office, 1963), 19, CSA.

24. "Washington at Work: Kennedy Administration," *WSJ,* January 18, 1961, 13. See also "John Horne," *Chicago Tribune,* January 10, 1985, n.p.

25. Ahmanson was not alone in his efforts to lavish cash on politicians to smooth the relationships between business and government. Farrell's series of investigative stories revealed that many of Ahmanson's friends in the savings and loan industry were members of a Los Angeles–based organization called United for California, which distributed an estimated one hundred thousand to two hundred thousand dollars to conservative, probusiness candidates in the early 1960s. Often this organization simply paid the bills of candidates it supported without ever making a recognized "contribution." Harry Farrell, "Phone Call—and Cash Arrives," *San Jose Evening News,* May 11, 1963, 1.

26. Harry Farrell, "Political 'Angel' Plays Dual Role," *San Jose Evening News,* May 16, 1963, 1.

27. The California Assembly Committee on Fire and Insurance launched a special investigation in October 1961. The committee, supported by a finding from the California attorney general, concluded that the contract had been awarded properly and determined that the agreement with H. F. Ahmanson & Co. "more adequately protects the interests of the State and, simultaneously, provides wider coverage than was otherwise possible at a lower premium to the Cal-Vet buyer." California, Interim Committee on Finance and Insurance, "Fire Insurance, Land Sale Contracts, Cal-Vet Insurance: Preliminary Report," in *Assembly Interim Committee Reports, 1961–1962,* vol. 15, no. 25 (Sacramento: Assembly of the State of California, 1962), 50.

28. Farrell, "Political 'Angel.' "

29. Senator Clark L. Bradley (R-San Jose), quoted in Harry Farrell, "A 'Gathering' of String-Pullers," *San Jose Evening News,* May 14, 1963, 1, 4.

30. Richard Harwood, "Government Lists Baker Misdeeds," *WP,* January 11, 1967, A1; Willard Edwards, "Baker Tells LBJ Role in Loan," *Chicago Tribune,* January 21, 1967, 1.

31. Richard Harwood, "Baker's Quest for S&L Donations Told," *WP,* January 13, 1967, A1.

32. The Senate Rules Committee launched an investigation into Baker's conduct. After Lyndon Johnson became president, Baker loomed as a considerable embarrassment to the new president. Although the Rules Committee heard testimony in February 1964 that suggested that Baker had received unethical, if not illegal, payoffs, Baker refused to reveal anything that would damage his powerful friends or incriminate himself. The Rules Committee found that Baker had committed "gross improprieties," but it took no further action. Mark Grossman, *Political Corruption in America: An Encyclopedia of Scandals, Power and Greed* (New York: ABC-CLIO, Inc., 2003), 19. See also Willard Edwards, "Tells of Cash on Baker Desk," *Chicago Tribune,* January 12, 1967, 1.

33. Grossman, *Political Corruption in America,* 19.

34. The case may have also alerted government investigators to look more closely at the political contributions of the savings and loans. The presidential campaign of

1964 came and went before investigators finally scoured the records of Ahmanson's public relations subsidiary. Ultimately, four separate entities within the Ahmanson empire pled guilty to making illegal campaign contributions of $50,026 during the presidential campaign of 1964 and of fraudulently deducting $177,469 from the companies' tax liabilities. "Ahmanson Firms Plead Guilty to Making Illegal Political Contributions," *WSJ*, October 29, 1969, 2.

35. Corporate spending on politicians had come under attack in the Progressive era, but laws seeking to limit or ban corporate election contributions had been largely ineffectual. Between 1925 and the end of the 1950s, the issue failed to produce significant new laws, in part because the public was increasingly comfortable with the relationship between business and government. Justin A. Nelson, "The Supply and Demand of Campaign Finance Reform," *Columbia Law Review* 100, no. 2 (March 2000), 524–57. See also Thomas E. Mann, "Linking Knowledge and Action: Political Science and Campaign Finance Reform," *Perspectives on Politics* 1, no. 1 (March, 2003): 69–83.

36. Office of Program Policy, Housing and Home Finance Agency, "Facts about the Housing of the Nonwhite Population: A Digest of Bureau of the Census Data," November 1962, in box 48, files of Federal Home Loan Bank Board Chairman McMurray, RG 195, NARA-CP.

37. Mark Brilliant, *The Color of America Has Changed: How Racial Diversity Shaped Civil Rights Reform in California, 1941–1978* (New York: Oxford University Press, 2010, 190–94.

38. Jackson K. Putnam, *Jess: The Political Career of Jesse Marvin Unruh* (Lanham, MD: University Press of America, 2005), 100.

39. "U.S. Directive on Civil Rights in Mortgage Lending Looms," *American Banker,* October 24, 1961, n.p., clipping in box 58, Records of the Office of the Chairman, Federal Home Loan Bank, General Correspondence of Chairman McMurray, RG 195, NARA-CP.

40. Housing and Home Finance Agency, "President's Executive Order 11063: Equal Opportunity in Housing," November 20, 1962, in box 48, Records of the Office of the Chairman, Federal Home Loan Bank, General Correspondence of Chairman McMurray, RG 195, NARA-CP.

41. "Torrance Picketers Will Continue Tract Protest," *LAT,* August 10, 1963, 10.

42. Kenneth Childs to Stephen Slipher, August 13, 1963, in box 58, Records of the Office of the Chairman, Federal Home Loan Bank, General Correspondence of Chairman McMurray, RG 195, NARA-CP.

43. Ibid.

44. Paul Weeks, "Negro Family Acquires Home in Disputed Tract," *LAT,* July 16, 1964, 20.

45. Millard Sheets, "Kenneth D. Childs," on reel 5704, in Millard Sheets Papers, AAA.

46. Richard Deihl, interview by author, September 25, 2009.

47. Ibid.

48. Jack Miller, "A Monotony in Making Millions," *San Francisco Examiner,* October 15, 1967, 10.

15. CRISIS OF THE MANAGED ECONOMY

1. E. Erich Heinemann, "Thrift Units Face California Test," *NYT,* July 17, 1966, 97.

2. Tom Cameron, "Southland Building Hits Lowest Level since '51," [no publication identified], clipping provided to John Horne by Norman Strunk, October 27, 1965, in box 6, Files of FHLBB Chairman John E. Horne, RG 195, NARA-CP.

3. California, Division of Savings and Loan, *Annual Report, 1963,* 27, and *Annual Report, 1964,* 5. The downturn was not limited to California. In 1964, a number of thrifts in Illinois failed and had to be bailed out by the FSLIC. When this happened, California regulators expressed concern. Balderston noted a major problem with the FSLIC: insurance premiums paid by thrifts did not reflect risk. Preston Silbaugh had proposed reforms to the federal system that would allow the FSLIC to charge higher premiums to institutions that took greater risks. Balderston suggested that such a system would help align management's interests with public policy. But California's suggestions were not heeded by federal lawmakers or regulators. In the absence of these pricing incentives, the burden of risk management fell primarily on regulators. F. E. Balderston, "Financial Regulation as a Control System Problem: The Case of the Savings and Loan Industry," *Management Science* 12, no. 10 (1966): B-427.

4. "Several Smaller S&Ls in Southern California Increase Savings Rates," *WSJ,* March 31, 1965, 9.

5. Cameron, "Southland Building.'"

6. Arelo Sederberg, "The Savings & Loan Problem: Are Mergers the Solution?" *LAT,* May 1, 1966, H1.

7. Some thrifts were able to turn to the secondary market for cash. In April 1965, for example, First Charter Financial announced that it would sell a 75 percent interest in $89 million of VA-backed real estate loans to Morgan Guaranty Trust Co. of New York. "First Charter Financial to Sell 75% of $80 Million of Loans Backed by VA," *WSJ,* April 21, 1965, 9.

8. Thomas W. Bush, "Ahmanson: What's This Talk of S&L Pinch?" *LAT,* June 5, 1966, H1.

9. "Federal Home Loan Bank Board Increasing Interest Rates Charged S&L Associations," *WSJ,* April 15, 1965, 32.

10. "Ex-Omahan Is a Giant in the Loan Industry," *[Omaha World-Herald],* June 6, 1965, n.p., clipping from Mary Jane Bettefreund.

11. Howard Edgerton to Franklin Hardinge Jr., August 19, 1965, in folder: Advertising General—1965, box 2, Files of FHLBB Chairman John E. Horne, RG 195, NARA-CP.

12. Henry A. Bubb to John E. Horne, December 22 and 27, 1965, in folder: Advertising General—1965, box 2, Files of FHLBB Chairman John E. Horne, RG 195, NARA-CP.

13. For a debate over the causes of the 1966 credit crisis, see articles by L. Randall Wray, "The 1966 Financial Crisis: Financial Instability or Political Economy?" and Martin H. Wolfson, "Financial Instability and the Credit Crunch of 1966," both in *Review of Political Economy* 11, no. 4 (1999).

14. "Reserve Board Lifts Discount Rate to 4½% From 4%, Directly Defying Administration," *WSJ*, December 6, 1965, 3.

15. In the meantime, Federal Reserve Board chairman William McChesney Martin, unwilling to backtrack, tried to fix the situation by suggesting that the Fed might increase the reserve requirement by discouraging banks from offering CDs in small denominations. But defensively, he criticized the savings and loans for overreacting. "Reserve Board to Mull Increase in Banks' Reserves behind Certificates of Deposit," *WSJ*, December 15, 1965, 2.

16. "Reserve Cautions Banks on Interest on Time Deposits: S&L Aid Grows," *WSJ*, December 20, 1965, 2.

17. "Savings Interest Lifted by Savings-Loans in Los Angeles, Detroit: Rate War Feared," *WSJ*, December 13, 1965, 4.

18. Ibid.

19. Gareth Sadler to Edmund G. Brown, June 7, 1966, in folder 67, box 4, RG 3739. CSA.

20. Staff Comments to L. E. Woodford, re: California FS&LA, August 17, 1966, in folder: California Federal, Los Angeles, CA—1966, box 6, Chairman John Horne's papers, RG 195, NARA-CP.

21. Home Savings had had some involvement with this 963-acre project in the late 1950s. Sales began in 1957 on a seven-hundred-home development. The project was shut down because of a construction strike in 1959. Long Beach Federal Savings & Loan apparently carried the financing at one point, but the thrift was seized by the FSLIC after regulators charged that the thrift was overextended and mismanaged. By 1966, the project was still unfinished. Home owners in the community were frustrated, and the developers owed money to the FSLIC. "Federal Suit Filed on Builders of Bellehurst," *LAT,* February 19, 1966, OC14; Hal Schulz, "Homeowners Request Action in Bellehurst," *LAT,* July 12, 1966, OC8; Thomas W. Bush and Paul Houston, "Renovation Finally on Horizon for Eyesore Bellehurst Tract," *LAT,* February 17, 1967, 3.

22. Jack Miller, "Tycoon Blasts Gimmicks," *San Francisco Sunday Examiner and Chronicle,* February 20, 1966, III-9.

23. "Home Savings Hits $2 Billion," *LAT,* March 10, 1966, B16.

24. John E. Horne to Howard F. Ahmanson, February 24, 1966, in box 6, Chairman John Horne's papers, box 4, RG 195, NARA-CP.

25. California Commissioner of Savings and Loan, "Lending Reports," June 15, 1966, in folder: [82] [Department of Savings and Loan, Los Angeles Office Records, 1964–66], box 4, F3739:63–86, CSA.

26. Richard H. K. Vietor, *Contrived Competition: Regulation and Deregulation in America* (Cambridge, MA: Harvard University Press, 1994), 257–60.

27. Gary Hector, *Breaking the Bank: The Decline of BankAmerica* (Boston: Little, Brown, 1988), 66–67.

28. Vietor, *Contrived Competition,* 257–60.

29. "Bank of America Offers 5% Savings Certificate in $5,000 Denomination," *WSJ,* March 22, 1966, 25.

30. "Two California S&Ls Raise Rates; More Banks Increase CD Interest," *WSJ,* March 23, 1966, 2.

31. Ibid.

32. "More California S&Ls Offer 5% Certificates to Compete with Banks," *WSJ,* March 28, 1966, 11.

33. Home Savings lowered the minimum threshold for these time deposits to $2,500. Ibid.

34. "Home Savings & Loan, Largest in Nation, Joins Others in West Paying 5% on Savings," *WSJ,* April 4, 1966, 7.

35. Ibid.

36. Heinemann, "Thrift Units." The *Los Angeles Times* reported a nearly $480.5 million outflow in April 1966 compared to a net positive inflow of over $161.7 million in May of 1965. Thomas W. Bush, "Higher Savings Rates Produce Little Switching," *LAT,* July 8, 1966, B11.

37. While other thrifts found it increasingly difficult to make loans because of the drain on their funds, Home Savings made $30 million of new loans on single-family homes in March and April, despite a depressed market. Sederberg, "Savings & Loan Problem" *LAT,* May 1, 1966, H1; "News," *House and Home,* July 1966, 5–6.

38. David L. Mason, *From Buildings and Loans to Bail-Outs: A History of the American Savings and Loan Industry, 1831–1995* (Cambridge: Cambridge University Press, 2004), 183–84.

39. Sadler sought to support the thrifts in their efforts to be competitive—authorizing them in June, for example, to advertise their high-rate bonus plans to attract depositors. H. Erich Heinemann, "Thrift-Rate War Looms," *NYT,* June 15, 1966, 63.

40. On May 17, the FHLB of San Francisco, recognizing that it too had to pay a higher cost for money, raised the interest rate it charged to member banks to 5⅜ percent. Thomas W. Bush, "Interest Rate at S.F. Federal Home Loan Bank Rises to 5⅜%," *LAT,* May 3, 1966, C9.

41. Testifying before a House committee in September 1966, Tom Bane, the lobbyist for the Council of Savings and Loan Financial Corporations, which represented state-chartered capital stock companies in eleven states, said that when the FHLBB refused to support an increase in savings deposit rates, "one or two S&Ls came to the conclusion that the Board's judgment was wrong, and to prevent serious damage to their institutions, gave up their borrowing privileges and

announced early, before the reinvestment period began, their intention to increase rates. These associations [including Home Savings] were successful in preventing a great outflow." The move was repeated in June and July. Tom Bane, "Prepared Statement," in U.S. Senate, Committee on Banking and Currency, *Regulation of Maximum Rates of Interest Paid on Savings,* hearing, 89th Cong., 2nd sess., September 13, 1966, 60–62.

42. Heinemann, "Thrift Units"; Thomas W. Bush, "Most Area S&Ls Reluctant to Follow Home Savings to 5¼%," *LAT,* June 25, 1966, A7.

43. "Ahmanson Considers Paying 5¼% on Home S&L Accounts," *LAT,* June 16, 1966, B10.

44. Bush, "Ahmanson."

45. Ibid.

46. John K. Horne to Robert DeKruif, June 13, 1966, in box 4, Chairman John E. Horne's papers, RG 195, NARA-CP.

47. Thomas W. Bush, "Home Savings Pushes Rate Higher—to 5¼%," *LAT,* June 24, 1966, B13.

48. "New York Savings Bank Lifts Rate to 5%; California S&L Joins Move above Ceiling," *WSJ,* June 27, 1966, 2; Arelo Sederberg, "Split Develops in S&L Ranks on Savings Rate," *LAT,* June 29, 1966, C10.

49. Bush, "Most Area S&Ls."

50. John E. Horne to Howard Ahmanson, June 24, 1966, in Chairman John Horne's papers, box 4, RG 195, NARA-CP.

51. Sederberg, "Split Develops."

52. Taper's First Charter Financial Corp. was under significant pressure throughout the crisis. The company's longtime president and CEO Charles Wellman resigned abruptly after Taper chose to take a conservative strategy that aligned with federal regulators. Several other top executives followed Wellman out of the company. Taper reorganized the company and closed down its tract development, apartments, and industrial and commercial construction units to concentrate primarily on single-family and smaller residential units. Bush, "Most Area S&Ls."

53. Arelo Sederberg, "Taper Urges S&Ls to Stop Boosting Rates," *LAT,* July 13, 1966, B8.

54. Heinemann, "Thrift Units."

55. Sederberg, "Split Develops."

56. "New York Savings Bank Lifts Rate."

57. Sederberg, "Split Develops."

58. Howard Edgerton to L. E. Woodford, August 9, 1966, in folder: California Federal, Los Angeles, CA—1966, box 6, Chairman John Horne's papers, RG 195, NARA-CP.

59. Sydney Barlow to L. E. Woodford, July 22, 1966, in box 15, Files of FHLBB Chairman John E. Horne, RG 195, NARA-CP.

60. Howard Edgerton to L. E. Woodford, August 16, 1966, in box 6, Files of FHLBB Chairman John E. Horne, RG 195, NARA-CP.

61. Gareth W. Sadler to John E. Horne, July 8, 1966, and John E. Horne to Gareth W. Sadler, July 21, 1966, both in folder: California State, 1965–66, box 6, Files of FHLBB Chairman John E. Horne, RG 195, NARA-CP.

62. Heinemann, "Thrift Units."

63. "More Major S&Ls Go Up to 5¼% Passbook Savings," *LAT,* July 1, 1966, B12.

64. Thomas W. Bush, "S&L 5¼% Rate Prevails; 8% Mortgage Seen," *LAT,* July 2, 1966, A9.

65. When California regulators totaled the winners and losers during the July reinvestment period, they said Home had a net gain in cash of $47,793,355, an increase of 2.58 percent. Lytton was the only other state-chartered association that also experienced a major gain—increasing $13,445,413 or 3.58 percent. Abner D. Goldstine to Gareth W. Sadler, July 22, 1966, in folder 83, box 4, collection 3719, CSA.

66. Bush, "Higher Savings Rates."

67. Display advertisement, *LAT,* July 19, 1966, 12.

68. H. P. Minsky, *Stabilizing an Unstable Economy* (New Haven: Yale University Press, 1986), 90, cited in Wray, "1966 Financial Crisis," 424.

69. Gareth W. Sadler to Luther E. Gibson, August 27, 1966, in folder 68, Department of Savings and Loan, Administrative Records, Records of the Los Angeles Office, Subject Files: Legislation, March 1966–Dec. 1966, box 4, collection F3739: 63–86, CSA.

70. Sydney Kossen, "Bills Ask Cal Bank, S&L Shakeup," *San Francisco Examiner,* April 8, 1965, 73.

71. Archie K. Davis to A. Willis Robertson, September 13, 1966, in U.S. Senate, Committee on Banking and Currency, *Regulation of Maximum Rates,* 50–52.

72. Larry Blackmon to A. Willis Robertson, n.d., in U.S. Senate, Committee on Banking and Currency, *Regulation of Maximum Rates,* 53.

73. Bane, "Prepared Statement," 60–62.

74. The act allowed for the payment of higher rates on CDs over one hundred thousand dollars and lower rates on deposits below that amount. Lyndon B. Johnson, "Message from the President of the United States Transmitting Proposals for Measures for Curbing Inflation and Preserving Our National Economy," September 8, 1966, in U.S. Senate, Committee on Banking and Currency, *Regulation of Maximum Rates,* 46.

75. Richard Deihl, interview by author, February 7, 2011. See also Richard K. Green and Susan M. Wachter, "The American Mortgage in Historical and International Context," *Journal of Economic Perspective* 19, no. 4 (2005): 97.

76. Lewis J. Spellman, "Deposit Ceilings and the Efficiency of Financial Intermediation," *Journal of Finance* 35, no. 1 (March 1980), 129–36.

77. Thomas F. Cargill, "U.S. Financial Policy in the Post–Bretton Woods Period," in *Money and the Nation State: The Financial Revolution, Government and the World Monetary System,* ed. Kevin Dowd and Richard H. Timberlake Jr. (Oakland, CA: Independent Institute, 1998), 197–98.

1. Franklin D. Murphy, interview by Margaret Bach, November 16, 1992, in TAFA. A number of scholars have looked at how "the arts became a key route by which the nouveaux riches were socialized into the upper class, and arts events became 'ritual occasions for the reaffirmation of elite solidarity.'" For a summary of this literature, see J. Allen Whitt, "Mozart in the Metropolis: The Arts Coalition and the Urban Growth Machine," *Urban Affairs Review* 23, no. 15 (1987): 17–18.

2. "Minutes of First Meeting of Board of Trustees of The Ahmanson Foundation," [December 22, 1952] in file: TAF Minutes, box: TAF History, TAFA.

3. The first contribution of shares of Guaranteed Stock of Home Savings and Loan Association was apparently made by Howard Ahmanson in December 1956. See Ahmanson Foundation Board of Directors Minutes in file: TAF Minutes, box: TAF History, TAFA.

4. Congressman Wright Patman criticized this growing practice of using tax-exempt foundations to hold the controlling assets in major corporations. In August 1961 he noted that the number of tax-exempt foundations in the United States had grown from 12,295 in 1952 to 45,124 in 1960 and that many of these foundations owned controlling interests in a number of major businesses. See A. James Casner, "Memorandum re Possible Investigation of the Rockefeller Foundation," May 7, 1962, in folder 87, box 14, series 900, RG3.2, Rockefeller Foundation Archives, Sleepy Hollow, NY. In 1948, the *Virginia Law Review* published an article on the use of charitable foundations to avoid taxes that also highlighted how business owners could maintain control of their companies. See B. C. E. Jr., "The Use of Charitable Foundations for the Avoidance of Taxes," *Virginia Law Review* 34, no. 2 (February 1948): 182–201.

5. Ahmanson Foundation Board of Directors, file: TAF Minutes, box: TAF History, TAFA.

6. For example, Dr. Edward Boland, his personal physician and a friend, who was researching rheumatic diseases, received support from the foundation. Evelyn C. Barty to Dr. Edward W. Boland and Dr. Nathan E. Headley, February 18, 1958, file: TAF Minutes, Box: TAF History, TAFA.

7. [Notes and statistics compiled from minutes, no author or date,] in file: Grants-statistics, box: TAF History, TAFA.

8. Francie Ostrower, *Why the Wealthy Give: The Culture of Elite Philanthropy* (Princeton: Princeton University Press, 1995), 28–49.

9. Howard Ahmanson to John A. McCone, n.d., in folder: Howard F. Ahmanson Sr., in box: TAF History, TAFA.

10. Howard Ahmanson to Dorothy "Buff" Chandler, February 7, 1958, in file: Southern California Symphony Association, Music Center Building Fund, TAFA.

11. Ernesto Chávez, *Mi Raza Primero: Nationalism, Identity, and Insurgency in the Chicano Movement in Los Angeles, 1966–1978* (Berkeley: University of California Press, 2002), 26–27. Urban redevelopment and downtown revitalization in many cities across the United States displaced low-income residents of color and

focused on this monumental and cultural approach in the 1960s and 1970s. Notable projects included the 1960s construction of Lincoln Center in New York. Eric Avila, *Popular Culture in the Age of White Flight: Fear and Fantasy in Suburban Los Angeles* (Berkeley: University of California Press, 2004), 60–61. Mike Davis asserts that these elites were motivated by their business and personal interests. Culture had become an important component of the land development process. It also played an important part in attaining social status. My own view is that these factors account for only part of Ahmanson's participation in this movement. Personal aesthetics and deep-seated beliefs about the nature of community, rooted in his upbringing in Omaha, also played a role. Mike Davis, *City of Quartz: Excavating the Future in Los Angeles* (London: Verso, 1990), 71. Ahmanson may have participated in the GLAPI conversations. Asa Call headed "an informal but influential Committee of Twenty-Five that met regularly for lunch at Perino's on Wilshire to discuss the issues of the day." Ahmanson knew Call and was a regular at Perino's. Kevin Starr, *Golden Dreams: California in the Age of Abundance, 1950–1963* (Oxford: Oxford University Press, 2009), 154.

12. Pereira's design of the new Union Oil high-rise downtown was celebrated by *Life* magazine in June 1960 as part of a transformation of a city that was finally "going up as well as out." "Los Angeles in a New Image," *Life,* June 20, 1968.

13. Henry Sutherland, "The Spirit That Built the Music Center," special insert, *LAT,* December 6, 1964, 29.

14. Davis, *City of Quartz,* 72.

15. Robert Gottlieb and Irene Wolt, *Thinking Big: The Story of the Los Angeles Times* (New York, G. P. Putnam and Sons, 1977), 306–20. See also Avila, *Popular Culture,* 61.

16. William Fulton, *The Reluctant Metropolis: The Politics of Urban Growth in Los Angeles* (Baltimore: Johns Hopkins University Press, 1997), 236. See also Davis, *City of Quartz,* 120–28.

17. Milton Goldin, "'Why the Square?' John D. Rockefeller 3rd and the Creation of Lincoln Center for the Performing Arts," *Journal of Popular Culture,* 21, no. 3 (Winter 1987): 19.

18. Ibid., 23, 27. See also Julia L. Foulkes, "Streets and Stages: Urban Renewal and the Arts after World War II," *Journal of Social History* 44, no. 2 (Winter 2010): 413–34.

19. "USC to Honor Ahmanson," *LAT,* April 9, 1967, I14.

20. In June 1961, he attended a reception honoring members of the committee and got a chance to see the architectural plans and a model for L.A.'s new cultural capital on Bunker Hill. Mrs. Norman Chandler to Mrs. Howard Ahmanson, June 13, 1961, in FA.

21. "Ahmanson Appointed to Culture Center Board," *LAT,* April 11, 1963, A2.

22. Howard F. Ahmanson Jr., interview by author, December 15, 2010.

23. Los Angeles businessman and Democratic contributor Ed Pauley was also added to the board. Judith Martin, "15 Named to Cultural Center," *WP,* August 28, 1964, C2.

24. "Where Oh Where Should We Revel in Art," *WP*, May 24, 1964, E2; "Trustees Approve Kennedy Center Plans," *WP*, May 18, 1965, A5. See also Elizabeth Stevens, "Battle over Kennedy Center Site Widens as Opponents Trade Shots," *WP*, August 22, 1965.

25. "Howard Ahmanson," *Valuator*, Fall 1966, 13, clipping in FA.

26. "A 'Potentially Great' Museum Opens," *This World*, April 4, 1965, 39–40, clipping in LACMA Archives, Balch Research Library, LACMA.

27. "Art Museum," *California Citizen News*, April 5, 1965, clipping in LACMA Archives, Balch Research Library, LACMA.

28. "Itinerary for Mr. and Mrs. Howard Ahmanson and Miss Evelyn Barty," on reel 5676, in Millard Sheets Papers, AAA.

29. Even after the opening of the museum, Lytton continued to pose problems for Brown and the institution. In June 1965, for example, he asked the Board of Supervisors to stop funding the museum's operations unless taxpayers gained direct representation on the museum's board of trustees. Ray Zeman, "Lytton Opposes Art Fund Unless Public Has Voice," *LAT*, June 17, 1965, A1.

30. Ibid.

31. The tensions at LACMA were experienced by other art museums and cultural institutions at this time. After the American Association of Museum Directors promulgated guidelines in 1963 to try and clarify these issues, the *Los Angeles Times* brought them to the public's attention to provide some structure to the local debate. Henry J. Seldis, "Drawing a Course through Art Museum Intricacy," *LAT*, June 20, 1965, B1.

32. Tom Goff, "Art Museum Upheaval Stirs Up Supervisors," *LAT*, November 9, 1965, A1.

33. Robert Wernick, "Wars of the Instant Medicis," *Life*, October 26, 1966, 112.

34. E. W. Carter to *LAT*, "Letter Page: Museum Controversy, Two Sides to Question Aired," *LAT*, November 13, 1965, B4.

35. "The Art Wagon," *Nation*, December 13, 1965.

36. Tom Goff, "Foundation Gives $1 Million to Music Center Fund," *LAT*, December 29, 1965, A1.

37. Charles Champlin, "A Fund for Cultural Opportunity," *LAT*, October 31, 1965, B1.

38. Howard Ahmanson to Kenneth Hahn, January 14, 1966, in folder: Music Center in box: TAF History, TAFA.

39. "The Music Center / Dedication Week" Program, April 1967, in file: Week of Dedication Taper-Ahmanson, April 9–15, 1967, box 14, collection 1421, Dorothy B. Chandler Papers, Special Collections Library, UCLA.

40. Peter Bart, "Los Angeles Prepares for Museum Opening," *NYT*, March 29, 1965, 42.

41. Ibid.

42. Frank Riley, "Ahmanson: A 1967 Interview," *Los Angeles Magazine* 12 (1967): 34.

43. "Prosperous Omaha Should Turn to Culture—Ahmanson," *[Omaha World-Herald]*, February 11, [1961], clipping provided by Mary Jane Bettefreund.

44. "Howard Ahmanson" *[Valuator]*, 13.

45. Riley, "Ahmanson," 34.

46. "Progress of Freeways on C of C Agenda," *LAT*, November 17, 1966, OC2.

47. Leonard Greenwood, "Rise in Bankruptcies: Too Many People Going for Broke," *LAT*, April 23, 1967, L1.

48. Seidenbaum wrote several pieces that articulated his idea that privacy was at the heart of Southern California culture. See "Man and His Materialistic Smog-castles," *LAT*, March 8, 1966, C1, and "California—As Others See Us," *LAT*, April 30, 1967, A21.

49. Riley, "Ahmanson," 34, 60.

50. Ann Forsyth, *Reforming Suburbia: the Planned Communities of Irvine, Columbia, and The Woodlands* (Berkeley: University of California Press, 2005).

51. James Gillies, "Some Preliminary Observations on the Publicly Held Company and Management in the Light Construction Industry," in *Essays in Urban Land Economics: In Honor of the Sixty-Fifth Birthday of Leo Grebler* (Los Angeles: Real Estate Research Program, University of California, 1966), 287–300.

52. In February 1964, *House and Home* reported on fifty new towns under construction across the country. Thirty-one of the fifty were being developed by publicly held companies. Cited in Gillies, "Some Preliminary Observations," 297.

53. Gillies, "Some Preliminary Observations," 292–93.

54. Greg Hise, *Magnetic Los Angeles: Planning the Twentieth Century Metropolis* (Baltimore: Johns Hopkins University Press, 1997).

55. Patrick Nuttgens, review of *The Community Builders,* by Edward P. Eichler and Marshall Kaplan, *Town Planning Review* 39, no. 4 (January 1969): 356–57.

56. Nicholas Dagen Bloom, *Merchant of Illusion: James Rouse, America's Salesman of the Businessman's Utopia* (Columbus: Ohio State University, 2004), 185.

57. The term *community builder* is used variously in academic literature. Marc Weiss used it to distinguish entrepreneurs like Mark Taper and Ben Weingert who planned, financed, built, and sold large-scale housing developments like Lakewood in Los Angeles. Others have used the term to refer to creators of planned development that incorporates community amenities like parks, recreational facilities, churches, and shopping. Marc A. Weiss, *The Rise of the Community Builders: The American Real Estate Industry and Urban Land Planning* (New York: Columbia University Press, 1987).

58. "Airport Development near Campus Cleared," *LAT*, September 20, 1953, A16.

59. Edward P. Eichler and Marshall Kaplan, *Community Builders* (Berkeley: University of California Press, 1967), 40.

60. Forsyth, *Reforming Suburbia.*

61. Fulton, *Reluctant Metropolis,* 9.

62. William L. Pereira and Associates, *A Master Land Use Plan of Fox Hills for Home Savings and Loan Association* (Los Angeles: William L. Pereira and Associ-

ates, 1960). See also Victor Gruen Associates, "Fox Hills Project: Exploratory Land Use Analysis for Home Savings and Loan Association," April 15, 1960.

63. Neighbors in the Ladera Heights community resisted this project, complaining that it would remove a recreational use from an area where recreational facilities were limited. Some citizens were unhappy that one of the area's few public golf courses that was open to minorities would be paved over to accommodate the plan. "Area Group to Fight Fox Hills Rezoning," *LAT,* January 14, 1962, CS1.

64. "Culver C of C Opposes Freeway, High-Rise Re-Zoning of Fox Hills," *LAT,* August 18, 1963, WS8.

65. "Fox Hills Rezone Plan Called 'Unsatisfactory,'" *LAT,* June 17, 1962, CS3. See also Charles Curtis, "Golfers Make Last-Ditch Appeal to Save Fox Hills Golf Courses," *LAT,* April 14, 1963, C5.

66. Walt Secor, "Plateau for Subdivision Draws Fire," *LAT,* May 3, 1962, H1.

67. "Rezoning Bid under Study," *LAT,* November 21, 1962, B8.

68. "Hughes Fights High-Rise Units in Baldwin Hills," *LAT,* January 12, 1964, E3.

69. Riley, "Ahmanson," 34, 60.

70. Ahmanson promised that the golf course would be developed early in the project. "One of the worst things that ever happened to Southern California," he said, "is that recreation facilities have not kept pace with home construction and growing populations." "New Community Planned on Ranch," *LAT,* June 12, 1963, E8.

71. Gordon Grant, "Call It Progress," *LAT,* June 13, 1963, G1.

72. Francis M. Carney, "The Decentralized Politics of Los Angeles," *Annals of the American Academy of Political and Social Science* 353 (May 1964): 118.

73. Ibid.

74. Even the *Los Angeles Times* embraced a less political or polemical position in the community under the leadership and influence of Otis Chandler and his mother Dorothy. Considered one of the worst major dailies in the mid-1950s, the *Times* ranked among the top ten by 1964. Dennis McDougal, *Privileged Son: Otis Chandler and the Rise and Fall of the L.A. Times Dynasty* (Cambridge, MA: Perseus, 2001), 219–34.

75. Speaking at the Carnegie Institute, John Gardner suggested that the most powerful individuals in cities across America had virtually abdicated their leadership responsibility. As a result, the federal government was increasingly filling the power vacuum. Gardner feared this trend would undermine local leadership. He advocated a new pluralism that would recognize the role of leaders from various constituencies within the urban community. Frank Riley, "The Power Structure: Who Runs Los Angeles?" *Los Angeles Magazine,* [December] 1966, 31, FA.

76. Ibid.

77. Riley, "Ahmanson," 34.

78. There's no record that Ahmanson's faith in elite experts created an intellectual conflict with his populist instincts. His perspective was certainly not uncommon for his generation.

79. Riley, "Ahmanson," 34.

80. Riley, "Power Structure," 29.

81. C. Wright Mills, *The Power Elite* (New York: Oxford University Press, 1956).

82. "Architect Stone a Self-Styled 'Migrant Worker,'" *LAT,* July 21, 1968, O1.

17. A PERSONAL EPIC

1. The list included John D. MacArthur, Edwin Land, John Mecom, Henry Crown, W. Clement Stone, Daniel K. Ludwig, Leo Corrigan, William Keck, R. E. Smith, Charles Allen Jr., James Abercrombie, and John Erik Jonsson. Stewart Alsop, "America's New Big Rich," *Saturday Evening Post* (July 17, 1965), 23–39.

2. Leon F. Scibilia, "The Wealthiest Man in California," *California Business,* January 4, 1966, 2.

3. Howard F. Ahmanson Jr., interview by Marc Nurre, [1993], in FA.

4. Margaret Leslie Davis, *The Culture Broker: Franklin D. Murphy and the Transformation of Los Angeles* (Berkeley: University of California Press, 2007), 114.

5. Howard Kushner, *A Cursing Brain? The Histories of Tourette Syndrome* (Cambridge, MA: Harvard University Press, 1999).

6. Howard F. Ahmanson Jr., interview by Marc Nurre [1993], in FA.

7. Howard F. Ahmanson Jr., interview by author, December 15, 2010.

8. "Black-Foxe: A Brief History," 2005 www.bfmi.org/history.html.

9. Davis, *Culture Broker,* 114–15. Howard Ahmanson Jr. says that his appointment to the board set a legal precedent.

10. Howard F. Ahmanson Jr., interview by author, December 15, 2010.

11. Howard F. Ahmanson Jr., interview by author, by Marc Nurre, [1993], in FA.

12. Howard F. Ahmanson Jr., interview by author, December 15, 2010.

13. Richard Deihl, interview by author, September 25, 2009.

14. Caroline Leonetti Ahmanson, interview by Roberta Ahmanson and Marc Nurre, August 23, 1993, notes by Marc Nurre, in FA.

15. Ibid.

16. "Faces behind the Figures," *Newsweek,* July 1, 1965, 26.

17. Caroline Leonetti Ahmanson, interview by Roberta Ahmanson and Marc Nurre, August 23, 1993, notes by Marc Nurre, in FA.

18. Richard Deihl, interview by author, December 19, 2009.

19. Davis, *Culture Broker,* 59.

20. Margo Leonetti O'Connell, interview by author, November 17, 2010.

21. Millard Sheets, interviews by Paul Karlstrom, October 1986–July 1988, in AAA.

22. "State of Mourning Proclaimed by Reagan," *LAT,* June 7, 1968, 24.

23. Robert DeKruif, interview by author, May 1, 2009.

24. Davis, *Culture Broker,* 100.

25. Franklin D. Murphy, interview by Margaret Bach, November 16, 1992, in TAFA.

26. Richard Deihl, interview by author, September 25, 2009.

27. Christy Fox, "Ahmanson and Courtright to Blow Out Candles Again," *LAT,* June 14, 1968, H3.

28. Caroline Leonetti Ahmanson, interview by Roberta Ahmanson and Marc Nurre, August 23, 1993, notes by Marc Nurre, in FA.

29. David Roe and Dial Torgerson, "2 Southland Fires Rage Uncontrolled," *LAT,* June 23, 1968, 1.

30. "Ahmanson Services Set for Saturday," *LAT,* June 21, 1968, A2; "More Than 500 at Rites for Financier Howard Ahmanson," *LAT,* June 23, 1968, B.

31. Funeral expenses totaled $105,558 (nearly $662,000 in 2010 dollars), the bulk of which was paid to Forest Lawn. "Inheritance Tax Affidavit," Court Proceeding No. P-541–088, copy in FA.

32. "More Than 500 at Rites for Financier Howard Ahmanson," *LAT,* June 23, 1968, B3.

33. Ibid.

34. Richard Deihl, interview by author, December 19, 2009.

35. "More Than 500 at Rites."

36. "Ahmanson Services Set for Saturday," *LAT,* June 21, 1968, A2.

37. Valuation comes from "Report of Inheritance Tax Referee," Superior Court of the State of California for the County of Los Angeles, Case Number 541 088.

38. *Ahmanson Foundation v. United States,* 674 F.2d 761 1981 US App.

39. "Directions for Partial Amendment," Ahmanson Bank and Trust Company Trust No. 28, Howard F. Ahmanson, April 17, 1967, copy in FA.

40. According to Ahmanson's will, until Howard junior reached the age of twenty-one, Dorothy Grannis Sullivan was given Howard senior's rights as guardian of Howard junior's person. "Last Will and Testament of Howard Fieldstad Ahmanson, June 3, 1968," copy in FA. "Application for Admission to The C.F. Menninger Memorial Hospital as a Voluntary Patient," July 14, 1968, copy in FA. See also Howard F. Ahmanson Jr., interview by author, December 15, 2010.

41. Howard F. Ahmanson Jr., interview by author, December 15, 2010. See also Davis, *Culture Broker,* 113–15.

42. H.F. Ahmanson & Co., *1993 Annual Report.*

43. This provision was included in California's Mortmain Statute. See "The Ahmanson Foundation—Detailed Statement of Need for Legislation," April 28, 1982 in FA.

44. *Ahmanson Foundation v. United States,* 674 F.2d 761 1981 US App.

45. H.F. Ahmanson & Co. sold 3.6 million shares worth about $101 million ($28/share). The underwriters were Goldman, Sachs & Co. and Kidder, Peabody & Co. After its financial restructuring, H.F. Ahmanson had about 22.7 million shares outstanding, 30.6 percent of which were owned by the Ahmanson Foundation. Another 44.6 percent interest was held by various trusts principally benefiting family members. "H.F. Ahmanson & Co.'s Initial Public Offer of Stock Sells Quickly," *WSJ,* October 18, 1972, 30. Of the 3.6 million shares offered, 800,000 were new issues to raise working capital, 857,421 were owned by the Ahmanson

Foundation, and 750,000 were shares in which the foundation and Dorothy Grannis Sullivan had joint interests. "The Ahmanson Foundation—Detailed Statement of Need for Legislation," April 28, 1982, in FA.

46. Franklin Murphy, interview by Margaret Bach, November 16, 1992, 2 in File: Trustees-Transcripts, box: TAF History, TAFA.

47. "The Ahmanson Foundation: Library Support," [1974–1990] in file: Grants-statistics in box: TAF History, TAFA.

48. "The Ahmanson Foundation: Research," [1974–90] and "The Ahmanson Foundation: Support to Hospital," [1974–90] in file: Grants-statistics in box: TAF History, TAFA.

49. Franklin Murphy, interview by Margaret Bach, November 16, 1992, 2 in file: Trustees-Transcripts, box: TAF History, TAFA.

50. Daniel M. Weintraub, "Charles Fletcher, 82, Dies: Founder of Home Federal," *LAT,* October 1, 1985, SD_A1.

51. John O'Dell, "Baldwin Co. Defaults on Property Loan," *LAT,* October 1, 1993, 7.

CONCLUSION

1. Walter Russell Mead, "The Death of the American Dream II," *The American Interest,* June 3, 2011, http://blogs.the-american-interest.com/wrm/2011/06/03/the-death-of-the-american-dream-ii/.

2. Tom Furlong, "Into the Home Stretch: Home Savings Faces Tough Problems as Its CEO Nears Retirement," *LAT,* December 20, 1992, 1.

INDEX

German Fire Underwriters of Omaha, 19

Germany, 1, 3, 71, 76, 81

Giannini, A. P., 93, 228, 300n3

GI Bill, 4, 86, 89, 124, 126, 170, 186, 238–39

Gibraltar Savings and Loan, 227, 228, 233

Gibson, Luther, 234

Glass, Carter, 52, 151, 268

Glass-Steagall Act. *See* Banking Act
of 1933

Glendale Federal Savings and Loan, 146,
289n63, 299n87, 322n6

Godfrey, Arthur, 225

Goldman, Sachs & Co., 343n45

Gottlieb, Robert, 238

Government entrepreneur, 6, 86, 112, 180.
As political entrepreneur, 112, 215, 251,
269, 274n18

Graham, Benjamin, 157

Grannis, Frank, 31, 281n21

Graves, Richard, 138

Greater Los Angeles Plans Incorporated
(GLPI), 237

Great Western Corporation, 149, 152,
217, 233

Great Western Fire & Marine Insurance
Company, 138, 146, 149

Great Western Savings and Loan, 227,
228, 229

Grebler, Leo, 194–96

Greendale, WI, 247

Green, Lucius Peyton, 177

Greenhills, OH, 246

Gross, Robert Frank, 64, 65, 73

Guaranty Savings and Loan, 150, 314n22

Gunnison, Foster, 80

Gunnison Magic Homes, 80

Hahn, Kenneth, 174, 176, 243, 261

Haldeman, Harry Francis "Bud," 53

Hancock, George Allan, 321n89

Hancock Park, 108, 176, 198, 199, 202,
209, 256

Hansen, Elwood, 150

Harbor Savings and Loan, 314n15

Harding, Warren G., 25

Harrison, William Preston, 319n65

Hearst, William Randolph, 173

Hegg, Roy, 140, 311nn40,41

Heifetz, Florence, 140

Heifetz, Jascha, 140

Henie, Sonja, 260

Hepburn, Katherine, 76

Hershey, Lewis, 66

H. F. Ahmanson & Company, 33, 35, 36, 42,
45, 46, 59, 60–61, 66, 71, 88, 93, 98, 102,
129, 150, 151, 152, 156, 157, 158, 159, 216,
258, 262, 298n82, 301n24, 315n17;
antitrust investigation, 139; headquarters on Wilshire, 162–66; holding
company structure, 109, 182, 184; initial
public offering, 264, 343n45

Heston, Charleton, 257

Highland Park, 83, 146, 295n51

Hillings, Patrick J., 137

Hinshaw, Carl, 136

Hiss, Alger, 132

Hoeft, J. E., 289n63, 299n87

Hoffman, Susan, 287n22

Holabird & Root, 178

Hollywood Advertising Club, 205

Hollywood Savings and Loan Association,
84, 123, 149, 296n55

Home Builders Emergency Committee,
80

Home Building and Loan Association, 6,
87. *See also* Home Savings and Loan
Association

Home Federal Savings and Loan, 2, 73, 84,
153, 154, 265

Home Mutual Savings and Loan (San
Francisco), 150

Home ownership: building boom, 5, 37;
costs, 79; federal policy, 5–6, 47–50,
52–53, 61; G.I. Bill, 4, 126, 139; Los
Angeles, 29, 111, 305n96; Omaha, 23, 29;
United States, 218

Home Owners Loan Act, 52

Home Savings and Loan Association, 6–7,
8, 87–88; acquisitions, 93–95, 102, 139,
149–51, 300n3; advertising, 88, 100–103;
assets, 87–88, 95, 127, 134, 139, 146, 147,
149, 161, 209, 233–34, 268, 299n86;
branch design, 103, 166–68, 257; branch
network, 146, 148, 149; complaints,
117–19; Congress on Racial Equality,
219–20; cost control, 99–100, 105, 230;

dividend (interest) rates, 88, 117, 228–35, 299n86; Federal Housing Administration (FHA) loans, 309n64; lending, 88–92, 104–8, 118–19, 120, 127–28, 227, 268; National American Fire Insurance, 119, 127–28, 156, 158; redlining, 107; regulation, 116–21, 299n89; tract development, 88–92, 246; Veterans Administration loans, 89, 126–27, 309n64; Washington Mutual, 268
Hoover Dam, 80, 102. *As* Boulder Dam, 28–29
Hoover, Herbert, 2, 25–26, 47–51, 52, 61, 281n18, 287n24
Hopalong Cassidy, 100
Hope, Mervyn, 123, 149, 296n55
Hopper, Hedda, 205
Horne, John, 215, 224–26, 227, 228, 230, 231, 232, 233
Hotchkiss, Preston, 53
Hounshell, David, 80, 294n23
House Banking and Currency Committee, 232
House Party (TV show), 204
House Un-American Activities Committee, 132
Housing Act of 1950, 308n55
Hughes, Charles M., 322n6
Hughes, Howard, 76, 248–49
Hunt, Leroy, 115

Insurance Managers, 61
Inter-Valley Savings and Loan, 314n23
Interest Rate Adjustment Act, 234
Iowa, 16, 21, 28, 51, 68–69, 157, 291n27, 296n60
Irwin, Robert, 170
It's a Wonderful Life, 37, 103, 211, 267
Izak, Ed, 83

Janns Investment Company, 248
Japan, 1, 3–4, 58, 60, 76, 96, 199
Japanese Americans, 107
Jefferson, Thomas, 6, 39, 40, 111, 188
Johnson, Lyndon B., 37, 215, 217, 234, 240, 330n32
Johnson, Philip, 178
Johnston, Laura, "Johnnie," 31

Jonathan Club, 34, 57, 138
Jones, Hayden, 50
Jonsson, John Erik, 342n1
JPMorgan Chase, 8, 268
Judson, Harold, 66

Kaiser Community Homes, 80–81, 82
Kaiser, Henry J., 4, 80–81, 82, 86, 112, 247
Kaplan, Jacob, "Jack" M., 316n29
Kaufmann, Milton, 99
Kauffman-Wilson, 318n28
Kavanaugh, Luke, 155
Keck, William, 342n1
Kefauver, Estes, 147
Kelton, Louis, 318n28
Kennedy Center (John F. Kennedy Center for the Performing Arts), 240
Kennedy, John F., 122, 185, 215, 217, 219, 239, 240
Kennedy, Robert, 257
Kent, Roger, 191
Keystone Savings and Loan, 314n15
Kidder, Peabody & Co., 343n45
Kienholz, Edward, 245
Kimbell Art Foundation, 242
King, T. Bert, 120
Klein, Gene, 188
Knight, Goodwin, 95, 115–16, 132–33, 134–38, 139, 142–44, 185, 190–91, 192, 215, 262
Knowland, William, 123, 134, 135, 136, 137, 139, 142–44, 190
Kuchel, Thomas, 134, 136
Kuhrts, Jack, 87

Ladera Heights, 341n63
Laguna Niguel, CA, 248
Lakewood, 82, 146, 340n57
Lanchester, Elsa, 257
Land, Edwin, 342n1
Landsberg, Morrie, 136
Langsner, Jules, 177
Lehman Brothers, 149
Lemon, Virginia June (Unruh), 186
Leonetti, Caroline. *See* Caroline Leonetti Ahmanson
Leonetti, Margo, 204, 256
Levine, Max, 318n28

Levitt, William, 81, 295n38
Liberty Savings and Loan, 109
Lifetime Savings and Loan, 314n15
Lincoln Center (New York), 240
Linkletter, Art, 10, 161, 204, 205, 262, 327n52
Linkletter, Lois, 205
Lockheed, 81
Long Beach Building and Loan, 94
Long Beach Federal Savings and Loan, 333n21
Los Angeles, 1, 6–7, 10, 46; Ahmanson's plans for, 245; building boom, 81–82; building codes, 128; development, 247–49; population, 28–29, 76–79; public housing battle, 122; red lining, 107–9; savings and loan market, 110–11, 223; VA loan capital, 127
Los Angeles American Building and Loan Association, 83
Los Angeles Art Committee, 177
Los Angeles Chamber of Commerce, 34, 122
Los Angeles Charm Clinic for Underprivileged Girls, 205
Los Angeles City Council, 170
Los Angeles Civic Light Opera Association, 243
Los Angeles County Art Fair, 170, 173
Los Angeles County Art Institute (also Otis Art Institute), 169–72, 239
Los Angeles County Board of Supervisors, 161, 171, 174, 238, 243, 320n79
Los Angeles County Museum of Art (LACMA), 173–79, 180, 236, 239, 241–43, 245, 250, 264, 339n31
Los Angeles County Museum of History, Science and Art, 170, 173
Los Angeles Examiner, 136, 177
Los Angeles Opera Company, 244
Los Angeles Sentinel, 108
Los Angeles Stock Club, 57
Los Angeles Times, 10, 46, 57, 66, 76, 101, 135, 159, 170, 172, 173, 183, 191, 198, 203, 220, 230, 234, 242, 245
Lowenstein, Roger, 158
Luckman, Charles, 178–79, 247
Ludwig, Daniel K., 342n1

Lytton, Bart, 179, 182, 188, 192, 226, 231–32, 241, 262, 339n29
Lytton Savings and Loan, 225, 336n65

MacArthur, General Douglas, 96
MacArthur, John D., 342n1
Mackin, Frank, 181, 182, 183, 189, 322n1, 324n33
Managed economy, 5–7, 50, 52, 55, 121, 151, 152, 154, 179, 183, 188, 194, 207, 209, 210, 212, 217, 218, 222, 250, 266, 269, 274n16, 325n59
Manship, Paul, 257
Markham, Henry H., 114
Mark Taper Forum, Music Center, 243,
Marshall Plan, 133
Marshall, Thurgood, 304n83
Marten, John, 217
Martin, William McChesney, 333n15
Massachusetts Institute of Technology (MIT), 67
Mass production: housing, 79, 80, 81–82, 128, 246, 266, 294n23; mortgages, 103–4, 266
Mayan Theater, 60
Mayo, Virginia, 204
McAllister, Walter W., 118, 120–21, 147, 151, 307n30, 314n26
McBean, Gladding, 167
McCone, John, 53, 237
McDonald Brothers, 318n28
McMurray, Joseph P., 215
McNeill, Don, 225
McWilliams, Carey, 28, 191–92
Mead, Walter Russell, 266
Mecom, John, 342n1
Mehta, Zubin, 243
Mellon, Andrew, 47
Mellon, Paul, 177, 254
Menninger Memorial Hospital, 263
Merriam, Frank, 132
Metropolitan Life, 282n40
Metz, Don, 318n28
Mexican Americans, 107, 122, 238, 280n2
Midwood Homes, 318n28
Miller, George, Jr., 155
Millier, Arthur, 173
Molotch, Harvey, 293n12